Strategic Ambiguities

What we want is not terms that avoid ambiguity, but terms that clearly reveal the strategic spots at which ambiguities necessarily arise. . . . Hence, instead of considering it our task to "dispose of" any ambiguity, we rather consider it our task to study and clarify the resources of ambiguity . . . it is in these areas of ambiguity that transformation takes place: in fact, without such areas, transformation would be impossible.

—Kenneth Burke, *A Grammar of Motives* (1962, pp. xx–xxi)

Inspirations have I none just to touch the flaming dove.

—David Bowie, *Soul Love* (1972)

Strategic Ambiguities

Essays on Communication, Organization, and Identity

Eric M. Eisenberg
University of South Florida

SAGE Publications
Thousand Oaks ▪ London ▪ New Delhi

For information:

Sage Publications, Inc.
2455 Teller Road
Thousand Oaks, California 91320
E-mail: order@sagepub.com

Sage Publications Ltd.
1 Oliver's Yard
55 City Road
London EC1Y 1SP
United Kingdom

Sage Publications India Pvt. Ltd.
B-42, Panchsheel Enclave
Post Box 4109
New Delhi 110 017   India

Printed in the United States of America.

Library of Congress Cataloging-in-Publication Data

Strategic ambiguities: essays on communication, organization, and identity / Eric M. Eisenberg.
    p. cm.
Includes bibliographical references and index.
ISBN 1-4129-2687-4 or 978-1-4129-2687-4 (cloth)
ISBN 1-4129-2688-2 or 978-1-4129-2688-1 (pbk.)
    1. Communication in organizations.
HD30.3.E38 2007
658.4'5—dc22

                                        2006022334
This book is printed on acid-free paper.

06   07   08   09   10   10   9   8   7   6   5   4   3   2   1

Acquiring Editor:	Todd R. Armstrong
Editorial Assistant:	Sarah K. Quesenberry
Project Editor:	Astrid Virding
Copyeditor:	April Wells-Hayes
Typesetter:	C&M Digitals (P) Ltd.
Proofreader:	Theresa Kay
Indexer:	Juniee Oneida
Cover Designer:	Michelle Kenny

Contents

Introduction

Laying Down a Path in Walking

Joy itself is a form of wisdom. . . . If people were nimble enough to move freely between different perceptions of reality and if they maintained a relaxed, playful attitude well-seasoned with laughter, then they would live in harmony with the universe; they would connect with all matter, organic and inorganic, at its purest, most basic level.

—Tom Robbins (2001)

When my son Joel was 7 years old, we visited an indoor climbing gym after school. There were 20-foot walls for climbing, each dotted with irregularly placed steps and handholds. I wrapped one end of a long, thick rope around my waist while my son slipped into a safety harness at the other. The first few ascents came easily, but as he struggled to complete the harder courses, I became frustrated and advised him on what looked to me to be the best route to the top. From my perspective on the ground, the optimal path along the rock face was clear. Nonetheless, as I tried to convey this information to my son, he cut me off. "It's not like that," he said from 20 feet in the air. "Until you *take* a step, you don't know where the next step should be."

Explanations and accounts provided outside of or following a stream of action can be wrong, misleading, and even harmful. This point has been made before through contrasting metaphors for leadership: the map and the compass (Weick, 2001). Using a map to lead presumes a deep level of prospective knowledge about the terrain one will encounter and a sure sense of the best route to take. In comparison, using a compass as one's guide suggests both a certainty about one's general direction and an openness toward alternative paths along the way. As much as the "logical next step" looks obvious in retrospect, it may not appear so in the ongoing stream of action. The urgent need to appreciate the "certain ambiguity" that characterizes contemporary human societies is both the alpha and the omega of this book.

Put more plainly, the specific impetus behind the essays in this collection—and indeed, the decision to collect them—is my frank desire to promote a more contingent style of living, one in which people are serious about their attachments but not seriously attached (Phillips, 1996). Making this case requires your indulgence for a brief recap of the nature of human being, focusing specifically on our species' trademark qualities, language and reflexive consciousness.

People emerge from worlds not of their making but, unlike other living creatures, are not content merely to participate in the ebb and flow of life. Instead, language and reflexive consciousness (the ability to think about our thinking) goad us to construct an überworld, an elaborate system of meanings in which (unlike the real world) all things appear possible. Much has been made of the essential link between language and civilization, yet considerably less attention has been paid to what is *lost* in learning to communicate, most notably the ability to live more simply in a world of signs (Phillips, 1999).

But as humans, we have no choice. We face the predicament of immortal souls trapped in mortal bodies (Becker, 1997). We are marked by an uneasy duality that both differentiates us from angels and evokes a host of expectations and desires. If there is a Creator, she is a co(s)mic tailor who carefully takes our measure and consistently produces suits that never quite fit. The secular version of this insight is not much different—even if we believe that reality is "socially constructed," it is so only in an ironic sense. We rarely get the reality we favor or set out to create (Ortner, 1984).

Human beings are unique among animals in their tendency to organize experience into plots (Bruner, 1990). These plots sprout from the gaps we perceive between our lived experience and our expectations (Ochs & Capps, 1996). The difference between the way things are—and how they could be—continually cries out for explanation. Language lures us out of the present tense into ornate images of the past and future, into talk of aspirations and traditions, dreams and regret. But it is the strength of our belief in these constructions—our degree of attachment to these beliefs—that has an overwhelming impact on how we live our lives, through its influence on our thoughts, actions, and relationships.

The call of language intoxicates even the sober. Although everyone is aware to some degree that we are subject to the hazards that affect all animals, we also imagine ourselves a breed apart, a species uniquely qualified to be stewards of the world, if not the universe. In our efforts to achieve *dominion* over the Earth, we come to believe that evolution ends with our species (Quinn, 1993). Sadly, this could turn out to be a self-fulfilling prophecy. There is a cruel irony to a species that can speak with such certainty but inhabits a world so ambiguous and unmanageable (Lennie, 1999).

The desire for certainty permeates every human psyche born of the West. We long to replace our internal conflicts and anxieties with "something clearer, simpler, and ultimately more permissive" (Edmunson, 2006, p. 16). As each individual soul struggles to make sense of his or her existence through identification with a transcendent set of institutions or beliefs (Taylor, 2000), however, the identities that emerge from this struggle diverge considerably in degree of certainty and attachment. On the one hand, some individuals declare adherence to what might be called "dominion narratives," characterized by single meaning, heroic individuals, and the importance of centralized and singular control. Fundamentalisms of every kind can be understood as dominion narratives, rigid responses to a perceived gap between one's ideals and the state of the world. Examples include certain extreme religious sects and corrupt governments that require the blind loyalty of their followers.

Others seek to live in accord with what might be called "engagement narratives," characterized by multiple meanings, vulnerability, participation, and inclusion. New organizational forms and network organizations use technology to open up lines of communication and encourage participation. Many local schools and communities promote the value of diversity and of holding space for difference. And certain religious sects are known for their commitment to inclusion (e.g., Quakers, Jesuits).

Problems invariably arise when people with differing narratives and attachments to their beliefs seek to live together. The central challenge in human relations is communicating with people who hold radically different worldviews from us and who are passionately attached to the veracity of their perspectives. The source of the difficulty, however, is less in the fact of the difference and more in the strength of the attachment, in one's certainty about certainty. Although we should encourage a wide diversity of beliefs among people, we must also make a fundamental commitment to oppose fundamentalism of any kind, a refusal to tolerate the intolerant (Popper, 1971).

Although this may seem like a logical contradiction (similar, for example, to promoting "serious play"), it is in fact a starting point for cultivating a new kind of systems logic. Consider this: In the Judeo-Christian tradition, it is not money per se but the "love of money" that is claimed to be the root of all evil. *The central problem is not belief but attachment.* For this reason, we should encourage the promulgation of beliefs worldwide but actively discourage fanatical attachment to any of them. There are distinct parallels to the call for ecological systems thinking; any overemphasis on the needs of the individual always impacts others and may over time destroy the whole. A more peaceful world begins with heightened systems consciousness (Lifton, 1993; Senge et al., 2005).

This collection of essays was assembled with this new story of identity and communication in mind. People are seeking new ways of coming together across differences, discovering commonalities, and learning to live and work together. To the extent that we cling to dominion narratives, we resemble the computer operator who seeks to make changes in an electronic document by dabbing Liquid Paper on the screen; the change is illusory, and the world rolls on. A certain degree of nonattachment and vulnerability with regard to one's identity and beliefs is essential to the survival of our planet and our species.

What follows is a series of essays organized chronologically, charting the development of a set of related ideas about communication, organization, and identity. Part I, "Embracing Ambiguity," includes four essays that seek to shift attention away from a focus on clarity and openness toward a very different definition of effective communication. Specifically, the notion of "strategic ambiguities" refers to the human capacity to use the resources of language to communicate in ways that are both inclusive and preserve important differences. Written in the 1980s, this work appeared at a time when interpretive research and qualitative methods were just gaining legitimacy in organizational studies. In this spirit, these essays attempt to shine a brighter light on questions and problems of meaning in organizations.

Part II, "Transcendence and Transformation," includes a broad range of work aimed at exploring the consequences of this expanded definition of communication. Many of the pieces are expressly counter-rational, celebrating miscommunication and interpretive diversity as sources of organizational and relational strength. Recalling Burke's quote from the beginning of this book, I seek to connect ambiguity with the potential for meaningful change while at the same time debunking attempts to "fix" meaning through communication.

The third part of the book, "A New Communication Aesthetic," takes this expanded definition of communication and develops it into an aesthetic for experiencing organization and identity. Bringing together work from numerous disciplines, I attempt to articulate an aesthetics of contingency that both edifies the value of nonattachment and has significant implications for individual identity and interpersonal relationships. To the extent that this aesthetic can be realized in communication, we stand a good chance of developing new models for human relationships that will sustain us in a complex, interdependent, and diverse world.

Acknowledgments

The theme of this book comes straight from my life, born out of the over-flowing possibilities afforded to me by the people I love. Specifically, I am thankful for the inspiration I get from my family—Lori, Evan, and Joel—and from my dear friends, Patti Riley, Steve Burch, Buddy Goodall, Art Bochner and Carolyn Ellis. In recent years, I have also learned a great deal about rein-vention and renewal from two other close relatives I love dearly, Lucille Roscoe and Florence Millon. Finally, I am grateful to Todd Armstrong for having the considerable wisdom and insight to appreciate the value of this collection, and to Sarah Quesenbery, Astrid Virding, and April Wells-Hayes for making it a reality.

SAGE Publications gratefully acknowledges the following reviewers: Gail T. Fairhurst, University of Cincinnati; H. L. (Budd) Goodall Jr., The Hugh Downs School of Human Communication, Arizona State University; Steve May, University of North Carolina at Chapel Hill; Linda L. Putnam, Texas A&M University; Paaige K. Turner, Saint Louis University; and Pam Shockley-Zalabak, University of Colorado at Colorado Springs.

References

Becker, E. (1997). *The denial of death*. New York: Free Press.

Bowie, D. (1972). Soul love. *Ziggy Stardust and the Spiders from Mars*. London, UK: Virgin.

Bruner, J. S. (1980). *Under five in Britain* (Oxford Preschool Research Project, vol. 1). Ypsilanti, MI: High/Scope Press.

Burke, K. B. (1962). *A grammar of motives*. Berkeley: University of California Press.

Edmundson, M. (2006, April 30). Freud and the fundamentalist urge. *New York Times Magazine*, pp. 15–18.

Lennie, I. (1999). *Beyond management*. London; Sage.

Lifton, R. (1993). *The protean self*. Chicago: University of Chicago Press.

Ochs, E., & Capp, L. (1996). Narrating the self. *Annual Review of Anthropology, 25*, 19–43.

Ortner, S. (1984). Theory in anthropology since the sixties. *Comparative Studies in Society and History, 26*, 126–167.

Phillips, A. (1996). *Terrors and experts*. Cambridge: Harvard University Press.

Phillips, A. (1999). *The beast in the nursery*. New York: Vintage Books.

Popper, K. (1971). *The open society and its enemies*. Princeton, NJ: Princeton University Press.

Quinn, D. (1993). *Ishmael.* New York: Bantam Books.

Robbins, T. (2001). *Fierce invalids home from hot climates.* New York: Bantam Books.

Senge, P., Scharmer, C., Jaworski, J., & Flowers, B. S. (2005). *Presence.* New York: Currency.

Taylor, C. (2005). *The ethics of authenticity* (Rev. ed.). Cambridge, MA: Harvard University Press.

Weick, K. (2001). Leadership as the legitimation of doubt. In W. Bennis, G. Spreitzer, & T. Cummings (Eds.), *The future of leadership* (pp. 91–102). San Francisco: Jossey-Bass.

PART I

Embracing Ambiguity

In 1980, the vast majority of writers on organizations subscribed to an ideology of communication that emphasized clarity as equivalent to effectiveness. Although clarity is without a doubt one important criterion for evaluating the effectiveness of communication, other considerations often apply. In this part of the book, I attempt to expose the ideological biases of this particular philosophy of communication, drawing connections among "information engineering" views of language, the growing interest in personal self-actualization through disclosure, and the emphasis on clarity, openness, and shared meaning. Starting from this critique, I lay the groundwork for a more nuanced view of effective organizational communication that emphasizes the potential value of ambiguity and selective disclosure.

1

Ambiguity as Strategy in Organizational Communication

Written more than two decades ago, this essay was my first attempt to counter the prevailing ideology of clarity and openness in organizational communication theory and research that stood in sharp contrast to most people's experience of organizational life. Cited hundreds of times in the fields of Communication and Organizational Studies, this essay identified four functions of strategic ambiguity—specifically, its capacity to promote unified diversity, to preserve privileged positions, to foster deniability, and to facilitate organizational change. The discussion of plausible deniability foreshadowed a central theme of the Iran-Contra hearings, during which an American Lieutenant Colonel (Oliver North) testified to the U.S. Congress about the role and importance of "plausible deniability" in the illegal sale of weapons to the Nicaraguan Contras. The lack of serious consequences for the Colonel or anyone else connected to the case showed the power as well as the potential for abuse inherent in this kind of communication.

In retrospect, this essay reflects my youthful desire to edify and explore the more mysterious and less rational aspects of human connection (I was 23 when I began work on it and 26 when it was published). In focusing on these things, I paid little attention to other dynamics, such as how ambiguity can mask and sustain abuses of power. Looking back, I am also unsure about my relational definition of strategic ambiguity; it seemed to make sense at the time, but has proven difficult to study. Nevertheless, the paper accomplished what I had hoped it would, prompting scholars and practitioners alike to reflect on their assumptions about the centrality of clarity and the potential uses of ambiguity in successful organizing.

SOURCE: Eisenberg, E. M. (1984). Ambiguity as strategy in organizational communication. *Communication Monographs, 51*, 227–242. Copyright © 1984. Reproduced by permission of Taylor & Francis Group, LLC., http://taylorandfrancis.com.

Conceptions of organizations have changed drastically in recent years. This change has occurred in two ways. First, while past conceptions paid little attention to the role of cognition in organizing, current work reflects a shift toward viewing organizational participants as thinking individuals with identifiable goals (Argyris & Schon, 1978; Harris & Cronen, 1979; Pfeffer, 1981; Smircich, 1983; Weick, 1978, 1979a). Second, whereas previous analyses of organizational behavior treated communication as an epiphenomenon, recent work focuses directly on communication processes in organizations (Dandridge, 1979; Farace, Monge, & Russell, 1977; Pacanowsky & O'Donnell-Trujillo, 1983; Pfeffer, 1981; Pondy, Frost, Morgan, & Dandridge, 1983; Smircich & Morgan, 1982). Interest in organizational symbolism has been far-reaching and is a central concern of students of Japanese management (Pascale & Athos, 1981) and of organizational culture (Jelinek, Smircich, & Hirsch, 1983). Pfeffer (1981, p. 44) provides a concise statement of this new emphasis: "If management involves the taking of symbolic action, then the skills required are political, dramaturgical, and language skills more than analytical or strictly quantitative skills."

This change in emphasis corresponds to developments in various fields. Researchers in communication (Bochner, 1982; Clark & Delia, 1979; Hart & Burks, 1972; Monge, Bachman, Dillard, & Eisenberg, 1982; Pearce, Cronen, & Conklin, 1979; Tracy & Moran, 1983) and linguistics (Brown & Levinson, 1978; Fowler, Hodge, Kress, & Trew, 1979; Levy, 1979) are studying communication competence in ways which have implications for organizational behavior. Most of these writers view competent communication as the strategic use of symbols to accomplish goals. Moreover, a communicator's goals are not assumed to be unitary or even consistent; rather, individuals have multiple, often conflicting goals which they orient toward in an effort to satisfy rather than to maximize attainment of any one goal in particular. This perspective has evolved largely as a critical response to the "optimal" model of communication which equates effectiveness with clarity and openness. Communication theorists have rejected this particular ideology in favor of a more rhetorical view of communicator as strategist (Bochner, 1982; Parks, 1982; Wilder, 1979).[1]

While the more practitioner-oriented journals continue to publish essays which equate effective communication with open communication (e.g., Bassett, 1974; Fisher, 1982; Frank, 1982; Lorey, 1976; Sigband, 1976; VonBergen & Shealy, 1982; Wycoff, 1981) recent theoretical work reflects a genuine willingness among leading scholars and practitioners to accept the notion that organizational members use symbols strategically to accomplish goals, and in doing so may not always be completely open or clear (e.g., Pascale & Athos, 1981; Pfeffer, 1981; Pondy et al., 1983).

The overemphasis on clarity and openness in organizational teaching and research is both non-normative *and* not a sensible standard against which to gauge communicative competence or effectiveness. People in organizations confront multiple situational requirements, develop multiple and often conflicting goals, and respond with communicative strategies which do not always minimize ambiguity, but may nonetheless be effective. This essay goes beyond the assertion that people in organizations manipulate symbols to achieve goals toward a more rigorous conceptualization of how this process operates, what strategies work under what conditions, and with what effects. Specifically, this paper explores how people in organizations use ambiguity strategically to accomplish their goals.

I am not suggesting a retreat from clarity. There are numerous occasions in organizations in which greater clarity is desirable. What I am advocating is a shift in emphasis away from an overly ideological adherence to clarity toward a more contingent, strategic orientation. Pascale and Athos (1981, p. 102) capture the sentiment: "Explicit communication is a cultural assumption; it is not a linguistic imperative. Skilled executives develop the ability to vary their language along the spectrum from explicitness to indirection depending upon their reading of the other person and the situation."

The idea that people choose communication strategies to accomplish multiple goals is in sharp contrast to the classical-structuralist view of organizational behavior, which sees communication as primarily facilitating production. In the multiple-goal approach, communication is instrumental in building and maintaining self-image, in facilitating interpersonal relationships, and in advancing innovation, as well as in aiding production (Farace et al., 1977). From this perspective, organizational communication is the process by which organizing occurs, not something which takes place *in* organizations (Johnson, 1977; Putnam, 1983). Furthermore, the problem facing the typical organizational member is one of striking a balance between being understood, not offending others, and maintaining one's self-image. Many different strategies are used to orient toward conflicting interactional goals; some examples include avoiding interaction altogether, remaining silent, or changing the topic. One intriguing strategy which is of key importance to organizing involves the application of one's "resources of ambiguity" (Burke, 1969). In the next section, a more precise definition of strategic ambiguity is offered.

Defining Strategic Ambiguity

Before a definition of strategic ambiguity can be considered, I must provide a philosophical context for its understanding. The present definition of ambiguity is a direct outgrowth of the relativist view of meaning. This perspective is critical of logical empiricism and the mirror metaphor of science (Rorty, 1979); it rejects the notion that an objective world exists which waits to be discovered. With no purely "objective" reality to describe, the existence of "literal" language becomes questionable, and all meaning is seen as fundamentally contextual and constructed, at least partly, by individuals. Language, perception, and knowledge are completely interdependent. Ortony (1979) provides an elegant summary of the argument: "Knowledge of reality, whether it is occasioned by perception, language, memory, or anything else, is a result of going beyond the information given. It arises through the interaction of that information with the *context* in which it is presented, and with the knower's pre-existing knowledge" (p. 1, italics added). The relativist position does not consider ambiguity to be a special problem, since meanings are constituted by individuals, not inherent in discourse. In contrast, the nonconstructivist position considers non-literal language to be unimportant and parasitic on "normal" usage (Ortony, 1979, p. 2).

Students of communication theory have found the relativist view of meaning to be appealing. It is reflected in the "interactional view" of communication advanced by Watzlawick and Weakland (1977). From this perspective, all action is seen as potentially communicative, and context is the key factor in determining meaning. This view is most suitable for the study of strategic ambiguity, the meaning of which is heavily dependent upon the interactional context.

Now that the important epistemological issues have been addressed, the definitional process can proceed. Ambiguity has been addressed under a variety of labels, including indirectness (Branham, 1980; Nofsinger, 1976; Szasz, 1974), vagueness (Pascale & Athos, 1981), disqualification (Bavelas, 1983; Bavelas & Smith, 1982), and unclarity (Wender, 1968). The distinctions among these terms have themselves been unclear, primarily due to an inconsistent view of meaning. Most writers have endorsed the *interactional* view while at the same time attempting to identify specific *messages* which are more or less ambiguous. This is an impossible task, and more than one researcher has glossed the issue by remaining vague about the locus of ambiguity, i.e., whether it resides in the source's intentions, the receiver's interpretations, or in the message itself.

Some examples will illustrate the problem. In their study of equivocal messages in organizations, Putnam and Sorenson (1982) define ambiguity both in terms of message attributes (lack of specific detail, abstract language, absence of a course of action) and receiver interpretation (perceived equivocality of the message). Bavelas and Smith (1982) and Fowler et al. (1979) both posit an ideal message which is complete and clear and examine the ways in which actual messages are disqualified (Bavelas & Smith, 1982) or deviate from this hypothetical ideal.

Unfortunately, the concept of an ideally clear message is misleading in fundamental ways. Clarity (and conversely, ambiguity) is not an attribute of messages; it is a *relational* variable which arises through a combination of source, message, and receiver factors. Clarity exists to the extent that the following conditions are met: (1) an individual has an idea; (2) he or she encodes the idea into language; and (3) the receiver understands the message as it was intended by the source.[2] In trying to be clear, individuals take into account the possible interpretive contexts which may be brought to bear on the message by the receiver and attempt to narrow the possible interpretations. Clarity, then, is a continuum which reflects the degree to which a source has narrowed the possible interpretations of a message and succeeded in achieving a correspondence between his or her intentions and the interpretation of the receiver.

Returning now to the central argument, people in organizations do not always try to promote this correspondence between intent and interpretation. It is often preferable to omit purposefully contextual cues and to allow for multiple interpretations on the part of receivers. Furthermore, *clarity is only a measure of communicative competence if the individual has as his or her goal to be clear.*

One important implication of accepting a contextual view of meaning is that ambiguity can be engendered through detailed, literal language as well as through imprecise, figurative language. The particular message strategy chosen is not equivalent to whether an individual has been relatively clear or ambiguous. When communicating with close friends, incomplete phrases and vague references may engender high degrees of clarity, through the use of a restricted code; the same message strategies applied in less close relationships may lead to confusion and ambiguity. Conceived of in this way, ambiguity is totally independent of *perceived* ambiguity, which is a psychological variable; in fact, low levels of perceived ambiguity may often accompany high levels of strategic ambiguity, and vice versa.

A final qualification is in order. The focus of this paper is on the *strategic* use of ambiguity in organizations; as such, I am limiting the discussion to those instances where individuals use ambiguity purposefully to accomplish their goals. Not all communication is strategic, as evidenced by recent work on mindlessness and scripts (cf., Weick, 1983). Alternatively, ambiguity may be unrecognized (the speaker has no idea to communicate) or inadvertent (the speaker intends to be clear, but is unable to do so).

The aspect of strategic ambiguity which makes it essential to organizing is that it promotes unified diversity. This process is described in the next section.

Strategic Ambiguity Promotes Unified Diversity

Within every social system there exists a tension between the individual and the aggregate, the parts and the whole. In a free society, a balance must be maintained between "the requirements for dependable patterns of action and for independent initiatives" (Hollander, 1975, p. 56). This balance is closely allied to the dialectic of self-actualization and self-transcendence through others, to the individual's need to feel both a part of the social world and to develop a unique sense of self apart from the social world.

A similar balance is necessary in formal organizations. While organizations must generate sufficient consensus to survive, it is not always necessary or desirable to promote high levels of consensus among individual attitudes and goals (Weick, 1979a). In summarizing one school of organizational thought, Mohr (1983) concludes that there can be many advantages to cultivating inconsistency among goals, such as increased creativity and flexibility. The same theme appears repeatedly in the literature: How can cohesion and coordination be promoted while at the same time maintaining sufficient individual freedom to ensure flexibility, creativity, and adaptability to environmental change? This paradox has been referred to as the simultaneous seeking of self-determination and security (Peters & Waterman, 1982) and as the "unresolvable conflict" between centralization and decentralization (Pascale & Athos, 1981).

Perhaps the most elegant expression of the tension between the individual and the aggregate is given by Kant (in Becker, 1968) who argued that social systems should have as their goal "Maximum individuality within maximum community." Becker contends that this paradox makes a fitting, if unreachable goal for social systems. Contrary to traditional arguments, the "problem" of divergent goals is not always best resolved through consensus (through socialization or accommodation) but instead through the development of strategies which preserve and manage these differences.

But how can this be accomplished? One way of managing this paradox is through the creative use of symbols. Organizational values are often implicit in myths, sagas, and stories which are used as points of symbolic convergence (Bormann, 1983). Values are expressed in this form because their equivocal expression allows for multiple interpretations while at the same time promoting a sense of unity. It is therefore not the case that people are moved toward the *same* views (in any objectively verifiable sense) but rather that the ambiguous statement of core values allows them to maintain individual interpretations while at the same time believing that they are in agreement.

Strategic ambiguity fosters the existence of multiple viewpoints in organizations. This use of ambiguity is commonly found in organizational missions, goals, and plans. When organizational goals are stated concretely, they are often strikingly ineffective (Edelman, 1977). Strategic ambiguity is essential to organizing because it allows for multiple interpretations to exist among people who contend that they are attending to the same message—i.e., perceive the message to be clear. It is a political necessity to engage in strategic ambiguity so that different constituent groups may apply different interpretations to the symbol.

Ambiguity is used strategically to foster agreement on abstractions without limiting specific interpretations. For example, university faculty on any campus may take as their rallying point "academic freedom," while at the same time maintaining markedly different interpretations of the concept. Similarly, organizational myths (Smith & Simmons, 1983) which convey core organizational values may have a mantra-like ability to bind a group together while at the same time not limiting specific interpretations.

Focusing on organizational symbolism casts leadership in a new light as well. While a primary responsibility of leaders is to make meanings for followers (Pfeffer, 1981; Pondy, 1978; Smircich, 1983) and to infuse employees with values and purpose (Peters & Waterman, 1982; Selznick, 1957) the process of doing so is less one of consensus-making and more one of using language strategically to express values at a level of abstraction at which agreement *can* occur. If leadership is the ability to make organizational activities meaningful to members, the language required for such a task is abstract, evangelical, and even poetic (Weick, 1978). Effective leaders use ambiguity strategically to encourage creativity and guard against the acceptance of one standard way of viewing organizational reality.

Pascale and Athos (1981) make a similar observation in their discussion of "Zen and the Art of Management." When confronted with difficult decisions, managers must often "juggle" multiple goals. This juggling involves using less than explicit language, being purposefully vague, and leaving key meanings implicit. "*Vagueness in communication* can cause problems, to be sure, but it can also serve to hold strained relations together and reduce unnecessary conflict. There is too much American trust in increasing the clarity of communication between people, especially when disagreements are substantive. Getting a currently hopeless impasse clear is often unwise and likely to make things worse" (Pascale & Athos, 1981, p. 94, italics in original).

The writing of group documents provides a final example of how unified diversity can be promoted through the use of strategic ambiguity. When a group composed of individuals with divergent perspectives on a topic convenes to author a document collectively, the final product is presumed to represent the will of the group. Strategic ambiguity is often employed to make the group appear to speak in a single voice. Group members appeal to a repertoire of increasingly ambiguous legitimations which both retain the appearance of unity and reasonably represent the opinions of the group.

In the above discussion, I have taken issue with the typical emphasis on consensus in organizations. Multiple interpretations are inevitable in social systems, and ambiguity allows for both agreement in the abstract and the preservation of diverse viewpoints. We have seen how strategic ambiguity can promote unified diversity which is essential to the process of organizing; now we turn our attention to how ambiguity functions to bring about more specific individual and organizational outcomes. The first is the facilitation of change; the second is the amplification of existing source attributions and the preservation of privileged positions. Each of these issues is discussed in detail below.

Strategic Ambiguity Facilitates Organizational Change

At the organizational level, strategic ambiguity facilitates change through shifting interpretations of organizational goals and central metaphors. At the interpersonal level, ambiguity facilitates change through the development of relationships among organizational members.

Organizational Goals and Central Metaphors

Organizational goals are articulated at many levels, from the specifics of daily operations to the general relationship of the organization to the society. One fundamental goal, regarding the image of the company as an entity, is developed both internally for organizational members and externally for organizational publics. The strategic use of ambiguity aids in the effective statement of this goal.

Organizations change when their members change their metaphors of thinking about them (Pondy, 1983). Metaphor structures our lives in pervasive and subtle ways (Lakoff & Johnson, 1980; Ortony, 1975). According to Nisbet (1969, p. 6), revolutions in thought are quite often "no more than the mutational replacement, at certain critical points in history, of one foundation metaphor by another in man's contemplation of universe, society, and self."

Much has been written of late about the metaphors which characterize American organizations. Many writers, notably Weick (1979a), have discouraged the perpetuation of the military metaphor for organizing, with its corresponding orders, tactics, and chain of command. Numerous organizations have turned away from the military metaphor and replaced it with the family (cf. Peters & Waterman, 1982). What Kanter (1983) refers to as "strategic eras" in organizations can be launched through the careful use of metaphor; a shift from military to family, for example, could have widespread implications for behavior in the organization. The organizing strength of any central metaphor lies in the way it promotes unified diversity; individuals believe that they agree on what it means to be part of a "family," yet their actual interpretations may remain quite different.

Organizations must be ambiguous in stating goals which concern their publics. A common goal of state-supported universities is to establish a reasonable domain of concern, a limited geographical area in which services, funds, and students are exchanged. The definition of this domain is always problematic; narrow definition excludes outlying regions which may have something to offer, and overly broad definition leaves local communities feeling deserted. A rational organizational strategy is to be ambiguous, employing a statement such as, "The University shall be responsive to its surrounding areas," in public documents so as to retain flexibility to adapt to future opportunities and to satisfy multiple constituencies.

Organizational goals are expressed ambiguously to allow organizations the freedom to alter operations which have become maladaptive over time. Naisbitt (1982) argues that the question facing organizations in the 1980s is, "What business are you really in?" When air travel replaced sea travel from the United States to Europe, those cruise lines that survived did so because they defined their goals broadly as entertainment or hospitality, not narrowly as transportation. In this case, an ambiguous goal allowed these organizations to adapt by providing new types of services, such as pleasure cruises to nowhere and activities on boats that never left the dock. This characteristic of ambiguity is especially important to organizations in turbulent environments, in which ambiguous goals can preserve a sense of continuity while allowing for the gradual change in interpretation over time.

One last point deserves mention. In her analysis of innovation, Kanter (1983) reminds us that while symbols are important to organizing, they are not the whole story. The creation of inspirational, durable meanings is a crucial part of the change process, but it is not usually sufficient to sustain innovation. While endorsing the spirit of Bormann's (1983) assertion that symbolic changes can often shape technological ones, a more realistic scenario entails a mutual relationship between symbolic and technological change, of ideas and actions, of a manager's ability to operate both at the symbolic and at the practical level. "The tools of change masters are creative and interactive; they have an intellectual, a conceptual, and a cultural aspect. Change masters deal in symbols and visions and shared understanding as well as the techniques and trappings of their own specialties" (Kanter, 1983, p. 305).

Interpersonal Relationships

At the interpersonal level, strategic ambiguity can facilitate relational development. This occurs when organizational members are purposefully ambiguous and those attending to the message "fill in" what they believe to be the appropriate context and meaning. The more ambiguous the message, the greater the room for projection. When an individual projects, he or she fills in the meaning of a message in a way which is consistent with his or her own beliefs. Projection results in greater perceived similarity between source and receiver; research has shown that perceived similarity can lead to increased attraction and hence facilitate relational development (Clore & Byrne, 1974).[3]

Strategic ambiguity can facilitate relational development through the emergence of a restricted code to which only certain individuals are privy. In organizations, jargon, nicknames, and in-jokes can serve this function. To those outside of the language community, the discourse is strange, technical, or purposefully ambiguous; to those inside, it acts as a kind of incantation, an implicit expression of loyalty to the group or organization (Broms & Gahmberg, 1983; Edelman, 1977). Put differently, one of the results of strategic ambiguity is that camaraderie may form among those for whom the messages are not ambiguous, who believe that their privileged interpretations qualify them as part of an in-group.

Strategic ambiguity may be used inclusively or exclusively in organizing. In the context of relational development, ambiguity may be used inclusively to build the cohesiveness of an in-group and exclusively to allow certain people access to the "correct" interpretation, while purposefully mystifying or alienating others.

Finally, co-workers may use strategic ambiguity to control what they share of their private opinions, beliefs, or feelings. This allows them to be more tactful, to avoid conflict, and to understand one another without jeopardizing the relationship. Pascale and Athos (1981) see this in terms of indirection versus "brute integrity"; particularly when we anticipate working with someone in the future, it is important to consider whether unrestricted candor is worth the price of "the listener's goodwill, open-mindedness, and receptivity to change" (Pascale & Athos, 1981, p. 102). Many relationships in social systems are noninterpersonal and rely on imprecise and incomplete information which allows untested assumptions to persist (Moore & Tumin, 1948; Parks, 1982; Weick, 1979b). As an alternative to unrestricted candor, secrecy, or living, information control is often accomplished through the strategic use of ambiguity.

In addition to facilitating change at the organizational and interpersonal levels, strategic ambiguity can also amplify existing attributions and preserve privileged positions. This use of ambiguity is examined in the next section.

Strategic Ambiguity Amplifies Existing Source Attributions and Preserves Privileged Positions

Throughout his life, George Orwell maintained that all societies are organized upon the principle of unequal power, and that this power differential is maintained largely through the use of language by elites (Hodge & Fowler, 1979). One common strategy for preserving existing impressions and protecting privileged positions is strategic ambiguity.

In his discussion of responses to ambiguous stimuli, Manis (1961, p. 76) states that "in interpreting an ambiguous statement or opinion, the average person would be more strikingly influenced by his own views than he would be when interpreting a non-ambiguous statement." In practice, this implies that the same communication directed at the same receiver by sources differing in credibility would be interpreted differently. While this is surely true for relatively clear communication as well, one would expect even greater distortion when ambiguous communication is considered. Beliefs tend to be self-sealing; once an initial attribution is made about an individual, the tendency is to select information which is consistent with the initial assessment. In particular, language usage is a strong determinant of receivers' inferences about sources (Bradac, Bowers, & Courtright, 1979). Ambiguous communication has been shown to amplify existing impressions (Rogers, 1978), increase the match between a reader and a literary work (Skinner, in Wilson, 1971), and help to preserve and enhance attributions of credibility (Weick, Gilfillen, & Keith, 1973; Williams & Goss, 1975).

Similar findings have been reported by attribution theorists (Jones & Nisbett, 1972). People act to maintain a consistent set of beliefs about others, and hence dispositional attributions have considerable inertia. Highly credible people have greater freedom in what they can say to maintain a positive impression. A source deemed credible who speaks ambiguously may be called a prophet, but a low-credible source speaking identically may be dubbed a fool.

In organizations, strategic ambiguity is one way in which supervisors and subordinates can take out "character insurance" in order to maintain their formal or informal standing in the company (Williams & Goss, 1975). For those who are highly credible, clarity is always risky, since it provides the receiver with new information which can result in a potentially negative reevaluation of character. For those with low credibility, the opposite is true; clear communication remains a risk, but it is one of the only ways they can improve other's impressions of them through communication. It is important to remember, however, that communicators do not always have maintenance of self-image as their primary goal. On the contrary, people are sometimes willing to lose face in order to get a particular point across. While strategic ambiguity may be thought of as a way of coping with multiple goals, the priorities individuals assign to these goals may be highly variable.

Strategically Ambiguous Communication Is Deniable

In organizations, the deniability of ambiguous communication is a key element in the maintenance of privileged positions and has both task and interpersonal implications.

Deniability of task-related communication. Strategic ambiguity in task-related communication can preserve future options. Disclosure of information in unequivocal terms limits options and may prematurely endanger plans (Bok, 1983). Examples of this are common in the realm of international politics. For example, the American ambassador to the United Nations recently stated that Central American allies are consistently too explicit in discussing their affairs, and therefore deny the U.S. the "comforts of ambiguity." Similarly, Yoder (1983) has argued that the exercise of power is impossible if political actors are denied the use of ambiguity.

Sophisticated managers seldom "lay down the law" in areas of great importance to the organization. Many supervisors who have been overly clear in setting policy have found that the slightest violation of a rule by a valued employee places the supervisor in the untenable position of having to make a good decision while remaining consistent. Ambiguity can be used to allow specific interpretations of policies which might do more harm than good to be denied, should they arise.

Rather than being entirely secretive or clear, organizational communicators often employ some form of deniable discourse, such as strategic ambiguity. What Wheelright (1968) argues to be true for expressive language is true for other forms of ambiguity as well; ambiguous communication is characterized by its "assertorial lightness" and hence is more easily denied than its less equivocal counterpart. This strategy applies to the interorganizational realm as well; in the formation of interorganizational agreements, ambiguity is called for when a clear formulation will reduce flexibility of decision-making or lead to costly commitments which are hard to terminate (Aldrich & Whetten, 1981; Gottfredson & White, 1981; Metcalfe, 1981).

Deniability of interpersonal communication. The deniable aspect of strategic ambiguity is essential to interpersonal relationships in organizations as well. Labov and Fanshel (1977) argue that people need a form of discourse which is deniable in order to communicate; if one did not exist, they claim, people would create one. Szasz (1974) contends that indirect communication serves as a useful compromise between total silence and clear, potentially offensive communication. Szasz views indirect strategies as especially common in significant relationships wherein dependency needs and monetary problems are discussed; this seems clearly applicable to superior-subordinate dyads. Indirectness works because it "permits the expression of a need and its simultaneous denial or disavowal" (Szasz, 1974, p. 141). In organizations, strategic ambiguity helps to preserve the "close-but-not-too-close" nature of organizationally sanctioned interpersonal relationships (Pacanowsky & O'Donnell-Trujillo, 1983) by allowing participants to express their thoughts and feelings and simultaneously to deny specific interpretations which may be especially face-threatening.

The use of strategic ambiguity complicates the task of interpretation for the receiver. For example, an individual can disclose an important piece of information ambiguously ("I feel uncomfortable in this job") and then deny specific interpretations should they arise ("You mean you can't get along with the boss?"). This interplay between ambiguous assertions and requests for clarification is common on news shows that feature interviews with politicians; interviewers attempt to narrow the interpretive context, while politicians try to retain multiple possible interpretations. By complicating the sense-making responsibilities of the receiver, strategically ambiguous communication allows the source to both reveal and conceal, to express and protect, should it become necessary to save face. While Goffman (1967) is astute in observing, "There is much to be gained in venturing nothing," there is often even more to be gained by giving the appearance of venturing something which, on closer inspection, may be made to seem like nothing.

Lastly, it is important to note that clear communication is also deniable; it is just more difficult to do so and at the same time save face. Strategic ambiguity must be viewed as a continuum, from most clear to most ambiguous; the more ambiguous the communication, the easier it is to deny specific interpretations.

Research Strategies

Thus far in this paper, I have defined strategic ambiguity and offered an explanation of how it promotes the unified diversity essential to organizing. Two pervasive applications of strategic ambiguity were described as well: the facilitation of change, and the maintenance of attributions and privileged positions. In this final section, suggestions for how these ideas might be evaluated through empirical research are presented.

In operationalizing strategic ambiguity, some popular approaches can be ruled out. Since ambiguity is defined relationally, and not as a property of messages, experiments which assign levels of ambiguity to specific messages should be avoided. Even the most literal-appearing utterance can become highly ambiguous given certain relational contexts. Alternatively, measurement of the construct requires a knowledge of communicative goals, linguistic choices, and receiver interpretation. When we know these three things, we can assess the level of correspondence between intent and interpretation, as well as examine the linguistic forms which are used to accomplish this correspondence.

One example of this type of operationalization can be found in a recent study of superior-subordinate communication.[4] In this study, students role-playing superiors and subordinates were instructed to give negative feedback on a letter that their partner had written. Information was collected concerning their communicative goals, the message strategies they used in giving the feedback, and the interpretations and attributions of receivers. From this information, differences in ambiguity were calculated and examined in relation to message strategies chosen and overall judgments of effectiveness in superior and subordinate roles.

This study should be followed up by field investigations which distinguish among the use of ambiguity in different communicative contexts. Two important dimensions of context are the type of audience (internal or external to the organization) and the level of formality of the communication (formal or informal). A four cell matrix suggested by these dimensions is presented in Figure 1.

In Cell 1, formal internal communication, the research focus should be on how ambiguity promotes unified diversity and maintains privileged positions. Examples of this type of communication are organized goals, rules, policies and procedures; texts of these messages are likely to be available for analysis. As a result, appropriate methodologies include naturalistic and critical research in the interpretative tradition (Bantz, 1983). Naturalistic research could aim to describe how goals, policies, and procedures structure the reality-definition of organizational members. Critical research might examine how these same messages perpetuate the status quo. Linguistic analysis such as that done by Fowler et al. (1979) could be used to examine how the microscopic aspects of the texts reflect attitudes and behavior. Finally, this communicative context is especially amenable to rhetorical analysis, which would focus on the role of ambiguity in the persuasive aspects of the texts.

In Cell 2, informal internal communication, the research focus should be on how ambiguity is used in the development of interpersonal relationships. Examples of communication of this kind are conversation, group discussion, and the telling of organizational stories. Since these kinds of communication are usually oral, a successful research strategy would be discourse or conversation analysis. Informal communication could be analyzed to reveal the ways in which individuals attempt to balance among multiple interactional goals, particularly getting the job done and preserving interpersonal relationships.

More traditional work with superior-subordinate communication is also appropriate here (cf. Jablin, 1979). One approach to the study of strategic ambiguity in this context is coorientation on communication rules (Eisenberg, Monge, & Farace, 1984; Farace et al., 1977; Poole & McPhee, 1983). Coorientation theory is well suited to the study of ambiguity since it cuts across systems levels and focuses on relational concepts such as agreement, accuracy, and perceived agreement. From the standpoint of coorientation theory, a major function of strategically ambiguous communication between superiors and subordinates may be the maintenance of metaperspectives which facilitate positive evaluation. People in organizations do not always seek consensus on rules and often avoid situations where conflicting perceptions would be apparent and might have a negative effect on relationships. If communicators balance among multiple goals, they may use strategic ambiguity to avoid exposing those areas where their attitudes diverge from others with whom they work.

In Cell 3, formal external communication, the research focus should be on the preservation of future options and the deniability of formal statements to external audiences. Examples of communication of this type are public relations campaigns, advertising and sales information, and interorganizational agreements. As in Cell 1, much of this communication is written and texts are available for naturalistic, critical, or rhetorical analysis. Theories of marketing and of the relationship between organizations and their environments (Aldrich, 1979) could also be helpful in this context.

In Cell 4, informal external communication, the focus should be on how strategic ambiguity is used to develop interorganizational linkages which

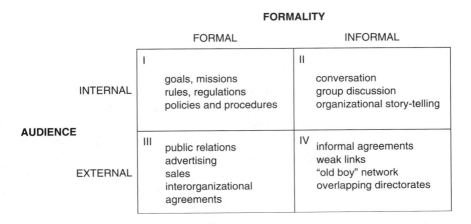

FORMALITY

	FORMAL	INFORMAL
INTERNAL	I goals, missions rules, regulations policies and procedures	II conversation group discussion organizational story-telling
EXTERNAL	III public relations advertising sales interorganizational agreements	IV informal agreements weak links "old boy" network overlapping directorates

AUDIENCE

Figure 1.1   Dimensions of Communicative Context Appropriate for the Study of Strategic Ambiguity

are often covert and highly political. The deniable aspect of this type of communication is extremely important. Examples of communication in this context are informal agreements, weak links, and interactions in the "old-boy" network. As in Cell 2, the key issues here are those of interpersonal politics and the balancing of individual, interpersonal, and organizational goals. Unlike internal communication, however, problems specific to this context include both legal ramifications and the difficulties encountered by boundary role occupants in maintaining loyalties and eliciting trust from co-workers (Adams, 1980). Studies in this area might focus on less obvious records of interorganizational communication, such as overlapping directorates, membership in professional clubs and associations, and informal agreements (Eisenberg et al., in press).

Regardless of which communicative context is chosen for study, researchers should focus on three basic questions: (1) What factors influence the formation of interactional goals? (2) How do people in organizations try to accomplish these goals through communication? and (3) How are different communicative strategies interpreted by others in and outside of the organization?

Some important questions remain. Once we gather a better understanding of how people use ambiguity in organizations, how will this affect what we tell managers and employees about what constitutes effective communication? What is the pedagogy of ambiguity, and what are its ethical constraints? Empirical research on strategic ambiguity should prompt further inquiry into these and related issues.

Conclusion

The model of meaning suggested in this paper is compatible with both a more realistic and desirable conception of organizations, one in which disagreement and idiosyncrasy are not necessarily minimized, but managed. Particularly in turbulent environments, ambiguous communication is not a kind of fudging, but rather a rational method used by communicators to orient toward multiple goals. It is easy to imagine the ethical problems that might result from the misuse of ambiguity. In the final analysis, however, both the effectiveness and the ethics of any particular communicative strategy are relative to the goals and values of the communicators in the situation. The use of more or less ambiguity is in itself not good or bad, effective or ineffective; whether a strategy is ethical depends upon the ends to which it is used, and whether it is effective depends upon the goals of the individual communicators.

As long as organizational scholars regard ambiguity as deviational rather than as contributing to normal interaction, they will remain unenlightened about the most dramatic aspects of organizations, those instances of communication which most influence our lives (Branham, 1980). Wheelright's (1968) commentary on metaphor and myth can be extended to apply to ambiguity:

> The metaphor and myth are necessary expressions of the human psyche's most central energy-tension; without it . . . mankind would succumb to the fate that the Forgotten Enemy holds ever in store for us, falling from the ambiguous grace of being human into the unisignative security of the reacting mechanism. (p. 123)

It is a common observation that humans are both social and symbolic animals. What is less frequently recognized is that the strategic use of symbols can facilitate the operation of the social order. We should turn our attention toward how this is accomplished in organizations.

AUTHOR'S NOTE: The author gratefully acknowledges the helpful comments and suggestions of Karen Tracy, Linda Putnam, Arthur Bochner, Lori Roscoe, Louis Cusella, Richard Buttny, James Dillard, and Patricia Riley.

Notes

1. An example of this perspective is given by Putnam and Jones (1982) in their discussion of the role of communication in bargaining. They conclude from the literature that open, honest communication is not a prerequisite for cooperation; in fact, more flexible commitment communicated via tentative, indirect language led to reciprocal concessions, whereas more firm commitments led to conflict escalation.

2. This definition is taken in part from a program of research Karen Tracy and I are conducting on the use of clarity in multiple goal situations.

3. Although he diverges from the definition of ambiguity offered in this paper, Cohen (1978) presents an intriguing argument about the relationship between metaphor and intimacy:

> There is a unique way in which the maker and the appreciator of a metaphor are drawn closer to one another. Three aspects are involved: (1) the speaker issues a kind of concealed invitation; (2) the hearer extends

a special effort to accept the invitation; and (3) this transaction constitutes the acknowledgment of a community. All three are involved in any communication, but in ordinary literal discourse their involvement is so pervasive and routine that they go unmarked. (p. 6)

4. This is the first in a series of studies mentioned in Note 2.

References

Adams, J. S. (1980). Interorganizational processes and organization boundary activities. In B. Staw & L. L. Cummings (Eds.), *Research in organizational behavior* (Vol. 2, pp. 321–355). Greenwich, CT: JAI Press.

Aldrich, H. E. (1979). *Organizations and environments.* Englewood Cliffs, NJ: Prentice Hall.

Aldrich, H. E., & Whetten, D. A. (1981). Organization-sets, action-sets, and networks: Making the most out of simplicity. In P. C. Nystrom & W. H. Starbuck (Eds.), *Handbook of organizational design* (Vol. 1, pp. 385–408). New York: Oxford University Press.

Argyris, C., & Schon, D. (1978). *Organizational learning.* Reading, MA: Addison-Wesley.

Bantz, C. R. (1983). Naturalistic research traditions. In L. Putnam & M. Pacanowsky (Eds.), *Communication and organizations: An interpretive approach* (pp. 55–72). Beverly Hills, CA: Sage.

Bassett, G. A. (1974). What is communication and how can I do it better? *Management Review,* February, 25–32.

Bavelas, J. B. (1983). Situations that lead to disqualification. *Human Communication Research, 9,* 130–145.

Bavelas, J. B., & Smith, B. J. (1982). A method for scaling verbal disqualification. *Human Communication Research, 8,* 214–227.

Becker, E. (1968). *The structure of evil.* New York: The Free Press.

Bochner, A.P. (1982). On the efficacy of openness in close relationships. In M. Burgoon (Ed.), *Communication yearbook 5* (pp. 109–124). New Brunswick, NJ: Transaction Books.

Bok, S. (1983). *Secrets: On the ethics of concealment and revelation.* New York: Pantheon Books.

Bormann, E. G. (1983). Symbolic convergence: Organizational communication an culture. In L. Putnam & M. Pacanowsky (Eds.), *Communication and organizations: An interpretive approach* (pp. 99–122). Beverly Hills, CA: Sage.

Bradac, J. J., Bowers, J. W., & Courtright, J. (1979). Three language variables in communication research: Intensity, immediately, and diversity. *Human Communication Research, 5,* 257–269.

Branham, R. J. (1980). Ineffability, creativity, and communication competence. *Communication Quarterly, 28,* 11–21.

Broms, H., & Gahmberg, H. (1983). Communication to self in organizations and cultures. *Administrative Science Quarterly, 28,* 482–495.

Brown, P., & Levinson, S. L. (1978). Universals in language usage: Politeness phenomena. In E. N. Goody (Ed.), *Questions and politeness: Strategies in social interaction* (pp. 56–289). New York: Cambridge University Press.

Burke, K. (1969). *A grammar of motives*. Berkeley: University of California Press.

Clark, R. A., & Delia, J. G. (1979). Topoi and rhetorical competence. *The Quarterly Journal of Speech, 65,* 187–206.

Clore, G., & Byrne, D. (1974). A reinforcement model of attraction. In T. L. Huston (Ed.), *Foundations of interpersonal attraction* (pp. 143–170). New York: Academic Press.

Cohen, T. (1978). Metaphor and the cultivation of intimacy. In S. Sacks (Ed.), *On metaphor* (pp. 1–10). Chicago: University of Illinois Press.

Dandridge, T. C. (1979). *Celebrations of corporate anniversaries: An example of modern organizational symbols*. Working paper, State University of New York at Albany.

Edelman, M. (1977). *Political language: Words that succeed and policies that fail*. New York: Academic Press.

Eisenberg, E. M., Farace, R. V., Monge, P. R., Bettinghaus, E. P., Kurchner-Hawkins, R., White, L., & Miller, K. I. (1985). Communication linkages in interorganizational systems. In M. Voight & B. Dervin (Eds.), *Progress in communication science*. Vol. 6. New York: Ablex.

Eisenberg, E. M., Monge, P. R., & Farace, R. V. (1984). *Co-orientation on communication rules as a predictor of interpersonal evaluations in managerial dyads*. Paper presented at the annual meeting of the International Communication Association, San Francisco, CA.

Farace, R. V., Monge, P. R., & Russell, H. (1977). *Communicating and organizing*. Reading, MA: Addison-Wesley.

Fisher, D. W. (1982). A model for better communication. *Supervisory Management, 27,* 24–29.

Fowler, R., Hodge, B., Kress, G., & Trew, T. (1979). *Language and control*. London: Routledge & Kegan Paul.

Frank, A. D. (1982). *Communicating on the job*. Glenview, IL: Scott Foresman.

Goffman, E. (1967). On facework. In E. Goffman, *Interaction ritual* (pp. 5–45). New York: Doubleday Anchor.

Gottfredson, L. S., & White, P. E. (1981). Interorganizational agreements. In P. C. Nystrom & W. H. Starbuck (Eds.), *Handbook of organizational design* (Vol. 1., pp. 471–486). New York: Oxford University Press.

Harris, L., & Cronen, V. (1979). A rules-based model for the analysis and evaluation of organizational communication. *Communication Quarterly, 27,* 12–28.

Hart, R. P., & Burks, D. M. (1972). Rhetorical sensitivity and social interaction. *Speech Monographs, 39,* 75–91.

Hodge, B., & Fowler, R. (1979). Orwellian linguistics. In R. Fowler, B. Hodge, G. Kress, & T. Trew (Eds.), *Language and control* (pp. 6–25). London: Routledge & Kegan Paul.

Hollander, E. P. (1975). Independence, conformity, and civil liberties: Some implications from social psychological research. *Journal of Social Issues, 31,* 55–67.

Jablin, F. M. (1979). Superior-subordinate communication: The state of the art. *Psychological Bulletin, 86,* 1201–1222.

Jelinek, M., Smircich, L., & Hirsch, P. (1983). Introduction: A code of many colors. *Administrative Science Quarterly, 28,* 331–338.

Johnson, B. M. (1977). *Communication: The process of organizing.* Boston: Allyn & Bacon.

Jones, E., & Nisbett, R. (1972). The actor and the observer: Divergent perceptions of the causes of behavior. In E. Jones, D. Kanouse, H. Kelley, R. Nisbett, S. Valins, & B. Weiner (Eds.), *Attribution: Perceiving the causes of behavior* (pp. 78–94). Morristown, NJ: General Learning Press.

Kanter, R. M. (1983). *The change masters.* New York: Simon and Schuster.

Labov, W., & Fanshel, D. (1977). *Therapeutic discourse: Psychotherapy as conversation.* New York: Academic Press.

Lakoff, G., & Johnson, M. (1980). *Metaphors we live by.* Chicago: University of Chicago Press.

Levy, D. M. (1979). Communication goals and strategies: Between discourse and syntax. In T. Givon (Ed.), *Syntax and semantics* (Vol. 12, pp. 183–210). New York: Academic Press.

Lorey, W. (1976). Mutual trust is the key to open communications. *Administrative Management, 92,* 70–74.

Manis, M. (1961). The interpretation of opinion statements as a function of message ambiguity and recipient attitude. *Journal of Abnormal and Social Psychology, 63,* 76–81.

Metcalfe, L. (1981). Designing precarious partnerships. In P. Nystrom & W. Starbuck (Eds.), *Handbook of organizational design* (Vol. 1, pp. 503–530). New York: Oxford University Press.

Mohr, L. B. (1983). The implications of effectiveness theory for managerial practice in the public sector. In K. S. Cameron & D. A. Whetten (Eds.), *Organizational effectiveness* (pp. 225–239). New York: Academic Press.

Monge, P. R., Bachman, S., Dillard, J. P., & Eisenberg, E. M. (1982). Communicator competence in the workplace: Model testing and scale development. In M. Burgoon (Ed.), *Communication yearbook 5* (pp. 505–528). New Brunswick, NJ: Transaction Books.

Moore, W., & Tumin, M. (1948). Some social functions of ignorance. *American Sociological Review, 14,* 787–795.

Naisbitt, J. (1982). *Megatrends.* New York: Warner Books.

Nisbet, R. A. (1969). *Social change and history: Aspects of the Western theory of development.* London: Oxford University Press.

Nofsinger, R. D., Jr. (1976). On answering questions indirectly: Some rules in the grammar of doing conversation. *Human Communication Research, 2,* 172–181.

Ortony, A. (1975). Why metaphors are necessary and not just nice. *Educational Theory, 25,* 45–53.

Ortony, A. (1979). Metaphor: A multidimensional problem. In A. Ortony (Ed.), *Metaphor and thought* (pp. 1–16). Cambridge: Cambridge University Press.

Pacanowsky, M. E., & O'Donnell-Trujillo, N. (1983). Organizational communication as cultural performance. *Communication Monographs, 50,* 186–147.

Parks, M. P. (1982). Ideology in interpersonal communication: Off the couch and into the world. In M. Burgoon (Ed.), *Communication yearbook 5* (pp. 79–108). New Brunswick, NJ: Transaction Books.

Pascale, R. T., & Athos, A. G. (1981). *The art of Japanese management.* New York: Simon and Schuster.

Pearce, W. B., Cronen, V., & Conklin, F. (1979). On what to look at when analyzing communication: A hierarchical model of actor's meanings. *Communication, 4,* 195–220.

Peters, T. J., & Waterman, R. H. (1982). *In search of excellence.* New York: Harper & Row.

Pfeffer, J. (1981). Management as symbolic action: The creation and maintenance of organizational paradigms. In B. Staw & L. L. Cummings (Eds.), *Research in organizational behavior* (Vol. 3, pp. 1–52). Greenwich, CT: JAI Press.

Pondy, L. R. (1978). Leadership is a language game. In M. M. Lombardo & M. W. McCall, Jr. (Eds.) *Leadership: Where else can we go* (pp. 87–99). Durham, NC: Duke University Press.

Pondy, L. R. (1983). The role of metaphors and myths in organization and the facilitation of change. In L. R. Pondy, P. J. Frost, G. Morgan, & T. C. Dandridge (Eds.), *Organizational symbolism* (pp. 157–166). Greenwich, CT: JAI Press.

Pondy, L. R., Frost, P. J., Morgan, G., & Dandridge, T. C. (1983). *Organizational symbolism.* Greenwich, CT: JAI Press.

Poole, M. S., & McPhee, R. D. (1983). A structurational analysis of organizational climate. In L. Putnam & M. Pacanowsky (Eds.), *Communication and organizations: An interpretive approach* (pp. 195–220). Beverly Hills, CA: Sage Publications.

Putnam, L. L. (1983). The interpretive perspective: An alternative to functionalism. In L. L. Putnam & M. Pacanowsky (Eds.), *Communication and organizations: An interpretive approach* (pp. 31–54). Beverly Hills, CA: Sage.

Putnam, L. L., & Jones, T. S. (1982). The role of communication in bargaining. *Human Communication Research, 8,* 262–280.

Putnam, L. L., & Sorenson, R. L. (1982). Equivocal messages in organizations. *Human Communication Research, 8,* 114–132.

Rogers, R. (1978). *Metaphor: A psychoanalytic view.* Berkeley: University of California Press.

Rorty, R. (1979). *Philosophy and the mirror of nature.* Princeton, NJ: Princeton University Press.

Selznick, P. *Leadership in administration: A sociological interpretation.* New York: Harper & Row.

Sigband, N. B. (1976). *Communication for management and business* (2nd Edition). Glenview, IL: Scott Foresman.

Smircich, L. (1983). Concepts of culture and organizational analysis. *Administrative Science Quarterly, 28,* 339–358.

Smircich, L., & Morgan, G. (1982). Leadership: The management of meaning. *Journal of Applied Behavioral Science, 18,* 257–273.

Smith, K. K., & Simmons, V. M. (1983). A Rumpelstiltskin organization: Metaphors on metaphors in field research. *Administrative Science Quarterly, 28,* 377–392.

Szasz, T. S. (1974). *The myth of mental illness.* New York: Harper & Row.

Tracy, K., & Moran, J. (1983). Conversational relevance in multiple goal settings. In R. Craig & K. Tracy (Eds.), *Conversational coherence: Form, structure, and strategy* (pp. 116–135). Beverly Hills, CA: Sage Publications.

Vonbergen, C. W., Jr., & Shealy, R. E. (1982). How's your empathy? *Training and Development Journal,* November, 22–32.

Watzlawick, P., & Weakland, J. (1977). *The interactional view.* New York: Norton.

Weick, K. E. (1978). The spines of leaders. In M. Lombardo & M. McCall (Eds.), *Leadership: Where else can we go* (pp. 37–61). Durham, NC: Duke University Press.

Weick, K. E. (1979a). Cognitive processes in organizations. In B. Staw & L. Cummings (Eds.), *Research in organizational behavior* (Vol. 1, pp. 41–74). Greenwich, CN: JAI Press.

Weick, K. E. (1979b). *The social psychology of organizing* (2nd Edition). Reading, MA: Addison-Wesley.

Weick, K. E. (1983). Organizational communication: Toward a research agenda. In L. Putnam and M. Pacanowsky (Eds.), *Communication and organizations: An interpretive approach* (pp. 13–30). Beverly Hills, CA: Sage.

Weick, K. E., Gilfillen, D., & Keith, T. (1973). The effect of composer credibility on orchestra performance. *Sociometry, 36,* 435–462.

Wender, P. (1968). Communicative unclarity: Some comments on the rhetoric of confusion. *Psychiatry, 31,* 247–274.

Wheelright, P. (1968) *The burning fountain: A study in the language of symbolism.* Bloomington, IN: Indiana University Press.

Wilder, C. (1979). The Palo Alto Group: Difficulties and directions of the interactional view for human communication. *Human Communication Research, 5,* 171–186.

Williams, M. L., & Goss, B. (1975). Equivocation: Character insurance. *Human Communication Research, 1,* 265–270.

Wilson, G. B. (1971). *Purposeful ambiguity as a persuasive message strategy.* Unpublished master's thesis, Department of Communication, Michigan State University.

Wycoff, E. B. (1981). Canons of communication. *Personnel Journal, 60,* 208–212.

Yoder, E. M. (1983). Foreign policy needs ambiguity. *Philadelphia Inquirer,* August 2.

2

Meaning and Interpretation in Organizations

Written as a book review, this short paper captured a unique moment in the development of organizational communication as a discipline, when scholars began to take a turn toward interpretive research marked by a greater acceptance of qualitative and critical methods. A central point of this essay was a critique of the idea of "shared meaning" as a criterion for evaluating the effectiveness of communication. Picking up on my earlier suggestion that there are certain conditions under which disagreements can be usefully masked through the use of ambiguous language, I argued that an evaluation of the degree of "shared meaning" is practically impossible and that concerns for this kind of alignment should yield to an approach that emphasizes the achievement of sufficient cognitive alignment to facilitate coordinated action.

Given its emphasis on traditional rhetorical studies, the Quarterly Journal of Speech *was an unusual outlet for this work, but the editor at the time (Walter Fisher) was aggressively seeking to broaden the scope of the journal. Nonetheless, I struggled to prepare a manuscript that was acceptable to a book review editor (and audience) that was more accustomed to rhetorical analysis. Since then, the connections between rhetoric and organizational communication have strengthened, but in 1986 they were, with very few exceptions (e.g., work by Phil Tompkins and George Cheney), different social worlds. This paper sought to build some small bridges between them.*

SOURCE: Eisenberg, E. M. (1986). Meaning and interpretation in organizations. *Quarterly Journal of Speech, 72,* 88–97. Copyright © 1986. Reproduced by permission of Taylor & Francis Group, LLC., http://taylorandfrancis.com.

Three beliefs have dominated theory and research in organizational communication: all problems in interpersonal relations are communication problems; "opening up lines of communication" is the solution to these problems; and organizational communication is a pervasive but tangential process, important only to the extent that it affects productivity and morale.[1] While these beliefs have not disappeared from the literature, they are being increasingly challenged by new studies, including the books reviewed in this essay. No longer are all interpersonal problems attributed to poor communication; no longer are organizational members expected to conform mindlessly to prescriptions of openness and honesty; and, perhaps most significantly, no longer is formal communication deemed more significant than informal communication. Indeed, "idle talk" is seen as the crucial stuff out of which organizations are constructed and sustained.[2]

The growing sophistication of organizational communication research is evident in other fundamental ways as well. The appropriateness of the "conduit" metaphor for studying communication has been challenged,[3] and message fidelity and shared beliefs are no longer taken to be the hallmarks of effective communication.[4] Rather than focusing on the short-term effects of messages as they once did, researchers instead are considering the practical force of messages to be a function of incremental, cyclical effects. Finally, organizational communication is no longer viewed in purely instrumental ways but rather as the ongoing evolution and negotiation of meaning.

Some important questions accompany this new emphasis on meaning. First, how do interpretations evolve in organizations, and what factors cause them to remain stable or to change? Second, how important are shared interpretations in effective organizing? Third, how can symbols be used in the service of power and control? Fourth, what methodologies are best suited to the study of symbols in organizations? Finally, what are the social and political implications of research on organizations as interpretation systems?

Preliminary answers to these questions are emerging in investigations throughout the discipline[5] and in the books reviewed here. The issues these authors choose to address highlight the continued maturation of the field and document its successes and failures in attempting to deal satisfactorily with the role of meaning in organizational life.

Despite the fact that investigators adopt somewhat different vocabularies (e.g., organizational symbolism, interpretive research, organizational culture, information processing in organizations), the central issue that emerges consistently is meaning.[6] These disagreements over vocabulary are important, however. They reflect the different goals each set of authors brings to his or her work. Linda Putnam and Michael Pacanowsky's *Communication and*

Organizations: An Interpretive Approach (PP), for example, is comprised mainly of essays by communication researchers searching for an alternative to functionalism. *Organizational Symbolism,* by Louis Pondy, Peter Frost, Greth Morgan, and Thomas Dandridge (PFMD), attempts to demarcate a new subfield within organizational behavior: "organizational symbolism." Finally, Lee Sproull and Patrick Larkey's *Advances in Information Processing in Organizations* (SL) reflects the dissatisfaction of researchers with information theory and their subsequent attempt to take a broader view of communication as a potential solution to their problems. Despite this diversity of orientations and concerns, each collection contains essays which address key aspects of the five questions posed above.

I

How do interpretations evolve in organizations? Through communication, individuals over time create, maintain, and transform the social realities they inhabit. Organizations are richly textured "symbolic fields" in which root-metaphors, stories, and myths continually generate interpretations for ongoing events.[7]

Two theoretical perspectives which typify this view of organizational reality are social constructionism[8] and structuration.[9] A critical feature of both perspectives is their attention to the nature of stability and change. Organizations achieve stability through the enactment of interaction cycles and the subsequent development of rules and recipes for appropriate behavior. Over time, these habitualized patterns of interaction are used to "achieve routine" by reducing the equivocality of novel events.[10]

A key to understanding how interpretations evolve is the role time plays in determining meaning. Time is critical because transactions have no meaning outside of their historical contexts; the expectations attendant upon an interactional moment are crucial for understanding the meaning of that interaction. A study of one such configuration is found in Patrick Larkey's and Richard Smith's history of budgetary misrepresentation in Pittsburgh's city government (SL). Their analysis of a forty-year time span reveals that (1) executives have strong incentives to misrepresent budgetary figures; (2) misrepresentation, over time, comes to be a sign of the experienced executive; and (3) some degree of misrepresentation is beneficial to the smooth operation of the city. While this example may seem extreme, it is in many ways typical of the complex political and historical contexts which must be taken into account in order to understand fully how communication works in organizations.

Over time, interpretations guide actions and actions shape interpretations, all within the framework of talk. As Karl Weick (PP) advises: "Until the linkage between talk and action is more clearly understood . . . conventional organizational wisdom will direct attention at conventional organizational variables—and not talk—to account for what goes on in organizations" (p. 17). One way to conceive of the communication-action relationship is as a mutually causal, deviation-amplifying cycle. Many organizations, unfortunately, learn too late about the potentially vicious nature of this cycle and how easy it is to fall into damaging ruts.

Another way of thinking about the interrelationship between talk and action is in terms of the metaphors, myths, and stories that guide interpretation (Harry Abravanel, PFMD; Joanne Martin & Melanie Powers, PFMD; Louis Pondy, PFMD; Alan Wilkins, PFMD). Metaphors generate meanings which can have a stabilizing effect on organizational behavior and suggest what behaviors are appropriate or inappropriate. Metaphors provide cues from other contexts (e.g., the family) which aid in the interpretation of events in the organization. Over time, root-metaphors may outlive their usefulness and eventually be replaced.

Changes in root-metaphors prompt individuals to reinterpret past events and to apply them to present conditions. Metaphors are particularly effective in facilitating change because they simultaneously reinforce existing values (by providing no literal challenge to the status quo) and suggest future possibilities. "Metaphor facilitates change by making the strange familiar, but in the very process [it] deepens the meaning of values in the organization by giving them expression in novel situations. . . . Because of its inherent ambivalence of meaning, metaphor can fulfill this dual function of enabling change and preserving continuity" (Pondy, PFMD. p. 164). It is worth noting that this dual function is served not only by metaphor, but by ambiguous language in general.[11]

In summary, research on the evaluation of interpretations in organizations is already well under way. Foundational theoretical perspectives (e.g., social constructionism, structuration) are evoked in these essays, but many details remain to be worked out. As Scott Poole and Robert McPhee suggest (PP), the key to understanding the process of interpretations in organizations is in the examination of the enactment of social structures and the ritualized creation of social reality through interaction cycles. Interpretations are cyclical, both because they cannot be understood outside of their historical context, and because they exist as part of a mutually causal relationship with communication and action. Interpretations develop both through the routinization of everyday interaction and through the emergence of root-metaphors that provide frameworks for making sense of the organizational world.

As interpretations develop in organizations, the degree of overlap between any two individuals' worldviews is not necessarily constant. Some organizations are more homogeneous than others, and within a given organization, one might find more overlap at different stages of development (i.e., shared interpretations may be more likely early in an organization's history).

II

How important are shared interpretations in organizations? With few exceptions researchers have argued that a primary function of communication in organizations is to facilitate the development of shared meanings, values, and beliefs. This theme appears repeatedly with different labels: coorientation, symbolic convergence, agreement, and "strong" cultures. Linda Smircich (PFMD), for example, argues that shared interpretations must be maintained for coordinated action to occur. Ernest Bormann (PP), in elaborating the notion of fantasy themes, stresses the importance of shared attitudes and emotions:

> When members of an organization share a fantasy, they have jointly experienced the same emotions; they developed the same attitudes and emotional responses to the personae of the drama; and they have interpreted some aspect of the experience in the same way. (p. 104)

The use of the words "same" and "share" here is problematic, however. If they are meant literally (as a one-to-one correspondence between cognitive states), the statement is wholly unverifiable. While people may share common modes of expression, it is hard to imagine how one would determine if they have in fact "jointly experienced the same emotion."

Making the argument for the importance of shared interpretations, Stanley Deetz and Astrid Kersten (PP) call for greater openness and increased participation in the workplace. This ideal has some potentially negative implications. Effective coordination of action is more often based on control and limitation of information than on the unrestricted exchange of ideas. The author's idealism—their hope that through open communications "agreement can be reached on fundamental ethical principles"—is a good example of the American bias toward ironing out differences rather than learning to live comfortably with diversity.[12]

The focus on persuasion, consensus, and the development of shared values can have other negative effects as well. J. Rounds (SL) and Larkey and Smith (SL) provide examples of how participation, when taken too far, can erode the common ground of discourse and lead to the revelation of conflicts which may be internally divisive and threaten the very legitimacy of the organization. In a culture that values professionalism and expertise, limited participation is a fact of life; acknowledging expertise implies a willingness to forgo full participation in a particular area. Full participation and "true consensus" do not appear to be either realistic or altogether desirable goals for organizations to pursue.

Equally problematic are calls for "strong organizational cultures" in which there is widespread agreement on core values and beliefs. The "excellent" companies studied by Thomas Peters and Robert Waterman are not the most livable for employees; *efforts to promote value consensus tend to be "top-down" and entail the construction of myths and stories by top management to manipulate employees.*[13] Terence Mitchell elaborates on this critique: "The orthodoxy underlying the 'excellence' position has serious negative consequences . . . the manipulative mode is detrimental to personal development . . . (it) violates the human essence, prohibits the expression of virtue and leads to personal and systemic corruption."[14] Attempts at building homogeneous cultures are reminiscent of efforts to regulate the production of art; the harder one pushes, the less likely one is to get the desired result. The collection of key organizational symbols at RCA by Gary Kreps to "speed up" socialization (PP) is an example of such an attempt to legislature culture; more than anything else, such an intervention makes too apparent a bias toward homogeneity and managerial control.

Some of the essays in these collections, rather than focusing on organizations as systems of shared interpretations, focus instead on the sharing of modes of expression. Such an approach, while implying a shared symbol system, does not require consensus on specific interpretations. Roger Evered (PFMD), for example, describes the vocabulary of the Navy and shows the importance of the ability to speak a common language to membership in that community. Similarly, Paul Hirsch and John Andrews (PFMD) describe the language of corporate takeovers as one in which the choice of a particular metaphor (e.g., war or seduction) carries with it expectations for behavior. Neither author presupposes that the use of a common vocabulary is necessarily isomorphic with shared interpretations.

Strong bonds can be created in organizations without shared interpretations, and efforts to promote sharing may in fact inhibit the formation of such bonds. Through the limitation of communication or use of ambiguous or metaphorical language, groups can focus on a sense of community, while at the same time preserving unique beliefs and interpretations. Barbara Myerhoff provides an example of this process in her discussion of "communitas" at Woodstock and among the Huichol Indians.[15] Communitas, the feeling of an ecstatic, common bond with a group, requires, above all, a *conviction* that important values are fully shared. For this reason, communication must be imprecise in order that members may assume that they are in fact sharing a vision. Meyerhoff concludes:

> Thus the Huichols will not discuss their peyote visions, and hippies often limit their description of their trips to comments such as "oh, wow." They are inarticulate from choice . . . ambiguity is absolutely necessary in order to allow individuals to project their private, most intense emotions and meanings into what is referred to. Though they are shared, symbols have multiple referents, and ambiguity is essential for their operation. Similarly, avoiding too much clarity and precision in language has the effect of minimizing the possibility of confrontation of unacceptable ideas and interpersonal conflicts. (pp. 55–56)

The study of organizational communication can benefit from the emphasis on commonality and complementarity. We must take care, however, to specify exactly *what* is shared, and to reserve judgment on the degree to which sharing exists in any particular organization. Rather than being a given in organizations, the degree to which interpretations are shared is an empirical question (Poole & McPhee, PP).

As part of the refinement of the notion of shared meanings and values, three distinctions might be made. First, the notion of sharing as a one-to-one correspondence should be rejected (many writers have already done so). Second, the temptation to encourage uniformity of belief should be resisted; diversity in interpretation of key symbols gives an organization adaptive strength.[16] Third, the presumption that shared understandings are necessary for smooth coordination should be questioned. It appears that smooth coordination can occur even under conditions of minimal sharing.[17] This phenomenon cannot be effectively understood so long as we continue to assume that widely shared interpretations are required for effective organizing.

Interpretations do not evolve in a social vacuum; at any given moment in an organization, one can identify numerous attempts at influencing perceptions and reforming worldviews. The next section explores the symbolic aspects of social influence.

III

Few topics in recent years have received as much enthusiastic attention from communication researchers as the question: how can symbols be used in the service of power and influence? Led by proponents of the critical school, writers in communication, philosophy, political science, and management are studying the use of symbols as instruments of domination. Needless to say, the symbolic exercise of power is far from an unusual occurrence; what *is* interesting is the growing popularity (and even politicization) of organizational research on the matter.

Building on the seminal work by Peter Bacharach, Charles Conrad (PP) provides a clear explication of the "symbological" approach to power. He rejects the commonly held view of power as overt and stable, and proposes instead a multi-layered, dynamic view in which covert strategies are considered as important as overt strategies in wielding influence. Conrad maintains that power inheres in language-in-use—in the metaphors, myths, stories, and rituals through which members of dominant coalitions control the issues that those with less power feel they may address.

Once one recognizes that power is often exercised through the unobtrusive control of premises and assumptions, the socialization of newcomers appears as one natural context for studying this process. Richard Boland and Raymond Hoffman (PFMD) explain how the sensibilities of the skilled machinist and the pecking order of the shop are communicated to new employees through physical humor. Similar to Pondy's earlier discussion of metaphor, Boland and Hoffman suggest that humor works as a socializing tool because it shields sensitive issues from challenge, while at the same time conveying important information about appropriate attitudes and behaviors.

Even with long-standing employees, management is continually concerned with fostering commitment. One way to promote commitment is through organizational stories. Through the telling and retelling of stories, employees may come to feel part of an in-group (Bormann, PP) or a language community (Evered, PFMD). Because they work in largely unconscious ways, stories can promote commitment better than other kinds of evidence (Wilkins, PFMD), especially when they confirm beliefs individuals in the organization already hold (Martin & Powers, PFMD).

Over time, some stories in organizations take on mythic proportions. Especially in organizations where evaluation is avoided, myths can play an important role in facilitating cohesiveness and a sense of "unified diversity."[18] This use of myths is common in educational institutions that forgo close examination of teaching and instead apply rigorous standards to administration (e.g., scheduling, certification, counting credits for graduation). In such organizations, it is tacitly acknowledged that interpretations may differ widely, and that confrontations which might undermine feelings of solidarity and legitimacy should be avoided.[19]

Even when feelings of solidarity exist within an organization, public pressure can present a challenge to legitimacy and thus bring about lasting change. Rounds (SL) chronicles such a change in the mental health delivery system in California. Contrary to popular mythology, change came about in this system not through individual heroics, but through a gradual diminishing of public confidence in the system's ability to meet their needs. In this situation, once again, we observe the operation of a causal loop involving communication, interpretation, and behavior. As the public increasingly sees the organization's performance as substandard, people are more likely to want a say in how the system should be changed. Since the dissatisfied clients vary widely in training, much of the common ground needed for meaningful discourse is lost. The breakdown of the homogeneous language community forces change at one level by interrupting current practices, but constrains meaningful discussion of solutions at another. As public interpretations become less favorable, there is an increased call for change in what the organization is doing. Whereas in more favorable times, professionals would be trusted to distribute resources according to "need" (i.e., according to their expert judgment), now there is a call for *equitable* distribution of resources, effectively removing the role of professional judgment from the distribution process. At this point, the public is exercising unusual control over the workings of the mental health system as a result of the ability to make professional opinion count for less in the decision-making process.

This scenario, however, is relatively rare. More often, organizations are able to dominate employee and public perceptions. Some writers have gone so far as to argue that symbolic domination is *the* critical process to study in organizations. But while most current research focuses on the impact of domination *within* organizations, the trend seems to be toward examining how communication and power in organizations affects and reflects inequities in society as a whole. For example, Gordon Walter (PFMD) argues that an unexpected by-product of the "information revolution" is a greater emphasis on impression management over genuine involvement, of style over substance. When we aspire toward symbols of success, Walter argues, we are in fact buying into a symbolism of narcissism, destructive in its capacity to rob our lives of real accomplishment and fulfillment.

In summary, power in organizations is seen as a symbolic process, through which individuals and groups control the interpretations and worldviews of others. Strategies for gaining power vary in their overtness. Through communication, power is exercised throughout the organizational life cycle and is manifested in stories, myths, and metaphors. While public opinion may at times dominate organizational interests, a more typical scenario is one in which organizations shape both public and employee perceptions. The trend in research in communication and power is to explore the relationship between power in organizations and patterns of inequality in society as a whole.

Whether one is concerned with exposing sources of domination in organizations, or simply in understanding how processes of domination work, the problem of how to best study interpretations is equally salient. We are in a transitional period regarding methodology in the social sciences generally. The next section addresses specific methodological problems peculiar to the study of symbols and interpretation in organizations.

IV

The critique of positivist social science is by now familiar to most readers and need not be repeated here. Two implications of this critique, however, are important to this review: first, that there is no single "Truth" with a capital "T"; communication researchers seek a variety of different kinds of knowledge and have different objectives in conducting research. Second, these different objectives do not have ironclad relationships to specific methodologies; a variety of choices is available for the researcher who wishes to study interpretations (Putnam, PP).

Putnam contrasts positivist and relativist methods and develops general requirements for interpretive study (i.e., studies should provide in-depth, richly contextual, nonlinear explanations). Similarly, Charles Bantz (PP) proposes appropriate research tools (participant observation, interviewing, document analysis) along with superordinate criteria for evaluating interpretive research. Neither author wishes to limit the choice of methods at this stage. Putnam rejects the claim that qualitative analysis is required by the interpretive approach and argues instead that there is a place for quantitative methods in the study of interpretation as well. There is a need to examine all the kinds of evidence (e.g., statistical, historical, anecdotal) that can be brought to bear on important questions about organizational communication.

While these suggestions provide us with needed direction, they leave unresolved the fundamental epistemological question which plagues all interpretive research: How can the validity or superiority of a particular explanation be established? Even with the demise of the "mirror" metaphor in the social sciences, we still need some way of choosing from among competing explanations. Nick Trujillo's study of a Dodge dealership (PP) epitomizes this problem. Trujillo presents sample dialogue as evidence that the dealership is a "fun" place to work. Unfortunately, his examples are equivocal, and one may see in them signs of strained interaction, manipulation, and power games. It is also difficult to evaluate a research report when the investigator's version appears as only one possible interpretation of the data. While the use of narrative examples may yield fruitful results, more rigorous argument and the anticipation and refutation of competing explanations could make such an account more convincing.

The extent to which an investigator's account is convincing sometimes seems to lie more with the form of presentation than with the method of data collection and analysis. Pacanowsky's short story on police work (PP), while similar in objectives to Trujillo's study, differs markedly in its presentation. Perhaps the familiarity of the traditional form of narrative fiction utilized by Pacanowsky (similar in familiarity to the conventional social science report) conditions a more positive response than is the case with the less familiar qualitative methods typified by Trujillo.

The issue here is not simply one of choosing the "right" method. At this stage, investigators need to be regarded with the kind of friendship which is simultaneously supportive and critical of their efforts. Researchers need to be encouraged to examine fully the criteria for excellence associated with a given method (whether it be factor analysis or ethnography), and where standards of quality do not exist, they must create some.

There are, of course, some especially hazardous pitfalls associated with the conduct of interpretive research. For example, whereas some investigators have been content to accept participants' corroboration of their interpretations as proof positive, there is suggestive evidence that people's perceptions may not be especially accurate regarding significant but potentially unflattering aspects of their behavior.[20] Differences among methods should be cultivated, so long as each is applied with attention to the specific pitfalls inherent in each approach. In studying organizations, a healthy mixture of pluralism and rigor is required.

V

One last issue, which has received limited attention in the literature, is the question of the impact research on interpretation might have on organizations and society. The main reason I am critical of models of organizational communication that indiscriminately promote openness, clarity, and sharing is that I believe them to be false utopias. I fear the promulgation of these ideas in our research adversely affects organizations and society through the way people think about themselves and their relationships. The history of management studies is filled with examples of attractive theories which lack empirical support, but nonetheless pervade the business world.[21] The recent push to create "excellent" organizations and "strong" cultures is such a case of an attractive theory, without empirical support, substantially influencing organizational life. This problem is not new, nor is it confined to organizational research. Research is a creative, social act, and the images of the world we create have important consequences for how human beings think about themselves.

Researchers studying organizational communication might ask themselves, "What effect do my theories, concepts, and questions have on individuals within and outside of the scholarly community?" Just as most of us expect managers to consider the implications of their communication for internal and external publics, so too should we insist that members of the academic community take responsibility for the social effects of their chosen concepts and theories.[22] In addition to evaluating the conduct of research (already the purview of human subject committees), the fundamental concepts, theories, and objectives of research should be scrutinized. To paraphrase Ernest Becker,[23] this juncture in human development requires not so much a science *of* man (sic) as a science *for* man. Despite their shortcomings, the essays reviewed here move us productively toward a more reflective view of organizational communication. In addition to identifying significant substantive and methodological issues, they highlight the fundamentally recursive relationship between the world of research and the social world which we must take responsibility for shaping.

Books Reviewed

COMMUNICATION AND ORGANIZATIONS: AN INTERPRETIVE APPROACH. Edited by Linda Putnam and Michael E. Pacanowsky. Beverly Hills, Sage Publications, 1983, pp. 303. Paper $14.95.

ORGANIZATIONAL SYMBOLISM. Edited by Louis R. Pondy, Peter J. Frost, Gareth Morgan, and Thomas C. Dandridge. Greenwich, CT: JAI Press, 1983, pp. xvii + 307. $24.75.

ADVANCES IN INFORMATION PROCESSING IN ORGANIZATIONS, VOL I. Edited by Lee S. Sproull and Patrick D. Larkey. Greenwich, CT: JAI Press, 1984. pp. ix + 171. $24.75.

Notes

1. See, for example, Lyman W. Porter and Karlene H. Roberts, "Communication in Organizations," in the *Handbook of Industrial and Organizational Psychology,* ed. M. Dunnette (Chicago, IL: Aldine, 1976), pp. 1553–1589; see also F. Stagnaro, "The Benefits of Leveling with Employees," *Management Review,* 71 (1982), 16–20; and C. VonBergen, Jr., and R. E. Shealy, "How's Your Empathy?" *Training and Development Journal,* November 1982, 22–32; and finally D. W. Fisher, "A Model for Better Communication," *Supervisory Management,* 27 (1982), 24–29.

2. James G. March and Guje Sevon, "Gossip, Information and Decision-Making," in *Advances in Information Processing in Organizations, Vol I.*, ed. Lee S. Sproull and Patrick D. Larkey (Greenwich, CT: JAI Press, 1984), pp. 95–108.

3. Stephen R. Axley, "Managerial and Organizational Communication in Terms of the Conduit Metaphor," *Academy of Management Review,* 9 (1984), 428–37.

4. Arthur P. Bochner, "The Functions of Human Communication in Interpersonal Bonding," In the *Handbook of Rhetoric and Communication Theory,* eds. Carroll Arnold and John W. Bowers (Newton, MA: Allyn & Bacon, 1984), pp. 544–621. See also Eric M. Eisenberg, "Ambiguity as Strategy in Organizational Communication," *Communication Monographs,* 51 (1984), 227–242.

5. Four recent conferences have addressed topics related to organizational symbolism, the first in Alta, Utah (Putnam & Pacanowsky, 1983), the second in Urbana, Illinois (Pondy et al., 1983), the third at Carnegie Mellon University (Sproull & Larkey, 1984) and the fourth in Vancouver, British Columbia (Front et al., 1985). In addition, a recent issue of the *Journal of Management* (11, 1985) was devoted entirely to the subject of organizational symbolism.

6. Karl Weick makes the argument, in his critique of the Vancouver conference, that concern with organizational culture is more correctly a concern with meaning. I think this renewed interest in meaning is even more pervasive and is central to organizational symbolism, interpretive research and information processing theory.

7. Per-Olof Berg, "Organization Change as a Symbolic Transformation Process," in Peter Frost, Larry Moore, Meryl Louis, Craig Lundberg, and Joanne Martin, eds., *Organizational Culture* (Beverly Hills, CA: Sage Publications, 1985), pp. 281–99.

8. Peter Berger and Thomas Luckmann, *The Social Construction of Reality* (Garden City, NY: Doubleday, 1966).

9. Anthony Giddens, *Central Problems in Social Theory* (Berkeley: University of California Press, 1979).

10. Louis Pondy and Anne Huff, "Achieving Routine in Organizational Change," *Journal of Management,* 11 (1985), 103–16.

11. Eisenberg, "Ambiguity as Strategy."

12. Mavor Moore, "Culture as Culture," In *Organizational Culture,* eds. Peter Frost, Larry Moore, Meryl Reis Louis, and Joanne Martin (Beverly Hills: Sage Publications, 1985), pp. 373–78.

13. Thomas Peters and Robert Waterman, *In Search of Excellence* (New York: Harper & Row, 1982).

14. Terence R. Mitchell, "In Search of Excellence versus The 100 Best Companies to Work for in America: A Question of Perspective and Values," *Academy of Management Review* 10, (1985), 350–54.

15. Barbara G. Myerhoff, "Organization and Ecstasy: Deliberate and Accidental Communitas among Huichol Indians and American Youth." In *Symbol and Politics in Communal Ideology,* eds. Sally Moore and Barbara Myerhoff (Ithaca, NY: Cornell University Press, 1975), pp. 33–67.

16. R. M. Keesing, "Theories of Culture," *Annual Review of Anthropology,* 3, (1974), 73–97.

17. This idea owes much to the discussion of minimal knowledge and mutual equivalence structures in Karl E. Weick. *The Social Psychology of Organizing,* 2nd Edition (Reading, MA: Addison-Wesley, 1979), pp. 98–109.

18. I developed this concept as a way of synthesizing what others had written on the subject. See Eisenberg, "Ambiguity as Strategy."

19. John Meyer and Brian Rowan, "Institutionalized Organizations: Formal Structure as Myth and Ceremony," *American Journal of Sociology,* 83 (1977), 340–63.

20. This insight is less pervasive in the study of formal organizations than it is in the literature on family systems. For a thorough introduction to the multitude of ways individuals can deceive themselves about their own perceptions, see Lynn Hoffman, *Foundations of Family Therapy* (New York: Basic Books, 1981).

21. Well-known examples include the application of Maslow's theory of human needs to organizational behavior (an application Maslow himself cautioned against) and Herzberg's two-factor theory of job satisfaction. Both theories have received mixed or no empirical support, yet both remain popular in management education and training.

22. Klaus Krippendorff, "On the Ethics of Constructing Communication," Presidential Address to the Annual Meeting of the International Communication Association, Honolulu, Hawaii, May 23–27, 1985.

23. Ernest Becker, *The Structure of Evil* (New York: Free Press, 1965).

3

Conflict at Disneyland

A Root-Metaphor Analysis

Co-authored with Ruth Smith (then a doctoral student at the University of Southern California), this was my first attempt to apply elements of strategic ambiguity to the analysis of a specific organization. We used the notion of root metaphor to interrogate the sense-making practices at Disneyland and to identify competing interpretive frameworks that seemed to underlie practical conflicts in the park. For many years, Disney management had invoked the "family" metaphor in ways that belied Walt Disney's original intentions; they exploited the resources of ambiguity in the idea of "family" to maintain control over employees and deflect challenges to their authority. Results revealed the utility of the root metaphor approach for understanding a serious labor dispute in the organization, and, more generally, for providing insights about latent tensions in the Disney culture.

Ruth Smith did the bulk of the interviewing for this paper, and it was challenging. Disney management refused to let her talk to employees in the park, so she met them in a diner across the street. Even after its publication, we feared a phone call from the Disney lawyers and even consulted general counsel at our university to determine how best to respond. But the call never came, and this paper joined a handful of other projects in organizational studies that investigated the dark side of Disney culture. In a way, this analysis begins to get at the power implications associated with the implicit or explicit endorsement of a particular metaphor for organizing.

SOURCE: Smith, R., & Eisenberg, E. M. (1987). Conflict at Disneyland: A root-metaphor analysis. *Communication Monographs, 54*, 367–380. Copyright © 1987 Reproduced by permission of Taylor & Francis Group, LLC., http://taylorand francis.com.

A world ends when its metaphor dies.

—Archibald MacLeish, *Hypocrite Auteur*

D isneyland occupies a special place in the American psyche. A favorite family vacation spot, its popularity is fueled by its clean-cut, "All-American" image. Disneyland, many believe, is "the happiest place on earth"; it represents much that is worth celebrating about traditional American values. Millions visit the park each year (and millions more Disneyworld and Disney's park in Tokyo) and most leave with this impression intact. Perhaps the values found along "Main Street, USA" are not gone forever, and it is "a small world after all."

But things are seldom what they seem. In recent years, internal conflict at Disneyland has provided a contrasting image to these public perceptions of the park. While dissatisfaction had been mounting for some time, internal strife peaked in late 1984 when a group of unionized employees voted to strike. Initial reports suggested the strike was centered around hiring and compensation issues, but on examination the differences appear to be more deep-seated. We argue in this paper that management and employees developed interpretive frameworks or worldviews that were incompatible. Our aim in this paper is to illuminate this incompatibility and its relationship to conflict at Disneyland through the use of a new interpretive methodology, root-metaphor analysis.

A Symbolic Approach to Organizational Conflict

In their recent review, Putnam and Poole (1987) characterized existing research on organizational conflict as overly mechanistic and static, and called for studies exploring the symbolic aspects of organizational conflict within a dynamic framework. Their sentiment reflects the recent "interpretive turn" in organizational studies (Geertz, 1985; Putnam & Pacanowsky, 1984). A primary goal of interpretive research on organizations is to articulate the taken-for-granted rules, assumptions, values, and beliefs that constitute organizational members' worldviews. Whether conducted under the rubric of organizational culture (Frost el al., 1985) or organizational symbolism (cf. Eisenberg & Riley, 1988; Pondy et al., 1983), all studies of this sort share a concern for the meanings and interpretations organizational members attach to events (Eisenberg, 1986; Weick, 1983). Furthermore, a key assumption of this approach is that these interpretations are not monolithic, but rather multiple worldviews can and do coexist within a single organization.

This last point has special relevance for conflict theory. Traditional conflict theories have been applied to organizations in ways that focus almost exclusively on overt goals, strategies, and resources. Much less attention has been paid to the differing worldviews that may underlie these disagreements. This deficiency of research in the organizational context is especially striking since theorists addressing smaller groups (notably families) have been successful in articulating multiple layers of conflict (e.g., Hoffman, 1981; Reiss, 1981).

The failure to investigate potential differences in worldviews may prevent researchers and practitioners from understanding the true sources of overt conflict, and as a result, from understanding why conflict may not be effectively managed over time. Researchers interested in motivating change in social systems should distinguish between first-order change, in overt attitudes and behaviors, and second-order change, in orientation, worldview, and the rules of the game (Argyris, 1982; Hoffman, 1981; Watzlawick, Weakland, & Fisch, 1974).

Organizational members sometimes hold divergent worldviews that can lead to deep-seated, unrecognized second-order conflicts. These worldviews function similarly to "group ideologies" (Billig, 1976; Putnam & Poole, in press) in that they constrain what count as legitimate topics for thought and action. Second-order differences can remain latent for long periods of time, and if and when they finally surface as conflict, their depth and nature are often misunderstood and mistaken for first-order conflict. Such misunderstandings are important since one result of unrecognized second-order conflict is a lingering inability to manage differences effectively.

As we see it, then, the challenge is to develop methods for identifying worldviews which enable us to anticipate, understand, and address second-order conflicts. Root-metaphor analysis is offered here as one such useful method. Root-metaphors are rich summaries of interpretive frameworks, and the identification of multiple root-metaphors operating within an organization can provide important insight into the underlying reasons for conflict. Furthermore, the change in root-metaphors over time—their ascendancy, adherence, and eventual demise—reflects the evolution in attitudes, beliefs, and values of organizational members. In other words, root-metaphors enable us to address the symbolic nature of organizational conflict in a dynamic framework. Changes in and competition among root-metaphors can illuminate organizational members' struggles over appropriate definitions of reality, over conceptions of what work life should be like. Applying this methodology at Disneyland, we identified two root-metaphors which had developed over a period of 30 years to the point where second-order conflict was inevitable. Before presenting the details of our analysis, however, we first provide some definitions and background on the utility of metaphor analysis for organizational research.

Metaphors and Organizing

Metaphors play a crucial role in the production, understanding, and communication of human thought and action. Their importance is evidenced by the growing number of scholars, from humanists to social and natural scientists, who are investigating the richness of metaphorical forms in a variety of human activities. Metaphors influence how we view and make sense of the world in general (Lakoff & Johnson, 1980; Langer, 1979), how we learn (Ortony, 1979), how we think (Honeck & Hoffman, 1980), how we create knowledge (Kuhn, 1970) and how we behave in social settings (Berg, 1985; Deetz & Mumby, 1985; Koch & Deetz, 1981; Owen, 1985). Furthermore, metaphors are not neutral representations of reality; they are manifestations of particular ideologies and worldviews, and have implications for what counts as information, and for what is thinkable (Deetz & Mumby, 1985). As a direct response to the increasing scholarly interest in metaphor, an interdisciplinary journal titled *Metaphor and Symbolic Activity* went into publication in 1986.

The symbolic role of metaphor in organizing has received increasing attention recently (Brown, 1986; Morgan, 1986; Smith & Simmons, 1983; Weick, 1979). Metaphors are important in organizing because they aid members in the interpretation of events; they allow cues from one context (e.g., the family) to be applied to the understanding of another (e.g., the organization). This usage is consistent with what Lakoff and Johnson (1980) call "structural" metaphors; they function by projecting the characteristics of one structured experience onto another. Over time, structural metaphors help "organization participants to infuse their organizational experiences with meaning" (Pondy, 1983, p. 157).

Organizational metaphors are useful for understanding how two central dialectics of organizing—stability-change, and autonomy-coordination—are managed. For each of these tensions, emphasis on one pole to the neglect of the other is risky; the challenge is in maintaining an effective balance. Metaphors help organizational participants to achieve this balance. Regarding the first dialectic, Pondy argues that "metaphor facilitates change by making the strange familiar, but in that process it deepens the meaning of values of the organization by giving them expression in novel situations. . . . Because of its inherent ambivalence of meaning, metaphor can fulfill the dual function of enabling change and preserving continuity" (p. 164). This ambivalence is also helpful in managing the tension between autonomy and coordination. Effective managers and employees use metaphors strategically to facilitate sense of cohesiveness and at the same time allow for a variety of individual interpretations (Eisenberg, 1984). Lastly, the two dialectics are clearly interdependent: Maintenance of a diversity of interpretations can aid an organization in adapting to change (Keesing, 1974).

Previous research on metaphor has often taken a static approach, offering little sense of the process whereby metaphors and their meanings evolve. This study employs metaphor analysis (Koch & Deetz, 1981) to reveal how root-metaphors guide the symbolic development of an organization, and to articulate a framework within which organizational conflict can be investigated.

The notion of "root-metaphors" in organizations is itself a metaphor. The roots of a plant are vital to its survival, but as a rule, are below ground and not immediately visible. Root-metaphors can be recognized by their ability to undergird a broad area of meaning. Root-metaphors are symbolic frames (Levinson, 1983) that provide an inferential base for understanding more discrete attitudes and behavior. They capture a fundamental, underlying worldview, but are often unobtrusive with regard to their frequency of usage in ordinary discourse. For example, a typical root-metaphor is "argument is war" (Lakoff & Johnson, 1980). This root-metaphor may guide our thinking, but we are mostly unconscious of its presence. We may say, "He needs to prepare a more convincing defense," "He destroyed my position," or "She was defeated," but we rarely think of the root-metaphor of war as informing our understanding of argument. Similarly, the root-metaphor of "organization as family" can be manifested in numerous surface references (e.g., "we should all take care of our own"), while the family metaphor may not be explicitly articulated.

The isolation of root-metaphors often results in a heightened appreciation of how meanings and interpretations develop over time, revealing not only "the current reality of the organization but also the possibilities open to it" (Koch & Deetz, p. 13). From any particular root-metaphor, multiple variations can evolve. For example, seeing an organization as a "living thing" leads quite naturally to discussions of organizational "births" and "deaths" (e.g., Harris & Sutton, 1986). In time, organizational members may reject one root-metaphor in favor of another. An alternative to the military metaphor of organizing, for example, is "organization as family," emphasizing nonviolence and intimacy over conflict and a strict hierarchy (Weick, 1979).

This study examines the symbolic aspects of conflict at Disneyland in four stages. First, we identify the root-metaphors underlying employee worldviews. Second, we reveal how specific groups within the organization have chosen to emphasize some root-metaphors over others. Third, we examine these differences in root-metaphors help us to understand overt conflict at the park. Fourth, and finally, we explore the implications of this conflict for the future of Disneyland.

Method

Our initial investigation of Disneyland began in March, 1983, with eight interviews of managers representing employment, training, publicity, and public relations. These interviews elicited general beliefs about organizational values, norms, and activities. In addition to these data, we were given access to a large number of documents describing the history and current activities of Disneyland. In late 1984, conflict came to a head in a 22-day strike by a group of unionized employees. Structured interviews were held with key figures in the strike, including negotiators and spokespeople for unions and management, and the federal mediator.[1] More focused data collection began in August, 1985. Thirty-five structured interviews with hourly employees were conducted. To maximize confidentiality, interviews were held in the lounge of a local restaurant, a favorite Disneyland haunt. Our sample included 25 men and 10 women, ranging in age from 21 to 45 and in tenure from two months to 20 years. Divisions represented in the sample were costuming, entertainment, foods, merchandising, services, and operations.[2]

Interviews were conducted in three parts. First, employees were asked general, open-ended questions like "What is it like working at Disneyland?" These questions were designed to build rapport and to solicit metaphors-in-use without introducing unnecessary bias from the researchers. Second, employees were given a list of metaphors that *management* had used in previous interviews and documents to describe the park,[3] and asked to identify those terms which currently seemed to be descriptive of the park. Third, and finally, employees were asked to complete the sentence "Life at Disneyland is like . . . " and in doing so were encouraged to discuss the reasons for the strike, their attitudes toward the strike, and the extent to which they thought the organization was changing.

All interviews were audiotaped and later transcribed; the average interview was 30 minutes in length. Root-metaphors were identified from the transcripts through a semantic sorting process in which coherent patterns or clusters of meaning emerged around specific metaphorical expressions (Koch & Deetz, 1981). For example,

Expressions:

"The cast members"

"The Show"

"Our costumes"

"The Disney image"

"The Disney role"

Shared understanding: Disneyland has actors, costumes, stories to be enacted on a stage and an audience to be entertained.

Organizational entailment: Disneyland puts on a show.

Root-metaphor: Disneyland is a drama.

A number of metaphors were initially identified (as shown in our original list of metaphors), but it soon became clear that there were two dominant metaphors which framed employee talk and which were classified as root-metaphors. Root-metaphors were chosen for their ability to provide a coherent summary of employee worldviews, which was not necessarily reflected in their *frequency* of usage by employees (i.e., while few employees used the term "drama" to describe their activities, many more talked about the Disney "family" explicitly). Once the root-metaphors were identified, records were made of (1) who used them and under what circumstances, (2) how users interpreted them, and (3) how these interpretations were similar to or different from one another.

Results

We do not claim to provide a complete history of Disneyland, which is available elsewhere.[4] More important for our purposes is what has *not* been documented about the symbolic, affective nature of the park. Disneyland has been characterized as an "excellent organization with a strong concern for the customer and widely shared core values and beliefs" (Peters & Waterman, 1982). These shared understandings are manifest in the idiosyncratic language of the organization. Visitors are not customers but "guests," personnel is known as "casting," and there is a clear distinction made between the park's "onstage" and "backstage" areas. This specialized vocabulary is repeated in orientation and training seminars as well as in ongoing development efforts, and as a consequence is readily used by both employees and management. More than in most organizations, the appropriate use of such symbols is crucial to Disneyland's image and day-to-day operation.

The two root-metaphors identified from our interview data were "drama" and "family." Other metaphors were initially considered, such as "magical," "teamwork," and "people experts," but further investigation revealed that they could be subsumed within employees' characterization of the park as either a drama or a family. For example,

The magic is part of the drama:

Magical—no doubt about it. Downtown Anaheim with two million people, in the middle of a town. . . there's something about walking into a place where there's sixty-six acres and Mark Twain's whistle blowing. . . .The costumes have something to do with it. You punch in dressed in t-shirt, shorts. . . [then you] get into your coonskin hat, leathers and stuff. . . you're home free (Ride Operator/Male/6 years tenure)

Teamwork comes from being a member of a family:

Teamwork—you have to have this to have things go as smooth as they do, it goes with family—like that's why people are so close. (Parking Lot/Female/ 5 years tenure)

No metaphors were volunteered by hourly employees that had not already been proposed by management, a surprising finding which underscores the important role management may play in providing interpretive frameworks for employees (Pfeffer, 1981; Pondy, 1978; Weick, 1980).

Root-Metaphor 1: The Disney Experience as Drama

Organizational documents, particularly those recording Disneyland's history (see note 4), largely explain the pervasiveness of the drama metaphor. It is clearly, consciously, and repeatedly stated in this literature that from the outset—the early 1950s—Walt Disney and his followers conceived of the park in dramatic terms. The design and construction of the park were influenced by the theatrical techniques learned in the Disney movie studios. Plans for the park were drawn up with the aid of "storyboard" techniques used by cartoonists. The parking lot was regarded as the "outer lobby," the ticket booths the theater's "box office," and the sixteen-foot wall surrounding the park, the "theater walls." Employee behavior and appearance were carefully regulated and justified by this dramatic context: Dress codes (known as "costuming") and rules for proper grooming were widely acknowledged as "all part of the show." Special ways of looking, talking, and acting comprised the Disney "role" and were part of the Disney "script." The park or "show" is the enactment of Walt Disney's utopian vision; it is "the happiest place on earth." Thus Disneyland was designed as a show, an escape from the real world, where paying customers are "guests," and every employee plays the role of host or hostess. Organizational documents and training seminars frequently cite Disney: "I don't want the public to see the real world they're living in. . . . I want them to feel they're in another world."

Our interview data reveal how successful management has been in getting employees adopt the drama metaphor. Most employees come to see their role at the park as not simply providing a service but as entertainment. Not one person we interviewed used the words "customer," "amusement park," or "uniforms" in describing life at Disneyland.

Despite this avoidance of traditional business terminology, the drama metaphor is not inconsistent with a business orientation. Dramas are highly structured, rule-governed presentations, in which individuals play clearly defined roles designed to bring about an intended effect. Moreover, all theatrical concerns have box office considerations. Introductory guidelines, manuals, and even a recent television commercial[5] stress the business orientation alongside drama; one management training manual concludes that "each member . . . must have a clear understanding of the 'business of show business.'"

The mid-1960s was a period of dramatic change for Disneyland. This period was marked by general growth and prosperity in the American economy, and the growing success of Walt Disney Productions. Gaining an international reputation as the "finest in family entertainment," Disneyland was hailed as the corporation's "flagship," secure in its popularity and emerging as a revered American institution. In this era of material well-being, however, the park suffered the loss of Walt Disney, who died in 1966.

The question of what happens to an organization when its founder departs is currently under debate (Martin et al., 1985; Rosenblatt et al., 1985; Schein, 1983, 1985; Siehl, 1985.) Martin et al. are particularly critical of the popular belief that a founder can leave an organizational culture as a legacy, calling it a "seductive promise" (p. 99). Disneyland is an interesting case. Disney was a charismatic founder and leader (still referred to by management and employees as "Walt"), and the organization struggled to adapt to his loss. In his absence, management reflected on and often reinterpreted Disney's life and achievements, as evidenced by the nostalgic histories in organizational documents, the commemorative exhibit housed inside the park, and the creation of the "Disney philosophy."

By the 1980s however, employees were casting themselves as the sole "caretakers" of Disney's legacy. They perceived management's actions as departing from Disney's original vision, and complained bitterly.

> It's their [management's] responsibility to maintain, preserve and project the image. . . ; we've seen a change in attitudes and beliefs during the last 16 years. . . . Facilities have to change but not the subtleties behind them: styles of management, the handling of its cast, the treatment of its employees. (Ride Operator/Male/20 years tenure)

Ironically, the employees' impulse to preserve Disney's founding vision resulted in a revised interpretation that even Disney may not have fully endorsed. Their interpretation placed primary emphasis on Disney employees as "family," and it was the protection and preservation of that interpretation that led ultimately to conflict with management.

Root-Metaphor II: The Disney Experience as Family

In response to the loss of Disney, documents reveal that management began to nurture the idea of a "Disney philosophy." The philosophy was intended to capture the spirit of and to act as a surrogate for Walt. Disneyland became known as a "friendly" place to work, an organization on a "first-name basis" in which "teamwork" was paramount. Current introductory guidelines read, "We are an informal, friendly organization and it is essential that we maintain this. Walt insisted that everyone call him 'Walt' and he applied his first-name philosophy to everyone in the organization." The organizational stories we were told depicted Disney as a caring family man who reserved his Saturdays for his two daughters and who designed the park to give his and other families a safe, clean, fun place to go. The establishment of "Disneyland University," offering career and extra-curricular activities along with generous compensation packages, reinforced Walt's philosophy of the caring employer. In short, Walt Disney was immortalized as the somewhat paternalistic, spiritual leader of an organization that, in turn, regarded itself as the caretaker of his beliefs. Friendly, wholesome, family entertainment had become synonymous with "Disney."

Our interview data suggest that the notions of friendliness (originally designed to refer to the employee-customer relationship) were interpreted by employees to refer to relationships among management and employees as well. While the notion of Disneyland as a tight-knit family existed to some extent in earlier years, the mid-1960s saw it receive emphasis that overshadowed even the drama metaphor. The friendly, family atmosphere was so convincing that most employees and many managers came to believe it uncritically, seeming at times to forget that Disneyland was a for-profit business selling a highly calculated fantasy world. Indeed, one long-term manager bemoaned the fact that people often forgot Disney was "a shrewd businessman, intolerant of incompetence, who certainly knew how to make a buck." Despite recent hard times, the feeling of the "Disney family" persists. Some typical employee comments:

> These people are like my brothers and sisters. (Ride Operator/Male/3 years tenure)

> It's family-like as far as the employees go. (Attractions Trainer/Female/8.5 years tenure)

> Real close knit . . . better than marriage. (Ride Operator/Male/6 months tenure)

> Yes, family-like: I feel so close to the employees. (Attractions Hostess/Female/5.5 years tenure)

> The people who work here treat each other as a family, there seems to be a common cause. . . . We're family presenting family entertainment: it's like we're inviting someone to our home to entertain them. (Entertainer/Male/2 years tenure)

As the family metaphor gained acceptance, employees not only continued to treat the public like personal guests but came to expect similar favored treatment from management. Management, in turn, did little to discourage this tendency; if anything, this close-knit feeling helped business, improved employee morale, and in some cases was even consistent with their personal dreams for what the park should be like. This is reflected in naming the annual party the "family picnic." Management continued its paternalistic style; according to one executive, the park became "so comfortable that employees were afraid to leave the womb." The dream of a familial utopia had become a fragile reality, and work at Disneyland was no longer just a role, but "a way of life" (Ride Operator/Male/7 years tenure).

Consequences of the Change in Metaphorical Emphasis

The years leading up to the 1984 strike were characterized by a change in emphasis of root-metaphors from drama to family, accompanied by parallel changes in the way management and employees interpreted their work experiences. In addition, general economic factors such as increased operating costs, reduced spending power, greater competition, takeover attempts and corporate-level resignations led to a growing sense of malaise and uncertainty at the park. By the 1980s financial problems were substantial and the economic aspects of the park became increasingly salient to management. This seemingly new emphasis on the "bottom line" offended some employees, and was perceived by many as constituting a breach of Disney's caring philosophy. Employee comments illustrate this resentment:

> Walt Disney's philosophy was to bring families together so that they could have fun. . . . The philosophy is now let's make as much money as [we] can. . . . We're numbers now, we're not people to them anymore. (Merchandising/Female/14 years tenure)

> It used to be, "let's try to make the employees as happy as possible so that they make the public happy" and now it's "let's save as much money as we can and make a buck." (Ride Operator/Male/7 years tenure)

> Management doesn't really care any more. . . . They keep going for the dollars and that's it. (Attractions Trainer/Female/8.5 years tenure)

> What management wanted from us ten years ago and what they want now are two different things. It's now more for the money and the employees are second. (Foods/Male/15 years tenure)

> Management doesn't care anymore. (Attractions Hostess/Female/8 years tenure)

> There was a time when the employee was very important to the company; now they're more of a company. . . . It's getting more like a business. . . . I don't think the park should be run like a business. (Services/Female/8 years tenure)

In late 1984, management proposed a two-year wage freeze and an elimination of benefits for some future employees, thereby creating a two-tier pay scale. Arguments presented by management were based on a 62% discrepancy between the amount Disneyland was paying its employees and comparable positions in the entertainment industry. Management's concerns were essentially economic, as they needed to improve the business aspects of the show in order to remain solvent. From the employees' point of view, management's preoccupation with economics had potentially disturbing implications. Employees perceived the underlying issue to be a threat to the Disney "family." Employees were shocked and claimed management's proposals violated the spirit of Disneyland, Walt's original vision. Accustomed to thinking of themselves as different and special, it was unthinkable to bring Disneyland employees in line with other amusement parks.

The people have made Disneyland what it is. Disneyland claims to be different, and it is different. Walt Disney said many times that the difference is in our people. (Spokesperson for five-union bargaining team)

Resentment of management decisions ran high and culminated in a 22-day strike by unions that had not struck for over 29 years. During this period, striking employees held a candlelight vigil to honor the memory of Disney and his philosophy, and bumper stickers were made which read, "Disneyland—Walt's dying dream." Employees claimed that management acted unfairly—that this was not the way one treats "family." Some typical employee reactions:

My family wouldn't treat me the way they [management] do. (Merchandising/Female/14 years tenure)

It's just totally business . . . they are not worried about the family thing. (Food/Male/3 years tenure)

Getting to be businesslike, especially this last year, we're a lot more towards the money making, let's go for the buck . . . we're losing a lot of the magic. (Sweeper/Female/2.5 years tenure)

They don't care. (Ride Operator/Male/4 years tenure)

It's all business now. (Parking/Female/9 years tenure)

The family-like thing is really dying . . . it's becoming more businesslike and less and less like a family. (Ride Operator/Male/8 years tenure)

It's getting farther away from family like . . . but it's one of the best-run business I've ever seen . . . everything's down to a science. (Attractions/Female/11 years tenure)

It's not fun to work at Disneyland any more . . . they gave us a cold slap in the face. (Merchandise/Female/14 years tenure)

Walt wanted family, but it's business now, not Walt's dream, that's shot, it's not what he wanted. (Ride Operator/Male/5 years tenure)

It's the end of an era . . . it's time to leave, they don't want us any more. (Ride Operator/Male/8.5 years tenure)

Management tried in vain to counteract the growing discontent with their own interpretation of "family." According to management, family life was sometimes hard, and truly close families must make sacrifices if they are to survive. This attempt at reinterpretation failed to catch on, however, and it soon become clear to management that the financial exigencies they faced would require some permanent changes in the way the park was run.

Forging New Interpretations: The Strike and Its Aftermath

During the strike, actions on both sides followed a predictable pattern: Unions picketed, management obtained restraining orders, union officials were arrested, management issued an ultimatum, letters of replacement were sent, and rehiring began. When the strike started, only a small percentage of employees crossed the picket line. Later on, management's ultimatum convinced a third of the striking employees to cross, which aggravated poor relations among employees.

Three days prior to the end of the strike, striking employees made their grievances more public; they paid their way into the park and distributed handbills to the guests. In the words of one union official, "It was a wowzer," and it had a profound effect on both management and the public. By going public with their complaints, the employees had effectively rejected the validity of the drama. This move was interpreted by some as a "clever strategy" but by others as "a cheap shot, a tacky move."

The striking employees were surprisingly unanimous over the specific issues, as was noted by the experienced union spokespersons. One commented, "I've never seen anything quite like the way they turned out. Ninety-nine percent of them showed at every meeting, very vocal, very much in unison, very much all felt the same way. . . . They really are a family."

For the striking employees, the overt conflict was over economics, but the deeper second-order issue was that their interpretation of the Disney philosophy, with family as its root-metaphor, was in danger of extinction. Consider this employee's representative opinion:

> It is not a strike over economics but policy and principle. It's the break of the family tradition: it's turning a family-oriented business into another cog of a large corporate structure and losing that identity. . . . There's no belief in the corporation's word whatsoever. . . . We should be able to conduct our business exactly as it was 20 years ago. . . . There's no reason why we can't be a family. (Ride Operator/Male/20 years tenure)

Moreover, the candlelight vigil in memory of Walt Disney held by employees during the strike further confirms the strikers' deeper concerns, their longing to preserve a threatened worldview: "Its purpose [the vigil] was a hint of exactly what this strike was all about. It was a remembrance of Walt's ideals" (Ride operator/Male/20 years tenure).

Since the strike, overt tensions have eased somewhat, but relations throughout the park seem greatly changed. Not only do some hourly employees view management as their adversaries, the employees themselves are now fractionated. In and around the period of the strike, the family metaphor was reinterpreted by many employees to exclude management. In the aftermath, some employees have been excluded from the family circle as well. Generational differences are now dividing employees; the two-tier pay scale which came out of the strike settlement ("grandfathering") makes a clear distinction between employees of three years or more, known informally as "the old timers," and recent employees.

Tensions are further aggravated by contradictory desires among employees. Disneyland employees resent being "treated like kids," and "not [being] allowed to have a personal opinion," yet at the same time miss the benefits of the paternalistic care of earlier years. In an attempt to facilitate interaction among employees, management initiated a circulating employee program, in which employees move through a variety of jobs. But the change in interpretive framework reflected by the revision of "who's in the family" has proven to be pervasive. Since many employees no longer trust management to look out for their best interests, the new program is seen as yet another attempt by management to destroy the family and to break the "Disney spirit." One employee complains, "When you move people away that love each other, how are you going to boost morale? . . . they are losing the family" (Ride operator/Male/5 years tenure).

Conclusions

Our purpose in this study was to illuminate recent conflicts at Disneyland through the use of a new interpretive methodology, root-metaphor analysis. Our major point has been that disagreements over policies and procedures are often better understood in the context of underlying worldviews of management and employees. In good times at Disneyland, the use of terms like "drama" or "family" caused few obvious problems. In light of harsh economics and scarce resources, however, the somewhat divergent behavioral implications of these symbols became clear. The managerial emphasis on drama and the "business of show business" implied structure, conformity, efficiency, and a concern for the bottom line. This was incompatible with the employees' emphasis on family, which suggested a transcendence of structure and an uncritical support of fellow employees. The strike at Disneyland, then, is traceable to a conflict over rival deep-seated, second-order issues, represented here as competing root-metaphors.

Our experience with root-metaphor analysis in this study makes us hopeful for its potential in future research. While other methods exist for studying organizational member's interpretations (e.g., analysis of organizational myths or stories), the concept of root-metaphor is elegant and easily understood by both researchers and practitioners. Naturally, care must be taken not to overgeneralize; interpretations may not always be representative, and perspectives may exist that are missed by the researchers. In all, however, we believe the strengths outweigh the limitations. Further, we feel that as a method for investigating organizational conflict, root-metaphor analysis captures the symbolic and dynamic character of organizational life.

Disneyland is sometimes singled out by organizational observers as possessing an especially "strong" or "excellent" culture. Most writers making this claim further contend that such a culture, once established, would be highly resistant to change. Wilkins (1984) takes exception to this conclusion, with important implications for this study. According to Wilkins, while so-called "strong cultures" with widely shared worldviews are difficult to build, they are relatively easy to destroy. Alternative interpretations are always available; people enter organizations with pre-existing frameworks for thinking about work (e.g., as stifling, unfair, adversarial) and even a single bad experience can trigger a dramatic shift such as that seen at Disneyland. This argument may explain the fast rate at which Disney employees have become disillusioned. Once there was trouble in paradise, employees had in mind the culturally shared interpretation of "management as adversary" to fall back on.

Successful organizations find ways of coping with multiple goals and of managing the stability-change and autonomy-coordination dialectics described earlier in this paper. The Disneyland experience is not atypical of our times: A large, successful company faces serious financial exigencies brought on by a failing economy and, in turn, cuts labor costs in an attempt to remain solvent. Similar examples can be found in the domestic airline and automobile industries. What makes Disneyland unique is the distance its employees perceive the company to have fallen, from a utopian vision to the cold reality of the bottom line. The problematic nature of their utopia is exacerbated by the particular interpretation of "family" the employees chose to advocate. There are many different types of families, but a central aspect of American mythology holds that happy families are tightly knit and conflict free. Recent research on family interaction reveals not only that this is a myth, but that perpetuation of the harmony-at-all-costs ideal can cause serious problems of adjustment (Reiss, 1981). In promoting a conflict-free work environment, and in particular one that was "on-stage" for all the world to see, Disneyland management and employees never learned to manage conflict effectively and were therefore seriously upset when disagreements finally surfaced. Of all the employees we interviewed, only two dancers were convinced that happiness was still the order of the day. Others had already made plans to leave, while still others were gearing up for the possibility of a second strike. Perhaps no organization can claim to be the "happiest place on earth" for long, especially if employees start to believe it.

In spite of all that has taken place, the future is not altogether bleak. From management's point of view, the key to Disneyland's future lies in a reconciliation of current economic realities with a distinctive tradition. One traditional image that may be worth preserving is that of "Walt" as the organizational hero:

He was a genius. (Ride Operator/Male/4 years tenure)

A lot of people [say] if Walt was here it would be different, and I have to agree with that. . . . He was a very special person. (Supervisor/Female/8 years tenure)

If Walt Disney was alive today he'd. . . . (Ride Operator/Male/3 years tenure)

A conscious reconsideration of the drama metaphor might help reconcile management with employees, and past with present. An appeal of the drama metaphor lies in its ability to subsume some of the interpretations of both management and employees; it simultaneously retains the image of the park as *family* entertainment and permits a *business* orientation. Alternatively, an altogether new root-metaphor may be needed, one that sees employees as neither "actors" nor "children" but as full participants in shaping the present and future of life at Disneyland.

Notes

1. The second round of interviews was designed to confirm results from the first round and to obtain data on the purposes, language, and actions of the 1984 strike. The interview schedule included the following questions: What are the characteristics of Disneyland that make it a unique organization, and in what ways is it similar to other organizations? Which of the following terms accurately describe the park and personnel? (Subjects were shown or read the list of terms listed in footnote 3); Have you heard personnel using any of these terms, in particular? Did you notice any discrepancies between the terms used and actions taken? What is the Disney philosophy? Do personnel agree on what it is? What does it mean that "the people make the place"? What were the issues in the strike from management's point of

view? From the union's point of view? From your point of view? What were the intentions and reactions of all parties to the respective strategies and moves in the strike? What are the short- and long-term implications of the strike?

2. The sample of hourly employees included members from all the principal divisions except maintenance. The latter were particularly inaccessible because they worked the graveyard shift. We decided, however, that their inclusion would be largely redundant given the tenure and age ranges of the present sample and the general consensus of opinion which existed among the interviewed.

3. Subjects were presented with the following list of terms and were told that they "had been used to describe Disneyland"; management was *not* identified as the source: *friendly, people experts, magical, family-like, informal, pioneering, teamwork, democratic, businesslike, wholesome, like a drama.*

4. See France, V.A. (1982). The spirit of Disneyland. Unpublished manuscript, Anaheim, CA; Morgenstern, J. (1966, December 26). Walt Disney (1901–1966): Imagineer of fun. *Newsweek*, p. 68–69; Walt Disney Productions. (1977). *The Disney theme show;* Walt Disney Productions. (1979). *Disneyland: The first quarter century;* Walt Disney Productions. (1981). *The Disney management style;* Walt Disney Productions. (1982). *Disneyland: A talented team;* Walt Disney Productions. (1982). *Your role in the Disneyland show.*

5. A recent TV commercial for Pacific Bell shows a Disneyland representative stressing the business side of his organization.

References

Argyris, C. (1982). *Reasoning, learning, and action.* San Francisco: Jossey-Bass.

Berg, P. (1985). Organization change as a symbolic transformation process. In P. Frost, L. Moore, M. Louis, C. Lundberg, & J. Martin (Eds.), *Organizational culture* (pp. 281–300). Beverly Hills, CA: Sage.

Billig, M. (1976). *The social psychology of intergroup relations,* London: Academic Press.

Brown, M. H. (1986). Sense-making and narrative forms. Reality construction in organizations. L. Thayer (Ed.), *Organization—communication: Emerging perspectives* (Vol. 1, pp. 71–84). Norwood, NJ: Ablex.

Deetz, S., & Mumby, D. (1985). Metaphors, information, and power. *Information and Behavior, 1,* 369–386.

Eisenberg, E. M. (1984). Ambiguity as strategy in organizational communication. *Communication Monographs, 51,* 227–242.

Eisenberg, E. M. (1986). Meaning and interpretation in organizations. *Quarterly Journal of Speech, 72,* 88–97.

Eisenberg, E. M., & Riley, P. A. (1988). Organizational symbolism and sense-making. In G. Goldhaber & G. Barnett (Eds.), *Handbook of organizational communication.* NJ: Ablex.

Frost, P., Moore, L., Louis, M., Lundberg, C., & Martin, S. (1985). *Organizational culture.* Beverly Hills, CA: Sage.

Geertz, C. (1983). *Local knowledge*. New York: Basic Books.

Harris, S. G., & Sutton, R. I. (1986). Functions of parting ceremonies in dying organizations. *Academy of Management Journal, 29,* 5–30.

Hoffmarr, L. (1981). *Foundations of family therapy*. New York: Basic Books.

Honeck, R. P., & Hoffman, R. R. (1980). *Cognition and figurative language*. Hillsdale, NJ: Erlbaum.

Keesing, R. M. (1974). Theories of culture. *Annual Review of Anthropology, 3,* 73–79.

Koch, S., & Deetz, S. (1981). Metaphor analysis of social reality in organizations. *Journal of Applied Communication Research, 9,* 1–15.

Kuhn, T. S. (1979). *The structure of scientific resolutions* (2nd ed.). Chicago: University of Chicago Press.

Lakoff, G., & Johnson, M. (1980). *Metaphors we lure by*. Chicago: University of Chicago Press.

Langer, S. K. (1979). *Philosophy in a new key*. Cambridge, MA: Harvard University Press.

Levinson, S. C. (1983). *Pragmatics*. Cambridge, England: Cambridge University Press.

Martin, J., Sitkin, S. B., & Boehm, M. (1985). Founders and the elusiveness of cultural legacy. In P. Frost, L. Moore, M. Louis, C. Lundberg, & J. Martin (Eds.), *Organizational culture* (pp. 99–124). Beverly Hills, CA: Sage.

Morgan, G. (1986). *Images of organization*. Beverly Hills, CA: Sage.

Morgan, G., Frost, P., & Pondy, L. (1983). Organizational symbolism. In L. Pond, P. Frost, G. Morgan, & T. Dandridge (Eds.), *Organizational symbolism* (pp. 3–35). Greenwich, CT: JAI Press.

Ortony, A. (1979). *Metaphor and thought*. Cambridge: Cambridge University Press.

Owen, W. F. (1985). Thematic metaphors in relational communication: A conceptual framework. *Western Journal of Speech Communication, 49, 1,* 1–13.

Peters, T. J., & Waterman, R. H., Jr. (1982). *In search of excellence*. New York: Harper & Row.

Pfeifer, J. (1981). Management as symbolic action: The creation and maintenance of organization paradigms. In B. Staw & L. L. Cummings (Eds.), *Research in organizational behavior* (Vol. 3, pp. 1–52). Greenwich, CT: JAI Press.

Pondy, L. R. (1978). Leadership is a language game. In M. M. Lombardo & M. W. McCall, Jr. (Eds.), *Leadership: Where else can we go?* (pp. 87–99). Durham, NC: Duke University Press.

Pondy, L. R. (1983). The role of metaphors and myths in organization and in the facilitation of change. In L. Pondy, P. Frost, G. Morgan, & T. Dandridge (Eds.), *Organizational symbolism* (pp. 157–166). Greenwich, CT: JAI Press.

Pondy, L., Frost, P., Morgan, G., & Dandridge, T. (1983). *Organizational symbolism*. Greenwich, CT: JAI Press.

Putnam, L. L. (1983). The interpretive perspective. An alternative to functionalism. In L. L. Putnam & M. E. Pacanowsky (Eds.), *Communication and organizations* (pp. 31–54). Beverly Hills, CA: Sage.

Putnam, L. L., & Pacanowsky, M. E. (1983). *Communication and organizations*. Beverly Hills, CA: Sage.

Putnam, L. L., & Poole, M. S. (1987). Conflict and negotiation. In F. M. Jablin, L. L. Putnam, K. H. Roberts, & I. W. Porter (Eds.), *Handbook of organizational communication*. Newbury Park, CA: Sage.

Reiss, D. (1981). *The family's construction of reality*. Cambridge, MA: Harvard University Press.

Rosenblatt, P. C., de Mik, L., Anderson, R. M., & Johnson, P. A. (1985). *The family in business*. San Francisco, CA: Jossey-Bass.

Rummel, R. J. (1976). *Understanding conflict and war* (Vol. 2). Beverly Hills, CA: Sage.

Schein, E. H. (1983). The role of the founder in creating organizational culture. *Organizational Dynamics*, 13–28.

Schein, E. H. (1985). *Organizational culture and leadership*. San Francisco, CA: Jossey-Bass.

Siehl, C. (1985). After the founder: An opportunity to manage culture. In P. Frost, L. Moore, M. Louis, C. Lundberg, & J. Martin (Eds.), *Organizational culture* (pp. 125–140). Beverly Hills, CA: Sage.

Smith, K. K., & Simmons, V. M. (1983). A Rumpelstiltskin organization: Metaphors on metaphors in field research. *Administrative Science Quarterly, 28*, 377–392.

Watzlawick, P., Weakland, J., & Fisch, R. (1974). *Change*. New York: Gardner Press.

Weick, K. E. (1979). *The social psychology of organizing* (2nd ed.). Reading, MA: Addison-Wesley.

Weick, K. E. (1980). The management of eloquence. *Executive, 6*, 18–21.

Weick, K. E. (1983). Organizational communication: Toward a research agenda. In L. Putnam & M. Pacanowsky (Eds.), *Communication and organizations* (pp. 13–29). Beverly Hills, CA: Sage.

Wilkins, A. L. (1984, November). *On stories and cultural change*. Paper presented at the annual meeting of the Speech Communication Association, Chicago, Illinois.

4

Reconsidering Openness in Organizational Communication

Written with Marsha Witten for a management audience, this essay extended my critique of the emphasis on clarity in communication to the ideology of openness that was ubiquitous at the time. Contrary to common belief, openness can have a significant downside, and effective communication as a rule seeks a balance between expression and protection, revelation and concealment. Specific occasions on which openness is undesirable were identified and discussed.

I was teaching a graduate seminar in Center City Philadelphia, and Marsha was one of the students. Early on in the class we watched in horror as a class member verbally eviscerated one of her peers, justifying her attack by insisting that she was "just being open and honest." After this experience, we essentially tried to adapt my work on ambiguity to apply more generally to questions of openness and honesty. It was difficult to prepare the final manuscript, as the editor insisted that we cut the length of the essay, resulting in a final product that is overly terse and somewhat bloodless. Nevertheless, the paper succeeded in complicating notions of effective communication for many in organizational studies.

SOURCE: Eisenberg, E. M., & Witten, M. (1987). Reconsidering openness in organizational communication. *Academy of Management Review, 12,* 418–426. Copyright © 1987, Academy of Management.

M any organizational theoreticians and researchers uncritically accept the efficacy of open communication. Recently, however, some writers (Eisenberg, 1984; March & Olsen, 1970; McCaskey, 1982; Pascale & Athos, 1981; Pfeffer, 1977) have argued that organizational participants are strategists oriented toward multiple goals who communicate in ways that may not be completely open, but nevertheless may be effective. This agrees with recent work that rejects simple models of communication in favor of a more complex view of managers and employees as strategic, symbolic actors (Pfeffer, 1981; Pondy, 1978; Putnam & Pacanowsky, 1983; Weick, 1979, 1980).

This essay extends these lines of argument by examining the key assumptions that underlie the idea that opening up lines of communication is a panacea for organizational ills. It traces the development of the ideology of openness in organizational communication from its origins in the human relations movement, describes its use in contemporary organizational research, and proposes an alternative, contingency model of communication in organizations.

The Legacy of Human Relations

Early Human Relations

The emphasis of the early human relations movement on open superior-subordinate communications stemmed from an assumption about the need for uniform goals among organizational members. Viewing workers as latent cooperators (Bendix, 1974), Harvard researchers saw open communication between manager and employee as an integrating mechanism (Mayo, 1945; Roethlisberger & Dickson, 1947). First, by persuading employees to disclose their feelings about their jobs and superiors, this talking would simultaneously relieve worker stress and allow management to discover untapped sources of worker motivation (Perrow, 1986). Second, by increasing frequency of contact between workers and management, the employee would identify with the goals of the company. Morale and productivity would improve.

To achieve these ends, early human relations practitioners stressed frequent downward communication from superiors to increase integration and show a sincere interest in the employee (Bendix, 1974) and disclosive communication upward on the part of the employee. The former could be achieved by developing a managerial elite trained to communicate lucidly and unemotionally with workers. The latter was facilitated by nondirective personnel interviews. In these interviews, employees were encouraged to achieve emotional relief by airing grievances and frustration to counselors, even though the counselors were powerless to change the employees' circumstances (Wilensky & Wilensky, 1951). Employees were encouraged specifically to discuss personal problems with interviewers, under the assumption that useless emotional complications and obsessive thinking that could interfere with work performance might be reduced (Mayo, 1945).

Reexaminations of early human relations research reveal that economic rewards, better discipline, and the anxieties caused by the national depression contributed more to improved performance than did improved communication (Carey, 1967; Conrad, 1985; Franke & Kaul, 1978). Peter Drucker (1974) spoke for many in management when he referred to early human relations as a kind of psychological manipulation in which the exploitation of "individual fears, anxieties, and personality needs replaces the old fear of being punished or of losing one's job" in controlling employees (p. 243).

Later Human Relations

The early human relations school has been criticized by those who view its goals and techniques as serving managerial interests over those of workers (Bendix, 1974; Edwards, 1979; Perrow, 1986). Later advocates of human relations emphasized the *mutual* responsibility of managers and employees to create "supportive relationships" through open communication (Likert, 1967).

Likert's concern for supportive relationships inspired much of the research on openness conducted in the communication field. Notable within this tradition is work by Redding (1972) and Jablin (1985), who defined an open communication relationship as one in which both parties perceive the other to be a willing and receptive listener and refrain from responses which might be seen as negative or nonaccepting. From this perspective, the ideal managerial climate is characterized by supportiveness, empathy, participation, and trust, achieved in part by the "candid disclosure of feelings" (Redding, 1972, p. 330).

When subjected to empirical tests, these later conceptions have fared only slightly better than the earlier human relations theories. Numerous contingencies moderate the relationship between openness and employee attitudes and behaviors. For example, Miner's (1982) review of research on Likert's System-4 model and other related theories found only mixed support for the importance of supportive relationships. He further concluded that their impact varied across hierarchical levels. While some studies indicate a linkage between supervisor openness and subordinate satisfaction (cf. Jablin, 1985), others indicate negative findings (e.g., Rabinowitz, Falkenbach, Travers, Valentine, & Weener, 1983). In one study, Wiio (cited in Goldhaber, 1983) found that open communication was associated with greater *dissatisfaction* with the job and the organization. Dissatisfaction is not necessarily a reason to be less open, since conflict can engender compromise and positive change, but it does indicate the relationship between open communication and employee attitudes is not as simple as is sometimes presumed. Instead, the effect of openness on attitudes is moderated by the nature of the information that is shared and the extent to which revelations expose points of significant disagreement.

Finally, subordinates' preferences for open communication vary depending upon characteristics of their superiors. While subordinates generally prefer open communication, they are less at ease disclosing information to superiors whom they perceive as "highly involved in political activities" (Jablin, 1981, p. 273). McGregor (1967) correctly anticipated the need for a contingency approach to communications: "virtually every variable associated with human interaction may be 'dysfunctional' at both extremes. Like other variables, the openness of communication is relative for all practical purposes, not absolute. . . . Even in the most intimate personal relationships—marriage, for example—absolutely open communication could destroy the relationship" (pp. 162–163).

Reconsidering Openness

Openness has been identified three different ways in the literature. First, openness has been treated as the *disclosure of personal information*. This is due to an emphasis from the early human relations movement, in which the disclosure of employees' feelings and the resultant emotional relief were important for effective superior-subordinate relationships. Secondly, openness involves *disclosure of nonpersonal information* (such as work plans or objectives). This is reflected in later work by Likert, Redding, and Jablin, in which openness is defined as supportiveness rather than unrestricted candor. A third view of openness overlaps the first two and addresses the linguistic choices associated with being more or less open; that is, how *clear or ambiguous* disclosure may be. This is most apparent in work on language and symbolism in organizations (cf. Eisenberg & Riley, 1988; Pondy, Frost, Morgan, & Dandridge, 1983).

Openness as Personal Disclosure

In advice that recalls Mayo's (1945) notion of nondirective interviewing, Imberman (1979) argued that frequent listening sessions that encourage employees to share their feelings lead to better labor-management relations and a decreased likelihood of strikes. Closer in spirit to the later human relations theorists, Stagnaro (1982) contended that managers should conduct leveling sessions in which they communicate openly with employees about their performance, skills, ability, and feelings. He believed that honesty would not backfire as long as managers listened carefully, avoided emotionalism, and viewed employees who left the organization as a result of leveling sessions as the "removal of stress from the organization" (p. 19).

Sessions of this kind can backfire for both managers and employees. While disclosure and directness are appropriate under certain circumstances, this approach can cause serious discomfort, confusion, emotional demands, and more stress than is alleviated. Those who prescribe disclosive communication assume that by understanding the other person better, one will be better able to get along with him or her. However, this assumption is counter to common sense and empirical evidence. Most work relationships are noninterpersonal, because participants are low in "intrinsic commitment" and, subsequently, little private psychological-level information is exchanged (Conrad, 1985; Parks, 1982). Furthermore, close relationships that result from mutual disclosure can complicate rather than simplify employees' work lives (Conrad, 1985). While it is possible that increased knowledge of another person may lead to an improved work relationship, it is also possible that knowing someone better may increase the probability of serious disagreement that could jeopardize the future of the relationship (Bochner, 1984).

The idea that open communication may not always be good is resisted by many because it contradicts deeply held beliefs about human relationships. When asked to describe their *ideal* superior-subordinate relationship, most people respond that it should be trusting, open, and honest (Jablin, 1985). Often, however, these beliefs about communication differ from actual behavior in organizations (Steele, 1975). Managers frequently use "manipulative persuasion" to disguise self-interest, to distort information, and to overwhelm others (Allen, Madison, Porter, Renwick, & Mayes, 1979). Although most managers believe they are supportive when dealing with poor performers, in actuality, their behavior may contradict this belief (Fairhurst, Green, & Snavely, 1984). Research about subordinates reveals a similar pattern. When communicating with superiors, subordinates deviate from openness to protect self-interests; messages directed upward in organizations are "largely edited, cautious, and inaccurate" (Krone, 1985, p. 9).

Openness as Disclosure of Nonpersonal Information

The assertion that the free flow of task-related, nonpersonal information increases organizational effectiveness is true only under certain conditions. Between superiors and subordinates, labor and management, and the organization and its publics, both individual and group goals can be promoted through the cautious disclosure of information.

In collective bargaining, seasoned negotiators use ambiguity and conceal-ment as a matter of course—research shows that open disclosure does not lead to better settlements and may reduce the likelihood of satisfactory agree-ments (Putnam & Jones, 1982). At times, norms against openness are a matter of convention. For example, in many organizations there are strict informal rules against the discussion of controversial topics at meetings; real differences are hammered out backstage (Steele, 1975). In organizations that depend on public perceptions of legitimacy for survival, communication about technical activities may be restricted to prevent internal conflicts that could damage the organization's image (Meyer & Rowan, 1977). Finally, openness must be restricted in the treatment of confidential or proprietary information (Steele, 1975).

Overly disclosive communication may be harmful to organizations during a crisis. Kleinfield (1985) explored the public disclosures of wrong-doing in corporations such as E. F. Hutton and General Electric. In such sit-uations, employees must be reassured that the organization will not repeat its mistakes and that the company is worthy of their continued commit-ment. Simple prescriptions of openness do little to help managers cope with such complex problems.

Perhaps the most publicized claim made about openness in organizations is that the free exchange of information equalizes power relationships and reduces the likelihood of political behavior. For example, Naisbitt (1982) argued that the open communication characteristic of his ideal network structures would help members to treat each other as peers, regardless of formal status. Similarly, Peters and Waterman (1982) contended that the informal, freewheeling communication that characterizes their excellent organizations reduces political maneuvering.

Increased exchange of information alone may not be sufficient to equal-ize power relationships. Power is derived from information only when the individual is able to make sense out of the raw data and has the opportunity and is willing to act on it (Blackburn, 1981; Mechanic, 1962). Members who have superior abilities and are in better positions to translate information into action will dominate those who lack this ability. Even in organizations where there is free exchange of information, power is manifested in the dynamics of ordinary interaction through who initiates, terminates, and sets the agenda for what gets talked about (Conrad & Ryan, 1985; Eisenberg, Monge, & Farace, 1984). Similarly, people have varying abilities based on position and credibility to make information salient for others (Weick, 1979). For these reasons, more disclosive communication alone cannot make people equal or remove the politics from organizational behavior.

Disclosure of technical information is especially risky for lower-level employees. Lower-level participants have few means of building power bases other than from the highly specialized information uniquely in their possession (Hickson, Hinings, Lee, Schneck, & Pennings, 1971). As a result, the sharing of technical information can reduce lower-level employees' access to informal power within the organization (Mechanic, 1962). In contrast, managers and executives can rely on legitimate authority (position power) if their technical knowledge becomes widely shared.

Upward communication in organizations presents a more fundamental dilemma for employees. Although the interests of the organization often are best served when employees reveal all they know about problems and opportunities, revealing such information can be damaging to the individual's job security and career aspirations. The disincentives to reveal negative information are well documented (e.g., the space shuttle tragedy) and less dramatically shown in research on the "mum effect" and on upward distortion in organizational hierarchies (cf. Jablin, 1979). Individuals may feel trapped between conflicting motivations, that is, to reveal what they know for the good of the company, but to do so at their own peril. Openness often involves risks people are unwilling to take, and they will resist strongly if openness is imposed (Zalzenik, 1971). While it is admirable to strive for an organizational climate in which people feel comfortable speaking openly with one another, such a goal is unreasonable unless we are realistic about the good reasons people have for concealment. According to Conrad (1985), "the norms and political realities of organizations thus reward people for closed, not open communication" (p. 104).

Openness as Clear, Unambiguous Communication

Many managers place excessive "trust in increasing the clarity of communication between people, especially when disagreements are substantive. Getting a currently hopeless impasse clear is often unwise and likely to make things worse" (Pascale & Athos, 1981, p. 94). At all levels, members of organizations stand to gain from the strategic use of ambiguity (Eisenberg, 1984). In this way, organizational participants can express their feelings ("I have some reservations about giving this assignment to Joe") and can deny specific interpretations, should they arise ("You mean, you don't think he's bright enough to do the job?").

It can be especially useful to use strategic ambiguity when coping with the multiple interactional goals associated with supervisory positions. The ability of a manager conducting a performance appraisal "to use strategically ambiguous statements and comments may improve subordinate performance by allowing him or her the freedom and creativity to excel" (Goodall, Wilson, & Waagen, 1986, p. 77). Vague, metaphorical, and humorous suggestions are methods of communicating multiple messages which could not be expressed as easily in a literal fashion. While one risk of such strategies is that the subtlety will be lost on the audience, employees tend to be sensitive to this kind of communication. Usually, they can tell, for example, when the boss is at the same time conveying a more serious message (Ullian, 1976; Winick, 1976).

Researchers of organizational evaluation processes found that beliefs tend to be self-perpetuating, despite managers' efforts to overcome their biases. Once an initial assessment of another person has been made, there is a tendency mainly to attend to information that supports this first impression (Jones & Nisbet, 1972). For this reason, full disclosure is risky, but equivocation can serve as a kind of character insurance for people who are perceived as credible (Williams & Goss, 1975).

Overly explicit communication can affect task-related decisions and attributions about character. Indiscriminate explicitness limits options and can endanger plans (Bok, 1983). Often, sophisticated managers learn the hard way about the liabilities of speaking too soon (Pascale & Athos, 1981). Many managers who have been overly explicit in their policies have paid dearly later on, when a violation by a valued employee forces them to choose between making a good decision and remaining consistent with previous pronouncements.

The manager who is overly explicit in the statement of missions and goals also takes a risk. When missions are couched in unequivocal terms, conflict is unavoidable; when goals are stated concretely, they often are strikingly ineffective (Edelman, 1977). Ambiguous missions and goals allow divergent interpretations to coexist and are more effective in allowing diverse groups to work together. Further, ambiguous missions allow organizations greater freedom to respond to environmental changes (Keesing, 1974).

In public sector organizations, formal agreements often are constructed as purposefully ambiguous so that representatives of various constituencies can claim victory for their respective groups (Ring & Perry, 1985). Clear articulation of strategy may be inappropriate, since such disclosure provides a rallying point for the opposition, and over time leads executives to exercise inadequate caution. "Ambiguity in strategy, characteristic of many public organizations, therefore, may be an asset" (Ring & Perry, 1985, p. 279). The need for ambiguity in communication extends beyond formal organizations. All societies require a degree of value-consensus in order to survive; as a rule, this consensus is engendered through the creative use of communication. Political discourse is rarely literal, and usually a psychological sense of community (Sarason, 1974) or sense of oneness (Becher, 1981) is sufficient in modern social life (Hart, 1984). In communities whose members strive for extreme levels of communitas, ambiguity is absolutely essential for the maintenance of a sense of common understanding (Myerhoff, 1975).

Toward a Contingency Perspective on Organizational Communication

In this paper, an undifferentiated view of the benefits of open communication has been critiqued. This is not an objection to all suggestions regarding the beneficial effects of open communication or a suggestion that managers stop talking with their employees. Some organizational activities, particularly those having safety or legal implications, require clear, complete communication. Here, concealing information would lead to the worsening of some problems over time, making them less manageable if confronted in the future.

It is laudable to sensitize employees and managers to the benefits of empathic listening; to create an atmosphere of mutual respect and willingness to entertain new ideas; to share feelings and sentiments when individuals so desire; and to establish as much as possible in a context of unequal power a climate of trust and mutual concern. Endorsement of these goals does not equal supporting openness in all circumstances. Instead, the development of a contingency perspective in which communication strategies reflect individual goals and situational characteristics is proposed. Future research should move systematically toward identifying appropriateness norms for open communication (Derlega & Grzelak, 1979), that is, the conditions under which managers and employees choose to be more or less open.

The reasoning behind an individual's decision to be more or less open can involve many different contingencies. Four types are suggested by this review: individual, relational, organizational, and environmental.

Individual contingencies are personal motives, preferences, and styles that affect communicative choices. If one knows that someone is highly ambitious in pursuing a career path or, alternatively, that one's primary concern is to keep his/her private life separate from his/her work life, his/her degree of openness can be explained regarding these desired ends. Similarly, it is expected that a communicator's personal style (e.g., loquacity or shyness) would affect the extent to which he or she communicates openly with others.

Relational contingencies refer to the closeness or shared history between organizational members. In part, choices to reveal or conceal information can be explained by an expediency model, since interactants in a relatively closed group with a long history can communicate less explicitly without compromising understanding (Bernstein, 1964). Attention to relational contingencies also may indicate tact, politeness, and the preservation of intimacy as possible explanations for one's degree of openness. For example, usually the decision to reveal highly personal information to another employee depends on the degree of trust and respect in the relationship.

Organizational contingencies are constraints on communication related to the job, the tasks at hand, or the interests of the organization as a whole. For example, a decision not to reveal company secrets or a decision to hold back information from employees about a tentative plan may be justified because it furthers or protects organizational interests. Alternatively, a decision to share information about the big picture with employees can be viewed as one way of promoting more participative, democratic decision making.

Lastly, *environmental* contingencies may constrain an organization's internal and external communication. Particularly in organizations that are highly regulated or those in the public eye, communicative choices must be considered in light of how they will be interpreted by various publics. For example, managers and CEOs monitor their degree of openness with the public as a way of protecting their organizations from possible threats to legitimacy or survival.

Often, the development of theories of human communication parallels the dominant values of society. Definitions of what constitutes *effective* communication have evolved from a concern with serving societal ends, to a focus on individual goal attainment, and most recently to a combined concern with personal goals and situational adaptation (Rawlins, 1985). The perspective presented here is consistent with this latter view. A contingent, differentiated view of organizational communication, one that eschews indiscriminate calls for openness in favor of a more subtle characterization of organizational life, is desirable.

AUTHORS' NOTE: The authors are grateful to Janet Fulk, Patricia Riley, Lori Roscoe, and Walter Fisher for their helpful comments and suggestions.

References

Allen, R. W., Madison, D. L., Porter, L. W., Renwick, P. A., & Mayes, B. T. (1979). Organizational politics: Tactics and characteristics of its actors. *California Management Review, 22*(1), 77–83.

Becher, T. (1981). Towards a definition of disciplinary cultures. *Studies in Higher Education, 6,* 109–122.

Bendix, R. (1974). *Work and authority in industry.* Berkeley: University of California Press.

Bernstein, B. (1964). Elaborated and restricted codes. *American Anthropologist, 66*(6), 55–69.

Blackburn, R. S. (1981). Lower participant power: Toward a conceptual integration. *Academy of Management Review, 6,* 127–131.

Bochner, A. P. (1984). The functions of human communication in interpersonal bonding. In C. Arnold & J. Bowers (Eds.), *Handbook of rhetorical and communication theory* (pp. 544–621). Boston: Allyn & Bacon.

Bok, S. (1983). *Secrets: On the ethics of concealment and revelation.* New York: Pantheon Books.

Carey, A. (1967). The Hawthorne studies: A radical criticism. *American Political Science Review, 32,* 403–416.

Conrad, C. (1985). *Strategic organizational communication.* New York: Holt, Rinehart & Winston.

Conrad, C., & Ryan, M. (1985). Power, praxis, and self in organizational communication theory. In R. McPhee & P. Tompkins (Eds.), *Organizational communication* (pp. 235–258). Beverly Hills, CA: Sage.

Derlega, V., & Grzelak, J. (1979). Appropriateness of self-disclosure. In G. J. Chelune (Ed.), *Self-disclosure* (pp. 151–176). San Francisco: Jossey-Bass.

Drucker, P. (1974). *Management: Tasks, responsibilities, practices.* New York: Harper & Row.

Edelman, M. (1977). *Political language: Words that succeed and policies that fail.* New York: Academic Press.

Eisenberg, E. M. (1984). Ambiguity as strategy in organizational communication. *Communication Monographs, 51,* 227–242.

Eisenberg, E. M., Monge, P. R., & Farace, R. V. (1984). Coorientation on communication rules in managerial dyads. *Human Communication Research, 11,* 261–271.

Eisenberg, E. M., & Riley, P. R. (1988). Symbols and sense-making in organizations. In G. Goldhaber (Ed.), *Handbook of organizational communication.* Norwood, NJ: Ablex.

Fairhurst, G. T., Green, S. G., & Snavely, B. K. (1984). Face support in controlling poor performance. *Human Communication Research, 11,* 272–295.

Franke, R., & Kaul, J. (1978). The Hawthorne experiments: First statistical interpretation. *American Sociological Review, 43,* 623–643.

Goldhaber, G. (1983). *Organizational communication* (3rd ed.). Dubuque, IA: Brown.

Goodall, H. L., Jr., Wilson, G. L., & Waagen, C. L. (1986). The performance appraisal interview: An interpretive reassessment. *Quarterly Journal of Speech, 72,* 74–87.

Hart, R. P. (1984). The functions of human communication in the maintenance of public values. In C. Arnold & J. Bowers (Eds.), *Handbook of rhetorical and communication theory* (pp. 749–791). Boston: Allyn & Bacon.

Hickson, D., Hinings, C., Lee. C., Schneck, R., & Pennings, J. (1971). A strategic contingencies theory of intraorganizational power. *Administrative Science Quarterly, 16,* 216–229.

Imberman, W. (1979). Strikes cost more than you think. *Harvard Business Review, 57*(3), 133–142.

Jablin, F. M. (1979). Superior-subordinate communications: The state of the art. *Psychological Bulletin, 86,* 1201–1222.

Jablin, F. M. (1981). An exploratory study of subordinates' perceptions of supervisory politics. *Communication Quarterly, 29,* 269–275.

Jablin, F. M. (1985). Task/work relationships: A life-span perspective. In M. L. Knapp & G. R. Miller (Eds.), *Handbook of interpersonal communication* (pp. 615–654). Beverly Hills, CA: Sage.

Jones, E., & Nisbet, R. (1972). The actor and the observer: Divergent perceptions of the causes of behavior. In E. Jones, D. Kanouse, H. Kelly, R. Nisbett, S. Valins, & B. Weiner (Eds.), *Attribution: Perceiving the causes of behavior* (pp. 78–94). Morristown, NJ: General Learning Press.

Keesing, R. M. (1974). Theories of culture. In B. Siegel, A. Beals, & S. Tyler (Eds.), *Annual review of anthropology* (Vol. 3, pp. 73–91). Palo Alto, CA: Annual Reviews.

Kleinfield, N. R. (1985, July). When scandal haunts the corridors. *New York Times,* pp. 1, 7.

Krone, K. (1985). *Subordinate influence in organizations: The differential use of upward influence messages in decision-making contexts.* Unpublished doctoral dissertation, University of Texas, Austin.

Likert, R. (1967). *The human organization.* New York: McGraw-Hill.

March, J. G., & Olsen, J. (1970). *Ambiguity and choice in organizations.* Bergen, Norway: Universitetsforlaget.

Mayo, E. (1945). *The social problems of an industrial civilization.* Cambridge, MA: Harvard University Press.

McCaskey, M. B. (1982). *The executive challenge: Managing change and ambiguity.* Boston: Pitman.

McGregor, D. (1967). *The professional manager.* New York: McGraw-Hill.

Mechanic, D. (1962). Sources of power of lower participants in complex organizations. *Administrative Science Quarterly 7,* 249–264.

Meyer, J., & Rowan, B. (1977). Institutionalized organizations: Formal structure as myth and ceremony. *American Journal of Sociology, 83,* 340–363.

Mine, J. (1982). *Theories of organizational structure and process.* Chicago: Dryden Press.

Myerhoff, B. (1975). Organization and ecstasy: Deliberate and accidental communitas among Huichol Indians and American youth. In S. Moore & B. Myerhoff (Eds.), *Symbol and politics in communal ideology* (pp. 33–67). Ithaca, NY: Cornell University Press.

Naisbitt, J. (1982). *Megatrends.* New York: Warner Books.

Parks, M. P. (1982). Ideology in interpersonal communication: Off the couch and into the world. In M. Burgoon (Ed.), *Communication Yearbook, 5* (pp. 79–108). New Brunswick, NJ: Transaction Books.

Pascale, R. T., & Athos, A. G. (1981). *The art of Japanese management.* New York: Simon & Schuster.

Perrow, C. (1986). *Complex organizations* (3rd ed.). New York: Random House.

Peters, T. J., & Waterman, R. H. (1982). *In search of excellence.* New York: Harper & Row.

Pfeffer, J. (1977). The ambiguity of leadership. *Academy of Management Review, 2,* 104–112.

Pfeffer, J. (1981). Management as symbolic action: The creation and maintenance of organizational paradigms. In B. Staw & L. L. Cummings (Eds.), *Research in organizational behavior* (Vol. 3., pp. 1–52). Greenwich, CT: JAI Press.

Pondy, L. R. (1978). Leadership is a language game. In M. Lombardo & M. McCall (Eds.), *Leadership: Where else can we go?* (pp. 87–99). Durham, NC: Duke University Press.

Pondy, L. R., Frost, P., Morgan, G., & Dandridge, T. (1983). *Organizational symbolism.* Greenwich, CT: JAI Press.

Putnam, L., & Jones, T. (1982). The role of communication in bargaining. *Human Communication Research,* 8, 262–280.

Putnam, L., & Pacanowsky, M. (1983). *Communication and organizations: An interpretive approach.* Beverly Hills, CA: Sage.

Rabinowitz, W., Falkenbach, K., Travers, J., Valentine, C., & Weener, P. (1983). Worker motivation: Unsolved problem or untapped resource? *California Management Review, 25*(2), 43–56.

Rawlins, W. K. (1985). Stalking interpersonal communication effectiveness: Social, individual, or situational integration? In T. Benson (Ed.), *Speech communication in the 20th century* (pp. 108–129). Carbondale: Southern Illinois University Press.

Redding, W. C. (1972). *Communication in the organization: An interpretive review of the research.* New York: Industrial Communication Council.

Ring, P. S., & Perry, J. L. (1985). Strategic management in public and private organizations: Implications of distinctive contexts and constraints. *Academy of Management Review, 10,* 276–287.

Roethlisberger, F., & Dickson, W. (1947). *Management and the worker.* Cambridge, MA: Harvard University Press.

Sarason, S. (1974). *The psychological sense of community: Prospects for a community psychology.* San Francisco: Jossey-Bass.

Stagnaro, F. (1982). The benefits of leveling with employees: ROLM's experience. *Management Review, 71*(7), 16–20.

Steele, F. (1975). *The open organization: The impact of secrecy and disclosure on people and organizations.* Reading, MA: Addison-Wesley.

Ullian, J. A. (1976). Joking at work. *Journal of Communication, 26*(3), 129–133.

Weick, K. (1979). *The social psychology of organizing* (2nd ed.). Reading, MA: Addison-Wesley.

Weick, K. (1980). The management of eloquence. *Executive, 6*(3), 18–21.

Weick, K. (1984). Organizational communication: Toward a research agenda. In L. Putnam & M. Pacanowsky (Eds.), *Communication and organizations: An interpretive approach* (pp. 13–29). Beverly Hills, CA: Sage.

Wilensky, J., & Wilensky, H. (1951). Personnel counseling: The Hawthorne case. *American Journal of Sociology, 57,* 265–280.

Williams, M. L., & Goss, B. (1975). Equivocation: Character insurance. *Human Communication Research, 1,* 265–270.

Winick, C. (1976). The social context of humor. *Journal of Communication, 26*(3), 124–128.

Zalzenik, A. (1971). Power and politics in organizational life. *Harvard Business Review, 49*(2), 51–59.

PART II

Transcendence and Transformation

This part of the book chronicles my diverse range of attempts to investigate the advantages of communication that is unclear, unfinished, and unplanned. Many of the papers explore the contrast between how communication happens in real life and how we make sense of it after the fact. I celebrate the type of interaction that purposefully postpones the fixing of meaning in favor of cultivating possible new interpretations. I argue that this more open-ended view of communication and meaning creates supportive conditions both for individual transcendence and for positive organizational and social transformation.

5

Jamming

Transcendence Through Organizing

*This paper sought to expand the original argument about ambiguity in organiza-
tions (see Chapter 1, "Ambiguity as Strategy") to include considerations of identity.
A prepublication version of the paper was presented at the Alta Conference for
Organizational Communication, which in part explains my desire to more fully
consider the role of the individual, as these conferences were always focused on
the lived experience of the scholar and organizational member. Borrowing a
metaphor from music and sports, this paper offered preconditions for jamming
experiences and stressed the importance of improvisation for successful organizing.
In so doing, I sought to emphasize the individual's role in coordinated action over
a more psychological notion of personal identity.*

*Despite its publication in a journal not known to feature organizational commu-
nication studies, this essay was well received and captured the imagination of many
scholars. Its publication marked the culmination of a commitment on my part to
make sense of the rare experience of communitas that can occur during organizing
and that often happens outside the usual stages of relational development. At one
professional meeting I introduced the paper as not being about "sex, God, or me
personally," but of course it is very much about all of these things, along with many
other kinds of transcendence. If the 1984 strategic ambiguity paper was mostly a
critique of current ideology, the jamming essay (published six years later) was my
attempt to articulate and edify a positive model of transcendence through organizing.*

SOURCE: Eisenberg, E. M. (1990). Jamming: Transcendence through organizing.
Communication Research, 17, 139–164. Copyright © 1990, Sage Publications, Inc.

Modern communication theory focuses to a disproportionate degree on the cultivation of shared meanings, interpretations, and emotions, and insufficiently on how coordinated action may occur under conditions of minimal self-disclosure and limited consensus. Borrowing a term from music and sports, this article describes characteristics of "jamming" experiences, instances of fluid behavioral coordination that occur without detailed knowledge of personality. Two biases in prior work—individual bias and strong culture bias—are cited as reasons why experiences like jamming have been ignored in the literature. Examples are given of how these experiences strike a balance between autonomy and interdependence, and can even be transcendent. Four preconditions for jamming—skill, structure, setting, and surrender—are also provided. Finally, possibilities for jamming in formal organizations and society are explored.

Our deeply held, implicit models of communication prevent us from fully appreciating the value of personally involving, minimally disclosive exchanges. One specific type of experience, often encountered but rarely acknowledged, does not follow the norms of communicative clarity and openness but may nonetheless be rewarding. After related notions in music and sports, I call these *jamming* experiences.

Jamming celebrates the closeness that can arise through coordinated action. Jamming is nondisclosive but fulfilling. Jamming experiences are worthy of study because they are an often ecstatic way of balancing autonomy and interdependence in organizing. As such, they offer a different route, other than reciprocal disclosure, to community.

I begin with a review of two contemporary biases in communication theory that lead us to ignore phenomena such as jamming. I then describe the jamming experience, the conditions under which it may occur, and its implications for organizing.

Two Biases

Individual Bias

> As concern for questions of selfhood has grown greater, participation with strangers for social ends has diminished; people feel they need to get to know each other as persons in order to act together; they then get caught up in the immobilizing processes of revealing themselves to each other as persons, and gradually lose their desire to act together. (Sennett, 1978, p. 11)

Whereas 18th-century thinkers for the most part agreed that "behaving with strangers in an emotionally satisfying way and yet remaining

aloof from them . . . [was] the means by which the human animal was transformed into a social being" (Sennett, 1978, p. 11), many today have lost their
appreciation for the emotional rewards of public life. Good manners and
public action are routinely characterized as phony, staged, and unfulfilling in
comparison with "deeper" relationships, that is, those forged with family and
friends. Drawing upon the work of de Tocqueville, Adorno, and Trilling, some
theorists (e.g., Bellah, Madsen, Sullivan, Swidler, & Tipton, 1985; Berger,
Berger, & Kellner, 1974; Parks, 1982; Philipsen, 1987; Sennett, 1978; Storr,
1988) now maintain that an overemphasis on the private realm denies us an
acceptable version of community, hinders coordinated action, and has over
time caused us to lose even our language for thinking and speaking in communal terms. Storr summarizes this point of view:

> The modern assumption that intimate relationships are essential to personal
> fulfillment tends to make us neglect the significance of relationships which are
> not so intimate. . . . In the course of daily life, we habitually encounter many
> people with whom we are not intimate, but who nevertheless contribute to our
> sense of self. (p. 13)

In addition, this privatization of public life shifts our criteria for evaluating
people's behavior away from the results of their actions, toward the desirabil-
ity of their personalities or motives. But motives and personality are often
beside the point: Communication can have as its goal not simply the intimacy
that comes through greater knowledge of the other, but also the satisfaction
born of acting together. *Without devaluing* the importance of deeper psychological exchange, a renewed respect for interaction with strangers can restore
an individual's ability to play an active part in a diverse public.

Theories of Meaning

The overemphasis on personality described above has its counterpart in
tacit theories of meaning. Personalist views of meaning, most common in
the Western world, suggest that individuals create and consequently "own"
meaning inside their heads and that the challenge of communication is to
transmit what is in one person's head to another, with minimal "spillage"
along the way (Axley, 1984). Research on meaning in non-Western cultures
reveals a much less intention- and speaker-oriented perspective (e.g.,
Duranti, 1984; Levine, 1985; Williams, 1987).

A more interactive view of meaning is advocated by Holquist (1983). From
his perspective, meaning is not owned, but "rented" by individuals, and is co-
constructed in social interaction. Furthermore, the social consequences of a

communicative act are seen as more important than the speaker's original intentions (cf. Duranti, 1984). This approach challenges the traditional view of the individual as autonomous actor and offers instead an intersubjective view of meaning: The speaker-subject is continually "constituted in and through a relationship" (May, 1988, p. 11).

One notable example of this perspective is Bakhtin's (1981) theory of language and social development, in which he argues that "language lies on the borderline between oneself and the other. The word in language is half someone else's" (p. 293). Vygotsky takes a similar approach in his socially based theory of mind. According to Vygotsky, mental functions can be carried out socially: "Speech is first and foremost a social phenomenon and is the source of much of the mental functioning on the intra-psychological plane" (Wertsch, 1988, p. 86). A final example is Gergen's (1985) "constructionism," a theory that translates traditionally psychological concepts into explicitly social processes. This translation requires a radical reformulation of epistemology, says Gergen, because it "challenges the concept of knowledge as mental representation. . . . From this perspective, knowledge is not something people possess in their heads, but rather, something people do together" (p. 270).

This shift is especially important because it directs our focus to the interactional character of communication. For example, a truly interactive approach to "organizational stories" would not view them as monologues or cultural artifacts but would focus instead on how they are told and the meanings, identities, and ideologies that emerge in their telling (Ochs, Smith, & Taylor, 1990). Similarly, the study of persuasion in organizations would not investigate any one individual's "compliance-gaining strategies" but rather how all parties contribute to the emerging pattern of behavior. In summary, recent developments in theories of meaning urge us toward studying social interaction and the development of novel meanings between people.

An interactive view of meaning also directs us to study joint practices, the things people *do* together, apart from the similarity of their values or beliefs (Geertz, 1983; Ortner, 1984). Giddens (1981) makes this distinction well:

> "Ideas" . . . are inherently embroiled in what people do, in the texture of the practices of daily life. Some of the most potent forms of ideological mobilisation do not rest upon shared beliefs (any more than shared normative commitments); rather, they operate in and through the forms in which daily life is organized. (p. 68)

In sum, the individual bias in social research robs us of possibilities for community and has the effect of making us more isolated and less able to act together. Furthermore, personalist views of meaning reinforce a monologic view of communication and neglect the novel ways in which meaning is co-constructed through interaction. The next section describes a different but related bias, the yearning for greater homogeneity, shared values, and "strong" cultures.

Strong Culture Bias

Originally dismissed as a "folk" notion in anthropology, the idea of value consensus as a precondition for community has enjoyed a resurgence in the organizational context. For example, many corporate leaders promote shared values and beliefs in their companies in the hopes of gaining an edge over threatening global competition. This strategy has gained some legitimacy under the rubric of "excellent," "strong" cultures, attitudinal monoliths wherein relative homogeneity of values and goals is seen as an ideal (e.g., Peters & Waterman, 1982).

Although the "dark side" of strong cultures has been duly noted (e.g., Mitchell, 1985), the temptation to promote homogeneity and limit diversity remains. One consequence of overemphasizing consensus on core values and beliefs is an often unrealistic desire to resolve differences, rather than learn to live with them (Lyotard, 1984; Moore, 1985). Managers "clone" themselves through personnel selection, assessment, and succession planning. In many organizations, "management knows best," loyalty is expected whether deserved or not, dissent is discouraged, and "boat-rockers" need not apply (Redding, 1985). Even when a new organizational culture is touted as highly participative, screening and assessment procedures are often designed to ensure that only those of like mind have the option to participate. These practices limit diversity in the system and prevent individuals and organizations alike from reaching their creative and adaptive potentials.

Diversity and Security

Why is diversity of such importance in organizational life? Beyond their bottom-line reasons for existence, organizations are social arenas in which individuals strive to attain some sense of personal significance (Pacanowsky & O'Donnell-Trujillo, 1983; Weick, 1979). Participation in organizations is critical to the development of individual identity, and prohibitions against organizational participation (as sometimes occur in retirement or unemployment) can have a devastating effect on mental health and self-esteem (e.g., Deal, 1984). Through our interactions with others, our sense of self is established and shaped, and we become more or less ontologically secure.

This sense of security can be elusive. Within the process of organizing lies the essential dialectic of social life. Through interaction with others, we struggle to establish a balance between feeling a part of a social world and developing a self-concept apart from that world. All social relationships move between autonomy and interdependence, individuation and fusion (Alberoni, 1983). Many have characterized this tension as at the heart of all social organization (e.g., Bellah et al., 1985; Bochner, 1984; Rawlins, 1985; Redding, 1985; Scarf, 1987; Storr, 1988).

Effective Communication Balances
Autonomy and Interdependence

Communicators in all social organizations—friendships (Rawlins, 1985), marriages (Scarf, 1987), families (Reiss, 1981), organizations (Eisenberg, 1984; Eisenberg & Phillips, 1990), and societies (Buber, 1965; Philipsen, 1987)—must walk the "narrow ridge" between self and other and seek to preserve a balance between the two (Arnett, 1986). Acknowledging this fact, we must appreciate the tendency of social actors to be selective in their communication, in decisions about when to get closer and when to become more distant, what to reveal and what to conceal, when to invite conflict and when to avoid it.

At the same time, attempts to limit diversity are understandable. Similarity breeds familiarity, which in turn decreases the likelihood of conflict. Similar others are easier to predict and to control. Perhaps our desire to promote shared goals and values is an easy (but ultimately misguided) answer to the larger question of how to restore a lost sense of community to American public life (Bellah et al., 1985).

But in every case, either too much or too little consensus can be dysfunctional. Groups that are overly interdependent (e.g., Peters and Waterman's [1982] "strong cultures" or Reiss's [1981] consensus-sensitive families) stifle creativity and can lead to emotional problems for individuals and adaptive problems for the group. Groups that promote excessive autonomy run the risk of dissolving or of becoming so conflict-ridden that nothing gets done. Every action brings us either closer together or farther apart; the challenge is to remain close but different (Scarf, 1987); "close-but-not-too-close" (Pacanowsky & O'Donnell-Trujillo, 1983).

What is required, then, is not shared goals, values, or meanings in the usual sense (Krippendorff, 1989). Instead, as Wentworth (1980) puts it:

> The opposite of anomie is not necessarily consensus, when consensus means simple agreement or similar viewpoints. People may, in effect, "agree to disagree" (Scheff, 1970, p. 363). The key to grasping the difference between order and consensus lies in the parallel difference between *shared* and *common* reality. To share an apple, for example, cannot mean taking the same bites . . . a shared definition of the situation or a shared reality does not declare a

condition of common values, but instead may be best thought of as a kind of compatibility, a working relationship coordinating and containing differences in subjective vantage points. (p. 97)

More important than common values or beliefs, concludes Wentworth, is a "sense of mutual presence" (p. 103) and an adherence to the rules of the context, whether or not one agrees with them fully. This conception is consistent with a political perspective on organizing, in which stability is engendered not through shared values but through the coordination and negotiation of dominant sectional interests with different value structures (Eisenberg & Riley, 1988; Morgan, 1986; Riley, 1983).

Individual and organizational effectiveness depend more on the conviction that goals or values are shared than on the actual extent of agreement (Eisenberg, 1984; Eisenberg & Riley, 1988; Hart, 1984; Myerhoff, 1975). More important, this perception of unity facilitates the smooth coordination of action: "Often, for action to be taken, it is sufficient for meanings to be compatible in terms of action implications even though the actors do not share the same interpretations about what the action will accomplish" (Donnelon, Gray, & Bougon, 1986). In studies of coorientation, perceived agreement has been shown to be a better predictor of relational satisfaction than actual agreement (Eisenberg, Monge, & Farace, 1983).

Diversity need not impede effective organization; coordinated action can often be more important than coordination of beliefs (Eisenberg, 1986; Eisenberg & Riley, 1988; Weick 1979). "In the absence of shared meaning, organized action is made possible by the shared repertoire of communication behaviors group members use while in the process of developing *equifinal meanings* for their joint experience" (Donnelon et al., 1986, p. 44).

The development of equifinal meanings requires some degree of ambiguity in communication (Eisenberg, 1984; Hazelton, 1975; Levine, 1985; Myerhoff, 1975). Myerhoff claims that ambiguity is "absolutely necessary in order to allow individuals to project their private, most intense emotions and meanings into what is referred to" (pp. 55–56). Flanagan (1985) makes a related observation in his analysis of Christian liturgies, which he claims have "functional ambiguity." This ambiguity is necessary, he argues, "to enable a self that would otherwise be fractured to remain unified" and also "as a means of preserving some element of indeterminacy and paradox that could otherwise not be disclosed" (p. 206). Ambiguity makes the particular generally available, and in doing so makes room for epiphany.

Effective organization, in sum, requires management of a dialectic between autonomy and interdependence. An overemphasis on intention and personality can paralyze action; excessive openness can jeopardize community; and overly strong cultures can stifle autonomy and impede adaptability. A different view of communicating and organizing is needed, one that considers both sides of the dialectic together and consequently does not privilege openness and consensus over selective disclosure and coordinated action.

Jamming

Traditional perspectives on communicating and organizing fail to account for important aspects of organized action, specifically experiences associated with minimally disclosive relationships. Although there have been a number of well-known attempts to describe forms of coordination under conditions of limited consensus (cf. Astley & Van de Ven, 1983; Thompson, 1967; Weick, 1979), none explicitly consider the connection between limited disclosure, coordinated action, and transcendence. This section presents a view of organizing that seriously considers this class of experience, which I call jamming.

Jamming encourages both cooperation and individuation. Jamming experiences provide an opportunity to transcend the autonomy-interdependence dialectic, simultaneously allowing for the possibility of both. These experiences are refreshing, as they satisfy cravings for both closeness and independence. Like Turner's (1969) "social dramas," jamming experiences occur predictably in a personalistic society where they provide some sense of reintegration into a communal life (Philipsen, 1987).

Jamming is characterized by fluid behavioral coordination unhindered by expectations for self-revelation. Similar to mutual equivalence structures (Weick, 1979), jamming experiences are highly rule-governed, structured activities in which little or no personal information is exchanged, yet important goals may be accomplished, and a strong, ecstatic bond is formed among participants.

Characteristics of the Jamming Experience

Jamming has four essential characteristics. Jamming (a) is transcendent, (b) embraces diversity, (c) is fragile, and (d) can be risky. Each characteristic is described in turn.

Jamming Is Transcendent

Jamming is appealing because it enables individuals temporarily to feel part of a larger community, but without the obligation to reveal much personal information. The feelings associated with such transcendence can be ecstatic.

In his study of how rock bands form, Bennett (1980, pp. 44–45) maintains that "every group is founded in a 'good jam,'" the occurrence of a "wholly other experience" in which participants experience total involvement in music making. Musician David Byrne hints at what it is like to jam in performance:

> In concert, where all the musicians are playing, and you kind of subsume yourself and become part of the community of musicians. They, in turn, become part of the audience. And everybody senses that. It's not a rational realization. It's a visceral realization that you're part of a larger whole. (Thompson, 1988, p. 49)

Maintaining a balance between surrender and active participation can sometimes be tricky, and moments out of balance are inevitable. The jazz bassist Red Mitchell (1987) comments on how such moments of imbalance may even jeopardize the definition of the situation:

> When—and I don't mean if—the cycle gets too far out of balance one way or the other (for example, too much or too little planning or form, or too little or too much freedom of improvisation) the musicians themselves will probably start saying, "This isn't really jazz." (p. 3)

Myerhoff (1975) gives two excellent illustrations of the rare combination of "organization and ecstasy" in her contrasting accounts of the peyote rituals of the Huichol Indians and the "Woodstock Nation." In both examples, there is a fragile moment out of time when alienation and self-consciousness disappear, and the participants "stand in relation" to one another as total human beings (Buber, 1958). In these moments, participants experience something akin to the French *presque vu*—an unquestionable feeling of rightness. The relatedness problem is solved; through activity with others people can transcend their separateness and live not only in themselves but also in community.

An impressive number of scholars have made similar observations about the social nature of transcendence (e.g., Turner's [1969] communitas and Csikszentmihalyi's [1975] flow experiences). But Buber's (1958) statement is perhaps most compelling. In contrast with traditional views of communicating and organizing, Buber asserted boldly that "all real living is meeting" (p. 11). By this he meant that a full, spiritual life was in part obtainable through immersion in social interaction. By "meetings," however, he did not refer solely to highly disclosive relationships. Instead, when an individual meets another, he or she directs full attention toward the other, but not necessarily to garner personal knowledge or experience. Instead, the attention is born of a desire to stand in relation to the other, with full respect for his or her individuality. Buber was searching for a way to find unity in diversity, identity in unity. Solovyov (1985) summarizes: "True individuality is a certain form of universal unity, a way of apprehending and assimilating the whole." In a fundamental way, jamming experiences both transcend the individual and enrich the life of the self.

The great basketball center Bill Russell spent his career searching for the jamming experience, which in sports is sometimes called flow, or zone. Some excerpts from his memoirs provide a vivid portrait of such an experience (Russell & Branch, 1979):

> Every so often a Celtic game would heat up so that it became more than a physical or even mental game, and would be magical. That feeling is difficult to describe, and I certainly never talked about it when I was playing. . . . It came rarely, and would last anywhere from five minutes to a whole quarter or more. [Sometimes] the game would just take off, and there'd be a natural ebb and flow that reminded you of how rhythmic and musical basketball is supposed to be. I'd find myself thinking, "This is it. I want this to keep going," and I'd actually be rooting for the other team.
>
> At that special level all sorts of odd things happened. The game would be in a white heat of competition, and yet somehow I wouldn't feel competitive. . . . The game would move so quickly that every fake, cut and pass would be surprising, and yet nothing would surprise me. It was almost as if we were playing in slow motion. . . . I always felt then that I not only knew all the Celtics by heart but also all the opposing players, and that they all knew me. There have been many times in my career when I felt moved or joyful, but these were the moments when I had chills pulsing up and down my spine. (pp. 156–157)

Some writers have observed that the capacity for transcendence may be inherent in the nature of certain types of games (Csikszentmihalyi, 1975; Csikszentmihalyi & Selega-Csikszentmihalyi, 1989; Gadamer, 1988; Grassi, 1987). Gadamer (1988) notes that a common characteristic of games is their tendency to dominate the individual. This suggests that when Russell comments that "the game took off," he is speaking literally.

> Play fulfills its purposes only if the player loses himself in the play. . . . all playing is a being-played. The attraction of a game, the fascination it exerts, consists precisely in the fact that the game tends to master the players. (Gadamer, 1988, pp. 92, 95)

Grassi (1987) further describes the transcendent aspects of play:

> By playing we experiment, we experience the power of the "project" that transforms everything; it is in the game that the player experiences the elation of being in the sphere of an order to which he not only submits but which he also carries out. . . . The playing cards are far from being simply "cards," the

dice are far from being "wooden boxes," the ball much more than a spherical shape made of leather and rubber filled with air. The metamorphosis of the beings arises from the metaphorical character of the game and of the language of playing. (p. 72)

Csikszentmihalyi (1975; Csikszentmihalyi & Selega-Csikszentmihalyi, 1989) seeks to identify the "intrinsic motivations" for engaging in a variety of play and work activities (e.g., chess, rock climbing, surgery, basketball). He concludes that one common reason is the opportunity each activity offers for experiencing flow, wherein people not only forget their problems but temporarily lose the self-consciousness that can intrude on everyday life. "At the most challenging levels, people actually report experiencing a *transcendence* of self, caused by the unusually high involvement with a system of action" (Csikszentmihalyi & Selega-Csikszentmihalyi, 1989, p. 33). Gadamer agrees that the transformational aspects of play are rooted in action: "Play itself is, rather, transformation of such a kind that the identity of the player does not continue to exist for anybody . . . the players no longer exist, but only what of theirs is played" (p. 101).

Jamming Embraces Diversity

In the novel *Merely Players,* Gregory MacDonald describes the lives of three American jazz musicians struggling to find work in Europe. What is most fascinating about these characters is their utter diversity. They cannot relate to each other except through music; in another context, they would never seek each other out, nor would they have anything to talk about if they did. Yet, in music, they find a kind of transcendent communion.

I remember vividly one Friday afternoon in October playing pick-up basketball at Lincoln Park in Santa Monica. A new player appeared who was a visiting IBM executive from St. Louis, in town for a conference. Whenever he was on the road, he searched the local schoolyards for a pick-up game. On his team was a homeless man in his 40s (reeking of wine and wearing long brown pants), a 15-year-old drug dealer, and me. On that day, we played together seamlessly—although there was no other setting or circumstance in which I could imagine this group interacting.

A Canadian colleague reports a gripping experience that further illustrates this point. While sailing with another man, whom he did not know well, a sudden storm overtook their boat. In the crisis that ensued, they both did what had to be done to keep the boat from capsizing, literally to stay alive. What my friend remembers most from the experience was a brief moment, as each of them was securing opposite sides of the boat, when they simultaneously looked up to see if the other was still holding on. In this moment, the sense of human affirmation made possible by doing what was necessary made all of the differences between them seem trivial.

Seamless performance conveys a joyful, encapsulated feeling of total involvement. When the experience is over, however, participants know not so much the details of each others' lives but mainly that they performed well together in a specific situation. Later, these same people may meet and have little to say to each other beyond a passionate retelling of the experience. Still, they can be grateful for the special bond that developed.

Crises make strange bedfellows—an office building fire, air raid, or earthquake often leads the chief executive officer to pitch in alongside the company janitor and to report later about the camaraderie that was formed, however fleeting. Descriptions and interpretations of the same experience may be diverse as well. This diversity of interpretation does not necessarily make the experience less satisfying. Just as weak ties are sometimes more important than strong ones (Granovetter, 1973), the stranger on the court, across the boat, or beside you at the piano may act in a way that is mysterious, exciting, and at the same time highly satisfying.

Jamming Is Fragile

Jamming experiences are both unusual and relatively rare. Pick-up games and musical jam sessions can be more like work than play, filled with selfishness, ego displays, and bad luck. Jamming may be the exception, not the rule—something to be hoped for but not expected. The fragility of jamming is evident in that it can never be routinized, habitual, linked to a specific set of antecedents, or necessarily self-sustaining once begun. On the other hand, it is possible to court these experiences and to cultivate the attitudes and expectations that make jamming most likely to occur.

Jamming requires clear rules, structures, and expectations (and especially expectations about appropriate levels of disclosure). Asymmetrical expectations can lead to mixed signals and disappointment. For jamming to occur, expectations are best kept low. To be successful, one must surrender to the experience, engage faithfully and respectfully in the interaction, and not use the exchange to unload on, show off, or control others.

In sports, for example, the "hot dog" who uses athletics to bolster his or her ego effectively blocks the possibility of jamming for everyone. In jazz, a distinction is made between jam sessions and cutting sessions (D. Bastien, 1989, personal communication). In a cutting session, the group's "star" or soloist expects the other musicians to cooperate in the development of his or her vision. In a jam session, the players cooperate in the formulation of a joint, emergent vision. Introducing elements from the cutting session into a jam session prevent jamming and can cause a break in the flow.

Returning to basketball, Russell laments a break in the flow:

> But these spells were fragile. An injury would break them, and so would a couple of bad plays or a bad call by a referee. Once a referee broke a run by making a bad call in my favor, which so irritated me that I protested it. . . . Still, I always suffered a letdown when one of those spells died, because I never knew how to bring them back; all I could do was keep playing my best and hope. They were sweet when they came, and the hope that one would come was one of my strongest motivations for walking out there. (p. 157)

Reluctance to accept the ebb and flow of social relationships often leads to attempts at institutionalizing these ecstatic encounters. But attempts at institutionalization are ultimately self-defeating. In practice, it is rare to be able to retain mystery and spontaneity alongside a workable routine. Following Myerhoff (1975), the difference between the Woodstock Nation's and the Huichol's experiences lies in the former's failed attempt to institutionalize ecstasy into everyday life. The Huichol tradition is more successful than Woodstock, she concluded, because the peyote rituals are held out of the mainstream of life, in a place members can visit and return from enlightened and refreshed. Although transcendence is a worthy goal of social interaction, it is ultimately not sustainable on an ongoing basis.

Jamming Can Be Risky

When engaged in jamming, something of one's self is on the line, although not in the usual way, not through revelation or verbal disclosure. Jamming can be both physically and psychologically risky.

Some of the physical risks of jamming are closely associated with gender. Men and women occupy different places in the social world, and women have less easy access to public places where jamming happens. Even when a woman has the needed skills to participate, questions of safety and morality may be raised. Altman (1989, personal communication) points out that women may approach interpersonal relationships differently from men. Whereas men are more comfortable getting to know one another through common activities, reciprocal disclosure is characteristic of women's social interactions in our society.

The psychological risks of jamming are somewhat more subtle. First, a player risks embarrassment if his or her skills are found to be insufficient for the game. Because skill levels differ markedly from game to game, it is often difficult to determine ahead of time whether one will fit in.

Second, in jamming one risks exposing unresolved emotional issues that may be triggered by the intensity of the game. "Perfect" players would play completely "within themselves," meaning that they would have a great deal of self-knowledge and attempt only things within their level of skill. But as mentioned above, many players use the arena of the game to work out problems and insecurities carried over from other aspects of their lives. Hence another risk of jamming is the revelation of emotional problems that show up in the game.

Third, when the game takes over, the resultant transcendence can have a dark side. Shepard (1988) explores this in his short story, "The Way It Sometimes Happens." What "happens" in the story is that a group of jazz musicians, jamming in Greenwich Village, approach transcendence. But the nature of the insight is for at least one of the players (the narrator) highly disturbing. Alongside the approaching epiphany, he sees the illusory nature of everyday life, the tragic mortality of the players, and the tremendous cost each has paid for a chance at this type of experience. As it sometimes happens with meditation, religion, psychedelics, even love, there is a risk of becoming so hooked on transcendence that it is hard to live otherwise.

This article began by locating the jamming experience in a particular intellectual context and by articulating four key aspects of the experience. This next section elaborates four conditions that must be met for jamming to occur. These conditions are necessary but not sufficient; some degree of grace or luck is also required.

Conditions for Jamming

Skill

In a tightly coordinated activity, the quality of the total experience is always limited by the skill of the weakest member. "The universal precondition for flow is that a person should perceive that there is something for him or her to do, and that he or she is capable of doing it" (Csikszentmihalyi & Selega-Csikszentmihalyi, 1989, p. 30). At a minimum, people must be skillful enough to be *unself-conscious*. Jamming also requires that skill levels be *comparable*. Professional athletes do not enjoy playing their sport with amateurs for this reason—people of inferior skill prevent them from reaching their limits. In rock bands around the country, players go through an elaborate weeding-out process through which they find their own level of expertise, which in turn allows the possibility of jamming (Bennett, 1980).

Saying that jamming requires minimal and comparable skill does not mean that all players must be equally talented. Instead, what is needed is for individuals to know and play within themselves, that is, doing the things and playing the roles for which they have sufficient skill. In some pick-up basketball games, there are role players who only pass the ball, never shoot—they do what they do well and consequently also participate in the jamming experience. Furthermore, the skill of any single individual is not stable from group to group; my ability to play well is conditioned by the level of talent of my fellow players. Better teammates or opponents bring out the best in most players. In any case, there is no greater obstacle to jamming than people who overestimate their skills or abilities and fail to play within themselves.

Although they focus on shared knowledge (rather than on comparable levels of skill or competence), Bastien and Hostager (1988) make a related point in their analysis of jazz:

> Because the group jazz process relies on *shared* musical and social knowledge, the total knowledge that is usable by the entire group can only equal or slightly exceed the knowledge of the least informed (i.e., the least competent) member of the group. . . . We predict that groups that include musicians of very different knowledge bases will either produce jazz that is not well integrated or will perform at a level roughly equivalent to that of the least competent member. (p. 596)

This has implications for work teams in organizations; for work groups to really "hum," minimal and comparable skill levels are essential. This skill requirement, however, applies only to the activity in question—skill in other areas is largely irrelevant. The result is personal diversity against a well-defined structure or backdrop, which is discussed next.

Structure

Whereas we typically think of structure as constraining, jamming illustrates how a highly defined structure can also be liberating. In jamming, there are minimal expectations for future interaction; a lack of emphasis on individual personalities frees people to engage unself-consciously in coordinated action. Precisely *because* they are highly structured and place few requirements on coping with individual personalities, jamming experiences permit a sense of community that is difficult to achieve through more disclosive interaction. In the jazz context: "Paradoxically, these structures enable collective musical innovation by constraining the range of musical and behavioral choice available to the players" (Bastien & Hostager, 1988, p. 586). Finally, there may be a connection between structure and skill; jamming usually occurs in more tightly structured activities in which the level of challenge and skill can more easily be varied and controlled (Csikszentmihalyi & Selega-Csikszentmihalyi, 1989).

Although it may at first seem paradoxical to equate a fixed structure with liberation, contradictions arise only if certain aspects of the system are inflexible. Meyer and Rowan's (1977) theory of institutional organizations (mainly schools and hospitals) provides a good example of this noncontradiction. School and hospital administrators have rigid rules of administration. Courses of study must be pursued to the letter, insurance regulations cannot be violated, and standards of admission and graduation are held firm. But although basic rules may exist, doctors and teachers are given the freedom to approach their work in a variety of ways because of the "logic of confidence" placed in them by their professional colleagues. In jamming, although the rules and roles may seem clear and inflexible, their enactment may be quite creative.

A key aspect of jamming, then, is its improvisational quality; it is forever interesting, because the options for individual moves are unlimited. During a musical jam session, there is great latitude for the players to shift musical styles midstream, to change tempos or melodies within an otherwise fairly structured experience. In other words, although you may predict 95% of what the other musicians will do (the structured part), the other 5% is the most exciting (the creative part).

This improvisational freedom is only possible against a well-defined (and often relatively simple) backdrop of rules and roles. In this sense, jamming is a kind of minimalist's view of organizing, of making do with minimal commonalities and elaborating simple structures in complex ways. Relying on the basic rule and role structure, each player sets up interesting possibilities for the others and keeps the action going. Following Gadamer (1988), "the attraction of the game, which it exercises on the player, lies in this risk. One enjoys a freedom of decision, which at the same time is endangered and irrevocably limited" (p. 95).

This notion of structure includes both formal rules (e.g., of the game, or of musical keys and progressions) and informal ones (e.g., how long can you play, how many points make a game, etc.). Bastien and Hostager (1988) provide an excellent description of these "structural conventions" in the jazz context. They divide these conventions into musical structures (the formal rules of jazz theory) and social practices. Social practices are further divided into behavioral norms (e.g., each musician gets a chance to solo sometime during the performance) and communicative codes (e.g., eye contact and hand signals that indicate a change in dynamics or tempo). In practice, additional "local agreements" may also be made before a performance (e.g., who will call the songs that are to be played).

In summary, although local conventions vary, there is generally a core set of rules and roles that a player must know and respect in order to allow the possibility of jamming. These rules include both formal aspects of the activity (e.g., in basketball, how many steps you are allowed before you dribble or shoot) and more variable behavioral and communicative norms (don't shoot every time you get the ball) and agreements (double-team their star player— he's really good). Too much attention to the rules, however, raises concerns of ego and increases self-consciousness. Only when this layered rule and role structure becomes taken for granted does jamming become possible.

Setting

As suggested by Myerhoff (1975), jamming is most likely to occur when a separation is made between "normal" life and some special contained setting (see also Turner, 1969). The function of this encapsulation is to allow people to shed the baggage of their daily lives and become ahistorical participants, judged mainly by their actions, not their personalities. In this context, we are more likely to associate with people we might normally avoid; aspects of their character that would otherwise discourage us from interacting with them are suppressed. This does suggest that jamming is easier with "strangers" than with friends or well-known acquaintances. But part of the challenge of jamming in longer-term relationships is finding ways to somehow set aside what we know about the details of another person's personality in order to create the possibility for seamless coordination.

Put another way, jamming dramatically alters the typical figure-ground relationship, in which personality, social role, and life history provide the context for understanding a person's actions. The result may be unusual but not necessarily ineffective. In her work on figure-ground relationships in the mass media, Cerulo (1988) concludes that upsetting normal expectations can sometimes enhance communication. She challenges "the assumption that clarity, compatibility, and balance achieve the most effective communication. Certain types of message distortion . . . can actually enhance communication effectiveness" (p. 100).

A related analogy can be made to recent developments in printing software design, specifically in the area of fuzzy fonts. Common sense suggests that the ideal type font recognizable by humans would be as crisp and clear as possible. But beyond a certain level of clarity, sharp edges negatively affect human comprehension. Consequently, computer designers now purposefully blur the edges of characters, creating the so-called fuzzy font, which is, paradoxically, easier to read. The analogy to jamming is important. Blurring the distinctions between people, purposefully not drawing sharp lines, can increase the ease of interaction and create a greater likelihood of community.

Encapsulation can involve a separation of home life from work life, spiritual retreats from daily life, or the creation of buffered work zones within an organization. Consequently, "intrapreneurial" work teams that are sheltered from normal organizational constraints would be more likely to jam than groups lacking this degree of encapsulation.

Surrender

Surrender of control is essential to the jamming experience. Like religious epiphany or artistic inspiration, efforts to force jamming to happen are counterproductive (Moore, 1985). It is precisely the fact that you cannot jam at will—that it depends on others and cannot be harnessed—that gives the experience its special mystery. But this does not mean that jamming is completely dependent on luck or fate. Much can be gained by preparation, sharpening skills, developing the right attitude, and seeking out partners with compatible skills and dispositions.

The idea of surrender as a positive force in facilitating action is consistent with current philosophical accounts of the "death of man." Consistent with Gadamer's (1988) aforementioned observation that we are often "played by the game," postmodern philosophers seriously oppose the Enlightenment assumption that human reason can attain certainty and control. With the demise of "man" as omnipotent subject and personalist repository of meanings, one consequence is that humans will have to learn more about surrender, in order to better live within the flow.

Eastern philosophy is less subject-centered than Western modernism and consequently has more to say about the importance of surrender. A typical example comes from Tsujimura's (1968) "Zen and the Art of Archery." He describes the evolution of the Master Archer:

> While he has self-consciousness to loose the shot excellently or hit the bull's-eye, right shots did not come off. When he let himself go to some transcendental strength, "It," and time was ripe, he would loose the correct shot. It is the last goal of practice to reach the stage of "free handling" where "self" is erased. Therefore, it is not important whether he hits the target or not. As the result, even if he missed the target, the Master bowed deeply and humbly, as long as the shot is loosed in the state of egolessness and spiritual freedom. (pp. 60–61)

This description says a great deal about the inhibiting role of self-consciousness in coordinated action. In his explanation of Morita psychotherapy, Reynolds (1982) emphasizes the need to "do what needs to be done" without concern for the outcome, which is ultimately beyond one's control. I am not going so far as to say that some kind of "ego-death" is required for jamming to occur, but a considerable degree of unself-consciousness is needed. Moreover, it is the surrender of personal control and the suspension of self-consciousness that facilitates seamless coordination and creates a clearing for the co-construction of community.

Implications

> Reality exists only in effective action, its power and depth in the power and depth of effective action. (Buber, 1958, p. 89)

One of my earliest jamming experiences was playing guitar with Brad in a summer camp in Albany, New York. Brad was a soccer coach from rural upstate, and I was a counselor from New York City. We sat on the steps of the camp canteen at twilight and played four-bar blues. While things started simply enough, it is hard to describe where they ended up. Some nights, it seemed he could anticipate every musical change I made and was even a step or two ahead. These nights, I felt as if we knew each other completely, although in the usual sense we did not "know" each other at all. On the nights we jammed, the music played us. Kids would gather, and although we sensed they were there, it was as if through a friendly curtain—we were so absorbed in the activity, they became part of the moment. The closeness I felt to Brad then stays with me today, more than 10 years later.

Implications for Formal Organizations

Although these personal feelings of closeness and connection are important, the value of jamming goes beyond personal benefits to the individual. Some theories of organizing acknowledge that organizations may be redundant, underorganized, loosely coupled, and at the same time effective (Meyer & Rowan, 1977; Morgan, 1986; Weick, 1979). Discussions of organizational subcultures (e.g., Gregory, 1983) and certain critical approaches (e.g., Deetz & Kersten, 1983) are also motivated in part by the desire to promote effectiveness without sacrificing autonomy or diversity.

Jamming can occur in many places and in many forms, from full-blown crises (e.g., when a manufacturing "red team" is asked to investigate a major production problem) to more routine situations (e.g., in lunchroom banter or at holiday office parties). Jamming can be task-related or more personal; it can be initiated by managers or employees; and it can focus on the status quo or on innovation.

Some authors are enthusiastic in their belief that work can be designed to improve the probability of jamming and flow (Csikszentmihalyi & Selega-Csikszentmihalyi, 1989). One major obstacle to doing so is the belief on the part of organizational members that more and more disclosive communication is the key to developing meaningful interpersonal relationships. Also, transcendence at work may be harder to achieve than transcendence at play. In the games described in this article, for example, most of the rule structure is given, and the basic nature of the activity is relatively clear. In formal organizations, there is more room for defining the context for employees' daily activities. The role of an organizational "leader" may include creating a framework within which individual employees can find meaning or significance (Bennis & Nanus, 1985). Work can be experienced in many different ways, and it is through this framing that a leader can create a context for jamming.

To facilitate jamming experiences, an organization must create a *structure for surrender,* within which risk is rewarded, not punished, and work groups are kept sufficiently autonomous to ensure the development and survival of novel ideas. At the same time, jamming requires careful selection of participants, especially relative to skill levels, so that poor performers unable to work within themselves do not limit the rest of the group.

Rarely are both of these conditions met in business. Most organizations reward closed communication and conservatism, not openness or risk. Consequently, individuals in search of jamming experiences avoid large corporations in favor of joining small, entrepreneurial firms, or going off to work on their own. Most report similar motivations for their decision—more stimulation, being part of a dynamic team, synergy, freedom, and challenge. As much as they are businesspeople, entrepreneurs are people looking to jam.

Such individuals are often frustrated in their search, however. The hard realities of the business world set it apart from musical jam sessions or pick-up games. In addition to everything else—the right people, skills, and attitude—jamming in organizations also requires a minimal level of basic resources. These resources are the equivalent of a ball and a hoop in basketball or musical instruments for jazz. The anxieties of limited capital, equipment, or support can frustrate jamming in the organizational context. As a result, building the requisite structure for surrender also means providing a structure of safeguards. Enough of the basics must be in place to allow participants the latitude to take risks.

Once an individual experiences jamming at work, the experience may become addictive. Much has been written about entrepreneurs who start business after business, openly admitting that they could never work for someone else. What they are really striving for is akin to Russell's "flow." Their search is motivated by the knowledge that most formal organizations are not designed to meet this need.

Implications for Society

I wish to be excessively clear about one point: Jamming, although ecstatic, should be seen as an addition to, not a substitute for, more disclosive intimate relationships. Needless to say, there is often great temptation to use jamming as a point of departure for just such relationships. But increased disclosure signals the entrance to a potentially long road along which we give up measures of autonomy and privacy in exchange for other emotional rewards. Humans cannot live by jamming alone. Some intimacy is born of knowing others well, some from simply acting in concert. In either case, we are fated to drift in and out of ecstasy, in accordance with our twofold nature (Buber, 1958).

Consistent with the times in which it emerged, modern communication theory is forward looking, focused to a disproportionate degree on the cultivation of shared interpretations, cognitions, and emotions and insufficiently focused on how action occurs under conditions of limited shared understandings. As the world grows smaller, we must deal with diverse, distant peoples. Consequently, we need theories of communication that edify action and humanize without offering openness, disclosure, and shared values as standards by which all social relationships must be judged. Organization is not always facilitated by greater understanding. Revelation of certain kinds of information can be futile or make matters worse. Given the incommensurability of languages and value systems, it is preferable in many cases to seek tolerance of diversity, coordination of activities, and respect for others than it is to work for shared understanding or agreement.

Returning to my opening argument, what is needed most of all is a renewed respect for the value of public life and, hence, for close, nondisclosive relationships (e.g., Philipsen, 1987; Sennett, 1978). Seasoned politicians and businesspeople understand the value of these relationships; our theories are substantially more naive. Highly disclosive relationships are valuable, without a doubt, but not for most of our encounters most of the time (Parks, 1982). Time and energy are limited; and the way to improve less disclosive relationships is not necessarily to tell more but to establish workable patterns of action that do not always involve greater sharing. Jamming is a third ideal type of relationship; between the cold nondisclosive relationship and the intimate disclosive one lies the close, nondisclosive relationship rooted in collective action. Jamming stresses coordination of action over the alignment of cognitions, mutual respect over agreement, trust over empathy, diversity over homogeneity, loose over tight coupling, and strategic communication over unrestricted candor.

This emphasis on coordinated action ultimately implicates *respect* as a key concept. But respecting someone's individuality is not the same as understanding them personally. Whereas the authenticity model (advocating complete honesty and openness) is unwieldy, unrealistic, and may leave us too vulnerable, the efficiency model (emphasizing the inevitability of politics and strategy) is too calculated and closed. What is needed is a workable middle ground, in which both highly disclosive and less disclosive relationships can be seen as legitimate and important.

From a humanistic perspective, the ultimate measure of communicative success is the degree to which members establish and maintain a balance between autonomy and interdependence and consequently secure a sense of meaning and purpose (Eisenberg & Phillips, 1990). In support of this process, we should develop proactive, humanizing theories of communicating and organizing, theories that acknowledge the multiple communicative avenues members may traverse in their pursuit of personal and social significance.

AUTHOR'S NOTE: The ideas in this article are the result of a most rewarding dialogue. For their thoughtful comments, I am grateful to Karen Altman, Steve Banks, David Bastien, Keith Freadhoff, Lisa Gates, Bruce Hyde, Linda Putnam, Bill Rawlins, Patti Riley, Lori Roscoe, Caren Siehl, and Karl Weick. I am especially indebted to John Stewart, everyone at the Alta Conference, the players at Lincoln Junior High, and the stars and reactors along the way.

References

Alberoni, F. (1983). *Falling in love.* New York: Random House.

Arnett, R. (1986). *Communication and community.* Carbondale: Southern Illinois University Press.

Astley, W. G., & Van de Ven, A. (1983). Central perspectives and debates in organizational theory. *Administrative Science Quarterly, 28,* 245–273.

Axley, S. (1984). Managerial and organizational communication in terms of the conduit metaphor. *Academy of Management Review, 9,* 428–437.

Bakhtin, M. (1981). *The dialogue of imagination: Four essays.* Austin: University of Texas Press.

Bastien, D., & Hostager, T. (1988). Jazz as a process of organizational innovation. *Communication Research, 15,* 582–602.

Bellah, R., Madsen, R., Sullivan, W., Swidler, A., & Tipton, S. (1985). *Habits of the heart.* Berkeley: University of California Press.

Bennett, H. S. (1980). *On becoming a rock musician.* Amherst: University of Massachusetts Press.

Bennis, W., & Nanus, B. (1985). *Leaders.* New York: Harper & Row.

Berger, P., Berger, B., & Kellner, H. (1974). *The homeless mind.* New York: Vintage.

Bochner, A. P. (1984). The functions of human communication in interpersonal bonding. In C. Arnold & J. Bowers (Eds.), *Handbook of rhetoric and communication theory* (pp. 544–621). Newton, MA: Allyn & Bacon.

Buber, M. (1958). *I and thou* (2nd ed). New York: Scribner.

Buber, M. (1965). *Between man and man.* New York: Collier.

Cerulo, K. (1988). What's wrong with this picture. *Communication Research, 15,* 93–101.

Csikszentmihalyi, M. (1975). *Beyond boredom and anxiety.* San Francisco: Jossey-Bass.

Csikszentmihalyi, M., & Selega-Csikszentmihalyi, I. (Eds.). (1989). *Optimal experience: Psychological studies of flow in consciousness.* New York: Cambridge University Press.

Deal, T. (1984). Culture change: Opportunity, silent killer, or metamorphosis? In R. Kilman, M. Saxton, & R. Serpa (Eds.), *Gaining control of the corporate culture* (pp. 292–231). San Francisco: Jossey-Bass.

Deetz, S., & Kersten, A. (1983). Critical models of interpretive research. In L. Putnam & M. Pacanowsky (Eds.), *Communication and organizations* (pp. 147–171). Beverly Hills: Sage.

Donnelon, A., Gray, B., & Bougon, M. (1986). Communication, meaning, and organized action. *Administrative Science Quarterly, 31,* 43–55.

Duranti, A. (1984). Intentions, self, and local theories of meaning: Words and actions in a Samoan context. *Center for Human Information Processing, 122,* 1–20.

Eisenberg, E. M. (1984). Ambiguity as strategy in organizational communication. *Communication Monographs, 51,* 227–242.

Eisenberg, E. M. (1986). Meaning and interpretation in organizations. *Quarterly Journal of Speech, 72,* 88–113.

Eisenberg, E. M., Monge, P. R., & Farace, R. V. (1983). Coorientation on communication rules in managerial dyads. *Human Communication Research, 11,* 261–271.

Eisenberg, E. M., & Phillips, S. R. (1990). What is organizational miscommunication? In J. Wiemann, N. Coupland, & H. Giles (Eds.), *Handbook of miscommunication and problematic talk.* Oxford, UK: Multilingual Matters.

Eisenberg, E. M., & Riley, P. (1988). Organizational symbols and sense-making. In G. Goldhaber & G. Barnett (Eds.), *Handbook of organizational communication* (pp. 131–150). Norwood, NJ: Ablex.

Flanagan, K. (1985). Liturgy, ambiguity, and silence: The ritual management of real absence. *British Journal of Sociology, 36,* 193–223.

Gadamer, H. G. (1988). *Truth and method.* New York: Crossroads.

Geertz, C. (1983). *Local knowledge.* New York: Basic Books.

Gergen, K. (1985). The social constructionist movement in modern psychology. *American Psychologist, 40,* 266–275.

Giddens, A. (1981). *A contemporary critique of historical materialism.* Berkeley: University of California Press.

Granovetter, M. (1973). The strength of weak ties. *American Journal of Sociology, 78,* 1360–1380.

Grassi, E. (1987). Why rhetoric is philosophy. *Philosophy and Rhetoric, 20,* 68–78.

Gregory, K. (1983). Native-view paradigms: Multiple cultures and culture conflicts in organizations. *Administrative Science Quarterly, 28,* 359–376.

Hart, R. (1984). The functions of human communication in the maintenance of public values. In C. Arnold & J. Bowers (Eds.), *Handbook of rhetoric and communication theory* (pp. 749–791). Newton, MA: Allyn & Bacon.

Hazelton, R. (1975). *Ascending flame, descending dove: An essay on creative transcendence.* Philadelphia: Westminster Press.

Holquist, M. (1983). The politics of representation. *Quarterly Newsletter of the Laboratory of Comparative Human Cognition, 5,* 2–9.

Krippendorff, K. (1989). On the ethics of constructing communication. In B. Dervin, L. Grossberg, J. O'Keefe, & E. Wartella (Eds.), *Rethinking communication: Paradigm issues* (pp. 66–96). Newbury Park, CA: Sage.

Levine, D. (1985). *The flight from ambiguity.* Chicago: University of Chicago Press.

Lyotard, J. (1984). *The postmodern condition: A report on knowledge.* Manchester, England: Manchester University Press.

May, S. (1988). *The modernist monologue in organizational communication research: The text, the subject, and the audience.* Paper presented at the annual meeting of the Speech Communication Association, New Orleans, LA.

Meyer, M., & Rowan, B. (1977). Institutionalized organizations: Formal structure as myth and ceremony. *American Journal of Sociology, 83,* 340–363.

Mitchell, R. (1987). And a happy new year, Mike. *Jazzletter, 6,* 3–5.

Mitchell, T. (1985). "In search of excellence" versus "The 100 best companies to work for in America": A question of perspective and values. *Academy of Management Review, 10,* 350–354.

Moore, M. (1985). Culture as culture. In P. Frost, L. Moore, M. Louis, C. Lundberg, & J. Martin (Eds.), *Organizational culture* (pp. 373–378). Beverly Hills, CA: Sage.

Morgan, G. (1986). *Images of organization.* Beverly Hills, CA: Sage.

Myerhoff, B. (1975). Organization and ecstasy. In S. Moore & B. Myerhoff (Eds.), *Symbol and politics in communal ideology* (pp. 33–67). Ithaca, NY: Cornell University Press.

Ochs, E., Smith, R., & Taylor, C. (1990). Detective stories at dinner: Problem-solving through co-narration. *Cultural Dynamics, 2,* 238–257.

Ortner, S. (1984). Theory in anthropology since the sixties. *Comparative Studies in Society and History, 26,* 126–167.

Pacanowsky, M., & O'Donnell-Trujillo, N. (1983). Organizational communication as cultural performance. *Communication Monographs, 50,* 126–147.

Parks, M. (1982). Ideology in interpersonal communication: Off the couch and into the world. In M. Burgoon (Ed.), *Communication Yearbook 5* (pp. 79–108). New Brunswick, NJ: Transaction Books.

Peters, T., & Waterman, R. (1982). *In search of excellence*. New York: Harper & Row.

Philipsen, G. (1987). The prospect for cultural communication. In D. L. Kincaid (Ed.), *Communication theory: Eastern and Western perspectives* (pp. 245–254). San Diego: Academic Press.

Rawlins, W. (1985). Stalking interpersonal communication effectiveness. In T. Benson (Ed.), *Speech communication in the 20th century* (pp. 109–129). Carbondale: Southern Illinois University Press.

Redding, W. C. (1985). Rocking boats, blowing whistles, teaching speech communication. *Communication Education, 34,* 245–258.

Reiss, D. (1981). *The family's construction of reality.* Cambridge, MA: Harvard University Press.

Reynolds, P. (1982). *Playing ball on running water.* New York: Quill.

Riley, P. (1983). A structurationist account of organizational culture. *Administrative Science Quarterly, 28,* 414–437.

Russell, B., & Branch, T. (1979). *Second wind: The memoirs of an opinionated man.* New York: Random House.

Scarf, M. (1987). *Intimate partners.* New York: Random House.

Sennett, R. (1978). *The fall of public man.* New York: Vintage.

Shepard, L. (1988). The way it sometimes happens. In I. Asimov (Ed.), *Isaac Asimov's science fiction* (Vol. 12). New York: Davis.

Solovyov, V. (1985). Love evolving. In J. Welwood (Ed.), *Challenge of the heart* (pp. 42–46). Boston: Shambhala.

Storr, A. (1988). *Solitude.* New York: Free Press.

Thompson, J. D. (1967). *Organizations in action.* New York: McGraw-Hill.

Thompson, R. F. (1988, April 21). David Byrne: The Rolling Stone interview. *Rolling Stone,* p. 49.

Tsujimura, A. (1968). *Japanese culture and communication.* Tokyo: NHK Books.

Turner, V. (1969). *The ritual process.* Chicago: Aldine.

Weick, K. (1979). *The social psychology of organizing* (2nd ed.). Reading, MA: Addison-Wesley.

Wentworth, W. (1980). *Context and understanding.* New York: Elsevier.

Wertsch, J. (1988). L. S. Vygotsky's "new" theory of mind. *The American Scholar, 57,* 81–89.

Williams, B. (1987). Humor, linguistic ambiguity, and disputing in a Guyanese community. *International Journal of the Sociology of Language, 65,* 79–94.

6

Miscommunication in Organizations

This invited chapter attempted to reach out to colleagues with a particular interest in language and discourse. The book's theme, miscommunication, had been established by its editors, and the idea was to examine the concept across a range of settings. Then-doctoral student Steve Phillips and I critiqued accepted definitions of effective communication to reveal how miscommunication could be defined situationally and relationally. We also showed how some exchanges that seemed like miscommunication might well be judged effective when considered in context.

It is hard to gauge the impact of a book chapter on the field. I was never entirely sure who read this book or how they may have reacted. At the time of its preparation, I was co-teaching a graduate seminar on language and work with the prominent sociolinguist Elinor Ochs. Consequently, I was seeing all kinds of connections between communication and sociolinguistics, and hoped that this paper could begin to reach audiences whose interests were centered more squarely in the study of language.

SOURCE: Eisenberg, E., & Phillips, S. (1991). Miscommunication in organizations. In N. Coupland, H. Giles, & J. Wiemann (Eds.), *"Miscommunication" and problematic talk*. (pp. 244–258). Newbury Park, CA: Sage. Copyright © 1991, Sage Publications, Inc.

Miscommunication in Organizations: Background

Most managers and organizational theorists view communication as extremely important in organizations, but difficult to address in any systematic way. Communication is praised or blamed although specific problems go unsolved, and opportunities for understanding the dynamics of effective communication are missed. The resultant state of affairs is frustrating to theorists and practitioners alike; like Mark Twain's comment about the weather, organizational communication is something about which everyone talks, but no one does anything.

Communication researchers are in a good position to provide a more detailed perspective on effective organizational communication, one that allows for specific analyses and actions. Such scrutiny will no doubt reveal some surprises. What is defined as problematic communication from the viewpoint of management, for example, may be seen as effective from an employee's perspective. However it is manifested, the complexities of organizational life make miscommunication inevitable.

In the sections to follow we discuss various forms of miscommunication from a variety of perspectives. Examples of organizational miscommunication occur at all levels and in all areas of companies. Here is a sampling we have encountered in our work.

- In an advertising agency, a receptionist makes a mistake in recording a phone message, leading to a missed meeting and a lost contract.
- In a utility company, a depressed employee attempts to tell her boss about some personal problems, only to be told curtly "get professional help if you can't cut it around here."
- In a leasing company, the sales department withholds some details about a big deal from the legal department. The deal goes through, but five years later the secret gets out, and the company and certain individuals suffer enormously.
- In a retail store, a manager doesn't tell a problem employee the whole truth about her performance in a performance appraisal interview. The employee's continued poor performance negatively affects the morale of peers and subordinates, as well as productivity of the store.
- In an aerospace firm, senior management feels ill-equipped to communicate with union employees, and hires an ad agency to do their internal communication. Employees are offended and cynical when they are told of this strategy.

Which of these examples is an example of *miscommunication*? Although we attempted to order them by increasing subtlety and complexity, the fact is that miscommunication can only be defined according to a specified set of criteria and in a certain context. For every communicative act, some individuals benefit, others lose; some in the short term, some later on. No single set of criteria has emerged that allows for a simple determination of what constitutes miscommunication (or for that matter, effective communication) in organizations. Even those examples that seem the most "obvious" at first (e.g., involving lying, secrecy, or a gross lack of empathy) can be judged as effective by certain criteria and in certain contexts.

Purpose of the Chapter

After briefly introducing the concept of miscommunication and showing its importance in organizations, we describe and evaluate four major attempts at defining miscommunication. Each approach to miscommunication identifies some kind of failure. Miscommunication has been defined as the failure:

- to be understood;
- to achieve one's communicative goals;
- to be authentic, honest, and disclosive; and
- to establish an open dialogue.

Table 6.1 summarizes the key ideas associated with each perspective, linking definitions of miscommunication to more general views of organizational behavior. After reviewing these four approaches, we offer a new definition of miscommunication that both subsumes prior definitions and better accounts for organizational reality.

We conclude that any acceptable definition of miscommunication must inevitably be relative to the social context—to a theory, worldview, set of values, group of stakeholders, or point in time. In our definition, *miscommunication* is the failure, in social interaction, to balance individual creative agency against the coordination and control that makes organizing possible.

The Machine Metaphor: Miscommunication as Failed Understanding

In his recent book on organizations, Morgan (1986) portrays the classical-structuralist school of organizational thought as motivated by a *machine* metaphor (see Table 6.1). Consequently, effectiveness is defined in terms of efficiency, and employees are seen as interchangeable and passive. In such a scenario, communication is regarded as the straightforward transmission

Table 6.1   Four Approaches to Miscommunication in Organizations

Approach	Key Terms	Criteria for Effectiveness	View of Miscommunication
Classical-Structuralist	Machine Conduit Efficiency	Clarity Understanding	Failed Understanding Overload Distortion Ambiguity
Pragmatic	Individual Goals Cost/Benefit Analysis	Goal Achievement	Failed Goal Achievement
Human Relations	Openness Disclosure Sharing Authenticity	Open Lines of Communication Unrestricted Candor	Failed Openness Dishonesty Secrecy Lack of Full Disclosure
Critical Theory	Dialogue Co-Construction Practice Activity	Open Dialogue Individual Emancipation Reveals Domination	Failed Dialogue Hegemony Oppression

of information. A manager has communicated well when he or she has transferred what is in his or her head to a subordinate, with minimal "spillage" along the way.

Axley (1984) characterized this view of communication as the *conduit* metaphor, pervasive in most discourse about organizations. Successful communication is clear and promotes understanding, and transfers necessary information for the "machine" to continue optimal operation. Miscommunication occurs when either no message is received (e.g., due to distracting physical or psychological noise) or when the message received is not understood in the way the speaker intended (e.g., the receptionist mentioned above who made a mistake with a phone message). Clarity is synonymous with competence, and ambiguity is to be avoided at all costs. Typical communication "breakdowns" from this perspective are message overload, distortion, and ambiguity (Stohl & Redding, 1987). In *message overload,* a receiver is overwhelmed by inputs and hence fails to comprehend the speaker's full intent. For example, if a secretary is simultaneously answering five phone calls and signing for a delivery, he or she may not clearly understand the boss's request. In *message distortion,* the serial transmission of information alters the original meaning so that the message does not arrive as intended. This is akin to the children's game, "Telephone," in which the first child is told a story and tries to retell the story to the second child, retaining as many of the details as possible. The second child then tries to retell the story to a third child, and so forth. The final version of the story often bears only a distant resemblance to the original story. In *message ambiguity,* the failure to choose words that establish easily understood symbol-referent connections allows receivers the latitude to interpret messages in ways that differ from the speaker's intent. This definition reflects the overriding concern of the classical-structuralist school with downward communication, and specifically with orders and instructions. Although there are many occasions in organizations when clarity promotes effectiveness, there are important exceptions as well: for example, a supervisor may need to maintain confidentiality about a strategic plan. Once we look beyond the accomplishment of simple, physical tasks, clarity must always be balanced against relational and political ends, both of which are sometimes better accomplished by choosing one's words carefully.

The machine or conduit definition of miscommunication is problematic in at least two ways. First, the recipient of the message is seen as largely *passive* and as playing no significant role in the co-construction of the meaning of the message. This is in line with "personalist" views of meaning in which individuals "own" meaning and pass it around, rather than constructing it in discourse (Gergen, 1985; Holquist, 1981). Second, this definition assumes message senders always *intend* to be clear. Although this is usually true in the case of technical instructions, it may not always be so. For example, in the conduct of a performance review, a manager may be intentionally unclear about negative aspects of the employee's performance in order to avoid confrontation (Goodall, Wilson, & Waagan, 1986). Similarly, this definition does not acknowledge that ambiguity may sometimes facilitate effective communication (Eisenberg, 1984; Levine, 1985).

The critique of the conduit metaphor in organizational communication has broader resonances in the analysis of conversation. Specifically, Grice's (1975) well-known *cooperative principles* of conversation include "avoid ambiguity," and "do not say what you believe to be false." Although Grice understood these principles to be an idealization of the communicative process, their existence does tend to minimize the fact that most people break these rules most of the time, and furthermore, *expect* others to break them in pursuit of their goals (Okabe, 1987). Simply put, competent communicators in complex organizations do much more than transfer information from point A to point B.

Others have endeavored to describe the ways organizational members deviate from cooperative principles and still succeed. In a previous paper (Eisenberg, 1984), the senior author of this chapter described some of the ways in which ambiguity may be used strategically by organizational members to accomplish important goals. Specifically, strategic ambiguity:

- promotes unified diversity;
- preserves privileged positions;
- is deniable; and
- facilitates organizational change.

An example of *unified diversity* can be found in an organization's mission statement. If made too clear, it can be divisive; like political platforms, most missions must be sufficiently abstract to allow a diversity of interpretations to coexist. Ambiguity *preserves privileged positions* in that once an employee has gained considerable stature or respect, he may be unclear in stating explicit views, relying on others to credit his past achievements and fill in the blanks. For example, if an executive has a track record of success, she may simply say that she is going to help the organization "achieve total quality" or "put the customer first," leaving everyone to construct their own interpretations of these equivocal expressions. What makes this especially interesting is that it is unlikely that anyone will question the goal or the means of achieving the goal if sufficient ambiguity exists in the credible executive's statements.

Ambiguity can also be used strategically to form in-groups, preserving privilege in a broader sense. When a group develops its own technical jargon, this technical talk is "ineffective" only from the standpoint of the outsider, who is mystified or confused. From the perspective of the insider, jargon is effective because it makes communication more efficient and builds camaraderie.

The *deniability* afforded by strategic ambiguity is especially important to managers and employers. By being less than clear, employees can protect confidentiality, avoid dysfunctional conflicts, and not reveal tactical information that might compromise the effectiveness of a decision. Finally, ambiguity can *facilitate organizational change* by allowing groups and individuals sufficient latitude to alter the focus of activity while at the same time appearing to be consistent.

The strategic use of ambiguity is but one illustration of how people make symbolic use of information in organizations (Feldman & March, 1981). Management is increasingly seen as requiring symbolic or strategic skills more akin to evangelism than accounting (Pfeffer, 1981; Pondy, 1978;

Weick, 1979). Communication is not always rational in the sense of maximizing understanding, but instead involves individuals acting to maximize gains and minimize losses. Consequently, rational, *information engineering* models of effectiveness should be replaced by broader theories of symbolic information control that address the more subtle roles of tact, politeness, white lies, and agenda control. This shift toward considering individual motivations leads us naturally to the pragmatic view.

A Pragmatic View: Miscommunication as Failed Goal Attainment

This widely held perspective on communication equates effectiveness with goal attainment. In an organization, communication is considered ineffective if it fails to help an employee achieve his or her goals (see Table 6.1).

The biggest problem with such an avowedly strategic perspective is ethical relativism; if effective communication is defined as goal attainment, *who* decides which goals are worth accomplishing? Note the shift in evaluative focus from the discourse toward the correspondence between goals and accomplishments. From this angle, if an organization's Chief Executive Officer (CEO) was strategically ambiguous to escape blame for poor performance, judgments of effectiveness would not be tied to the lack of clarity in his or her language (as they would under the conduit or machine metaphor definition) but instead to whether or not the CEO was able to escape blame.

A second concern with the pragmatic perspective is determining the appropriate *time* to evaluate the effectiveness of communication. For example, if one's goal is to change the "underlying beliefs of managers and employees," how long should it take for this change to occur? A critical performance review, for example, may first prompt a defensive reaction, and only some months later show any improvement in productivity.

From this pragmatic perspective, competent communicators are adaptive and say the appropriate thing for the situation. Inappropriateness signifies a poor fit between strategy choice and goal achievement, and is synonymous with miscommunication. But inappropriate for whom? This question has important ethical implications. In a condemnation of double-talk among managers, *Fortune* magazine quoted an executive's definition of effective communication: "All you have to remember is . . . let the language be ambiguous enough that if the job is successfully carried out, all credit can be claimed, and if not, a technical alibi (can) be found" (Whyte, 1948). From a goal-oriented perspective, an employee who lies about employment history or a manager who withholds important information about the safety of working conditions might both be communicating effectively, if the goal is to succeed by hiding some uncomfortable truths. For this reason, there are serious ethical problems with a blanket endorsement of this perspective on miscommunication.

Finally, scholars are coming to see that communicators never have a single, overarching goal, and consequently, effectiveness always means balancing between multiple goals (cf. Dillard, Segrin, & Harden, 1989; O'Keefe, 1988; Phillips, 1989; Tracy & Eisenberg, 1989). A single message can serve a variety of functions. A subordinate communicating negative information about the competition to his or her boss, for example, must balance the importance of getting the information across against the face needs of the boss and his or her own personal career concerns. Performance reviews are another place where a multiple goals model applies. When appraising an employee's performance, a supervisor is challenged both to give clear feedback about the employee's weaknesses, and to maintain a positive working relationship. This calls for substantial tact and communicative skill. Consequently, many managers avoid or trivialize this activity. The performance appraisal is an archetypal example of the rule in organizational communication—the requirement to balance numerous motivations in discourse. Poor communicators fail to recognize tradeoffs and consequently ignore the face concerns of the other in getting their point across, or tiptoe through the conversation and fail to accomplish their primary goal. But although the acknowledgment of multiple goals makes the pragmatic perspective a better match to the reality of organizational communication, it fails to free us from the ethical relativism inherent in any goal orientation.

Human Relations: Miscommunication as Failed Openness

Some organizational scholars focus on the importance of *openness* and *self-disclosure* in defining organizational communication effectiveness (cf. Eisenberg & Witten, 1987). Based in the human relations movement, these authors argue that what is missing from most organizations is personal disclosure and authenticity. Furthermore, these authors propose that greater candor is tantamount to communicative effectiveness. In some organizations, openness continues to be seen as fundamental to building an effective work group (see Table 6.1).

There is, however, a tendency to overstate the applicability and positive effects of increased openness in organizations. A number of writers have critiqued the "ideology of openness" (Brown & Rogers, 1991), offering numerous contexts in which greater openness hurts, rather than helps individuals *and* organizations (Bochner, 1984; Eisenberg & Witten, 1987; Parks, 1982). Parks (1982) maintains that people have neither the time, energy, nor sufficiently good reasons to be completely open with their colleagues. In most organizations, people are rewarded for closed, not open communication (Conrad, 1985).

A typical situation in which the use of candor might backfire is when an employee is asked for feedback on a report by their boss or close colleague. How should they respond? Too blunt a response may alienate the other person and decrease the likelihood that any suggestion will be considered. A vague response may be problematic as well, especially if the employee has a stake in making the final report as good as possible. A second example involves a senior manager preparing to quit to take a job with a competitor, but at the same time continuing daily activities in his or her current firm, including hiring and recruitment. Should the manager be honest with new recruits about the possibility of his or her departure?

These and similar questions are commonly asked in organizations, and they do not have easy answers. What is obvious *is* that as simple prescriptions of clarity or openness, they are inadequate. Although one might *assert the general rule* that open communication allows for smoother working relationships and better decisions, there is no clear empirical evidence documenting this claim. Furthermore, the most interesting communicative challenges at work entail deciding *how much* to reveal (or conceal), *how* to reveal, *what* to reveal, *when* to reveal, and *to whom* to reveal. While our striving for openness may be well-intentioned, most real-life communication situations present more complex social dilemmas.

Limitations to the efficacy of openness are not restricted solely to personal disclosure, but extend to more general incidences of concealment and revelation. Florida's "Sunshine Laws" are a case in point. Sunshine Laws force government agencies to open their meetings to the public. McLaughlin and Riesman (1985) conducted a case study of public hearings to select a new president for the University of Florida. What they found did not provide unequivocal support for the efficacy of openness. Rather, the Sunshine Laws led to evasive, ambiguous behavior in "open" meetings, leaving the public even less informed than before. The reality of Sunshine Laws illustrates that nothing may be gained (on a practical or theoretical level) when the mismatch between theory and reality is too great.

Another reason organizational participants and theorists uncritically endorse open communication is an implicit belief in the *sharing* metaphor of social relationships (Eisenberg, 1986; Eisenberg & Riley, 1988; Krippendorff, 1985). The sharing metaphor implies that effective communication requires the cultivation of shared cognitions and emotions between interactants. Recently, this tendency has surfaced in arguments supporting the development of so-called *strong* cultures—attitudinal monoliths marked by a homogeneity of understandings, values, and beliefs (e.g., Peters & Waterman, 1982).

The tendency toward consensus models of communication is uniquely American (Moore, 1985), distinctly modern (Lyotard, 1984), and reflects a desire to resolve differences rather than learn to live with them. But shared understandings are *not* necessary for effective organization (Eisenberg & Riley, 1988; Weick, 1979); coordination of action is often more important than coordination of beliefs (Duranti, 1984; Weick, 1979). So long as organizational members agree on the implications for action of a particular communication, meanings may be *equifinal* (Donnellon, Gray, & Bougon, 1986; Gray, Bougon, & Donnellon, 1985). That is, congruent actions may result from divergent interpretations. Furthermore, not only is shared meaning unverifiable (Krippendorff, 1985) and not essential to effective organization (Weick, 1979), the lack of shared understanding may provide an atmosphere supportive of diversity and even transcendence (Eisenberg, 1990). That is, the lack of shared understanding may actually allow employees to connect and collaborate with each other in ways that would be blocked if they came to know each other better.

The emphasis on openness advanced by the human relations school was revised over time, as it became clear that most managers were asking employees to communicate openly mainly as a means of manipulation and control (cf. Eisenberg & Witten, 1987). Unrestricted self-disclosure witnessed a resurgence in the 1960s, but recent developments have caused people to be more modest in their claims about the efficacy of openness. One interesting consequence is that we are again forced to examine goals; some degree of openness may be appropriate toward one end, but not another. Furthermore, the way in which information is expressed (i.e., paralinguistically, nonverbally, through a communicator's style) has an effect. But just as simple endorsements of clarity are not helpful in real organizations, so too do simple prescriptions of openness reflect a naive view of what constitutes real-life organizational communication. Consequently, it is inappropriate to brand some piece of talk "miscommunication" simply because it is not open, disclosive, or honest. More must be known about the local context before such judgments can be made.

A Critical Perspective:
Miscommunication as Failed Dialogue

Although arguments against blanket endorsements of clarity, goal achievement, and openness have received some attention of late, critiques of the *monologic* character of communication theory and research are relatively new (May, 1989a). In this section we first briefly narrate the transition from the monologic to the dialogic view. Then we explore the implications of the dialogic view for definitions of effective and ineffective communication.

Although most writers are explicit in their definition of communication as a transactional process, research practice typically reduces its study to monologue. Two areas of organizational research are illustrative. In the study of organizational stories (see Martin, Feldman, Hatch, & Sitkin, 1983), writers tend to see stories as canned monologues, emerging "fully cooked" from a speaker's mouth. Although this approach renders the subject easier to study, most real stories are not told this way. Instead, stories are usually co-constructed in dialogue, with "listeners" playing an active verbal and nonverbal role. The "story" gets constructed in the process (see May, 1989b; Ochs, 1988b).

Similarly, most studies of organizational compliance-gaining (see Kipnis, Schmidt, & Wilkinson, 1980) view persuasion as something one person does *to* another, despite the fact that the other may play an active role in resisting, modifying, or cooperating with the compliance-gaining attempt. This weakness is exemplified in the use of the terms *agent* and *target*. In reality, compliance-gaining can be highly interactive and requires shifting between these roles as well as the balancing of multiple goals.

The monologic view of communication is deeply rooted in personalist models of meaning, which reify individuals as "owning" meaning inside their heads (Holquist, 1981). As such, it is consistent with the conduit metaphor discussed above. What is missed most from this perspective is the socially *emergent* character of communication, effective or ineffective. Also lost is the potential for dialogue, the social co-construction of meaning over time. From a *dialogic* perspective, miscommunication is failed dialogue, or a one-sided definition of the situation; precisely the kind of situation much of our current research is unfortunately designed to study (see Table 6.1).

Because it eschews simple prescriptions of consensus and acknowledges the fluid negotiation of meaning and interpretation, the dialogic perspective is both more democratic and action-oriented than the other viewpoints we have described. It is action-oriented in the sense that it focuses on what people do together, whether they agree or not (cf. Eisenberg, 1990; Giddens, 1981). This move in communication studies echoes developments on a broader scale, what Ortner (1984) calls the master metaphor of *practice,* the leading theme of anthropological research in the 1980s.

This concern with practice and activity is only one connection between the dialogic perspective and its Soviet roots (e.g., Bakhtin, 1973; Vygotsky, cited in Wertsch, 1988). Another is its similarities to critical theory in general (e.g., Deetz & Kersten, 1983). Critical theorists see organizations as systems of domination in which the hegemony of taken-for-granted decision premises prevents participants from attaining their full potential. From this perspective, effective communication is *open dialogue* which creates a clearing for individual emancipation. For the critical theorist, miscommunication is any communication that oppresses individuals and supports domination (Henley & Kramarae, 1991).

Unfortunately, in adopting a dialogic or critical perspective, the problem of ethical relativism is not solved, only dodged. Note, for example, that the locus for evaluating communicative effectiveness has shifted away from the *discourse* (because domination is usually covert) and from explicit goals (because participants on both sides are usually unaware of the forces of domination that are controlling them) to a *critic's judgment* of the positive or negative effects of communication on individuals. In addition to changing the locus of evaluation, we have changed the evaluator by privileging the role of the critic (Smircich & Calas, 1987).

But ethical relativism is not the only shortcoming of the dialogic perspective. Another relates to the question: *Who* is involved in the dialogue? All communication can be evaluated relative to multiple audiences, and different audiences (or stakeholders) make different assessments. This point is especially important from a dialogic perspective, where being excluded from the dialogue is the same as being disenfranchised. In a broad sense, miscommunication occurs not only when dialogue fails, but more fundamentally, when certain parties are excluded from the conversation altogether.

An Alternative Definition: Miscommunication as Failed Balance

The history of definitions of effective organizational communication is difficult to track and largely implicit. This may be because many organizational theorists and practitioners see communication as unproblematic or undifferentiated. At the same time, most people share at least an implicit appreciation for the trade-offs and subtleties required for organizational survival, and the strategic role communication can play in organizational politics. Most writers, however, are simply not accustomed to thinking about communication in this way. Instead, a dual reality is maintained: one motivated by theoretical formulations in which good communicators are open, honest, and clear; and one rooted in real life in which people are constantly adapting what they say to cope with the emerging situation. Developing useful theories of organizational communication necessitates finding a point of convergence between these two views.

Communication plays a dual role in organizing. On the one hand, communication is an expression of constraint, promoting organized action, accountability, and task accomplishment. On the other, communication expresses creativity; through interaction, individuals can exercise autonomy and exhibit innovativeness. The interplay between organized action and individual agency is present in all social organization. The individual strives to retain sufficient independence for growth and well-being, while simultaneously cooperating enough to do the job and feel a part of the group. For the organization, coordination is obviously important. But so too is individual autonomy, because it grants the organization greater flexibility, innovation, and the ability to adapt to change (Weick, 1979). The last thing an individual or an organization wants is employees who cooperate only according to formal rules (Katz & Kahn, 1978).

The delicate balance between individual agency and organizational constraint is enacted in communication. Every moment, in every organization, employees choose to reveal or conceal, express or protect themselves, and in so doing shape this balance. Effective communication achieves a proper balance of autonomy and control, and miscommunication is failed balance—too much freedom, and the organization becomes dysfunctional—too little freedom, the individual suffers, and the organization stagnates.

In our view of miscommunication, the locus of evaluation shifts away from goals, discourse, and the critic to a systematic or dialectical assessment. We define effective communication as discourse that promotes a balance between agency and constraint. Any assessment of miscommunication requires observers to tie a number of judgments together in determining the degree to which this balance has been achieved.

Although we feel our definition of miscommunication corresponds closely to the realities of organizational life, we have in no way escaped ethical relativism; we have simply traded one type (involving goals) for another (involving the "proper" balance between autonomy and control). Further, definitions of what counts as the "proper" balance between autonomy and control are always:

(1) *actor-bound* (i.e., more autonomy may be desired by employees but feared by management and stockholders);

(2) *time-bound* (i.e., a certain balance may be problematic in one time period and make better sense in another); and

(3) *culture-bound* (i.e., what is viewed as an appropriate degree of employee freedom in Asia may be seen as overly restrictive in the United States).

These points warrant further elaboration.

First, to say that a proper balance between autonomy and control is *actor-bound* indicates that organizational members will have differing perceptions of what constitutes the appropriate level of autonomy, and consequently, will hold different views of miscommunication. In her book on family systems, Hoffman (1981) demonstrated how the same message or action will be perceived as positive or negative, constructive or destructive, depending upon the system level (e.g., child, parent, grandparent) from which it is judged. For example, a cost-cutting method that saves the company money but significantly alters job descriptions may be seen as effective by senior management but ineffective by a union.

Second, the *time-bound* nature of our definition suggests that judgments of effectiveness are always historical; they are not invariant over time (Gergen, 1985). Organizations are often thought of as having life cycles (Kimberly & Miles, 1980). At different points in an organization's life cycle, different activities are expected and desirable. Temporal differences in what counts as miscommunication are to be expected as well. For example, it would be premature to institute strict management systems or accountabilities in the entrepreneurial phase of development, just as high levels of autonomy and a low degree of control would be inappropriate in the "mature" stage. The right balance between autonomy and coordination depends in part on where an organization is in its development.

Finally, substantial work exists to illustrate the *culture-bound* nature of communication (Banks, Gudykunst, Ge, & Baker, 1991; Cushman & Kincaid, 1987). Judgments of miscommunication are culture-bound in at least three ways—national culture, organizational culture, and organizational sub-cultures. Regarding national culture, what constitutes miscommunication in one country might be construed as effective in another. For example, Pascale and Athos (1981), Hirokawa (1987), and others have noted the Asian tendency toward indirect speech and preservation of the other's "face." Japanese and Korean managers rarely say "no" directly, which leads to considerable confusion when dealing with Western cultures. Representatives of Chinese organizations focus much more on the creative side of communication than do their American counterparts. And should they enter the global marketplace, countries like Samoa or Guyana can be expected to add even more diversity. Ambiguity is critical to Guyanese communication (Williams, 1987), for example, and Samoan culture has no concept of intent or even personality (Duranti, 1984), making the Western strategy of assessing goals or motives futile.

Much has been written about how organizations *are* cultures (e.g., Frost, Moore, Louis, Lundberg, & Martin, 1985), and as such are characterized by their own unique set of attitudes and practices. Conceptions of miscommunication in one company (e.g., Apple Computer) will vary considerably from conceptions in another (e.g., IBM). Whereas some companies highly value autonomy (e.g., 3M's intrapreneurial teams), others emphasize coordination and even suppress individual expression as part of their corporate strategy (e.g., McDonald's). Finally, organizational cultures are *not* monoliths; they contain subcultures. This means that what might count as miscommunication in one part of the company may be effective somewhere else.

In sum, no adequate definition of miscommunication escapes relativism or context-dependence. The problem of defining effective communication is similar to the contemporary problem facing epistemology—what counts as firm knowledge in a post-positivist, post-modern world? According to Rorty (1979), the best we can do is "continue the conversation"—"effectiveness" is whatever helps us to cope. Dialogue, community, and coping may be appropriate descriptors of effective communication in an increasingly complex business world, especially because any more descriptive definition necessarily privileges specific stakeholders.

McGuire's (1983) theory of contextualism provides a slightly different way of thinking about miscommunication. According to McGuire, no theory or hypothesis is ever altogether right or wrong; rather, we should proceed as if all theories are true somewhere. The purpose of research, then, is to discover the contexts in which the various theories apply. Relating back to the present argument, there may be no definitive definition of miscommunication in organizations. Instead, there is only a continual discovery of contexts wherein certain kinds of communication are more or less problematic.

AUTHOR'S NOTE: The authors acknowledge Lori Roscoe and Terry Albrecht for their insightful critiques.

References

Axley, S. (1984). Managerial and organizational communication in terms of the conduit metaphor. *Academy of Management Review, 9*, 428–437.

Bakhtin, M. (1973). *Marxism and the philosophy of language.* New York: Seminar Press.

Bochner, A. (1984). The functions of human communication in interpersonal bonding. In C. Arnold & J. Bowers (Eds.), *Handbook of rhetoric and communication theory* (pp. 544–621). Boston: Allyn & Bacon.

Conrad, C. (1985). *Strategic organizational communication.* New York: Holt, Rinehart & Winston.

Cushman, D., & Kincaid, L. (1987). Introduction and initial insights. In L. Kincaid (Ed.), *Communication theory: Eastern and western perspectives* (pp. 1–10). San Diego, CA: Academic Press.

Deetz, S., & Kersten, A. (1983). Critical models of interpretive research. In L. L. Putnam & M. Pacanowsky (Eds.), *Communication and organization: An interpretive approach* (pp. 147–171). Beverly Hills, CA: Sage.

Dillard, J., Segrin, C., & Harden, J. (1989). Primary and secondary goals in the production of interpersonal influence messages. *Communication Monographs, 56,* 19–38.

Donnelon, A., Gray, B., & Bougon, M. (1986). Communication, meaning, and organized action. *Administrative Science Quarterly, 31,* 43–55.

Duranti, A. (1984). *Intentions, self, and local theories of meaning.* Center for Human Information Processing, 122-1-20.

Eisenberg, E. (1984). Ambiguity as strategy in organizational communication. *Communication Monographs, 51,* 227–242.

Eisenberg, E. (1986). Meaning and interpretation in organizations. *Quarterly Journal of Speech, 72,* 88–113.

Eisenberg, E. (1990). Jamming: Transcendence through organizing. *Communication Research, 17,* 139–164.

Eisenberg, E., & Riley, P. (1988). Organizational symbols and sense making. In G. Goldhaber & G. Barnett (Eds.), *Handbook of organizational communication* (pp. 131–150). Norwood, NJ: Ablex.

Eisenberg, E., & Witten, M. (1987). Reconsidering openness in organizational communication. *Academy of Management Review, 12,* 418–426.

Feldman, M., & March, J. (1981). Information in organizations as signal and symbol. *Administrative Science Quarterly, 26,* 171–186.

Frost, P., Moore, L., Louis, M., Lundberg, C., & Martin, J. (1985). *Organizational culture.* Beverly Hills, CA: Sage.

Gergen, K. (1985). The social constructionist movement in modern psychology. *American Psychologist, 40,* 266–275.

Giddens, A. (1981). *A contemporary critique of historical materialism.* Berkeley: University of California Press.

Goodall, H. L., Wilson, G., & Waagan, C. (1986). The performance appraisal interview: An interpretive reassessment. *Quarterly Journal of Speech, 72,* 74–87.

Gray, B., Bougon, M., & Donnelon, A. (1985). Organizations as constructions and destructions of meaning. *Journal of Management, 11,* 83–98.

Grice, J. (1975). Logic and conversation. In P. Cole & J. Morgan (Eds.), *Syntax and semantics, Vol. 3: Speech Acts* (pp. 41–58). New York: Academic Press.

Hirokawa, R. (1987). Communication within the Japanese organization. In L. Kincaid (Ed.), *Communication theory* (pp. 137–150). San Diego, CA: Academic Press.

Hoffman, L. (1981). *Foundations of family therapy.* New York: Basic Books.

Holquist, M. (1981). The politics of representation. *Quarterly Journal of the Laboratory of Human Cognition, 5,* 2–9.

Katz, D., & Kahn, R. (1978). *The social psychology of organizations.* New York: Wiley.

Kimberly, J., & Miles, R. (1980). *The organizational life cycle.* San Francisco: Jossey-Bass.

Kipnis, D., Schmidt, S., & Wilkinson, I. (1980). Intraorganizational influence tactics: Explorations in getting one's way. *Journal of Applied Psychology, 65,* 440–452.

Krippendorff, K. (1985). *On the ethics of constructing communication.* Presidential address, annual meeting of the International Communication Association, Honolulu, HI.

Levine, D. (1985). *The flight from ambiguity.* Chicago: University of Chicago Press.

Lyotard, F. (1984). *The postmodern condition: A report on knowledge.* Minneapolis: University of Minnesota Press.

Martin, J., Feldman, M., Hatch, M., & Sitkin, S. (1983). The uniqueness paradox in organizational stories. *Administrative Science Quarterly, 28,* 438–453.

May, S. (1989a). *The modernist monologue in organizational communication research.* Paper presented at the annual meeting of the International Communication Association, New Orleans, LA.

May, S. (1989b). *Performing narratives of work.* Paper presented at the annual meeting of the Speech Communication Association, San Francisco.

McGuire, W. (1983). A contextualist theory of knowledge. In L. Berkowitz (Ed.), *Advances in experimental social psychology, 16* (pp. 1–47). New York: Academic Press.

McLaughlin, J., & Riesman, D. (1985). The shady side of sunshine. *Teacher's College Record, 87,* 471–494.

Moore, M. (1985). Culture as culture. In P. Frost et al. (Eds.), *Organizational culture* (pp. 373–378). Beverly Hills, CA: Sage.

Morgan, G. (1986). *Images of organization.* Beverly Hills, CA: Sage.

Ochs, E. (1988b). *Language, affect, and knowledge.* Cambridge, MA: Oxford University Press.

Okabe, K. (1987). Indirect speech acts of the Japanese. In L. Kincaid (Ed.), *Communication theory* (pp. 127–136). San Diego, CA: Academic Press.

Ortner, S. (1984). Theory in anthropology since the sixties. *Comparative Studies in Society and History, 26,* 126–166.

Parks, M. (1982). Ideology in interpersonal communication. In M. Burgoon (Ed.), *Communication Yearbook, 5* (pp. 79–101). New Brunswick, NJ: Transaction Books.

Pascale, R., & Athos, A. (1981). *The art of Japanese management.* New York: Simon & Schuster.

Peters, T., & Waterman, R. (1982). In search of excellence. New York: Harper & Row.

Pfeffer, J. (1981). Management as symbolic action. In B. Staw & L. Cummings (Eds.), *Research in organizational behavior, 3* (pp. 1–52). Greenwich, CT: Jai Press.

Phillips, S. (1989). *Electronic persuasion: The uses of electronic mail for interpersonal influence in organizations.* Unpublished doctoral dissertation, Department of Communication, University of Southern California.

Pondy, L. (1978). Leadership is a language game. In M. Lombardo & M. McCall (Eds.), *Leadership: Where else can we go?* (pp. 87–99). Durham, NC: Duke University Press.

Rorty, R. (1979). *Philosophy and the mirror of nature.* Princeton, NJ: Princeton University Press.

Smircich, L., & Calas, M. (1987). Organizational culture: A critical assessment. In F. Jablin et al. (Eds.), *Handbook of organizational communication* (pp. 228–263). Newbury Park, CA: Sage.

Stohl, C., & Redding, W. C. (1987). Messages and message exchange processes. In F. Jablin et al. (Eds.), *Handbook of organizational communication* (pp. 451–502). Newbury Park, CA: Sage.

Tracy, K., & Eisenberg, E. (1989). *Multiple goals: Unpacking a commonplace.* Paper presented at the annual meeting of the International Communication Association, San Francisco.

Weick, K. (1979). *The social psychology of organizing* (2nd ed.). New York: Random House.

Wertsch, J. (1988, Winter). L. S. Vygotsky's "new" theory of mind. *American Scholar,* 81–89.

White, W. F. (1948). *Human relations in the restaurant industry.* New York: McGraw-Hill.

Williams, B. (1987). Humor, linguistic ambiguity, and disputing in a Guyanese community. *International Journal of the Sociology of Language, 65,* 79–94.

7

Dialogue as Democratic Discourse

This essay marked another stage in the development of a critical consciousness in my work. I chose this response paper for my first brief foray into the relationship between certain forms of communication and democracy. Specifically, I examined different democratic organizational forms and attempted to articulate the close connection between dialogic communication and democratic discourse. Both dialogue and democracy depend heavily on the purposeful use of language to create the possibility for multiple voices to be heard.

The concept of dialogue provided some useful links among organizational and interpersonal communication, rhetoric, and philosophy. Big-name scholars at MIT (notably Peter Senge) were successfully placing dialogic practices on the agendas of organizational leaders worldwide, but they were doing so without regard for the history of theories of dialogue, usually traced to the work of Martin Buber. This essay was a first step toward bringing these two streams of work together; this integration was further realized in Chapter 2 of my (then forthcoming) textbook, Organizational Communication: Balancing Creativity and Constraint, *5th edition (with H. L. Goodall Jr. and Angela Tretheway).*

SOURCE: Eisenberg, E. (1994). Dialogue as democratic discourse: Affirming Harrison. In S. Deetz (Ed.), *Communication Yearbook 17* (pp. 275–284). Newbury Park, CA: Sage. Copyright © 1994 by the International Communication Association. Reprinted by permission of Sage Publications, Inc.

The unequal distribution of power in most organizations presents an enduring ideological problem for the United States. Describing the early twentieth century, Charles Perrow (1986) identifies the issue succinctly: "On the one hand, democracy stressed liberty and equality for all. On the other hand, large masses of workers and nonsalaried personnel had to submit to apparently arbitrary authority, backed up by local and national police forces and legal powers, for ten to twelve hours a day, six days a week" (p. 53). While working conditions have improved for most Americans over the years, this fundamental contradiction persists. In a society that is committed in the abstract to democratic values, it is at the very least ironic that most U.S. workers have both few liberties at work and little power to influence the decisions that most affect their work lives.

It is clear that Teresa Harrison would like to see this situation change. In her superb essay, she offers three arguments:

a. that academics have focused disproportionately on the kinds of communication that create and maintain hierarchies and not enough on alternative forms of interdependence,

b. that Giddens' metatheory of structuration is especially useful in analyzing both bureaucratic and democratic organizational systems, and

c. that two types of democratic organizational systems may be identified and the role of communication in fostering these alternatives to traditional hierarchy can be effectively demonstrated.

The Academic Bias Toward Hierarchy

According to Harrison, academics are complicit in the maintenance of hierarchical, bureaucratic organizations in which power is closely held at the top. She argues that while there are many alternative ways to organize, academic theorists have focused almost exclusively on one kind of interdependence, bureaucratic hierarchy. In so doing, we have systematically decreased the likelihood of discovering communication practices that might produce workable alternatives. Harrison sees a need for new "democratic" discourses that will enable us to envision alternatives to hierarchy.

I agree with Harrison and can offer something of an explanation. It is useful to remember that early organizations were fashioned after armies (Morgan, 1986) and that the field of organizational communication was to a large extent launched by the "Triple Alliance" of academics, managers, and the military (Redding, 1985). Even today, the military plays a significant role as both a customer and an overseer of work processes. Hence it is not all that surprising that we have inherited a bias toward classical, hierarchical models of organizing.

Alternatives to classical models are not as unexplored, however, as Harrison makes them out to be. Outside of the academy, the search for new structures is well under way. Following a decade of downsizing and flattening of hierarchies, most contemporary organizations are experimenting with some form of increased employee participation and involvement. These changes are well reflected in the popular press, but Harrison is indeed correct that academic theory and research have lagged behind practice.

Further consideration of these practical initiatives reveals Harrison's review of different types of democratic organizations to be somewhat limited in scope. Contemporary attempts to create alternatives to hierarchy take many forms other than employee-owned organizations. Initiatives of this sort are occurring with increasing regularity and at many levels. For example, at the *interorganizational* level, strategic alliances and joint ventures are increasingly common. High levels of vertical integration, through which companies strive to be relatively self-sufficient by bringing component parts and processes in-house, are giving way to a more flexible, "modular" style of organizing that seeks alliances on an as-needed basis. The result is that organizations that formerly had many hierarchical levels and functions assume flatter, simpler structures by vending out aspects of their operations to strategic partners.

At the *organizational* level, some of our best known companies (e.g., Dana, 3M, Hughes Aircraft) are restructuring to minimize centralized control through the creation of autonomous business units that are allowed to operate independently so long as they meet financial goals. Power is delegated to strategic business units in the hopes of avoiding the "giantism" (Peters, 1987) that leaves big organizations inflexible and unresponsive to customers and changing market conditions. Within these business units, management often attempts to create "high-involvement organizations" in which decision-making authority is pushed down to the lowest possible level (Lawler, 1986).

Finally, at the *work group* level, there is a widespread desire to replace individual work with high-performance work teams. This may have something to do with the decline of individualism and the rise of community as a guiding philosophy for the United States (Bellah, Madsen, Sullivan, Swidler, & Tipton, 1991). Although not without their problems, these "self-directed" work teams are expected over a period of time to take control of their schedules, budgets, and in some cases the hiring and firing of team members (Eisenberg & Goodall, 1993; Wellins, Byham, & Wilson, 1991).

The most radical alternatives to hierarchy in formal organizations may not originate in the United States. In Scandinavian countries, for example, participative action research (PAR) has for some time explored forms of organizing that involve greater power sharing and the overturning of hierarchies (e.g., Elden & Levin, 1991). One notable example is a Swedish company called Skaltek AB. Skaltek AB has 90 employees and revenues of $17 million annually; it also has no hierarchy or titles. All staff members are called "responsible persons," not employees, and everyone is personally responsible for the quality of their work. When a customer has a complaint, he or she contacts the "responsible person" who did the work (Osterberg, 1992).

There are still other places to look for novel ideas of this sort. The World Business Academy publishes a journal (*Perspectives*) and a newsletter, *At Work: Stories of Tomorrow's Workplace,* devoted exclusively to providing proven examples of these new organizational forms. Finally, ecofeminists (e.g., Eisler, 1987) have taken a leadership role in promoting a "partnership" model of interdependence. For these writers, hierarchy is the common enemy of both women and nature. The ecofeminists' program is based on a critique of hierarchy, which they believe exists mainly to support the dominator societies of today and those who run them (Eisler, 1987).

In summary, while Harrison's concern about the lack of research on alternative forms of interdependence is accurate, it is also true that the problem is receiving significant attention from others outside of the academic community.

Analyzing Communication
in Hierarchical and Democratic Systems

Harrison begins her discussion of "models of interdependence" with the claim that, over time, perspectives on organizational structure that were fundamentally processual became corrupted and steadily more static. In response to this unfortunate trend, Karl Weick's (1979) model of equivocality reduction stands as an important corrective; it "reclaimed the processual nature of structure for organizational studies" (Harrison, p. 251). Harrison is frustrated with Weick's model, however, in that it constitutes "a framework without specific content" (p. 253). In an attempt to locate more specific content implications, she invokes Giddens's metatheory of structuration.

Harrison's explication of Giddens's work is excellent. She both places the work in compelling intellectual context and provides definitions and examples that make the otherwise daunting vocabulary comprehensible. She also explains in detail the balancing act in which all social actors are continually engaged, both invoking social rules and resources and modifying and constructing new ones. Central to her ideas (and Giddens's) about how this process occurs is the notion of a "reproduction circuit."

According to Giddens (1984), a reproduction circuit is "a cycle of routinised activities and consequences which are reproduced across time-space within and between institutionalised locales" (p. 124). Harrison gives a good example of how a particular kind of circuit—that which reproduces bureaucratic hierarchy—works in an organization. She observes further that the work of generations of educators has echoed these ideas about the nature and necessity of hierarchy, which in turn produces college graduates ready and eager to draw on precisely these rules and resources in the further reproduction of bureaucracies.

From my perspective, two things are missing from Harrison's otherwise compelling account of the reproduction of bureaucratic hierarchies: a sense of struggle, and an expanded role for the environment. First, with the exception of one brief caveat ("each cycle of reproduction introduces the possibility of change into the system"; p. 259), I found the discussion of *how* certain organizational forms come to be reproduced rather bloodless. My own experience "inside" these reproduction circuits is that there is much conflict, shifting coalitions, confusion, and just plain hanging around.

Along these lines, I find work by Patricia Riley (1983) and Stephen Barley (1986) to be especially resonant. Both revel in the marked differences between subgroups as the negotiated order unfolds. I am *not* saying that Giddens's framework is incapable of handling the decidedly ungraceful way in which reproduction proceeds, only that the vocabulary of structuration, at least as Harrison applies it, feels to me overly sanitized. Put differently, I would like to see more about the circuits of *resistance* alongside the circuits of dominance.

My second point has to do with a lack of emphasis on the external environment, including legal, political, and social forces. For example, significant obstacles to the implementation of democratic organizations are federal and state laws concerning the hiring, firing, and overall treatment of employees. In addition, union contracts may discourage the significant work redesign that often accompanies decentralization of power. Both kinds of hurdles exist at a level that transcends individual organizations but are at the same time two of the most serious obstacles in altering traditional hierarchical structures.

Writers such as Stanley Deetz (1992) and Stewart Clegg (1989) offer a more sweeping consideration of the relationship between an organization's form and its social environment. Deetz, for example, argues that the suppression of democracy by bureaucratic forms is not limited to any individual organization but is instead symptomatic of the larger corporate "colonization of the lifeworld." According to Deetz, this broader kind of control pervades the organization of contemporary Western society and applies to families and the media as well as to businesses.

Also worth mention is Clegg's application of Giddens's notion of circuits of power and resistance. While similar to Harrison's in many respects, one important difference is Clegg's emphasis on the impact of changes and events in the broader consumer culture on the reproduction of power within organizations. As such, he sees the pull of the marketplace and the dominant values of a consumer society as in large part responsible for the organizational forms that appear. In the "postmodern postscript" to his book on power, Clegg (1989) writes:

> In the post-modern world, power consists less in the control of the relational field of force in each circuit and more in the way in which the obligatory passage point of the market has become a "black hole," sucking in ever more agency and spewing out an ever more diffuse power as the pursuit of things becomes an all encompassing passion. . . . The conceptual execution of sovereign power heralded only superficially a new realm of freedom; the easing of surveillance seems sure to offer even less freedom as these old concepts are reborn in the unity of the self-regarding and ceaselessly restless consumer sovereign reflexively monitoring the appearance of things through one's self and one's self through things. (p. 275)

While the application of structuration theory to organizational reproduction is no doubt valuable, we must not when doing so forget the more straightforward lessons of open systems theory. Specifically, the rules and resources one draws upon in constituting organizational reality come from far and wide and may at times be better seen as features of society than of any single organization or industry.

Types of Democratic Organizational Systems

I have little to say about what is perhaps the most significant contribution of Harrison's essay, the typology of democratic systems in employee-owned organizations. She draws important distinctions between two types of organizations that are often grouped together—those committed to equal power and alternatives to hierarchy (Type 1) and those more accurately seen as modifications of traditional organizations wherein the primary commitment is to improved productivity and survival of the organization, not to democratic principles per se (Type 2). Not only does this distinction make a lot of sense, Harrison does a fine job of using Giddens's work to fully explore all relevant implications.

Beginning with the section on system integration, however, Harrison raises some deeper issues that ought perhaps to be the basis of another paper, as they are not sufficiently developed here. First, she discusses the key role played by homogeneity, trust, and cultural control as instruments of coordination in democratic systems. Each of these processes is problematic, however, with costs and benefits to both employees and other stakeholders. Her argument is reminiscent of Meyer and Rowan's (1977) groundbreaking work on institutional organizations. From their perspective, institutions (e.g., hospitals, schools) operate from a "logic of confidence" and a presumption of "good faith" among professionals (e.g., physicians, teachers) who work for the most part on their own. Institutions use trust as an organizing strategy to buffer the technical core of the organization from public scrutiny, because opening up a public discussion of the actual quality of teaching or health care risks their social legitimacy.

Meyer and Rowan did their initial work in the 1970s, however, and the ability of any organization to resist public scrutiny has steadily eroded since. Institutions of all kinds are increasingly being asked, and in many cases forced, to be more accountable for the quality of their outcomes. Certainly this is true in hospitals and universities. Consequently, we may have cause to wonder whether it is socially and politically possible to endorse things like homogeneity and trust as practical mechanisms of organizational self-regulation. While these strategies can indeed work internally in an organization, they raise suspicions externally. And, while we may find familiar the scenario Harrison presents of a relatively homogeneous group achieving self-regulation through social pacts and groans of protests at meetings, this form of control runs counter to some of the realities of diversity in organizations as well as to the more rigorous protections against particularism that were the positive legacy of bureaucracy. I would hate to see the formation of democratic organizations that were exclusionary in their hiring (to foster homogeneity) or that used informal social pressure to evict or to intimidate those who fail to "trust" enough to support the will of the group.

I don't think that Harrison is unaware of these problems, only that she has downplayed them in favor of emphasizing the benefits and appeal of democratic organizations. I am curious, however, about the types of businesses or industries in which such democratic organizations could thrive, given the time pressures placed on decision making. Time is the ultimate competitive advantage these days—the current business environment rewards managers who can consistently make high-quality decisions with inadequate information and little opportunity to discuss the pros and cons with employees. Real democracy takes time, as every voice can claim a right to be heard. Organizations I have known that are most democratic (e.g., the Santa Monica

California City Council) are nearly comic in this regard—their ideological support for self-expression leads predictably to citizens testifying weekly to alien invasions and the second coming of the messiah. But how and where would a similar set of values and practices work in industry? Is modern (or postmodern) capitalism really compatible with democracy?

As this question is no doubt an empirical one, I am especially intrigued by Harrison's assertion that democracy is constituted in interactional practices. She says very little about the nature of such practices, however; hence I would like to end this piece with a personal nomination of dialogue as a kind of democratic discourse.

Dialogue as Democratic Discourse

[Dialogue] is one of the richest activities that human beings can engage in. It is the thing that gives meaning to life, it's the sharing of humanity, it's creating something. And there is this magical thing in an organization, or in a team, or in a group, where you get unrestricted interaction, unrestricted dialog, and this synergy happening that results in more productivity, and satisfaction, and seemingly magical levels of output from a team. (Evered & Tannenbaum, 1992, p. 8)

Humans are neither entirely social nor entirely private. To be human means to live in between, to establish a sense of self apart from the world and a sense of self as part of the world (Eisenberg & Goodall, 1993). Along these lines, the central challenge facing all organizations is one of balance, between individual autonomy and agency, on the one hand, and social coordination and constraint, on the other. This challenge is magnified in democratic organizations where, at least in principle, the support for freedom of expression and diverse viewpoints is in some way expected to constitute a superior form of coordination.

But this is easier said than done. Few organizations have learned *how* to foster productive conflict and to remain profitable and competitive while at the same time promoting a diversity of options (and, in Harrison's terms, "minimizing deleterious psychological impacts on organizational members"). Few individuals are able to see beyond their personal worldviews to accept and understand the viewpoints of others. In the beginning of this commentary, I described a number of different approaches currently being taken to reconcile competitive pressures with empowerment. I now conclude with my own approach, which focuses specifically on promoting dialogue in organizations.

In my opinion, the litmus test for a democratic organization is its ability to handle diversity. It is currently in style to speak of "managing" diversity in organizations, but the meaning behind such statements is often more abstract, legalistic, or ideological than practical. A better question might be this: What practical steps can a democratic organization take to reap the benefits of its diverse membership? One answer is to promote dialogue. Doing so requires one to shape communication practices in a number of different ways, involving issues of voice, empathy, and experience. Each is described below.

First, it is well known that in organizations some people's voices count more than others. The first step in establishing dialogue (and, I would argue, democracy) is through the equalization of opportunities for employee voice. Much of the work on employee participation, empowerment, and involvement has this as a primary goal, and changes are made in job design and organizational structure to allow employees at all levels to speak their minds on important issues.

A second step in establishing dialogue in organizations is to promote empathy for differing ideas, opinions, and worldviews. Perhaps the greatest obstacle to progress in most organizations is the stubborn belief on the part of those in power that their view of organizational reality is the one, correct view. According to management theorist Peter Drucker (1993), most organizations today are in trouble because their fundamental "business theory" that worked some years ago no longer makes sense. The only way such theories can change is if people are willing to risk letting go of some of their most treasured beliefs and to truly listen to others who hold different positions. Listening skills must be learned. Many have the mistaken belief that simply bringing people together and giving them the opportunity to speak will lead to quality dialogue—in fact, this is only the first step. People must also learn to listen openly to others' ideas and opinions.

The third step in cultivating dialogue in organizations has to do with how the personal experiences of organizational members are handled in conversation. All too often, managers treat discussions with peers or subordinates as a kind of "marketplace of ideas" in which individuals critique others' perceptions in an attempt to win the argument and elevate their own point of view. In the process, individuals rarely speak from experience. They say things like the following: "We need a new compensation policy for these reasons . . . " rather than "The people in my work group feel underpaid and so do I."

Conversations about ideas usually alternate between constructive and destructive comments, often leading to some partial consensus on a course of action. Alternatively, a dialogue of experience leads people to speak from their experience and listen for the experiences of others, which may be very different than their own. This both limits defensiveness by reducing attacking communication and, more important, gives people insight into the ways in which others frame their opinions and behavior—the personal and cultural context that can help others seem different, yet sensible.

A dialogue of experience is additive. Each person's experience is a contribution to the whole, and, while others' experiences do indeed make one think differently about one's own, no person's experience can invalidate another's. Four different accounts of the same problem, if seen as complementary and not competing, can lead to a complex, sophisticated solution. What is more, there is no goal of consensus or integration of experience—in fact, the rich tapestry of experience that emerges from such dialogue properly resists such attempts at synthesis.

An example is in order. I once facilitated a weekend retreat for the executive team of a major construction company. The company had asked me to help them improve the quality of their communication, which translated into an attempt on the part of the vice-presidents to resist the president's autocratic, militaristic decision-making style. The first thing I did was to structure the meeting so that everyone had an equal chance to speak. While this was a step forward, most of the participants remained frustrated, because whatever they said was immediately judged by the president to be useless or impractical. Next, I taught them the principles of active listening and gave them ample opportunity to practice. While there were many fewer interruptions, I felt that their newfound "tolerance" for one another's opinions was more superficial than real. Then there was a turning point.

The conversation turned to the management abilities of one member of the team. There was a heated discussion, with radically different opinions on both sides. I stopped the conversation and asked them to switch from talking about "how the manager really is" to "your experience with the manager."

The consequences of this small change were remarkable. As each person told his or her experience with this manager, it became clear to all participants that the person in question behaved differently in different situations and that they were all partly "right" about him. When customers were present, he tended to act condescending to employees; with the boss present, he was formal and kept himself at a distance; one on one with direct reports, he was warm and supportive. The point I wish to make is that this complex view of "the real situation" and the excellent solutions that were tried as a result *did not and could not come out of the traditional kind of "meeting" common to most organizations.* It was only when people spoke from and listened to others' experiences that the fullest range of information about the situation became available. In the world of ideas and opinions, differences in experience get inappropriately transformed into differences of opinion, which in turn the group may try to "resolve."

In summary, Harrison has sounded the alarm for a more thoroughgoing consideration of alternative kinds of interdependence. She has described in detail some of the democratic organizational forms that are being tried today and drawn important distinctions among companies that might otherwise appear similar. Finally, she has opened the door for an analysis of the specific communication practices that constitute democratic organizing. I offer dialogue as one potentially fruitful practice; there are surely many others to be explored.

References

Barley, S. (1986). Technology as an occasion for structuring: Evidence from observations of CT scanners and the social order of radiology departments. *Administrative Science Quarterly, 31,* 78–108.

Bellah, R., Madsen, R., Sullivan, W., Swidler, A., & Tipton, S. (1991). *The good society.* New York: Knopf.

Clegg, S. (1989). *Frameworks of power.* Newbury Park, CA: Sage.

Deetz, S. (1992). *Democracy in an age of corporate colonization.* Albany: State University New York Press.

Drucker, P. (1993, February 2). A turnaround primer. *Wall Street Journal.*

Eisenberg, E., & Goodall, H. L. (1993). *Organizational communication: Balancing creativity and constraint.* New York: St. Martin's Press.

Eisler, R. (1987). *The chalice and the blade.* San Francisco: HarperCollins.

Elden, M., & Levin, M. (1991). Cogenerative learning: Bringing participation into action research. In W. F. Whyte (Ed.), *Participatory action research* (pp. 127–142). Newbury Park, CA: Sage.

Evered, R., & Tannenbaum, R. (1992). A dialog on dialog. *Journal of Management Inquiry, 1,* 43–55.

Giddens, A. (1984). *The constitution of society.* Berkeley: University of California Press.

Harrison, T. (1994). Communication and interdependence in democratic organizations. In S. Deetz (Ed.), *Communication Yearbook, 17* (pp. 247–274). Newbury Park, CA: Sage.

Lawler, E. (1986). *High involvement management.* San Francisco: Jossey-Bass.

Meyer, J., & Rowan, B. (1977). Institutionalized organizations: Formal structure as myth and ceremony. *American Journal of Sociology, 83,* 340–363.

Morgan, G. (1986). *Images of organization.* Newbury Park, CA: Sage.

Osterberg, R. (1992). A company without hierarchy. *At Work: Stories of Tomorrow's Workplace, 1,* 9–10.

Perrow, C. (1986). *Complex organizations: A critical essay* (3rd ed.). New York: Random House.

Peters, T. (1987). *Thriving on chaos.* New York: Knopf.

Redding, W. C. (1985). Stumbling toward identity: The emergence of organizational as a field of study. In R. McPhee & P. Tompkins (Eds.), *Organizational communication: Traditional themes and new directions* (pp. 15–54). Beverly Hills, CA: Sage.

Riley, P. (1983). A structurationist account of political cultures. *Administrative Science Quarterly, 28,* 414–437.

Weick, K. (1979). *The social psychology of organizing* (2nd ed.). Reading, MA: Addison-Wesley.

Wellins, R., Byham, W., & Wilson, J. (1991). *Empowered teams.* San Francisco: Jossey-Bass.

8

A Communication Perspective on Interorganizational Cooperation and Inner-City Education

This essay presents the argument for the usefulness of ambiguity to a different audience: educational scholars and practitioners. The paper is notable for its accessible style and bold counter-rational claims about the (un)importance of clarity and understanding in effective coordination.

At this point, I was becoming frustrated with the lack of response to what I thought were controversial essays; if people were reacting to my work, they certainly weren't doing it in print. So I took my show on the road, attending a range of conferences outside of (but related to) the communication field to determine what impact I might have. In addition, I took a more strident tone to see if I could stir up some response. The particular conference featuring this paper eventually decided to publish selected essays (including this one) in an edited book.

SOURCE: Eisenberg, E. (1995). A communication perspective on interorganizational cooperation and inner-city education. In. L. Rigsby et al. (Eds.), *School/community connections: Exploring issues for research and practice* (pp. 101–120). San Francisco: Jossey-Bass. Copyright © 1995, Jossey Bass. Reprinted with permission of John Wiley & Sons, Inc.

As a society and as a species, we have entered an age of limits. Whereas past generations were afforded the slack to make bad decisions and still survive—even thrive—we no longer have this luxury. Shrinking resources have led managers and administrators to seek ways (and the rhetoric is by now painfully familiar) to "do more with less" and to "work smarter, not harder." Of course, for some people scarce resources have always been a way of life. What is different now is the near-universal scarcity of resources across every type of organization and industry, from hospitals and schools to private businesses and government agencies (Eisenberg & Goodall, 1993).

When times are tough, one natural tendency is to pull together to support one another. The 1990s have thus far been marked by an explosion in joint ventures, partnerships, and strategic alliances that shows no sign of abating. A fair conclusion would be that in good times, plentiful resources permit agencies and organizations to conduct their business independently with little concern for one another. Given scarce resources, however, interorganizational cooperation becomes essential as a means of managing a turbulent organizational environment.

While noble in concept, interorganizational cooperation is risky business in practice. The success rate of such partnerships, whether private-private, public-private, or public-public, is in fact quite low. Interorganizational arrangements share a common characteristic: they require participating organizations to give up some degree of autonomy in exchange for the potential synergies and rewards that may come from the partnership. Once this reality of collaboration becomes clear to all parties, there is often a steady withdrawal from cooperation and communication. Consequently, the number of organizations that consider various forms of interorganizational arrangements far exceeds the number that actually goes through with them. Over time, the actual realized benefits from cooperation fail as a rule to outweigh the considerable costs. For these reasons, I am tempted to begin with the assertion that interorganizational cooperation *does not* work, and to consider instead some fundamentally different alternatives.

This view seems overly pessimistic, however, particularly in light of Carol Truesdell's comments (1995). In regard to her work with the Minneapolis Youth Trust, she feels a "real readiness for doing something radically different," and that frustration is reaching such a level that the "need to cooperate is greater than any sacrifices that may be required" (p. 151). A similar sort of hopefulness is associated with the New Beginnings program in San Diego, where preliminary data collection on interagency collaboration revealed that change was necessary since service delivery agencies could hardly do any worse than current arrangements. While I share this perception of the growing motivation for change, I realize that there are not as yet reliable models for successful interorganizational cooperation. More to the point, I will argue in this chapter that interorganizational cooperation may indeed be possible, but only if we come to think differently about how and why it might work. Specifically, *current approaches to interorganizational cooperation are based on fundamentally flawed ways of thinking about the nature of effective communication, and of the relationship between communication and coordinated action.* An alternate view of these processes will allow us to foster interorganizational arrangements that have a greater chance of success.

Historically, the dominant approach to interorganizational cooperation has been a rational one, based on an ideologically motivated, modernist view of communication that values agreement, openness, and prospective planning as the preferred route to coordinated action (Eisenberg, 1984, 1990). The payoff from this approach has been minimal. As an alternative, I offer a *counter-rational* approach to cooperation, one that values dialogue, diversity of experience, and coordinated action over agreement and open communication. Specific implications for school-community connections are offered throughout.

Rational Approaches to Interorganizational Cooperation

Traditionally, interorganizational cooperation is viewed as an attempt by one or more organizations to address perceived uncertainty in the environment. Two models have been applied to understanding the process of interorganizational cooperation: *resource flow and information flow.* The resource flow model "treats environments as consisting of resources for which organizations compete . . . the process through which information about environments is apprehended by decision-makers is not given much attention" (Aldrich, 1979, p. 110). By contrast, the information flow model "relies heavily on theories of perception, cognition, and decision making, focusing on environment as seen through the eyes of organizational members" (Aldrich, 1979, p. 110).

Many types of information and resource flows can be established between organizations. In manufacturing organizations, a common strategy is to promote vertical linkages between assembly houses and suppliers to ensure a reliable flow of high-quality parts and sub-assemblies. Among service organizations, horizontal linkages are more common. Agencies involved in treating cancer patients, for example, may cooperate to make it easier for an individual to navigate the journey from the screening clinic to a physician, then to a hospital, and finally to a hospice or support group for cancer survivors. Schools may cooperate with community-based social service agencies to increase the likelihood that disadvantaged students come to classes physically and emotionally prepared to learn.

It is misleading, of course, to consider interorganizational linkages as if they were all the same. In an earlier study (Eisenberg et al., 1985), my colleagues and I devised a classification scheme identifying three levels of interorganizational cooperation. First, an *institutional* linkage occurs when information or resources are exchanged between organizations without the immediate involvement of specific organizational roles or personalities (for example, data exchange between bank computers). These types of exchanges are becoming much more frequent. Second, a *representative* linkage occurs when a person who officially represents one organization has contact with the official representative of another organization (for example, a labor union leader meets with a school principal to work out a job training program). These contacts are common, and the emphasis is on the official nature of the individual's purpose and roles. Third, a *personal* linkage occurs when an individual from one organization exchanges information or resources with someone in another organization but in a non-representative and unofficial capacity (for example, friendship, kinship, old-school ties). Personal linkages, while risky and difficult to control, are at times the most likely source of successful cooperation.

The level at which the linkage between organizations takes place is only one way of characterizing differences among types of collaboration. Michael Grady makes the excellent suggestion that, at least in the realm of school-community connections, there are many different "flavors" of interorganizational relationships. Specifically, Grady argues that such ventures can be classified along a continuum, reflecting the extent to which each participating organization is required to change its "deep structure" in order to cooperate. For example, one kind of school/industry partnership might simply provide information and role models for students through a guest speakers program, necessitating no significant changes on the part of either the school or the business. Alternatively, a business might offer an extensive scholarship and apprenticeship program for students, but only on the condition that the school revamps its curriculum (as well as its methods of evaluation) to better prepare students for the business world. This latter arrangement would require much more substantial change on each partner's behalf. Collaborative ventures requiring deep structure changes are more likely to fail, but are also most likely to bring about breakthroughs in large-scale systems change.

Whatever the degree of change required, underlying the traditional approach to interorganizational cooperation is the belief that interorganizational arrangements are undertaken for mainly rational reasons, with each agency attempting to maximize its own goals while at the same time giving up as little autonomy as possible. In some cases, entire communities

(Ackoff, 1981) and industries (Emery & Trist, 1965) have come together to develop superordinate goals and plan methods of cooperation. Such efforts are rational and prospective, and involve, in general, the identification of key stakeholders, joint definition of the problem, and a commitment to reach agreement on a chosen course of action. The practical value of each of these activities is critiqued in the next section.

Critique of the Rational Approach

With rare exception, the rational approach to interorganizational cooperation is problematic. The difficulties are by now quite familiar to those who have tried it:

• Differences in professional training and background result in widely divergent values and priorities, expressed as incommensurable vocabularies (that is, the stakeholders don't "speak the same language").

• Fear of loss of autonomy leads to stalling and an unwillingness to carry through on planned actions, especially when deep structure changes are called for.

• In general, there is an "inefficiency" of cross-professional dialogue that results from misguided attempts to reach agreement on values, beliefs, and terminology.

This is the problem in a nutshell: efforts to lead diverse groups toward agreement on core values or assumptions naturally result in a focus on differences, which are often divisive (Weick, 1979); in watered-down plans that can amount to bad compromises satisfying no one; and in a lack of follow-through on actions, since once the planning is over, it is very hard to apply these agreements back in each organization's specific culture.

I have seen the rational approach to interorganizational cooperation fail dramatically in a number of different settings; two examples are especially memorable. In the early 1980s, the National Cancer Institute funded the Metropolitan Detroit Cancer Control Project (MDCCP) to improve coordination across diverse professions dealing with cancer in Detroit. The grant was made for a five-year period. Initial obstacles to communication were significant—physicians and hospital administrators felt little motivation to speak with members of social service organizations with vastly different training, status, and goals. Nevertheless, new linkages were forged among these individuals, discussions were held, cooperative plans were made, and a sense of hopefulness pervaded the community—until the money ran out. The fourth and fifth years of the grant were marked by a rapid retreat from cooperation to renewed isolation. By the time the five years was up, although a few improvements were made, one was hard-pressed to find evidence that the project had ever happened.

A second experience with the limitations of the rational approach to cooperation involved a federally funded seminar to promote school-industry collaboration on student career readiness. I remember this work-shop especially well because I was co-facilitator. Rather than identify and discuss the differences in values and opinions between labor leaders and sixth-grade teachers, I struggled to keep the focus on joint actions that could be implemented immediately. We had two excellent days to work, until the senior project manager showed up. He opened the final session by asking people to "communicate openly" and to share their strongest feel-ings about how well things were working in the field and about what needed to change. Things degenerated quickly into a shouting match, with each "side" blaming the other, mouthing well-worn positions. I was appalled to see the fragile connections that had been built for two days bro-ken apart; but the project manager thought the outcome was somehow healthy in that at least now they had "cleared the air."

I fear these examples are typical. The reason the rational approach is so difficult to implement is because it is grounded in faulty models of human communication that also pervade American culture. Specifically, it is based on the following three assumptions, which I discuss in turn: (1) the goal of "effective" communication is to reach agreement; (2) effective communica-tion is open and honest; and (3) it is best to plan before you act.

Effective communication seeks to reach agreement. The idea that organiza-tions should communicate to create shared assumptions, values, and beliefs gained popularity in the 1980s, with the publication of Peters and Waterman's (1982) *In Search of Excellence* and Deal and Kennedy's (1982) *Corporate Cultures.* Overnight, businesspeople were talking about the benefits of "strong cultures," homogenous monoliths characterized by a high degree of value consensus. It did not take long, however, to see the problems and abuses that accompany such a commitment to agreement, such as the loss of diver-sity and the potential for groupthink. Many of Peters and Waterman's excel-lent companies have failed, or have been tagged as unpleasant places to work. What is more, the desire to resolve differences and to strive for agreement (rather than learning to live with differences) has been recognized as peculiarly American and far from the standard worldwide (Moore, 1983). Most impor-tant, the idea of a "strong" culture was dismissed as a folk notion borrowed from anthropology with little supporting evidence for either its actual prevalence or effectiveness. In contrast, some extraordinary examples of coordinated action can occur under conditions of limited agreement and shared understanding (Eisenberg, 1990). People can understand, appreciate, and respect one another's experiences and worldviews *without* seeking agreement.

Effective communication is open and honest. Closely allied with the drive for agreement is an ideology of openness that pervades American social life (Eisenberg & Witten, 1987). The ideology of openness says that (despite considerable research and lived experience to the contrary—see Bochner, 1982) effective communication is open, clear, and honest. In real organizations, however, closed communication is as a rule rewarded over open communication (Conrad, 1983). Nevertheless, people maintain the ideal of openness as the best way to approach organizational communication. But there is neither the time nor often a good reason to be open in organizational communication (Parks, 1982). Openness reveals differences that are not easily resolvable and may consequently lead to paralysis. In opening up fully to one another, we may lose the ability to act together.

Planning is key to the rational interorganizational project. The complete argument goes something like this: effective cooperation depends on getting the right people together to communicate openly and build a shared understanding that will serve as a basis for action. While there is considerable anecdotal evidence to suggest that planning actually works, research has in many cases supported just the opposite—that people act first, then make sense of their actions later. Karl Weick (1979) calls this "retrospective sensemaking" and argues that, in many cases, people figure out what they think only *after* seeing what they do and say. In other words, plans are myths, or "useful fictions." Things rarely work out as planned.

It has been my experience that, counter to rational arguments, an emphasis on open communication, a drive toward agreement, and a desire to plan before acting can create more roadblocks to effective interorganizational cooperation than they remove. The rational approach might be classified as modernist in that it puts faith in rational thought and discourse to solve the problems at hand. By contrast, I wish to offer a counter-rational, postmodern view of interorganizational cooperation, one that focuses less on planning, agreement, and open communication and more on coordinated action.

A Counter-Rational Alternative

In my experience, effective interorganizational cooperation does not require shared purposes, common goals, common language, an agreed-on plan, or even open communication. Instead, it requires a commitment to coordinated action. Although this commitment *can* be reached through fostering agreement on goals, plans, and beliefs, this may in fact be the most difficult approach—sort of like climbing the sheer face of a mountain when there is a well-maintained road that runs up the other side. Attempts at fostering agreement may be motivated more by ideology than pragmatics, the result of an unquestioned set of beliefs about communication. But aren't there alternative routes to coordinated action?

I am sure you will have noticed by now that I have avoided using the word *consensus* thus far in this chapter, since the concept is often misunderstood in important ways. The technical definition of consensus is "agreement to implement," which is not the same as agreement on a set of values, beliefs, or assumptions. While this definition of consensus allows for coordinated action despite diverse ideas and opinions, the term is usually applied incorrectly to mean a process of reaching unanimous agreement. I have no problem with consensus building that seeks as its primary goal the cultivation of *sufficient* understanding to permit coordinated action. I do object when consensus is used as a synonym for unanimity.

Following are guidelines that I have used effectively to promote collaboration that does not depend on agreement, openness, or a common plan.

Begin with the client's voice. The goal of many interorganizational efforts is to have a positive impact on the perceptions and experience of the end user or client. One good way to build this goal into cooperative efforts is to begin by introducing to the stakeholder group the *voice* of these clients' experience. This tactic also minimizes irrelevant tangents and professional crosstalk. If inner-city families are the concern, begin the meeting with *their* talk, through interviews, ethnography, films, tapes, or even better, *their participation in person.* For example, conferences on education could as a matter of course begin with the testimony of students. Conferences on the reproductive choices of unwed Latino women could include such women. Make the language and priorities of the end user the common denominator for the group.

The effects of such a shift in perspective are significant, with two implications being especially notable. First, when this approach is adopted, the burden of "translation"—from technical to non-technical language—is where it should be: with the service provider. Technical language either gets demystified through such an encounter or is revealed to be superfluous. Second, including the client in the conversation influences *how and where* such conversations take place. This process alone is instructive, as the coordinating groups are forced to address some of the obstacles facing their target population (for example, transportation, child care) in an immediate way.

Postpone master plans. Explicitly and purposefully avoid drafting any master plan of interorganizational cooperation. Table, defer, and filibuster all attempts to do so. Focus instead on small, definable, achievable joint actions— "small wins"—that over time will build upon each other (Weick, 1979). Reorient your definition of success to mean incremental action sustained over a long period of time. Commit yourself to celebrating these successes, and to identifying them publicly as "wins," examples of how cooperation can work.

Once significant progress has been made, then and only then should a plan be constructed, when it is no longer a threat to action and will at the same time inform others (and yourself) about what you have been doing all along. In this sense, planning in interorganizational efforts is a kind of "retrospective sense-making" (Weick, 1979) wherein the stakeholders create a story about how well they worked together (and how they didn't). The actual nature of cooperation is, of course, quite unlike this "plan." Instead, it is lumpy, serendipitous, messy, and unpredictable. This should not be seen as a problem since the formulation of better up-front plans does not make the coordination process more rational or manageable in any case.

Cultivate weak ties. One of the first steps people take in orchestrating an interagency effort is to make a list of the key stakeholders who must be involved in the planning process. As is the case in the private sector, within any reasonably defined community or region of the country, the same people keep showing up on such lists. These are the "movers and shakers" in industry, government, and education who have the expertise to make such a program work, and/or the power and influence to promote it (or potentially stop it).

A problem exists, however, if coordination efforts are limited to these "key players." Mark Granovetter (1973) found that for many organizational decisions, the people you think of first—those who are most familiar with the issue at hand—are also least useful in providing critical, novel information needed to make good decisions. This is because these "strong ties" already share the same knowledge base, and most likely have access to information that is already familiar to you.

Consequently, in contemplating any interorganizational effort, first make a list of the twenty or so "key players" who are most identified with the issue. Then set this list aside. Next, make a list of twenty other intelligent, powerful people in (and outside) the community who are at most tangentially related to the problem at hand. Spend your time cultivating them.

Create joint plots. Walter Fisher (1987) argues that humans operate using "narrative rationality" more than formal logic. In other words, what is of primary importance in human decision making is whether the "story" being told rings true. View the task of interorganizational cooperation not as one of fostering agreement among people speaking diverse vocabularies, but rather as an effort to craft a joint plot or story that all agencies and organizations will find resonant. Stress experience over ideas—both the experience of the end clients or users and the experiences of the various professionals. Write in prose what the "story of their cooperation" might look like, and avoid attempts to move the conversation to abstract ideas, values, or commitments. Be tolerant of subplots that run in different directions; the story should work like a web that weaves together experience without declaring any one individual or group's account superior (there is more on this point in the final section on dialogue).

This idea also works well with pictures. I once saw a cartoonist document the past, present, and potential future of an organization on a long sheet of paper hung across a huge wall. All the critical events that contributed to the development of the organization were there, along with the likenesses of key people. The result was that people focused more on the fact that there was a coherent story that they could all refer to and laugh about than they did on their specific interpretations of key individuals or events.

Act globally, reap locally. An overly narrow focus on the defined problem and the most immediately affected population may blind us to broader social patterns that hinder cooperation. Always keep your project out in front of you, bigger than whatever problem you are working on at the moment. Rather than focus on the constituency of interest (for example, stressed families from the inner city), try addressing a broader client population than you are directly interested in serving (for example, the Korean-American community). Working at higher levels of generality can help build political support for change. Some believe, for example, that the social programs of the 1960s had limited success because they focused too narrowly on the poor to gain a significant political constituency. In addition, envisioning a different client population from the one you think you are targeting works similarly to cultivating weak ties—it opens you up to a far greater number of ideas and possibilities than you might uncover otherwise.

Cultivate boundary spanners. One important legacy of open systems theory is the conception of organizations as existing in continuous interaction with environments across permeable boundaries (see Adams, 1980). Some jobs are especially focused on communication across boundaries. For example, a social worker or parole officer who has most of his or her contacts with individuals outside the organization is clearly a boundary spanner. In for-profit organizations, receptionists, salespeople, customer service representatives, and market researchers are all examples of boundary spanners.

It is important to remember that boundary spanners have significant power because they provide a communication linkage between disparate groups. Unfortunately, their training and development is often neglected by their employers. This is why the reputation of a multimillion-dollar bank, for example, can be adversely affected by the poor communication skills of a single teller or telephone receptionist who is earning minimum wage.

Similarly, in interorganizational efforts, new interfaces among organizations are often worked out at the higher levels, but rarely taken into account are the boundary spanners who will actually facilitate the day-to-day connections. For example, a high school may have an arrangement with a job training program to refer their non-college-bound students for job-specific training. The specific people who will make the arrangement work—teachers, guidance counselors, secretaries, administrators and their assistants—must all be involved and informed (especially about the ways in which their jobs will change) to ensure the greatest likelihood of success. Boundary spanners may be identified through communication network analysis (see Monge & Eisenberg, 1987) and explicitly involved in planning and implementing the details of the collaboration.

Think the unthinkable. Whether or not you are willing to buy into this idea, I would nevertheless urge you to spend at least some time considering seriously the statement I made earlier—that interorganizational cooperation and cross-professional dialogue is impossible. If this were a true statement, what would you do then? This way of thinking refocuses your energies on the goals of cooperation, when all too often we get caught up in the politics of the process, which are not at all the concern of the clients or end users. For reasons I have already suggested, the likelihood of successful interorganizational cooperation is sufficiently low that if viable alternatives exist, they should be carefully considered.

Foster dialogue. Adopting a counter-rational approach to interorganizational communication does not mean avoiding communication or regarding interaction as futile—quite the contrary. This is the key difference: instead of seeing communication as a tool for building shared attitudes, values, or beliefs, one can see communication as *dialogue.* But what are the defining characteristics of interorganizational dialogue? The three dimensions of dialogue that I consider to be most important have to do with equalization of voice, empathy for another's perspective, and respect for another's experiences (Eisenberg & Goodall, 1993). I discuss each of these in turn.

First, at the outset of any interorganizational effort, it is a given that some people's voices will "count" more than others. In fact, the systematic exclusion of the client population from such sessions is an extreme case of this phenomenon. But even among invited participants, preexisting power relations often lead to uneven participation. The first step in establishing dialogue is to promote and allow for equalization of participant voices through the strategic use of facilitation techniques and the agenda. A necessary but not sufficient condition for interorganizational dialogue is that all parties have a comparable opportunity to speak.

Second, interorganizational dialogue requires participants to empathize with others' positions and perspectives. The most common obstacle to cooperation is the individual's entrenched belief that his or her worldview is the only correct one. In practice, a change in this area requires participants to be trained in active listening skills so they may get beyond the initial resistance that naturally comes from being exposed to a different position from their own. Empathy is another necessary but not sufficient condition for dialogue, although it is harder to achieve than comparable opportunities for voice, since it exists in the realm of emotions and egos.

The third step in cultivating interorganizational dialogue regards the treatment of personal experience in conversation. The key notion here is that fostering dialogue is not so much about sharing ideas as it is a way of cultivating experience. Much too often, participants treat conversations with each other as a kind of free market of ideas in which different perceptions are in competition with one another and the goal is to advance one's own perspective at the expense of all others. In the process, people rarely speak directly from experience.

Alternatively, in dialogue people speak from their experience and listen for the experiences of others. In this way, dialogue is additive; each new experience that is recounted is a contribution to the whole, and no individual's remarks invalidate what has come previously. The result is a varied collection of multiple "voices" that form a richly textured account of "how things really are" without forcing adherence to any one viewpoint or perspective (Eisenberg & Goodall, 1993). What is more, there is no goal of integration of experience, and such attempts at synthesis are resisted. In dialogue, what is fostered is not agreement but mutual understanding; interestingly, it is this mutual understanding and respect that is most likely to lead to coordinated action. In dialogue, participants feel they have had their say, feel their voices have been heard, feel they have truly heard others, and despite apparent differences, are ready to work together.

Interorganizational dialogue is possible—I have seen it work. What is needed to make it work is an advocate or group of advocates who encourage the expression of experience by all participants, including clients, and discourage attempts to reach agreement that are based on the devaluation of some individuals' experience. This is another way of saying that the mechanics of valuing "diversity" occur in communication, and with repetition become normative within a group. What is most needed (and most difficult, it must be said) is a shift away from arguments over ideas and values toward the expression of experience, away from plans for action and toward acting in the absence of plans.

Needless to say, dialogue "feels" very different from the typical arguments and debates among stakeholders, and if judged by modernist standards, seems unfocused and unresolved. What is most persuasive from my perspective, however, is that successful and sustained joint action follows more surely from dialogue rooted in diversity and mutual understanding than it does from traditional attempts at fostering agreement.

Implications for School-Community Connections

The document outlining the purpose of the conference for which [this chapter was] originally written underscores the need to "mobilize school and community resources in the service of children and youth" (Rigsby, 1992, p. 3). The importance of such an effort is unquestionable. What *can* be questioned further are useful routes to such mobilization. The document reflects further on "the complexities of communication" but concludes that the goal should be "*coherent* [italics added] multiagency support and assistance . . . to the children and their families" (pp. 2–3). Whereas the need for such support is undeniable, I am always skeptical of calls for coherence. The history of many academic disciplines, for example, is an unending struggle for coherence that is in the end unattainable in any specific way due to multiple incommensurable language communities. Preferable to coherence in promoting coordinated action is *cohesiveness*, the willingness to work together in the absence of shared understanding (Bochner & Eisenberg, 1984). In business, and in politics, for me one key to effective coordination is a strategically ambiguous vision or mission, which simultaneously motivates action and permits individuals to retain their idiosyncratic meanings and beliefs (Eisenberg, 1984).

The idea of an improved "cross-professional dialogue" is also mentioned repeatedly in the purpose statement for the conference. This is clearly needed, not just in relationship to this set of issues, but globally in regard to many interest groups. Two things are worth noting about how such a dialogue is operationalized. First, professionalization itself may prove an obstacle to dialogue, both among members of organizations and between such individuals and the stressed population of concern. As mentioned earlier, the common denominator should be the experience and vocabulary of the client. Professionalization is a concept that isolates individuals physically, attitudinally, and linguistically from many kinds of dialogue by erecting disciplinary language barriers. Second, we should consider carefully the precise definition of dialogue that we wish to advocate. As I have described above, dialogue for me has a very specific meaning—it is a conversation that is not oriented toward agreement, but instead toward cultivating the diversity of experience.

And it is precisely this diversity of experience—the fact that people representing businesses, families, churches, schools, and government agencies have partial and different readings of the current situation—that should be the starting point for a productive interorganizational dialogue. A well-meaning sense of urgency may lead us to attempt to orchestrate this dialogue in ways that produce greater openness, agreement, and plans. We should resist these temptations, inasmuch as experience teaches us that such efforts as a rule backfire. Instead, we should concentrate on transforming attempts at interorganizational communication into dialogue, and on promoting coordinated action in the explicit absence of agreement.

References

Ackoff, R. (1981). *Creating the corporate future.* New York: Wiley.

Adams, J. S. (1980). Interorganizational processes and organization boundary activities. *Research in Organizational Behavior, 2,* 321–355.

Aldrich, H. (1979). *Organizations and environments.* Englewood Cliffs, NJ: Prentice Hall.

Bochner, A. (1982). The functions of human communication in interpersonal bonding. In C. Arnold & J. Bowers (Eds.), *Handbook of rhetoric and communication theory* (pp. 544–621). Newton, MA: Allyn & Bacon.

Bochner, A., & Eisenberg, E. (1984). Legitimizing speech communication: An examination of coherence and cohesion in the development of the discipline. In T. Benson (Ed.), *Speech communication in the 20th century* (pp. 299–321). Carbondale: Southern Illinois University Press.

Conrad, C. (1983). Organizational power: Faces and symbolic forms. In L. Putnam & M. Pacanowsky (Eds.), *Communication and organizations: An interpretive approach* (pp. 173–194). Newbury Park, CA: Sage.

Deal, T., & Kennedy, A. (1982). *Corporate cultures.* Reading, MA: Addison-Wesley.

Eisenberg, E. (1984). Ambiguity as strategy in organizational communication. *Communication Monographs, 51*(3), 227–242.

Eisenberg, E. (1990). Jamming: Transcendence through organizing. *Communication Research, 17*(2), 139–164.

Eisenberg, E., Farace, R. V., Monge, P., Bettinghaus, E., Kurchner-Hawkins, R., Miller, K., & Rothman, L. (1985). Communication linkages in inter-organizational systems: Review and synthesis. In M. Voight & B. Dervin (Eds.), *Progress in communication science* (Vol. 6, pp. 231–261). Norwood, NJ: Ablex.

Eisenberg, E., & Goodall, H. L. (1993). *Organizational communication: Balancing creativity and constraint.* New York: St. Martin's Press.

Eisenberg, E., & Witten, M. (1987). Reconsidering openness in organizational communication. *Academy of Management Review, 12*(3), 418–426.

Emery, F., & Trist, E. (1965). The causal texture of organizational environments. *Human Relations, 18*(1), 21–32.

Fisher, W. (1987). *Human communication as narration: Toward a philosophy of reason, value, and action.* Columbia, SC: University of South Carolina Press.

Granovetter, M. (1973). The strength of weak ties. *American Journal of Sociology, 78*(6), 1360–1380.

Monge, P., & Eisenberg, E. (1987). Emergent communication networks. In F. Jablin, L. Putnam, K. Roberts, & L. Porter (Eds.), *Handbook of organizational communication* (pp. 304–342). Newbury Park, CA: Sage.

Moore, M. (1983). Culture as culture. In P. Frost, L. Moore, M. Lewis, C. Lundenberg, & J. Martin (Eds.), *Organizational culture* (pp. 373–378). Newbury Park, CA: Sage.

Parks, M. (1982). Ideology in interpersonal communication: Off the couch and into the world. In M. Burgoon (Ed.), *Communication Yearbook* (Vol. 5, pp. 79–108). New Brunswick, NJ: Transaction Books.

Peters, T., & Waterman, R. (1982). *In search of excellence.* New York: HarperCollins.

Rigsby, L. (1995). *School-community connections: Exploring issues for research and practice.* (Prospectus for a conference on school-community connections. Philadelphia: National Center on Education in the Inner Cities). In L. Rigsby et al. (Eds.), (1995), *School-community connections.* San Francisco: Jossey-Bass.

Truesdell, C. (1995). Commentary: On building trusting and mutually beneficial partnerships. In. L. Rigsby et al. (Eds.), *School/community connections: Exploring issues for research and practice.* San Francisco: Jossey-Bass.

Weick, K. (1979). *The social psychology of organizing* (2nd ed.). Reading, MA: Addison-Wesley.

9

From Anxiety to Possibility

Poems 1987–1997

Although I was always open to exploring the deeper motives for my scholarly perspective in informal conversation with others, I never did so in writing—until the following set of poems. Former doctoral student Steve Banks called to say that he was putting together a collection of alternative forms of scholarly writing, and I signed on without having any idea what I would do. I ultimately sent him a series of poems I wrote about my inner emotional life during the late 1980s and most of the 1990s. Although the poems are open to multiple readings, my sense is that they show something about why I am drawn to a philosophy of communication that features ambiguity and contingency. A second reason I published this work at this time was to encourage my colleagues to explore multiple modes of presentation for their work.

SOURCE: Eisenberg, E. (1998). From anxiety to possibility: Poems 1987–1997. In A. Banks & S. Banks (Eds.), Fiction and Social Research. Copyright © 1998, Lanham, MD: AltaMira Press.

If I were to wish for anything, I should not wish for wealth and power, but for the passionate sense of potential—for the eye which, ever young and ardent, sees the possible. Pleasure disappoints; possibility, never.

—Søren Kierkegaard

In this late modern era, each of us lives in the shadows of numerous powerful institutions and organizations. These institutions and organizations both constrain and enable our behavior, and in so doing provide us with a sense of identity. Claiming to be a lawyer, teacher, mother, or baseball fan asserts a recognizable identity along with a code of conduct (and a broad set of practices) which make that role intelligible. What is more, each of us maintains multiple memberships of this kind, giving rise to contradictions. How can I be a good teacher, father, son, spouse, sibling, and citizen—all at the same time? How can I cope with the sometimes competing emotional, spiritual, professional, sexual, and political expectations associated with each institutional field?

We usually strive to make our professional roles and performances appear seamless. Framed this way, I have spent the last twenty years learning about communication in organizations, with the goal of becoming an effective change agent. During this time, I worked with a dozen or so organizations and other institutions, including aerospace manufacturers, medical centers, local governments, hotels, and high schools. In each case, my singular goal was to improve the internal communication of these organizations to help them become more effective.

But this shiny summary hides much about my personal development as a change agent. When I began this work, I acted mostly as a facilitator, and regularly doubted my qualifications. What could I possibly know that would be useful to my clients, who for the most part had been in business for decades? Over time, and with the help of key mentors and partners, I came to realize that I did possess a particular knowledge of human relationships that was both rare and helpful to business executives. As a consequence, in 1990 I began identifying myself as an "expert" in communication and organizational change. While at some level I understood that my expertise was based more on trial and error than on any inviolate truths, this shift helped both me and my clients to relax. Today, I have softened this position somewhat, as my experience speaks for itself. I partner with organizational leaders and share stories about what has (and has not) worked for me in the past, and they use this knowledge to advance their own learning. Most of the time, it works.

But how much easier it is to forge these partnerships in Florida, where I have lived since 1993, than it was in Los Angeles! Another way of telling my story is in terms of the impact of a peculiarly amoral city—and a doubly amoral time—on a confused young man at the beginning of his career. My decade in Southern California was marked by harrowing earthquakes, choking smog, insane greed—and fleeting moments of ecstasy. Success as an Angeleno is directly and unequivocally linked to one's capacity for denial. Mine was strong for a time, but the economic collapse of 1989 revealed the raw trade-offs I had been making. The civil unrest of the early 1990s was the last straw placed on the strained back of an already teetering camel. For three anxious days, I watched the fires on television and smelled the smoke through my back window. Once the curfew was lifted, I returned to the university and encountered block after block of burned-out buildings. Driving those streets, I slumped down in my car seat and, for the first time in my life, seriously considered getting a gun. It clearly was time to go. Shortly after I moved to Florida, my advisor's house in Malibu burned to the ground and my old condominium in Santa Monica was badly damaged by an earthquake (but still not "The Big One").

But even this detailed story fails to reflect key aspects of what really happened. During these same two decades I got married, my mother died, and my two sons were born. My mother's messy death from emphysema produced what was for me a profound crisis of anxiety, depression, and self-doubt, followed by two years of weekly psychotherapy augmented by biofeedback, aromatherapy, personal trainers, and kundalini yoga (it was, after all, LA!). In retrospect, from 1985 to 1989 I was perpetually on the verge of a nervous breakdown, although you wouldn't know it from my *Vita* or from how I looked to my students and clients at the time.

The energy one spends keeping the story together! All too often, the face we show to the world masks deep truths about what animates our behavior. Each day of the last twenty years I have been confronted with hard choices that test my resolve to become the person I would most like to be— joyful, honest, authentic, humble, and firmly connected to the world. But each interaction, whether with a student, client, colleague, or family member, still resonates with possibility, both positive and negative. Will I tell the whole truth today? Why am I speaking with this person? Where am I going? Is this my path? Does it have a heart?

The ten poems that follow were written during this turbulent time. While I "accomplished" many things during these years (again, see the *Vita*), these poems are the sole record of the interior struggle with anxiety that energized my outer activities. Seen this way, they are a view from the bottom of a deep pool from which you can barely see the surface. These poems reflect the submerged truths of my experience during this period, which suggest connections among the various aspects of my emotional, spiritual, and professional life. For me, these connections were mostly about replacing an overly rational, prospective, and strategic view of life with a more unstructured, improvisational, and contingent one, all the while maintaining a continuity of values that would form the basis of my new, much-expanded identity.

You may be wondering: Why poetry? For me, writing this way was less a movement toward something new and more a recovery of something old, which, thankfully, had not yet completely disappeared. Poetry was my constant companion since grade school, where an immense, angry English teacher had accused me of plagiarizing e.e. cummings when I experimented with lower-case letters. Somehow, I persisted. I was a poetry major for a year at Rutgers College, where my writing improved and my teachers—working poets themselves—encouraged me to pursue a career in creative writing. I was deeply flattered.

But in the end, I did not choose the path of the poet. Despite the sheer joy I experienced exploring the perverse mysteries of Eliot and Coleridge, Donleavy and Brautigan, I chose what was for me an even stranger path—not toward text, art, or the life of the mind (which everyone, including my parents, expected) but toward science, commerce, and the empirical world. By my senior year at Rutgers, I had learned how to write. Graduate school training in communication as a social science destroyed all that. In their efforts to substitute rigor for imagination, protocol for substance, theory for story, my professors helped me to forget most of what I really had to say.

Fortunately, the flame was never quite extinguished. The distinction between art and science had always seemed absurd to me, and not really a choice at all. Graduate school prepared me to be an excellent technician: the twenty years since have been a sort of salvage operation aimed at recovering the content of what I want most to contribute.

Which returns us to poetry. The poems that follow are a map of my heart in the world. Each one encodes a feeling or insight that emerged in the middle of a thousand commitments, decisions, dilemmas, and things to do. In this sense, there is no isomorphic relationship between a poem and a client, a person, or even an experience. Instead, they constitute a succinct interpretation of my emotional development as a communication consultant and change agent, marking as they do a kind of interior movement from anxiety of possibility.

I would like nothing more than for these poems to cause you to reflect on your own depths of experience, revealing both the profound ordinariness and the sacred mysteries that animate all of our lives.

L.A. (1987)

L.A. is street cocaine

so pure one day it'll kill you

so whacked speedy the next

you'll want to kill yourself

L.A. is strangled inner child

melanoma waiting to happen

Along The Coast (1988)

There's a fine line

between love and addiction.

There's a fine line

in a world without direction.

There's a long path

from the first step to the mission—

along a very fine line.

When I hold you

my soul comes to the surface.

When I touch you

it's the other side of nervous.

All those people standing in the shadows say

it's a very fine line.

Here in the kitchen I stare at my hands

thinking of love songs and unfinished plans.

Here in my car now I head for the night

the stars and reactors are my guiding light.

Sometimes I wonder

can you lead a double life?

Explored the insides

of a husband and a wife.

The beach is quiet now

as the tide comes rushing in

along a very fine line.

Love's Hometown (1991)

Can this be love's hometown?
A tiny undistinguished suburb
halfway between the zoo and the temple?

Mirror Poem (1991)

Familiar stranger
will you be my friend?
Will you take the way you look to me
and wash it, shave it,
post it in soft light to make me feel at ease?

Each day I spot
you bearded on motorcycle gruff and overdressed
or sexy and distracted
more or less wanton than I can imagine

You confuse me
you scare me
you are me

Brake Light (1990)

Every day is a dance of revelation and denial

of God drenched anxiety—

90 miles per hour down blacktop

with the emergency brake on.

How can I turn toward the truth of my life

without noticing the turn in old ways?

How can I make myself anew?

The cobwebs I sweep aside are my veins

and fearsome spiders reluctant handholds in a brave new world.

Or . . .

Nothing like this, more babies and music

soft words of comfort and the prospect of love

wedged inside this dance of approaching despair—

my happy life.

Tuesday, For Bruce (1991)

Who am I?

If not some strong possibility

born each moment of the world?

Surely not just some old story

of success and failure

triumph and neurosis

alive but already dust.

What I know about life

(is not life)

What I know about myself

(is not me)

I am the clearing in which these sentences exist—

not sentenced

to exist

in this clearing

Morning (1996)

Waking up to the kingdom again
the duties of the day announce themselves
like distant waters
rushing to fill an underground cave.

Only today I hear the surf in time
and before it's too late
swing a heavy green door
in its path.

Morning, now
I dwell for the first time
in the empty space of not knowing,
not doing,
not
caring
about the rising tide.

I am happy.

Between Mars and Venus (1996)

Brown scrub, yellow grass
White bird, spotted cow
Young son asking: What is love?

The Point (1996)

Identify
a golden
opportunity
and miss it.
Being
a human
being
is enough.

Untitled (1997)

Hot day
Cool night
The rest is extra.

10

Openness and Decision Making in the Search for a University Provost

This study used management scholar Joanne Martin's well-known taxonomy of organizational cultures as a tool to deconstruct the usual representations of a major university's search for a new Provost (Chief Academic Officer). Our analysis revealed that participants in the search process articulated multiple versions of what "really" happened in the search, expressed in three alternative narrative forms: integration, differentiation, and fragmentation. Different accounts were chosen for rhetorical reasons and tailored to the audience and the situation. Strategic ambiguity functioned to permit these alternate versions of reality to coexist.

Florida is a great place to study the conflict between the ideology of openness and the practical realities of organizational communication. The Florida Sunshine Laws are among the most radical in the nation and opened nearly every aspect of the provost's search process to public view. As a consequence, we were able to examine closely the specific communication behind the committee's decision making. Although we were shocked at first by what looked like capricious and illogical behavior, we eventually came to believe that most, if not all, complex organizational decisions resemble this one. They simultaneously contain rational, political, and other random elements and can be described in any one of these ways depending upon the situation.

SOURCE: Eisenberg, E. M., Murphy, A., & Andrews, L. (1998). Openness and decision-making in the search for a university provost. *Communication Monographs*, 65, 1–23. Copyright © 1998. Reproduced by permission of Taylor & Francis Group, LLC., http://taylorandfrancis.com.

The past twenty years have been marked by a wide-ranging reconsideration of the structure and purposes of social institutions and organizations. Beginning with the impact of global competition on American manufacturing operations in the 1970s, organizations in every industry have been challenged to reinvent themselves in ways that not only improve quality and reduce costs, but do so in a way that is both dramatic and renewable. Continuous learning is the key to business success in the 1990s.

Just as the pressure to compete transformed the manufacturing sector, similar changes are taking place in the service industries, notably health care and education. Health care practitioners, whose "principles of practice" previously went unchallenged, suddenly find themselves needing to alter their methods of working to adapt to a much constrained economic environment. The development of strict insurance regulations and the rapid emergence of managed care are two of the more obvious indications of this change.

Like hospitals, educational organizations qualify as institutions, i.e., groups that traditionally rely more on perceptions of public legitimacy than on bottom-line performance. Soon after the institutional status of health care organizations was first challenged (making them more accountable for financial performance), educational institutions followed. Like "principles of practice," phrases like "academic freedom" and "liberal education" were now placed in a context of limited resources. The resulting challenge was somehow to preserve the core values of the institution while becoming fiscally and financially competitive.

Leadership is key to facing this challenge. Only an effective leader can provide the operational guidance and the positive symbolic framework to promote the vision and values of the institution in a climate of limited resources (Fairhurst & Sarr, 1995). Consequently, the need for educational leadership in recent years has increased dramatically. Many senior scholars and administrators, understanding the extreme difficulty of the task, are unwilling to serve. Others believe themselves capable of bringing out the best in their institution within a limited financial envelope.

The general question that arises is, how does an educational institution—a university, for example—go about *locating, selecting, and attracting* such leaders? More specifically, what kinds of people do they aspire to hire, how do they find and qualify them for the job, and how do they select the best candidate from those available? What is the nature of the decision-making process? What perspectives do different individuals involved in the search process bring to bear during and after the search? These and related questions motivated us to investigate the dynamics of one university's search for its chief academic officer, the university Provost.

Core Assumptions About Organizational Communication

We approached the Provost search committee's decision-making process from a communication perspective. To this end, we wish to be explicit about our core assumptions regarding organizational communication. The reader will then be able to take our views into account in considering our results.

First, we maintain that communication constitutes organizational reality. In other words, organizational meanings do not exist as "brute data" awaiting discovery; meanings are manufactured rather than found. While the world exists independently, descriptions of the world cannot exist apart from the human mind. Since only descriptions of the world can be true or false, then the world on its own—unaided by the describing activities of human beings—cannot be true or false (Rorty, 1979). Truth is not "out there" waiting to be discovered—it can only be made socially. In this light, we sought to explore how meanings of the search process were manufactured socially through the communicative actions of participants. This process revealed the centrality of "meetings" as sites where organizational meaning is created. In fact, we concur with Schwartzman (1989) that an organization cannot be "understood apart from its meetings that both constitute and maintain it in an unpredictable environment" (p. 8). Organizational participants author their experience through sense-making practices; they generate what they interpret (Weick, 1995).

Second, we believe that all meaning is constructed in local, social, and historical context. Meaning is local, in that what makes sense in one organization can be completely alien to another. It is social, in that meanings are public, not located in individual heads, but rather in dialogue between people (cf., Eisenberg & Goodall, 1997). Meaning is historical, in that past meanings influence present and future interpretations and actions. Given these assumptions, we make no [generalizations] about *all* search processes. When we enlarge experience to the extent that all becomes typical, we risk losing insights into the very contexts that gave rise to the meaning attached to the experience. Therefore, what we offer is a highly situated account of one university search that is both rich in historical detail and exemplifies general macro-processes, such as the interplay between legal constraints and political agendas, common to most if not all searches. Much as we can learn something about the body by studying the hand (Geertz, 1973), we can learn about the nature of human decision making by studying one university's search for a Provost. The specific ways in which these processes are manifested in this search remain to be seen.

Third, we aimed to demonstrate that different groups and individuals construct their view of the search differently and that these alternative descriptions and interpretations compete for acceptance in an ongoing negotiation over definitions of reality. In other words, we expected a "plural present" (Goodall, 1991), in which different views of the search coexist. We were interested in the varying goals and objectives represented by different committee members and how these various interests influenced their interpretations of the process. Our focus, to a large degree, was on search committee meetings and the cultural "baggage" members bring. Following Schwartzman (1989),

> Individuals do not and cannot act outside of communicative events like meetings that they use to generate interaction as well as to interpret what it means (we are chatting, we are playing, we are meeting). It is in these forms, and only in these forms that individuals are able to transact, negotiate, strategize, and attempt to realize their specific aims, but cultural systems and social structures are "bred into" these forms. (p. 37)

We do not, however, suggest that interpretations are clear, unitary, or constant. The link between communicator goals and interpretations is complicated because communicators have multiple and even contradictory goals (e.g., relational and identity goals) in any situation that can influence the direction of discourse (Eisenberg, 1984; Tracy, 1991). In addition to maintaining the integrity of multiple and competing interpretations, we recognize the political aspects of "vying" interpretations—not all participants have an equal voice.

Fourth, we maintain that communication is best defined as the moment-to-moment working out of the tension between individual creativity and organizational constraint (Eisenberg & Goodall, 1997). As we have already argued, communication is a symbolic process whereby organizational reality is produced, maintained, negotiated, and transformed. Although reality is not given a priori, it is constrained by prior actions and predefined typifications of meaning that take on an objective character (Berger & Luckmann, 1967). Therefore, the order by which individuals come to perceive and define their world appears chosen in part *for* them, not by them.

The socially constructed world must be continually and creatively realized by individuals so that it can become and remain their world as well. In terms of the search process, this means that the communicative choices of the search committee at each moment are simultaneously shaped by individual agendas and by legal, organizational, social, and relational constraints. Put differently: "As sense makers and social and cultural validators, meetings play an important role in reconciling the practices of tradition and change, as they may be a place for maintaining tradition, whereas at the same time learning new practices" (Schwartzman, 1989, p. 43). We will show how communicative practices in the search process clearly reflect the balance between forces of creativity and constraint.

Finally, we maintain that no one best way exists to view organizational communication. Instead, communication appears different through different metaphors and lenses (Martin, 1992; Morgan, 1986). One's perceptions are limited by "requisite variety" (Weick, 1995)—we can only perceive as much complexity in our environment as our perceptual frameworks allow. Consequently, one purpose was to complicate our tools for perception to enable us to bring multiple perspectives to the search process. Juxtaposing differing viewpoints, we embrace the "plural present" and, consequently, provide a richer picture of the decision-making process. We feel that this expansion of perspectives is a sound route to developing more useful theoretical and practical lessons about communication.

Research on University Search Processes

Before we address our particular setting, we first review studies that have addressed the nature and effectiveness of processes by which universities search for key administrators. Much of this work is prescriptive, and most of it focuses on the search for a university President. This research is further distinguished by a concern with legal constraints on the decision-making process, notably the "Sunshine Laws" that regulate (on a state-by-state basis) the degree to which search-related communication must be open to the public. Particularly in the more restrictive states (such as Florida), a number of studies have examined the impact of "decision-making in the sunshine" on the Presidential search process.

Much of the literature on academic search processes has a markedly practical bent. A number of articles and books have been published to help guide institutions in their search for a President (McLaughlin & Riesman, 1990; Nason, 1984; Neff, 1992). Similar principles can be applied to the search for a university Provost. These principles, about which there is some consensus, constitute a series of steps in an "ideal search" as outlined in the literature. Following, we review the basic steps common to most searches so that the reader can have a framework to compare the progression of events in our case study with those of an "ideal" search.

According to these guides, the first step in selecting a leader is *to organize a search committee* (McLaughlin & Riesman, 1990; Nason, 1984; Neff, 1992). The most effective committee will consist of nine to ten people.

Next, a *committee chair* must be chosen. This person will "set the tone of the committee, smooth ruffled feelings, cope with any emergencies, and divert political pressures" (Nason, 1984, p. 8). This done, the search committee must *develop the criteria* against which the candidates will be evaluated. This includes both job and leadership criteria.

The next step is to *announce the search*. Individuals can apply directly or be nominated for the position. Nason (1984) points out that "the ideal candidate is functioning successfully in his/her present position and will most likely not respond to advertisements or form letters to apply" (p. 38). Such candidates may need to be wooed (McLaughlin & Riesman, 1990). McLaughlin and Riesman do, however, warn committees not to overpursue; when individuals say no, they may indeed mean it. Naturally, candidates may come from within or outside the university. Internal candidates are sometimes believed to be favored; as a result, good external candidates tend to drop out on the suspicion that an insider already has the position (Nason, 1984).

The next step is to *evaluate the candidates* and cut the initial number to a manageable size. Nason (1984) cautions against cutting too far on the grounds that candidates may withdraw and leave the committee short of choices. Nason (1984) further suggests keeping a written record of all oral transactions for future reference. Once the first cut has been determined, the screening process continues. References should be checked and cross-checked. The committee then needs to *narrow the list once more*, preferably to single digits. Some or all of these candidates are next invited *for a campus tour and interview*. The final step is to *recommend candidates* to a Board or President, who will make the final selection. Although this is the recommended process, each search progresses differently according to the individuals involved, the fields of candidates, and the setting and history of the institution.

The Setting

This study was an investigation into the search for the Provost (Chief Academic Officer) of a major university in Florida. To give context to the actions that took place during the search, we describe political, social, and historical forces acting on the committee.

Confidentiality and the Sunshine Laws

Florida is one of about twenty states that have developed "Sunshine Laws" as a reaction to perceived abuse and corruption in the political system. Kaplowitz (1978) defines them as:

statutes that require meetings of public bodies to be held in public. Generally, they include provisions requiring advance public notice as to time, place and agenda items of meetings of public bodies; that such meetings be held open to the public; that the public have some format for contributing to the discussions of issues; and that an official record of such meetings must be available to the public. (p. 2)

Although established as a reaction to perceived abuse in the political system (the majority of these laws were put in place post-Watergate), "Sunshine Laws" have been implicated for contributing to one of the most significant problems associated with a search—violations of confidentiality. McLaughlin and Riesman (1985) note that, "this is one of the most important decisions of the search committee—how will confidentiality be maintained through the search and selection process" (p. 346). The issue of confidentiality is especially problematic in states that operate under governmental regulations requiring searches to be conducted in public.

McLaughlin and Riesman (1989) explored the impact of the "Sunshine Laws" on a Presidential search in Florida. Florida has the most comprehensive "Sunshine Laws" in the nation as applied to institutions of higher learning. Cleveland (1985) lists four ways "Sunshine Laws" typically affect the decision-making process: (1) the public may put pressure on the committee to make a decision before it is ready, (2) peer pressure and fear may cause the committee members to listen to people they would have ordinarily ignored, (3) decisions may be altered because information might be repressed in the open forum, and (4) decisions may change because of power shifts from the committee to the public.

Studies that focus directly on the search process are to be recommended for the way in which they complicate our understanding of how open communications—which reflects ideological commitments—can also have unintended and unwelcome consequences. This conclusion is in line with arguments made more generally about openness in organizational communication (cf., Eisenberg, 1984; Eisenberg & Phillips, 1991; Eisenberg & Witten, 1987). It seems that in university searches, as in communication more generally, the unquestioned acceptance of values such as openness reveals an insensitivity to the potentially ironic consequences of how this communication can occur in practice. Although no one can dispute the public's right to know about the activities and decisions of public institutions, the multiple and problematic effects of openness often go unnoticed. We considered some of these effects in this study.

Institutional History

The university under study is a Comprehensive Research I institution located in a rapidly growing metropolitan area. The university was founded in 1957 with 1,000 students and grew dramatically to nearly 39,000 students by 1995. Growth has brought with it considerable debate about the mission of the institution. Founded mainly as a teaching college, various administrators over the years tried and mostly succeeded to move the mission toward that of a research university. Debates over this issue continue today. The culture of the university feels simultaneously like one of significant value dissensus and of limitless possibility.

The Provost of a university is the chief academic officer. In some ways, the Provost is the most important internal leadership position in a university, since in most universities, the President's job is outwardly-focused, dealing mostly with the public and with regents or trustees. In contrast, the Provost is the "inside" person in charge of academic affairs. The President and Provost must work together to coordinate their internal and external visions and actions.

In the late 1980s, a previous President of this university made a dramatic commitment to becoming a research institution, with a public statement that it would become a "top 25" research university by the year 2000. Not only was this an unlikely time frame for such a significant achievement, many stakeholders were not certain they even endorsed the goal. In time, this vision was discounted by many. The President was limited in his effectiveness, and before long, he stepped down and was replaced by an Interim President.

Prior to leaving his post, the President commissioned a broad study of the university and its administration, guided by an internal steering committee and conducted by an external consulting firm, the twin purposes of which were to diagnose problems resulting from too rapid growth and to develop a sensible focus for the future. As a result of the study, a detailed plan was developed that suggested streamlining the administrative side of the University. At the same time, the search for a new President began.

Feeling an acute need for leadership, the local and university community saw the Presidential search as pivotal. Interest in the search grew when it surfaced that a leading candidate for the position was a well-known, accomplished politician who (while formerly State Commissioner of Education) lacked a doctoral degree (although she held a Master's). Most university Presidents (particularly at major research universities) have a doctorate as the terminal degree, but since this candidate did not, many of the struggles that existed within the culture came to the surface by her nomination. A number of faculty publicly challenged the idea of hiring a President lacking a doctoral degree. In the end, the candidate prevailed and became the next President.

Those who supported the new President's appointment (and most seemed to) nevertheless recognized that she must appoint an exceptionally strong academic Provost to succeed. Shortly after her selection as President, the sitting Provost stepped down. An Interim Provost, then serving a successful term as Dean of Engineering, was appointed to the job. Shortly thereafter, at the instruction of the new President, the Interim Provost convened a search committee to identify a permanent Provost. The committee consisted of 25 members appointed by the university President. Membership included representation from Academic Affairs, Administrative Affairs, Health Services, regional campuses, deans, faculty, the Faculty Senate, staff, the Alumni Association, and graduate and undergraduate students. The Interim Provost was appointed chair of the Provost search committee. In accepting this responsibility, he assured all parties that he would *under no circumstances* be a candidate for the permanent position. It was April of 1994.

Methodology

Our research team consisted of one faculty member, two graduate students, and an undergraduate student, all affiliated with the Department of Communication. Our research process was as follows:

1. We reviewed the research literature on university searches and received approval from the university to conduct study;

2. We reviewed the initial charge given to the search committee by the Chancellor, including the emphasis on conducting all business in the "sunshine";

3. We attended all meetings of the Provost search committee;

4. We attended most of the interview sessions for the final 5 candidates;

5. We interviewed most of the 25 members of the search committee after the final decision had been made and asked for their description and impressions of the process. We also interviewed other university employees who were not members of the search committee when their names were suggested to us by search committee members.

Our belief was that the search process represented an exceptional example of "pure organizing," sense making in a limited time frame with a zero-history group that had both to design its own process and live with the consequences of its decisions. We were not disappointed. From the outset, we were struck by the differences in perspectives, the large discrepancies in perceptions of the search process. Notably, the differences were not so much in specific interpretations of a commonly agreed upon set of events, but rather in the frameworks for describing the search process altogether. Put differently, no single narrative captured "what actually happened" during the search; instead, multiple stories were invented and gained favor in line with individual biases and beliefs. Furthermore, this multiplicity of viewpoints was in no way resolved once a candidate was selected; *vying narratives persisted* despite what others might have seen as unequivocally disconfirming information.

Of course, not every story of the search process we heard was unique. Descriptions and interpretations clustered around some major themes and explanations. To capture these similarities, we used Joanne Martin's (1992) tripartite typology of organizational culture as an organizing framework. According to Martin, there is no one "correct" definition of organizational culture; different phenomena come into view as a result of different ways of seeing. She identifies three general perspectives on organizational culture: integration, differentiation, and fragmentation. Each approach differs in its view of organizational consistency, consensus, and ambiguity. For example, an integration perspective assumes that culture is shared and monolithic. Organizational culture is based on a high level of consistency and consensus in meaning. Ambiguity is excluded or seen as irrelevant—i.e., that which is not shared is not seen as part of the culture.

A differentiation perspective challenges notions of organization-wide agreement by arguing that consensus exists only at the subcultural level. Organizational culture, then, consists of multiple subcultures that may be inconsistent with or conflict with one another. At the same time ambiguity exists outside of the subcultures. Seen this way, organizational culture is comprised of "islands of clarity, surrounded by a sea of ambiguity" (Martin, 1992, p. 13).

A fragmentation perspective takes ambiguity as the *essence* of organizational culture. No consensus is presumed to exist at any organizational level. A fragmentation perspective views culture as a web of ambiguities "in which individuals [are] sporadically and loosely connected by their changing positions on a variety of issues" (p. 153).

We address our research questions concerning the nature of the Provost search through three summary narratives of the search process. Even with the help of Martin's broad framework, constructing the narratives was a struggle. We first attempted to read through each person's responses and sort search committee members according to the three different perspectives, so as to identify a "representative voice" for each person. This was unsuccessful. Over time, we recognized that rarely does one individual present a single perspective. Although each narrative operates from fundamentally different assumptions, the stories are not those of a different set of characters. A single individual was capable of explaining the process as both political and fragmented, usually at different times. This finding has significant implications for identity construction, which we discuss later. Practically speaking, we sorted committee members' statements into the three different types of narratives, while at the same time looking out for any comments that lay outside Martin's typology, as well as for specific instances in which a single individual endorsed multiple perspectives. These individuals, we reasoned, would provide a unique lens through which to view the motivations behind and consequences for taking differing perspectives.

Another complication in constructing narratives was the difference in interpretations held by members of our research team. Like the search committee itself, members of our small group approached the study in different ways. For example, whereas one member was mostly interested in the practical implications of the study for other searches, two others were more

Table 10.1   A Chronological Table of Events

Date	Committee Action
4/5/94	Initial meeting of the search committee (rules, charge, search plan, subcommittee, write and place ads)
8/21/94 (verbal)	Interim Provost decided to enter the race
9/15/94 (official)	
9/16/94	Appointment of new co-chairs
10/7/94	Copying and distributing 127 applicant files, 2/3 of committee sees each file.
10/10/94	Meeting to cut pool from 127 to 16 (the business building meeting)
10/10/94–10/26/94	Reference checking of 16, letters to other 111
10/26/94	Meeting to develop a short list, pool cut from 16 to 6 (the pizza meeting)
12/3–7/94	Interviews with 5; one candidate drops out before interview
1/11–2/3/95	
2/3/95	Final meeting to make recommendations to the President
2/11–14/95	President visits campuses of two finalists. Expectation of a return visit to Branch campuses
3/23/95	Appointment of Provost

interested in exposing the effects of unequal power relationships in the decision-making process. Our own sense-making process, then, revealed elements of both an integration and differentiation perspective. Taking our own advice, we resolved not to minimize or ignore these differences, but rather to pursue them both.

Narrative 1 follows a rational, integration perspective—it is the sanitized, realist tale (Van Maanen, 1988) that might be told to the public or press to inspire confidence in the rationality of the search process—i.e., the best candidates were recruited, rational criteria were developed and fairly applied, and the best candidate was chosen for the job. Interviews and observations revealed many instances of people giving voice to this perspective.

Narrative 2 reflects a differentiation perspective and emphasizes politics and negotiated order, the struggle among competing interests and subcultures for control over outcomes. This story reveals the possible ulterior motives behind various actions and statements, as well as the attempts at control that influenced the decision process.

Finally, *Narrative 3* takes a fragmentation perspective; it emphasizes the ambiguities in the process and how at many points of the process confusion was the rule and rationality the exception. Echoing Martin, our intention is not to present these perspectives as a means for *choosing* among them. Each perspective adds a different way of understanding the search process, and each offers both theoretical and practical lessons about the search (see also Morgan, 1986). To embrace fully the "plural present," our methodology had to parallel our epistemology. By maintaining the integrity of all views in our presentation and analysis of this search process, we challenge other researchers to wear multiple lenses when approaching a study.

Before relating the narratives, we present a table of events. The chronology is important since each of the three perspectives highlights different moments in the process. The reader may wish to refer to this table when reading the various descriptions and interpretations.

Three Views of a University Search Process

Integration Narrative

Several committee members captured the search experience this way: "Overall, we worked expeditiously. The committee was formed last spring, and by late summer we had ads and closing dates with our time lines set up. We were criticized for not working faster, but we obeyed guidelines and worked as quickly as possible." A junior faculty member described the process as "complete": [we] wrote an ad, received applications, divided applications into groups, reviewed, chose 16 people as a medium-sized pool, called references, based on discussion of references selected 6, one dropped out, conducted interviews and campus visits, and then had final meeting for those recommended. The strong point of our process was that the candidates were fairly reviewed in discussion with members of the committee. The people we brought to interview were all good and then the two presented finally were excellent candidates.

Members also described the communication of the committee as "clear." One experienced committee member said the process was "straightforward. The criteria were clear: prior experience and fiscal responsibility, a multi-campus environment or a similar model, and scholarship." Several mentioned that the process was "efficient," with the "procedures spelled out clearly." They felt the chairs "ran the internal and external communication very well." People believed they could express themselves. Some even talked about enjoying "the experience of talking and deliberating over the candidates."

Committee work over the summer was light. With the return of the faculty in the fall, the committee began work in earnest. The Interim Provost/Chair of the Search Committee surprised many people when he decided to "throw his hat into the ring" as a candidate. He said he decided "while thinking that this was the right thing." He had been a strong dean, perhaps the strongest at the university, and had dedicated his career to the institution.

The candidacy of the Interim Provost made it imperative that someone replace him as chair of the search committee. The committee took nominations from the floor, and two faculty agreed to serve, one man and one woman. The woman, a management professor, presided over the remaining meetings. When viewing interaction from an integration perspective, we saw evidence of a strong facilitative chair who "conducted herself with honor." She was most often described as an "outstanding facilitator" who ensured that "everyone participated" and had an opportunity to be heard. Between meetings, she "kept people well informed."

The new co-chairs implemented a committee-wide process to distribute documents as the resumés began pouring in. The easy availability of information ensured candidates a fair hearing and supported the search plan. Copying and distribution were accomplished efficiently and did not rely on people to share documents. Everyone received a separate set of files, and each application was scrutinized by two-thirds of the committee. The committee considered 127 completed applications in all.

Held in the center of the Business Building, a sprawling complex, the first significant evaluation began as the group divided into three subgroups, each

assigned a color name. Each group then discussed its sub-group of appli-
cants and made recommendations. Once the groups re-convened, they
decided it made more sense to decide first which candidates should in no
case be advanced. If anyone disagreed and thought a candidate had potential, the name stayed on the list. The group considered a wide variety of
arguments about each candidate pertaining to his or her range and type of
experience, strength of scholarship, and so on. Said one member:

> I was pleased with the first meeting. We color-coded groups and divided up the
> files. Some groups overlapped, and I think it was as fair a process as possible.
> There was little controversy, and I was amazed at how quickly that was done.
> But I was comfortable with the results. There was an obvious group of people
> who should be carried on who had the background and experience needed.

By the conclusion of the meeting, the 16 best candidates remained.
Rejection letters were sent to the remaining 111. Because the process was
open, it was important to reach them directly before press coverage became
widespread.

The next meeting, referred to as "the pizza meeting" by several committee members, occurred after work at an off-campus location. The pizza
meeting was relatively open and informal, and was preceded by a casual
spread of food, including pizza, cookies, and beverages. "The meeting was
one where criticism was aired, concerns were raised, and some candidates
were resurrected. The Interim Provost was out and then in and then out several times. I was impressed with the debate." This meeting, in particular,
tested the group members' ability to work together, and the speedy progress
bolstered the sense of a fair, rational process. Many left this meeting feeling
it was "one of the most important times—the most significant. We came up
with five [actually six but one dropped out] finalists. We listened to what
others said. We reported back about talking with the references." Others
talked positively about the process of the meeting itself and the learning
that took place. One member put it this way:

> About decision making—interesting dynamics. As a group, we wanted to do
> right and the discussion helps you make a decision. You come to the meeting
> with some information you've gathered, and then you listen to what others
> have. The first formulation is sterile with just resumes to go on, then when you
> discuss criteria—experience, accomplishments, notoriety, complications, what
> they had done, how they had dealt with faculty. Like with one candidate and
> his ability to attract bio-tech industry to work with the university. I learned
> through listening. Learned how to look at a piece of paper to get a sense of a
> candidate. The advantage of a large group is the variety of perspectives. I felt

very comfortable with decisions because we had various disciplines and perspectives I had not considered. And I appreciated their comments—women's studies, for example. I changed my mind because of diversity issues and was more comfortable with voting.

By the end of the pizza meeting, the group had reduced the number of candidates from 16 to 6.

The committee invited the six remaining candidates to visit the campus. They planned a series of interview activities, presentations, and meetings with faculty and staff. In the flurry of activity, many on the committee felt they were making significant progress.

After the candidates left, the committee met for the final time late in February on a Friday afternoon. Their task was to forward a short list of recommended names to the President. The four remaining candidates were listed on the chalkboard in front of the small conference room. Members of the committee could vote to forward as many candidates as they wanted from the four. They took their first vote by secret, written ballot. Members took a break while the votes were counted and posted on the board beside the candidate names. Three candidates had a clear lead. With 22 voting, two of the four candidates received 21 and 20 votes for recommendation to the President. The third candidate, receiving 9 votes, was the Interim Provost. The final candidate received no votes from the committee.

Upon the committee's return from a brief break, a local reporter "reminded" them that all votes had to be open and "in the sunshine." The group considered two options to remedy their slip-up: to sign the secret ballots submitted prior to the break or to re-vote in an open signed ballot. They decided to re-vote "in the sunshine," and while the votes remained mostly the same, the Interim Provost received two additional votes. At that point, a dean spoke up: "I move that we advance all three of these names." The group discussed the implications, such as the legitimacy of the search if they advanced the Interim Provost, the possibility of a candidate's dropping from the search, and the inequality of the number of votes. Someone commented, "If we advance three names, it will appear that they are three equal names, and these are *obviously* not equal." This argument carried the day, and the group decided to advance only the top two. When interviewed later, one administrator commented:

The final session was again open, and concerns were expressed. I appreciated the reporter who provided what I saw as helpful and practical information. Even the man who spoke at the end [a faculty member who spoke against the Interim Provost] demonstrated how comfortable people were with expressing their stand. I believe people voted their conscience, and I believe all their concerns were expressed.

Although diverse opinions were expressed in the meeting, many people there remarked how positive it was that such a heated discussion could lead to a clear consensus.

Differentiation Narrative

Upon attending the first meeting, one dean commented to the faculty researcher that a critical concern of his was the effect of the Sunshine Laws. He felt that these laws "had a major effect on the quality of the pool because people are unwilling to be subjected to this sort of public scrutiny."

The Interim Provost's entry into the race also raised serious concerns. Was the search rigged? Would the President, who liked him and had worked well with him as Interim Provost, select him no matter whom the committee recommended? (A similar situation had recently occurred at another Florida university.) And why did the Interim Provost go back on his word to not enter the race?

The search committee members were not the only ones asking these questions. The student daily newspaper, as well as community papers, began questioning the legitimacy of the process. A committee member from a satellite campus told us later,

> We read [about it] in papers and chatted with the committee members. The President had told us the Interim Provost was not going to apply because he had agreed to chair and be interim. It was really a shock when he did apply. After that, myself [sic] and others began to receive notes about a disagreement, about how he had handled a situation in his department. When the committee interviewed the Interim, I could see those concerns in [their] questions.

Furthermore, calls came in to the Chancellor's office asking if the process was rigged in favor of the Interim Provost. Adding to this turmoil and suspicion, another internal candidate, the Dean of the College of Arts and Sciences, withdrew his application without explanation.

The composition of the search committee concerned some people. With its wide representation, it included some members with search experience, but also many with none; some with hierarchical power and some with little status; some highly articulate members and some very uncomfortable speaking in large groups; and many from the faculty but few from the community.

This composition affected the perception of the process in different ways. One junior faculty member explained:

> I entered the process naively and learned a lot about politics and about criteria for selection. For example, during the process my emphasis on scholarship changed because I learned how important administrative experience was.

I learned about politics and the way people deal with each other. I saw how things get done in an important committee. I was probably the most junior person and one of the youngest. I learned about power. For example, the deans, all men, always wore expensive suits and ties while the chairs and faculty dressed more casually. As time passed, however, I began to dress more formally for our meetings. No dean would ever wear jeans! The women were more homogeneously dressed, but none of the women were deans.

In addition to divisions of power within the university, departmental divisions also manifested themselves. The discussion at the "pizza meeting" sometimes split to reflect "our departmental biases. You know, those liberal arts and sciences and we linear engineers."

Another division emerged between community members and university members. Said one member:

I was the token alumni, civic, community representative. My perspective and values were so different from the committee's strong academic emphasis, while mine lacked advocates. We debated about the advertisement and the vision statement. We have different decision-making styles. Faculty wanted a collaborative decision style. I see the Provost position as a bridge between faculty and the community, town and gown. My viewpoint got short shrift, and I became less involved as time went on.

When the committee selected the new co-chairs, some wondered about their political interests. The new chair of the search committee was nominated by her dean, who was also a member of the committee. He may have felt that given her skills she would make the best candidate; he may also have felt that he would have more influence on the outcome were she in charge. In any case, the nomination occurred by surprise and in public with the press in attendance. Although she did not want the position under the circumstances, she found herself caught between refusing to serve (which might have further undercut the legitimacy of the process in the eyes of the faculty at large) or agreeing to serve and making the best of it. The fact that this decision was revealed in the presence of the press also made it harder for her to say no. Others on the committee also reported being tempted to resign from the group once the Interim Provost entered the race, but none did so because they decided it was better to have a voice in a potentially compromised process than to lose one's voice altogether.

Issues of voice became increasingly important as more weighty decisions arose. One junior faculty member observed that "the most powerful members were ones who spoke the most. I didn't say a word the first few meetings. I was a little bit intimidated in general by such a committee. I also worried about my accent and being understood." Another said:

I did not go to the last 5 candidate meetings. I don't think that had much effect. I would have delivered the message in favor of the Interim. My constituencies were strongly in favor of him—if it ain't broke, don't fix it. The problem is the process of becoming a candidate, the way he came up. If he had kept out, the process would have seemed far more credible. I didn't think I'd make a difference so I didn't participate as much. The faculty had an agenda, and I felt out of the loop. I did enjoy reading the candidates' qualifications and really liked talking with one of the candidate's [supervisor, who was a] President at another university. I do feel the final decision was a good one, but the process was disturbing.

One particularly clear moment of tension occurred at the "pizza meeting." When the question of whether to advance the Interim Provost to the list of 16 came up, the room fell silent. A long five seconds later, there was one, very clear, "Get real." One member said, "I think it was significant that people were silent." Some felt the Interim Provost situation led to a feeling among the university community that the search was rigged. "My colleagues were concerned. They thought it was a 'done deal' and questioned whether it was a serious search. People did not believe the President would go with the committee's recommendation." Committee members sought reassurance from the co-chairs. Said one prominent member:

What was difficult though was that the Interim was still there [on the list] when we cut [to 16]. I got a lot of feedback from my colleagues at that point. It was difficult, and I was questioned outright about whether a real search was going on. I contacted the Chair [of the search committee] to get reassurance. She said as far as she knew the search was real and open. The Interim Provost had done a good job as interim but outside candidates were strong too. I was pleasantly surprised at the quality, and we did all we could to demonstrate an open search. I wondered if people feared fallout from not recommending [the Interim Provost], but it was not evident.

The impression of a "done deal" led to a division between the search committee and the university community. One member commented, "The open forums and chairperson meetings with the candidates who visited the campus were very poorly attended. The search committee was very disappointed and felt the university community did not really believe our efforts."

The final meeting reminded the committee of its image in the community when a reporter succeeded in forcing a repeat balloting. It also revealed the lack of a coordinated coalition behind the Interim Provost. The main reason for this is that the Sunshine Laws prohibit discussion of the candidates by committee members outside meetings. "About the communication among the members? Not much outside meetings. Maybe I'm naive, but

I didn't sense any subgroups except at the end when it was obvious there was a group very pro-Interim Provost and then those who were not." One dean did suspect such outside contact and noted feeling "blind-sided" by the apparent formation of an anti-Interim Provost coalition. The pro-Interim Provost members did not meet to discuss any strategies of support. Apparently, then, openness played one key role in the decision process—the Sunshine Laws discouraged the collaboration of a pro-Interim Provost coalition that might have changed the outcome of the voting.

Fragmentation Narrative

In the beginning, the process seemed logical and hopeful. The main unspoken issue was the qualifications for search committee membership and makeup of the group. Do we have the right experience? Some never knew why they had been chosen to serve. "I wish I had been told why I was chosen. The criteria for committee selection were never made clear."

When the Interim Provost entered the race, numerous rumors popped up overnight. This event was a turning point for the search process. His entry created significant uncertainty and further complicated still emerging impressions of the new President. It brought out the worst cynicism among faculty, who as a group are already predisposed toward cynicism.

> My major concern was that we started out with the Interim Provost as our chair, and he presented himself with no interest in being a candidate. He felt major support so he changed. He was naive not to expect such a situation to occur and should not have ever taken the chair position. It was unfortunate, and people questioned me. Those outside the search process assumed that the job was filled and that there was no real effort to find a candidate. I sensed a lot of ambivalence and the question of the search being over before it really got under way.

Another committee member told us "the hardest part of our search was the Interim Provost issue and what it did to the perception of the search's legitimacy." The replacement co-chair held several one-on-one meetings with the President to seek reassurance of the legitimacy of the process.

The issue was not easily put to rest. It remained an ongoing concern with faculty who now doubted the credibility of the process: what is more, it became something of a self-fulfilling prophecy. Fears of a "done deal" led to lack of university-wide faculty participation in candidate interviews and dampened enthusiasm for the search. Even those who strongly supported the Interim Provost had problems with the meaning of search itself. "I thought the process was followed even if the end result was not to my liking. The [Interim Provost's] arm was twisted [by the President], so it was not his fault. He had no interest in the position and did not show interest. I think he was made a scapegoat or something."

Months earlier, when he was chair of the search committee, the Interim Provost has requested input from the faculty about the composition of the search committee. One of the few to respond (via e-mail) was the person ultimately nominated as the next chair. She had some strong feelings about the importance of the search, the need to keep the committee small (she suggested no more than 12 people), and the necessity of strong faculty representation. Later on, when the Interim Provost entered the race, he may have remembered this note in suggesting her to the President.

Several events led to confusion at the first round of candidate consideration held in the Business Building. When the candidate documents were distributed, four of the 25 search committee members never picked up the materials in advance of the meeting.

> I didn't participate in the first process—defer, consider, not consider—because I didn't read the fax. They sent info but didn't follow up. I didn't understand I was supposed to go get the packets, so I didn't have one. I blame both of us a little bit. That was the only time we messed up. Overall, the communication was very good with phone calls and faxes.

A handful of members missed meetings and critical votes throughout the process. One of the most remarkable aspects of the meeting (when the group made the initial cuts in the candidate pool) was in the differences among the color-coded sub-groups as they made their recommendations. One group used a mathematical formula that quickly separated the "possibles" from the "rejects"; they were finished in 20 minutes. The other groups took nearly 90 minutes to perform the "same" task; they discussed each candidate in detail before making a decision. Rating sheets accompanied the original packets, and these scores were summarized, which led to what came to be called the "50% rule." The 50% rule emerged during the defer/advance stage of the discussion. It stated that a candidate would not be deferred or advanced without 50% of the vote—but it was not applied consistently.

Seen from a fragmentation perspective, the "pizza meeting" was especially confusing. A member from the community told us:

> The easy part was first—absolute consensus on two of the candidates. But to me it seemed chaotic—send resumes, do sound bytes. We needed criteria, and we needed to get references in writing and distribute them. What the

committee seemed to have decided was they wanted similarity—similar type
university, similar job with branch experience, some medical school/health
emphasis.

Most thought the original criteria outlined in the search plan were clear,
but now they were not so certain. For instance, one member stated, "I suddenly realized we weren't all on the same page." Throughout the meeting
interpretations of ambiguous criteria shifted. Some were "concerned about
our objectivity"; criteria were "not consistent" but "elastic." Basic criteria
were "open to interpretation." "For the process to work, we had to articulate and discuss it. In the beginning, we were as liberal as possible; then
people were cut out later by consensus." In listening to others' opinions,
some became even more confused. "I have been trying to think about the
best way to use other groups' votes. They are based on perception. What
weight do you give to that? To individual members who decide based upon
their impressions. How much weight do they play in the vote?" One of our
interviewees summed up the confusion:

> Most people met the basic criteria, so how do you judge academic values?
> Does that mean respect or intellectual curiosity or cross-cultural sensitivity?
> One could hold those values and not be top notch in one's field. How do you
> compare years of experience, for example? How do you compare someone
> who has been dean for five years with someone who has been a Provost for one
> year? Criteria must be applied, yet it depends on the rationality and judgment
> of those applying it—it's not a simple checklist.

The issue of the Interim Provost's part in the process surfaced as yet
another fuzzy piece of the picture in the pizza meeting. One person told us
the committee

> did not have the guts to reject his application. Instead, we advanced him. I felt
> the committee was intimidated that there would be retaliation. I learned—back
> to politics—that people were not in jeopardy but that they felt intimidated. The
> effect was that we looked terrible. I heard repeatedly that "the deal is done"—
> so much so that I began to believe it myself. I began to wonder if he already
> had the job. It made me feel powerless even though I knew I had not been pres-
> sured. People began to see us as a "puppet committee," I mean, they used that
> phrase, "puppet." I still think he should not have been advanced to the
> semi-final list.

One of the most remarkable aspects of the decision-making process had
to do with how candidates were treated once they failed to make the short

list. Despite highly ambiguous criteria and unreliable data, once candidates were advanced, the differences between them and those not selected were greatly exaggerated. Those not forwarded to the next level were demonized by the committee as a way of creating confidence in the rationality of the decision process and the unimpeachable quality of those who survived the cut. On the face of it, the differences between many of those chosen and those passed over were not great.

Because the definite number of candidates selected to present to the President had not been previously determined, the committee members had differing expectations of the outcome of their year's efforts. One member said, "I preferred to advance a list of three, not two. We should have had ground rules from the beginning that said how many we would advance. [The President] wanted three, and I think the committee should have sent the number she wanted. But the end result was good." Another felt the advancement of two not including the Interim Provost cleared up any previous ambiguity about the committee's legitimacy. She said, "I do feel very good about the final meeting. The committee was not a puppet. We really showed that we were not under pressure from the Administration."

Even after the committee fulfilled its charge, many were left wondering about the aftermath. "I understood that we would invite [the two leading candidates] back, but the President went out West to meet with [one candidate] and did not invite him back. [The other candidate] had impressive credentials and academic experience. Now we'll just wait and see."

Performing the Cultural Nexus

In their final form, each perspective appears as a very different version of the same event. From an integration perspective, the search process was a sensible progression of events based on clearly articulated criteria and shared meanings. From a differentiation perspective, the process revealed cultures within cultures, people and groups divided with inconsistent meanings and goals. Finally, the fragmentation narrative exposed the search process as rife with confusion and ambiguity. So what does it mean to look at the same event from diverse viewpoints?

> Society is a very mysterious animal with many faces and hidden potentialities, and . . . it's extremely shortsighted to believe that the face society happens to be presenting to you at a given moment is its only true face. None of us knows all the potentialities that slumber in the spirit of the population. (Vaclav Havel, May 31, 1990, as cited in Scott, 1990, p. v)

The Provost search committee became a microcosm of society through which three different "faces"—integration, differentiation, and fragmentation—were presented. As has been shown, a reliance on any one "face" or interpretation of "what really happened" is shortsighted. A consideration of all three faces or perspectives together opens up richer possibilities for learning. For example, we can explore such questions as:

1. Why are some narratives favored over others?

2. How can a group appear highly integrated at one level, yet also reveal suppressed conflict and ambiguities at another?

3. How can individuals speak of clear consensus, yet reveal contradictory criteria in the next breath?

4. And, finally, how do these varying interpretations relate to issues of audience, rationality, role, and identity?

To explore these questions, we return to Martin (1992) who states, "[I]n many ways an organization is a microcosm of the surrounding societal culture, many external influences will therefore permeate the organization's boundary and be enacted within it" (p. 111). An organization [or committee] becomes a "*nexus* where a variety of cultural influences come together within a [permeable and arbitrary] boundary" (p. 111, emphasis added).

Martin's discussion of cultural nexus provides a break in her otherwise categorical approach toward culture. We believe that the cultural nexus idea offers an approach to cultures in organizations that problematizes notions of organizational boundaries and uniqueness. This expanded view transcends all three narratives. We further believe that the cultural nexus carries implications for individual identity construction. Finally, we argue communication is the key process through which the cultural nexus is performed.

People come to social life telling a range of varied, often competing stories about themselves and the world. The intersection of these stories forms a nexus that can be bounded at various levels: the institution (or university) level, the organizational (or group) level, and the individual level. Meetings are sites where institutional, organizational, and individual levels interplay. "Meetings are also an important context for the display and validation of cultural beliefs. In American society, meetings assume great significance because they are a major setting for displaying the cultural value of the use of reason and logic in the development of decisions and policies" (Schwartzman, 1989, p. 42).

For our purposes, we will focus on the organizational and individual levels. The organizational level reflects the story the group tells as a whole. We found this level revealed most clearly by our observations. Through interviews, we identified individual perspectives and compared them to the "group" story that was publicly presented. The individual level emerged during our interview process. We found competing perspectives of the process both between and within individual accounts.

We suggest that perspectives are chosen for rhetorical reasons: perspectives are resources that organizational actors use to communicate with multiple audiences. For example, an organization may present an integration perspective to promote a consistent decision-making process to a public audience. At the individual level, an individual may provide an integration account to the media, while maintaining a differentiation account to colleagues (letting them know their specific interests were represented).

Organizational Level

Working as an autonomous, ad hoc group, the Provost search committee and its process were still deeply embedded within the university context (Putnam, 1992). This is not unique to this search committee. When a search begins, "[E]ach step along the way highlights both the internal complexities of the institution and the attitudes and ideologies of its environment" (McLaughlin & Riesman, 1984, p. 342).

We found that three broad environmental attitudes and ideologies influenced the communicative practices in the Provost search committee. We first address the effects of openness or "Sunshine Laws." We then examine how the history of rationality shaped individual and group decision making. Finally, we consider how social and political hierarchy affected this particular group. These three forces intersect to form a cultural nexus which in one sense "is" the Provost search committee.

Surveillance in the Sunshine. We began this study with the expectation that the "Sunshine Laws" would greatly affect the communication and decision-making process of the Provost search committee. The primary effect of these laws was to reframe the search process as a kind of public performance. Sunshine laws can be understood as a "panoptic gaze": the exercise of societal power through a constant yet unpredictable surveillance (Foucault, 1977). According to Foucault (1977), "The seeing machine was once a sort of dark room into which individuals spied; it has become a transparent building in which the exercise of power may be supervised by society as a whole" (p. 207). In this way, power is not individualized but publicized. As with the Provost search committee, there is no one individual exerting power on the committee. Any decision the committee makes is subject to the scrutiny and supervision in plain view of "society as a whole."

In his study of power and resistance, Scott (1990) notes that "one of the key survival skills . . . [in coping with social power] has been impression management in power-laden situations" (p. 3). Impression management activities are evident in the search committee's actions. At first glance, the committee communicated a convincing performance of an integrated culture. Each organizational member presumably has an equal voice and an equal vote. The formal search plan promised open communication and clearly explicated the organization's goals and evaluation criteria. There characteristics appeared shared in the committee's public performance. Newspaper reported the committee's goals as unified. For example, the campus newspaper quoted the co-chair, "We were looking at their academic credentials, previous experience in academia, their philosophy of education. Basically, we were thinking about how they would lead us into the future."

Attempts to tell an integration story may also be considered a form of impression management. Before the first meeting, the committee chair stated, "It is really kind of weird; a lot of communication censoring going on when the press is there. If you want to give negative feedback people are a lot more careful when the press is there. [They] would be a lot more candid if the press were not there." Another committee member remarked, "You have to temper your feelings a bit, choose your words carefully. We give a lot of lip service to open voice, but in fact there is a lot of reluctance to do that."

During the "pizza meeting" the chair exclaimed, "I am astonished the press is not here." Since the media were not there, the committee openly discussed strategies about the impact of open communication on the list of candidates. One strategy including writing a "wishy-washy" letter. Others hesitated putting things in a public letter, "particularly in the sunshine as we are here." The committee finally recommended phone calls over letters since calls are not part of "public records" and hence might lead to more honest opinions. Although the public display characterized the committee as an unbroken monolith, internal discourse and strategies revealed cracks in this picture.

History of Rationality. People seek security in sense making (Geertz, 1973; Weick, 1995). Geertz explains this by analogy to religion. Religion gives order to chaos: "[Man] can adapt himself somehow to anything his imagination can cope with; but he cannot deal with Chaos. Because his characteristic function and highest asset is conception, his greatest fright is to meet what he cannot construe" (Langer, 1960, cited in Geertz, 1973, p. 99).

Above all, the integration narrative displays order and predictability. Individuals take turns speaking, orderly conduct is followed, and decisions are presented as shared. However, the fragmentation narrative reveals that the criteria for evaluating candidates were far from shared and certain. Many decisions were accepted more on faith than on the basis of rational judgment. Comments like, "We've made good decisions," "Can't see us going back into that pool again," and "Once we cut the list, those people were not recoverable," reflect a kind of retrospective sense making that gives order to a web of ambiguities and inconsistencies and substitutes rational motivations after the fact (Weick, 1979). "Motivations are made meaningful with reference to the ends toward which they are conceived to conduce" (Geertz, 1973, p. 97).

We observed how rules emerged from chaotic processes that were retrospectively described and experienced as orderly and rational. "Thus rationality, rather than being the guiding rule of organization life, turns out to be an achievement—a symbolic product that is constructed through actions that in themselves are nonrational. We could even say that the dichotomy between rationality and nonrationality is itself ultimately unfounded, emerging mainly from the legitimacy in our culture of 'rational,' and the illegitimacy of 'nonrational,' conduct" (Brown, 1978, p. 370). The committee affirmed the choices they made as the *only* rational choices that could have been made. One member recounted, "We were looking for someone with experience as a sitting Provost, and in the end we hired the only applicant who did." They reinforced the appearance of an integrated and orderly culture. Through these practices, the Provost search committee was a microcosm of a larger human search for rationality and order.

Social Hierarchy. Any search for rational order inevitably leads to hierarchy. Further, hierarchy is embedded within our language system. As humans we are "goaded by the spirit of hierarchy" (Burke, 1989, p. 69). Through discourse and action, we create and sustain hierarchical systems. Because we are "moved by the sense of social order" (p. 69), these systems are as a rule treated as natural and inevitable.

A social hierarchy influenced the Provost search committee through university politics and practices:

> Meetings are a successful social validating mechanism because acceptance of the form requires, at least in part, acceptance of the current social and cultural order. A formal meeting requires the negotiation and ultimately the acceptance of a set of social relationships that define someone's right to call and arrange a meeting, to specify time and location, someone(s) or some way to start and end a meeting, a series of rules and conventions for ordering and regulating talk, and recognition of this as talk that may be legitimated by the meeting frame. (Schwartzman, 1989, p. 41)

For example, the initial committee charge came from the President—not a member of the group. Whether the Provost search committee members themselves ever had a "real" voice is questionable. "Typically [committees] recommend courses of action to other units rather than make the final decision on their own" (Putnam, 1992, p. 62). In this case, rumors existed that the university President had already chosen the candidate, and the campus newspaper had even endorsed him.

To combat images of an illegitimate search, a unified story emerged. Despite the fact that (1) members from satellite campuses were de facto excluded from the first round of voting (due to their not receiving materials in time), (2) student representatives did not feel comfortable to speak, and (3) community representatives felt they were not taken seriously, the publicly displayed narrative was still one of consensus.

A senior faculty member noted, "It is unfortunate nonacademics and students don't participate to the level that they should. Those folks that are appointed should be carefully scrutinized so they will participate." But as members attempted to participate in the decision-making process, they were constrained by the desires of others: what the President wants, what their department may want, and by what the public expects. These "other" wants position themselves within a political hierarchy that strongly influenced the decision-making process.

The cultural influences of "Sunshine Laws," a history of rationality and social hierarchy intersected to enable and constrain the committee. Exploration of these influences reveals that the appearance of an integrated culture may be just that—an appearance, carefully crafted for a public audience. It is a ritualistic display promoting what the broader cultural public expects to see—a rational decision based on shared and objective criteria.

The organizational level relies on the group presentation of competing perspectives drawn primarily through our observations. Yet, as we noted earlier, the competing perspectives are not told separately by different individuals. An exploration of the individual accounts of the Provost search committee follows. They are drawn primarily from our interviews with the committee members and other interested parties.

Individual Level

We were intrigued by the way individual stories shifted during the interview. Competing perspectives showed up in the same interviews. We suggest that the interviews are not doorways back to a time or event that can be "accurately" represented. Instead, they are moments in the present through which someone assigns significance to what has happened in the past. The presentation of the event and the event are not the same thing. Therefore, we should not try to judge these interview accounts for truth or accuracy. The value of each lies in how people assign meaning to a past event in the present and in how they locate themselves in relation to their perceived audience.

As interviewers, we witnessed numerous instances of people constituting the meanings of events. The tales they told were told to us in context. In light of this, we found Martin's (1992) three perspectives (integration, differentiation, and fragmentation) to best be thought of as rhetorical resources that organizational actors use to communicate with an audience. From a rhetorical view, different participants choose a perspective because it works at a given time for a given audience. They shift their accounts when the perceived audience changes and when they have different communication demands.

As we noted earlier in our discussion of the cultural nexus, the Provost search committee members could hardly check their respective cultural experiences at the door. Members were chosen for the breadth of representation they could add to the group. Therefore, each person represented a larger voice (e.g., student body, department of engineering, or administrative staff). "Members bring to their group settings divergent interests, disparate values, and specialized jargon that reflects occupational and departmental differences" (Putnam, 1992, p. 64). The statements members make about the search process must answer to the different communication demands of a department, a university, a President, and a community.

For example, most of the integration perspective quotations came from administrative staff. The administrators represent the University and first must "tell the party line," e.g., "The process was efficient" with the "procedures spelled out clearly." Only later, in private interviews, did they reveal less than unified perspectives, e.g., "I wish the criteria had been a little clearer." On the other hand, the faculty comments constituted a large portion of the differentiated and fragmented narratives. Academics do not represent the University in the same way as administrators. They are inclined to criticize politics first and to admit to a sensible selection process later, if at all.

For example, during the meetings, the committee did not discuss the Interim Provost situation openly. During interviews with us, however, academics tended to note immediately the controversial nature of his candidacy. People knew they might have to answer to him as a Provost or as a returning dean to their college. They did not want to go "on record" as criticizing him. Said one dean, "I wondered if people feared fallout from not recommending him, but it was not evident." A junior faculty member stated that the committee "did not have the guts to reject the Interim's application. I felt the committee was intimidated that there would be retaliation."

Conflicting stories have strong implications for identity construction. As such, Calas and Smircich describe the individual nexus as a "fragmented composite of external influences": "It does not matter how unique an individual we think we are, we are nothing but the discourses through and in which we live. In a sense, we are nothing more than traversing points in networks of discourses" (as cited in Martin, 1992, p. 157).

If we are no more "than the discourses through and in which we live," the identities of committee members are constructed and maintained through unique rhetorical choices. Our uniqueness lies in the particular configuration of these optional discourses. The individual self becomes enacted when a life story is communicated and is therefore subject to continual change (Kondo, 1990). Notably, the "networks of discourses" within which we exist depend on the audience(s) which we are addressing at any point in time.

Summary

We have offered a detailed account of one university's search for a Provost. We found different views of the search (integration, differentiation, and fragmentation) to coexist in a "plural present" (Goodall, 1991). Further, we were a group of diverse individuals studying a group of diverse individuals and interests. As such, we must acknowledge our own roles in constructing the very perspectives we describe. Culture is "always multivocal and overdetermined, and both the *observer* and the *observed* are always enmeshed in it. . . . There is no privileged position, no absolute perspective, no final recounting" (Rabinow & Sullivan, 1979, p. 6, emphasis added). Any attempt to reduce data to a single explanation risks losing the richness offered by alternate perspectives.

We encourage future observers of search and other such processes to take advantage of the broader range of insights made possible by considering multiple interpretations. Not all searches will face the same challenges that this university's committee did, i.e., an interim Provost stepping unexpectedly into the race. However, we do believe that most, if not all, searches will have to face an interplay between creativity, political interests, and legal constraints. The specific ways in which these processes show up in future searches remains to be seen.

References

Berger, P., & Luckmann, T. (1967). *The social construction of reality.* Garden City, NY: Anchor Books.

Brown, R. H. (1978). Bureaucracy as praxis: Toward a political phenomenology of formal organizations. *Administrative Science Quarterly, 23*, 365–382.

Burke, K. (1989). *Kenneth Burke on symbols and society.* Chicago: University of Chicago Press.

Cleveland, H. (1985). *The costs and benefits of openness: Sunshine laws and higher education.* Washington, DC: Association of Governing Boards of Universities and Colleges.

Eisenberg, E. (1984). Ambiguity as strategy in organizational communication. *Communication Monographs, 51*, 227–241.

Eisenberg, E., & Goodall, H. L., Jr. (1997). *Organizational communication: Balancing creativity and constraint* (2nd ed.). New York: St. Martin's Press.

Eisenberg, E., & Phillips, S. (1991). Miscommunication in organizations. In N. Coupland, H. Giles, & J. Wiemann (Eds.), *"Miscommunication" and problematic talk* (pp. 244–258). Newbury Park, CA: Sage.

Eisenberg, E., & Witten, M. (1987). Reconsidering openness in organizational communication. *Academy of Management Review, 12*, 418–426.

Fairhurst, G., & Sarr, R. (1995). *The art of framing.* San Francisco: Jossey-Bass.

Foucault, M. (1977). *Discipline and punish: The birth of a prison.* New York: Pantheon.

Geertz, C. (1973). *The interpretation of cultures.* New York: HarperCollins.

Goodall, H. L., Jr. (1991). *Living in the rock n roll mystery: Reading context, self, and others as clues.* Carbondale, IL: Southern Illinois University Press.

Kaplowitz, R. A. (1978). *The impact of sunshine/open meetings on the governing boards of public colleges and universities.* Washington, DC: Association of Governing Boards of Universities and Colleges.

Kondo, D. (1990). *Crafting selves: Power, gender, and discourses of identity in a Japanese workplace.* Chicago: University of Chicago Press.

Manganaro, M. (1990). *Modernist anthropology: From fieldwork to text.* Princeton, NJ: University of Princeton Press.

Martin, J. (1992). *Cultures in organizations: Three perspectives.* New York: Oxford University Press.

McLaughlin, J. B., & Riesman, D. (1984). A primer on the use of consultants in Presidential recruitment. *Change, 2*, 12–23.

McLaughlin, J. B., & Riesman, D. (1985). The vicissitudes of the search process. *The Review of Higher Education, 8*, 341–355.

McLaughlin, J. B., & Riesman, D. (1989). The shady side of sunshine. *Change, 21*, 44–57.

McLaughlin, J. B., & Riesman, D. (1990). *Choosing a college: Opportunities and constraints.* Carnegie Foundation.

Morgan, G. (1986). *Images of organization.* Newbury Park, CA: Sage.

Nason, J. W. (1984). *Presidential search: A guide to the process of selecting and appointing college and university Presidents.* Washington, DC: Association of Governing Boards of Universities and Colleges.

Neff, C. (1992). *Presidential search: A guide to the process of selecting and appointing college and university Presidents.* Washington, DC: Association of Governing Boards of Universities and Colleges.

Putnam, L. L. (1992). Rethinking the nature of groups in organizations. In R. S. Cathcart & L. A. Samovar (Eds.), *Small group communication: A reader* (6th ed., pp. 57–66). Dubuque, IA: Wm. C. Brown Publishers.

Rabinow, P., & Sullivan, W. M. (1979). *Interpretive social science: A reader.* Berkeley, CA: University of California Press.

Rorty, R. (1979). *Philosophy and the mirror of nature.* Princeton, NJ: Princeton University Press.

Schwartzman, H. B. (1989). *The meeting: Gatherings in organizations and communities.* New York: Plenum Press.

Scott, J. C. (1990). *Domination and the arts of resistance: Hidden transcripts.* New Haven, CT: Yale University Press.

Tracy, K. (1991). *Understanding face to face interaction: Issues linking goals and discourse.* Hillsdale, NJ: Erlbaum.

Van Maanen, J. (1988). *Tales of the field: On writing ethnography.* Chicago: University of Chicago Press.

Weick, K. E. (1979). *The social psychology of organizing* (2nd ed.). Reading, MA: Addison-Wesley.

Weick, K. (1995). *Sensemaking in organizations.* Thousand Oaks, CA: Sage.

11

Transforming Organizations Through Communication

One way I interact with organizations outside the research enterprise is as consultant or advisor to institutions contemplating significant changes. The aim of this essay was to examine the relationship between theories of organizational communication and theories of planned organizational change. In so doing, parallels emerged between newer, more democratic theories of change and dialogic forms of communication.

This paper was initially prepared for a conference on the future of organizational communication held in San Antonio, Texas. The meeting was memorable for its clashes between people who sought to explore the practical utility of various communicative forms (people such as me and my co-authors) and those who wanted to talk about abuses of power and the plight of the disenfranchised. Looking back, I think this was a pretty fair representation of an emerging duality in the field in that it focused simultaneously on both the economic and the cultural consequences of discursive choices.

SOURCE: Eisenberg, E., Andrews, L., Murphy, A., & Timmerman, L. (1999). Transforming organizations through communication. In P. Salem (Ed.), *Organizational communication and change* (pp. 125–147). New York: Hampton Press. Copyright © 1999, Hampton Press.

Man is a singular creature. He has a set of gifts which make him unique among the animals: so that, unlike them, he is not a figure of the landscape—he is a shaper of the landscape. In body and in mind he is the explorer of nature, the ubiquitous animal, who did not find but has made his home in every continent.

—J. Bronowski, *The Ascent of Man*

This is a strange world, and it promises to get stranger. . . . So we must live with the strange and the bizarre, even as we climb stairs that we want to bring us to a clearer vantage point. Every step requires that we stay comfortable with uncertainty, and confident of confusion's role. After all is said and done, we will have to muddle our way through. But in the midst of the muddle—and I hope I remember this—we can walk with a sure step. For these stairs we climb only take us deeper and deeper into a universe of inherent order.

—Margaret Wheatley, *Leadership and the New Science*

Ishmael said, "We know what happens if you take the Taker premise, that the world belongs to man." "Yes, that's a disaster." "And what happens if you take the Leaver premise, that man belongs to the world?" "Then creation goes on forever." "How does that sound?" "It has my vote."

—Daniel Quinn, *Ishmael*

The natural state of the universe is one of constant change—of transformation and mutation, degradation and decay. Each life form is challenged to adapt to these changing conditions. Adaptation, for most species, takes place over many generations. Order is introduced by trial and error. Human organizing, however, is qualitatively different. For human beings, language and communication offer a relatively speedy tool for creating order. Communication is such a powerful organizing force that a very few people communicating in particular ways can and have had enormous influence on organizations, societies, and the planet.

Attempts at organization are made against a backdrop of unlimited variation and possibility. For this reason, what is most remarkable is not change, but stability—how certain patterns of thought, talk, and behavior persist over time. For example, when we contrast Classical approaches to organizing with Human Resources approaches (cf., Eisenberg & Goodall, 1997), we are characterizing distinct world views and interaction patterns, each of which dominated consciousness and practice for decades before yielding to other patterns. But how did each scheme gain prominence? How is it that people achieve routine through communication? How do we organize in ways that construct the "taken for granted" across a series of historical moments?

Posed at this level of abstraction, the question of what makes for persistent patterns seems straightforward. But when we move to consider the enduring nature of specific organizational changes—and to questions of why, how, and when they might be made—we are cast immediately into an ocean of complexity. The complication comes about for at least two reasons. First, all patterns and structures favor some individuals and species over others. Consequently, we must attend to the *political* consequences of all change efforts. Second, people generally *resist* change, particularly when initiated by someone other than themselves. The combined result of these two tendencies is that most planned change efforts fail, as people resist them both because they are uncomfortable with new forms of behavior and because they perceive that the proposed change may not be in their best interest.

The purpose of this chapter is to outline some basic elements of a theory of organizational communication and change. We begin with a review of what is by now familiar territory, a discussion of how the collapse of traditional paradigms has created a special urgency for holistic thinking and for revolutionary, second-order change. Next, we reframe the challenge of coping with organizational stability and change as a special case of the more general human problem of negentropy—creating order out of chaos. Third, we consider in detail the pragmatics of organizational transformation, revealing parallels between evolving conceptions of communication and changing models of organization. Our favored approach features dialogue as a driving force in promoting lasting organizational transformation.

Why Change?

This century has been characterized as a period of rapid, radical and dramatic change—perhaps the most profound revolution ever experienced

(Osterberg, 1993). Discoveries in quantum mechanics have shifted our picture of the universe from one consisting of solid, discrete objects separated by space to a field of constantly varying and intimately connected energy. The universe vibrates and flows in unbroken waves. When we perceive the universe as complex, creative, and whole, we can conceptualize organizations as the same—communities of people interpreting complex and interconnected stimuli to respond creatively to continual change (Bohm, 1980; Henderson, 1993; Isaacs, 1993a, 1993b; Ray, 1993; Wheatley, 1992).

In a world undergoing enormous technological, economic, and political change, many of the established ways we have of living together are not working well (Bellah, Madsen, Sullivan, Swidler, & Tipton, 1992). The source of many of our problems is the fragmented way in which we conceive of our world. This fragmentation results in nations that consider themselves separate from others, and members of nations divided from other members (Bohm & Edwards, 1991). Fragmented ways of thinking create organizations that function as discrete entities scrambling for resources, innovation, and customers. Within this competitive context, organizational members refuse to share information. They construct boundaries to protect perceived power bases. Organizations react to crises without considering the global consequences of their actions. In contrast, holistic thinking can create organizations that exist primarily as "structures within which people come together to learn cooperatively" (Osterberg, 1993, p. 69).

To become more civil, humans must become ever more conscious of themselves, of others, and of the organizations that bring us together (Peck, 1993). We live on a planet that demands we develop better ways of living and working together. Searching for ways to structure interdependent lives more responsibly is no longer, if it ever was, the province of idealism—it has become the fundamental need we all share (Bellah et al., 1992). We tend to believe that somebody else's part of the boat is sinking and that it will not affect us. Instead we must talk together, cooperate, or we will destroy ourselves. Our problems are not "out there," they are "in here" (Bohm & Edwards, 1991).

Although there have been major crises on Earth in the past, it now seems that we face a unique historical moment in which most if not all traditional paradigms are collapsing simultaneously (Lyotard, 1984; Ventura, 1993). This situation is both terrifying and exhilarating. The need for change has never been greater, but the process of organizational transformation is in no sense easy or straightforward. The difficulties of altering routine, of challenging the taken-for-granted assumptions and practices of any culture are formidable. Many people are reluctant to abandon routines for psychological reasons, preferring *certain* dysfunctionality to an *uncertain* future.

A less apparent source of resistance comes from the larger framework of justifications and constraints that runs through every society and culture. In this way, any proposed new pattern of organizational behavior (e.g., building daycare centers at work sites; inviting employees to participate in decision making) can only be understood within a set of cultural stories and assumptions concerning appropriate behavior for mothers, fathers, workers, bosses, businesses, and countries.

Having said this, the usual conclusion is that organizational behavior is hard to change precisely because these various cultural stories have significant staying power of inertia. Today, however, *growing fissures in each of these canonical stories diminishes resistance to change at the organizational level.* This is why the current moment is one of great possibility, and even suggests that changes made at the organizational level may in turn have significant consequences for the reshaping of larger, taken-for-granted stories about society as a whole.

One recent example of the interaction between organizational change and broader social developments can be found in the decline of the "old social contract" between employers and employees in America (Chilton & Weidenbaum, 1994). Researchers observe that until a few years ago, employees were loyal to their employers and expected loyalty in return— stable employment, benefits, and decent treatment. Increased global competition, advanced technology, and the development of a global workforce created conditions that made possible the termination of this invisible contract; workers who had been employed by a company for years were unceremoniously replaced by employees from another country at a fraction of the cost (cf., Goodall & Eisenberg, 1997). By now, even the pretense of loyalty is gone from most companies, as employees are hired and fired (or used as independent contractors) in accord with rapidly fluctuating business conditions. These changes have resulted in a widespread questioning of the nature of jobs, work, human rights, and capitalism.

Pursuing Second-Order Change

The nature of this questioning—of considering our current predicament and deciding how to best move forward—varies considerably. Although it is clear that the era of ever-expanding growth and limited competition is over, management models developed in the waning years of that era continue to enjoy popularity. Total Quality Management, with its emphasis on continuous improvement, is notable for its reliance on evolutionary or first-order change. For many of today's organizations, however, the choices to be made are more similar to the situation facing boat transport companies at the dawn of commercial air travel. The first response of these companies to the invention of the airplane was denial, followed by desperate attempts at improvement (e.g., faster boats, better food, cheaper prices). In the end, *no amount of continuous improvement can save a company with an obsolete goal.* Even the speediest boats with the tastiest food could not compete with affordable overseas travel by air. Second-order change involves reexamining and changing your goals, not just the effectiveness with which you reach them. Those boat companies that did survive redefined their business as entertainment, not transportation, and created the cruise industry. This is not an isolated story. In organizations around the world, radical ideas about the purpose and organization of schools, churches, and government are facing heated discussion.

But how do you imagine the first person who suggested the idea of a "cruise to nowhere" was received by his or her peers? Timing and readiness for change is crucial, and most people's natural tendencies toward resistance often mean that second-order change, when it comes at all, comes too late (Handy, 1993). The best time to make second-order change is sooner—and the change required more dramatic—than most of us are prepared to face. If we wait until our current pattern no longer works, however, we will most likely have missed the boat.

Although a specific organizational arrangement may work today, our hypercompetitive business environment dictates that no single configuration can be successful for long. This is a marked departure from generations past, when placid organizational environments allowed companies to conduct "business as usual" for years, even decades. In 1980, for example, banking, air transportation, and fast food were all relatively stable industries in placid environments. Today, sea changes in technology, customer preferences, global competition, and employee expectations challenge organizations to be in a continual state of reinvention and renewal. This is one reason why TQM approaches have been in large part usurped by "reengineering" approaches (Hammer & Champy, 1993) that begin with a clean sheet of paper in redesigning work processes.

The lessons of reinvention and second-order change echo outside the world of organizations. In the realm of children's toys, the most popular action figures no longer use conventional weaponry. Instead, in responding to threat, Ninja Turtles mutate, Transformers transform, and Power Rangers morph. Our children and grandchildren receive the clear message that speedy, structural change is the optimal response to adversity. We may in time thank the toy manufacturers for propagating this orientation. After all, the organism currently atop the food chain—the virus—succeeds by second-order change. Viruses are enormously difficult to fight because they change structure in response to attack. Perhaps the only way we will learn to compete with such organisms is through second-order thinking—by designing "smart" medicines that can morph along with viruses as they change structure.

Courting Holism in an Era of Limits

We have thus far maintained that change is essential to survival, and that second-order change—the reexamination of our aims and goals—is especially critical today. What we have not yet mentioned is the unifying theme behind many if not most change efforts, both in and outside of organizations. This theme has to do with the rediscovery of our radical interdependence and with it the recognition that social problems can only be addressed by taking into account whole systems (Senge, 1990). The nuclear destruction at the close of World War II made clear how devastating our technological attempts at adaptation could turn out; the world has not been the same since. In the near future, we predict that in any system which does violence to the species or planet as a whole (e.g., nationalism, capitalism) will come under suspicion, if not attack.

One might call this situation a crisis of habitat, or perhaps a crisis of identity. At the same time that we assemble in small (ethnic, gender, religious, professional, socioeconomic) groups to assert our differences, we are being pushed daily to discover our common concerns. Recall that the "tragedy of the commons" occurred when farmers sought foolishly to maximize their individual gains at the expense of the common pasture. Today, multinational corporations and national governments do similar harm to human rights and ecosystems in the name of profitability and survival. How will this strategy play out in the long run? The time has come to begin thinking in a planetary way about issues of employment, human rights, and habitat.

Evidence of such a capacity emerging in either the political or organizational arenas has been minimal. What is more, many observers maintain that leadership of this sort will not come from a single source, or even in a unified way. Instead, they claim that new models of organization are emerging at a grass-roots level, through the efforts of like-minded people focused on organizing in ways that are protective of "the commons" (Barnet & Cavanaugh, 1993; Handy, 1994).

Chaos, Order, and Management

One reason why the types of changes we are proposing are so hard to consider is that current patterns of organizational behavior are deeply rooted in the fundamental characteristics of our species, and specifically in the ways in which language and rationality construct our relationship to the rest of the world. Particularly in the West, language and reflexive consciousness lead us to conceive of ourselves as *separate* and apart from the world, despite vivid sensory evidence to the contrary (Watts, 1967). The enduring belief that we are somehow "in" rather than "of" the world results in two related responses. On the one hand, we tend to behave *irresponsibly,* destroying other species and habitats (and as a consequence seriously depleting our own). On the other, we claim *responsibility* for managing the future of the Earth, and in this role engage in various projects of ecological repair and planetary escape (e.g., cleaning up bodies of water, planning to colonize other planets, building underground communities and international space stations).

This ambivalent relationship between humans and the world is written into Western culture's best known story, the book of Genesis in the Old Testament. There it is told that God gave order to the world before humans came on the scene, but that when man appeared, he was given "dominion" over the world. But what is meant by dominion? The charge to human beings from such a statement is ambiguous. One way of interpreting this passage is that we have been selected as *managers of the world.* Most Westerners probably do interpret the Genesis story in this way.

However, there is at least one alternative interpretation worth considering. In her book *The Chalice and the Blade,* Eisler (1987) offered a different reading of human history, exploring times past in which not all cultures sought to dominate the world. In other, partnership societies, women played a more central role and people lived in harmony with the Earth. Similarly, in his book about a teacher (who also happens to be a gorilla!), Quinn (1992) traced our species' current challenges to the critical difference between apprehending order and taking control. He argued that before there were human beings, there was already an order in the world, and consequently effective "dominion" must mean *learning this order and guiding behavior within it.* This interpretation has not been popular, however, at least in Western history. Instead, convinced that creation ends with us and that the world was made for humans and humans made to manage it, we seek to take control. With few exceptions, these attempts to manage the world are failures, rife with unanticipated consequences and ironies resulting from ignorance of the natural order.

Recent developments in organizational theory have witnessed a growing sensitivity to this distinction between order and control. Notably, Wheatley's (1992) application of chaos theory to organizations presents a forceful case for creating order in human behavior through the development of guiding principles and other "conceptual controls" (such as organizational vision and values), as opposed to through supervision or surveillance. Senge's (1990) description of the "learning organization" further promotes the idea that people do best when enrolled in a common vision and given sufficient autonomy to accomplish the vision in their own way.

As we noted earlier, the development of language and rationality provides humans with a powerful tool for creating routine patterns of behavior. Unfortunately, we have for the most part become convinced either that the patterns we create take precedence over nonhuman patterns, or worse yet, fail to see the existence of patterns other than the ones we have created. In so doing, we cast ourselves as managers of the world, a job no single species is equipped to perform. An alternative that has received limited consideration thus far would be to seek out patterns of order already present in the world and to live within them in ways that preserve life and the planet as a whole.

However you see the role of humankind, the story of Genesis is itself fundamentally one of creating order out of chaos. If we were to extend the story to imagine creation continuing through the present day, perhaps we can also see humans' role in the story differently. Rather than being called on to manage the world, we might instead become benevolent and enlightened guardians or facilitators of a creative process that *does not end with our species* (Quinn, 1992).

Contrasting Models of Communication and Change

We have argued so far for the necessity of holistic thinking and second-order change, and situated such change within a set of canonical stories that function to construct and reinforce current practices and routines. We have also suggested that the moment is ripe for change in a whole system of stories, and furthermore that specific changes in organizational life may have implications for more widespread transformation in social life. What we have not as yet discussed are the specific ways such changes can be achieved in real organizations through communication. The remainder of this chapter is dedicated to identifying the various models relating communication to organizational change, exploring their underlying assumptions, and comparing their likely effectiveness.

Our main point is that models of organizational change are inextricably linked to models of communication. To demonstrate this relationship, we begin with an early model of change—that of the charismatic leader—and show how it corresponds to the conduit model of communication. Next, we show how transformational models of leadership align with transactional models of communication. Finally, we describe how facilitative models of change parallel dialogic communication processes. We present the relationship between these existing theories of organizational change and communication as a kind of paradox—the simultaneous existence of what appear to be opposing and even contradictory forces.

Figure 11.1 reflects the relationship between organizational communication and organizational change through parallel continua. The top line represents the tension between approaches that see communication as a tool and those that see communication as generative or constitutive of social reality. The bottom line represents the tension between theories that view organizational change as a discrete event and those that see it as an ongoing process. The arrows indicate the general flow of communication efforts.

The left side of the figure, where communication is viewed as a tool and change as an event, is labeled monologic approaches to organizational change. Seen this way, change happens to an organization in the form of an event which a strong leader must manage and control. The event can take place either through naturally occurring events or through strategic intervention on the part of the leader or management team. In a monologic model, communication is the process of information transfer from the top

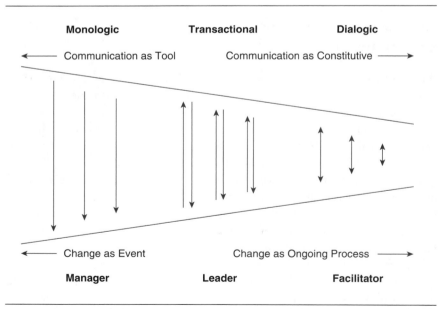

Figure 11.1   Parallels Between Theories of Organizational Communication and Organizational Change

down or informational orientation (Deetz, 1995). The manager attempts to control the change process using a linear model of communication. There are some situations in which such an approach may be most effective. For example, a monologic orientation may prove useful for dealing with first-order changes—incremental changes that occur within a constant framework (Bartunek & Louis, 1988). It may also work well for solving convergent problems for which there is only one right answer (Senge, 1990), and in emergencies when a quick response is vital.

The lines begin to converge in the middle, marking transactional perspectives in which employee participation is encouraged. Transformational change models focus on second-order organizational change—transforming organizational frameworks and structures. Organizational transformation emerges as "large scale changes in organizational form that occur throughout an organization's life cycle" (Bartunek & Louis, 1988, p. 98). In contrast to the monologic approach, transformational change parallels a more transactional communication model represented by arrows in each direction in the figure. With increased employee participation, the boundaries between senders and receivers blur as each simultaneously influences the other. Nevertheless, transformational approaches still require ongoing managerial direction.

On the right side of the diagram, where change is continual and communication is constitutive of meaning, the lines converge, representing dialogic approaches to change. This approach is most consistent with the notion of eliciting order out of chaos, rather than imposing a pattern by taking control. Dialogic models challenge conceptions of changes as a "thing" that happens "in" or "to" an organization. Outside pressures do not instigate change, the *perception* or enactment of these pressures do (Kanter, 1983; Weick, 1979). Ongoing change is more difficult to delineate, demarcate, or define. "Change is bound to meanings that are attached to events and action possibilities that follow from those meanings" (Kanter, 1983, p. 281). If we believe that communication is fundamentally the process of creating meaning, it follows that perception of change is tightly bound to communication, hence the two-headed arrows.

In most of the literature on organizational change, scholars do not explicitly address communication. We assert that communication forms the implied but neglected foundation of the change literature. Explicit or not, this literature reflects a paradox through which communication is presented both as a tool through which leaders promote change "events" and as an ongoing process through which new meanings and new practices are collaboratively generated. We next go into more detail about each of the three approaches in the model.

The Monologic Approach

Within the monologic approach, change is conceived as something that happens to an organization. Change is largely seen as an event such as a budget cut, a restructuring, a shift in the market, or a new governmental regulation rather than as an outgrowth of everyday activity. From this perspective, change is something to be managed. Important change management tools include the behavior of the manager, the vision, and the strategic use of communication.

Managers play the central role in monologic approaches—from this perspective, leadership drives change (Bass, 1981). First, managers execute and control change by scanning the environmental, assessing needs, and creating strategies (Kanter, Stein, & Jick, 1992). In other words, they decide which changes they will address and create strategies to predict and control the environment. Managers, sometimes with the help of experts, facilitate change for their employees to help them adapt quickly and remain productive. The leader's task is to make change as smooth as possible for employees. For change to be effective, production, profits, and service must remain at high levels.

Second, these managers must have a clear vision of what the organization is going to become. They know where they are going and how to get there:

> If there is a spark of genius in the leadership function at all, it must lie in this transcending ability, a kind of magic, to assemble—out of all the variety of images, signals, forecasts and alternatives—a clearly articulated vision of the future that is at once simple, easily understood, clearly desirable, and energizing. (Bennis & Nanus, 1985, p. 103)

Furthermore, managers must create a vision that will be inspiring to their members:

> They breathe life into what are the hopes and dreams of others and enable them to see the exciting possibilities that the future holds. Leaders get others to buy into their dreams by showing how all will be served by a common purpose. (Kouzes & Posner, 1987, p. 9)

The CEO creates the vision and hands it down to organizational members (Kanter et al., 1992; Stata, 1988). To keep the employees productive and the organization profitable through change events, managers must continually communicate and inspire.

From the monologic perspective, communication functions as a tool, and is used to disseminate the managers' vision for change. The messages managers choose to communicate generally flow downward and can be described according to a linear or conduit model of information transfer (Shannon & Weaver, 1949). At times, these communication strategies may be assessed and changed in order to increase efficiency and productivity. To increase effectiveness, managers continually sharpen their communication skills.

In one well-known model of change, communication shapes how organizations "adapt to the environment, make sense of external changes and implement strategic initiatives" (Daft, Bettenhausen, & Tyler, 1993, p. 143). Daft et al. offered a four-cell model that differentiates the type of information the leader should communicate to employees in response to varying environmental conditions. When the volume of external information is low and ambiguity is high (cell 1), managers develop common grammar, gather opinions, and define questions and actions. When the volume and ambiguity of information from the environment are both high (cell 2), managers gather opinions and analyze data to establish common grammar and answer explicit questions. When volume and ambiguity are both low (cell 3), managers gather and analyze routine objective data and answer objective questions. However, in an environmental state of rapid change with low ambiguity and high volume of information (cell 4), managers use scanning systems and high technology to answer explicit questions. *Different types of changes demand that managers use different channels and types of information.*

Another way of managing change which falls within the monologic perspective suggests that communication strategies depend on the type of movement (macroevolutionary, microevolutionary, or revolutionary); the type of change (identity, coordination, or control); and who is involved (change strategists, implementors, or recipients) (Kanter et al., 1992). Finally, a related model recommends tailoring communication strategies to potential psychological reactions (of employees) to change. This approach helps managers deal with employee denial, dodging, doing, and sustaining change (Rashford & Coghlan, 1994). Each of these models assumes the manager who communicates in appropriate ways promotes change with the least interruption to the organization.

For many years now, both in communication and organizational studies, writers have sought to revise the monologic perspective. For example, it has been observed that to be effective, employees must participate in making the leader's vision a reality (Beer, Eisenstat, & Spector, 1990; Bennis & Nanus, 1985). The process for doing so can hardly be monologic. People enroll in organizational visions only when they are ready (Senge, 1990). Managers must persuade employees and encourage participation, information sharing, and shop-floor-level decision making to implement their vision

(Beer et al., 1990). Tension emerges as leaders seek to drive organizational change, but at the same time require employee participation and involvement to make it happen.

This tension is felt by managers and employees alike. For example, many employees want quick solutions in the form of managerial decision making and directives. However, they may also wish to be involved in shaping their work by participating in decisions that affect them. Relatedly, the leader may experience discomfort and frustration as he or she attempts to involve organizational members and is met with distrust, lack of decision making and communication skills, or resistance to taking accountability.

Thus emerges the tension between change as located in leadership or management and change as located throughout the organization. The tension lies between wanting the sense of control and predictability that comes from a monologic, manager-focused approach to change, and realizing the need for participation and order—order that managers do not, and in fact, *cannot* control. This tension is played out as managers recognize the employees' powerful role in promoting successful change. In the transactional approach we began to widen our focus on the sender (leader) and message (vision) to further include the receiver (employee). The monologic stance gives way to a more transactional one as the need for employee input in the form of feedback is recognized (Kanter et al., 1992).

The Transactional Approach

Perhaps the best example of an approach to planned change that incorporates employee involvement but maintains the leadership role for managers is the theory of transformational leadership. In this section, we first define transformational leadership and explore the transactional role of communication in the transformed organization. Next, we present the leader and follower(s) as participants in effecting system-wide change.

Transformational Leadership. Contemporary organizations seek leadership that can guide them through the enormous social changes described earlier. Leadership transform is rapidly being redefined as having the capacity for transforming social systems, and new relationships between leadership and followers are emerging. From this perspective, the leader's job is to organize and mobilize them to create something new out of something old (Bass, 1981; Tichy & Ulrich, 1984; Zaleznik, 1977, 1990). Whereas many managers seek to make marginal improvements in quantity and quality of performance, transformational leaders inspire and motivate followers to perform above clearly communicated expectations. Accordingly, transformational leadership is based on more than the compliance of followers: it involves shifts in their beliefs, needs, and values. "The result of transforming leadership is a relationship of mutual stimulation and elevation that converts followers into leaders and may convert leaders into moral agents" (Burns, 1978, p. 4). The transformational leader raises followers' level of consciousness about the values of outcomes, and persuades followers to transcend self-interest.

In contrast to the managerial emphasis in the monologic perspective, transformational leadership recognizes that "one great man (or woman)" is not sufficient to accomplish any vision. Leaders and followers must develop new ways of working together which transform their organizations into safe learning environments equipped to respond to a turbulent world. This challenge requires leadership which recognizes the value of followers and encourages both innovation and independent decision making.

Transformational leadership is well known and has been widely researched across a variety of disciplines (Conger & Kanungo, 1987; Deluga, 1988; House, 1977; Kuhnert & Lewis, 1987; O. F. White & McSwain, 1983). The notion of transformational leadership developed from Downton's idea of "Rebel leadership," to political leadership (Burns, 1978), to its application in corporations (Bass, 1985; Bennis & Nanus, 1985; Tichy & Devanna, 1986), to a concept that includes the entire "learning organization" (Senge, 1990) as a dynamic system in which leadership is but one element in the set.

Close examination of research on transformational leadership reveals the following findings:

1. Significant and positive relationships exist between transformational leadership and organizational effectiveness (Avolio, Waldman, & Einstein, 1988; Hater & Bass, 1988; Seltzer & Bass, 1990; Yammarino & Bass, 1990).

2. Multiple levels of analysis in leader-follower interaction reveal that transformational leadership as compared to traditional forms was related more strongly to followers' extra effort and satisfaction (Yammarino & Bass, 1990). Transformational leaders were viewed as being more effective, and team members had greater levels of satisfaction with their leadership (Avolio & Bass, 1988).

3. The degree of transformational leadership behavior observed at one level of management tended also to be seen at the next lower level of management—called the "falling dominoes effect" (Bass, Waldman, Avolio, & Bebb, 1987).

4. In general, transformational leaders have more effective organizations (Avolio & Bass, 1988; Avolio et al., 1988).

As these findings reveal, for transformational leaders change is less an event to be managed than a process that requires leaders and followers to work and learn together. Communication is less monologic and more interactive. The next section continues to explore how a transformed organization requires the participation of followers and leaders in a transactional communication process.

Transactional Communication and Systems of Change. Transformational leaders simultaneously want control and participation. Toward this end, communication functions to "align attitudes, share knowledge, and manage information" (Quirke, 1995, p. 32). Leaders are responsible for communication; however, employees must simultaneously participate in organizational decision making. As the degree of change increases, so too does the level of involvement that is needed. When the degree of change is low, involvement can be limited to creating employee awareness. As the degree of desired change increases, employee understanding, support, and commitment are required. As the degree of involvement increases, the communication model employed must proceed from a one-way model to a more dynamic, transactional one.

The transformational leader is a perpetual learner. "The most marked characteristic of self-actualizers as potential leaders is their capacity to learn from others and the environment—the capacity to be taught" (Burns, 1978, p. 380). Learning is a system-wide activity as members obtain feedback from the environment and anticipate further changes. "At all levels, newly learned knowledge is translated into new goals, procedures, expectations, role structures, and measures of success" (Bennis & Nanus, 1985, p. 191). Innovative learning moves through six processes: reinterpreting history, experimenting, observing experiences of analogous organizations, using analytical processes, thinking and educating, and unlearning. These interdependent processes bring leaders and members of the organization closer together. They "nurture each other, guiding the process of creative self-discovery by which each learns how to be most effective in a complex and changing environment" (p. 205).

Transformational leadership features constant change, innovation, and entrepreneurship. Its advocates claim that this approach to leadership can be learned and managed; that it is "systematic, consisting of purposeful and organized search for changes, systematic analysis, and the capacity to move resources from areas of lesser to greater productivity" (Tichy & Devanna, 1986, p. vii). Only recently has literature focused specifically on the leader as part of a system that explicitly includes followers and their contributions. Within the transformational leadership approach, vision, purposes, beliefs, and other aspects of organizational culture assume prime importance

(Bennis, 1984). Symbolic expression becomes the major tool of leadership, as leadership effectiveness is:

> no longer defined as "9–9 grid score" or "system 4" position. Effectiveness is instead measured by the extent to which a "compelling vision" empowers others to excel; the extent to which meanings are found in one's work; and the extent to which individual and organization are bonded together by common commitment in a mutually rewarding symbiotic relationship. (p. 70)

Leadership reveals itself in interaction between people and necessarily implies its complement, "followership." The leader is simultaneously a follower serving the interest of multiple groups, such as shareholders, subordinates, and customers. For one to influence, another must permit him or herself to be influenced—reflecting a transactional communication model where interactants become involved in an interdependent relationship with no clearly defined senders or receivers. Moreover, leader and follower(s) must be at least loosely organized around some common or agreed-on purpose or mission, the achievement of which depends in part on the quality of the leader-follower relationship.

Related to the inspirational, visionary, and innovative aspects of transformational leadership, our traditional views of leaders—as special people who set the direction, make the key decisions, and energize the troops—are deeply rooted in an individualistic and fragmented world view. Especially in the West, leaders are usually heroes—great men (and occasionally women) who rise up in times of crises. Our prevailing leadership myths are still captured by the westernized image of the cavalry captain leading the charge to rescue settlers from attackers. So long as such myths prevail, they reinforce a focus on short-term success and charismatic heroes rather than on systemic forces and collective learning. At its heart, traditional views of leadership are based on assumptions of people's powerlessness, their lack of personal vision, and inability to master the forces of change, deficits that can be remedied only by a few great leaders (Senge, 1990).

When organizations emphasize learning together, leaders function as designers, stewards, coaches, and teachers who grow organizations through which people expand their capacities. This concept of leadership drastically alters the rationale for and the roles of managers. Communication and change become even more closely intertwined as lines of our model converge. The transformational leader helps create a space for members of the organization to create, learn, and build individual meaning in work. However, these tensions between control and creativity, authority and democracy, individuality and collectivity continue to pull in opposite directions (Eisenberg & Goodall, 1997).

For example, many attempts at implementing Total Quality Management have failed because of these conflicting tensions. Leaders have encouraged individuality and creativity and have devoted countless resources to team meetings only to override, ignore, or sabotage the resultant suggestions for change. These moments of disillusionment deflate the growing excitement and participation at work and can cause alienation between managers and managed. All too often organizational members participate in decision making and visioning only to find their voices go unheard. Transformational leaders usually discover that trust is hard to win and easy to lose. This type of leader must consistently value and practice the inclusion of members in complex decision making that effects the entire organization.

The Dialogic Approach

In our third approach, communication and change are so closely intertwined that they are nearly indistinguishable. Communication generates the organization's interpretations, contexts, and practices. Emphasis shifts from management to facilitation as the literature challenges and redefines images of leadership. Organizations, seen as dynamic work communities, continually develop and change as people interact interdependently. The right side of the figure pictures this close connection between constitutive communication and continual change. Nonetheless, those with power can disproportionately shape organizational symbols and meanings.

Co-constructing Organizations Through Dialogue. As organizational members work together, talk through daily situations, and act interdependently, the organization is continually under construction. Communication generates the organization's interpretation of its context, its identity, and its practices. In doing so, communication generates the organization itself. Put another way, "our symbol systems construct what we call the reality of a given situation, and words are the most taken-for-granted facts of those constructions" (Cheney & Tompkins, 1988, p. 466). Many organizational studies explore how symbolism creates organizational realities and environments (Berg, 1985; Goodall & Eisenberg, 1997). When we conceptualize communication as the core process which generates the organization, organizational change appears as "a transformation of the underlying symbolic field" (Berg, 1985, p. 289).

An organization's environments serve as symbolic contexts that provide meaning for members. These collective meanings are made manifest in the practices of the organization's members and effectively structure the organization. Strategy emerges as a "collective image that can be acted upon"

(Berg, 1985, p. 295). Change is "bound to meanings attached to events and action possibilities that flow from those meanings" (Kanter, 1983, p. 281).

Organizational members engaged in dialogue recognize heterogeneity and face significant points of contention. They confront the tensions between authority and democracy, profit and caring, creating and constraining. "As we are increasingly challenged to change our ways or perish, we must begin to entertain questions that, even in the asking, will open us to new possibilities" (Mandel, 1993, p. 169). When people balance advocacy and inquiry by explaining their reasoning and inquiring into that of others, they are able to create a safe space for learning and risking together (Senge, 1990). Communication of this sort allows "dialogic, collaborative constructions of self, other, and world in the process of making collective decisions" (Deetz, 1995, p. 107). When we listen both individually and collectively, we can build lasting relationships as the foundation of work. "Instead of glorifying transactions at the expense of relationships, business can re-energize itself as a high voltage conduit of human connectedness" (Mandel, 1993, p. 170). In the dialogic approach to communication, people function as essential information and idea resources, creating solutions we have never seen before. Human labor is no longer "a disposable commodity, but a creative resource, in which an individual's development is as valuable as the organization's growth" (Land & Jarman, 1993, p. 265).

Assumptions and Practices of Dialogic Approaches to Organization. Laying out some of the "ground rules" of dialogue may be helpful here. Bohm and Edwards (1991) discussed these in their book, *Changing Consciousness,* and Senge (1990) elaborated in *The Fifth Discipline.* The following is a summary:

1. Before beginning talk, we need to talk about the meaning of dialogue and its importance, usefulness, and risks.

2. We buy into the belief that our opinions and those of others are discussable and alterable. We are willing to hang them in front of us for consideration and questions. We listen seriously to opinion whether or not we agree. Only in this way can we learn to think together.

3. We recognize that dialogue is a commitment to time, to the group, and to the process.

4. Having no leader, no hierarchy, and no predetermined agenda enhances spontaneity. Imposing a question on the group is unnecessary—questions will grow out of the dialogue.

5. Exploring meanings together bonds the group and creates new ways of knowing.

Dialogic inquiry can lead to transformation. Generally speaking, the process leads from impersonal fellowship to friendship. Our emotions are integral. We change the nature of consciousness as we share content and think together. "I suggest that if we can sustain a real dialogue, we will find in the end that talking and thinking together is very like a kind of improvised singing and dancing together" (Bohm & Edwards, 1991, p. 192). We must be able to talk about and acknowledge our differences in a negotiable way if we are to stay together.

"The way people talk together in organizations is rapidly becoming acknowledged as central to the creation and management of knowledge" (Isaacs, 1993a, p. 1). Because complex issues require the combined intelligence of multiple individuals, dialogue is essential to the survival of today's organizations. In the tradition of dialogue as a way of knowing, William Isaacs of the MIT Dialogue Project asserts that dialogue is a discipline of collective learning and inquiry. It leads to new levels of understanding as well as to coordinated action. Although dialogue allows greater coherence among people, it does not impose it. People can agree on a direction but for different reasons. Dialogue is inquiry that can lead to a common vision. "The core of the theory of dialogue builds on the premise that changes in people's shared attention can alter the quality and level of inquiry that is possible" (p. 3). More than a mere problem-solving technique, dialogue is a means of exploring incoherent thoughts that underlie our problems.

In dialogue, people become observers of their own thinking (Senge, 1990). The suspension of assumptions, of hanging them in the air apart from specific egos, allows members to question and examine how and why they think the way they do. The collective conversation of colleagues who can question their own thinking is a powerful way of discovering new possibilities. In another popular management book, *The 7 Habits of Highly Effective People,* Covey (1989) called the highest level of communication synergy. At this level openness and communication, creativity is exciting and differences are both valued and transcended.

Dialogue and the Experience of Work. What does this kind of communication mean in our experience of work? "Most . . . people desperately want to do more than just bring home a paycheck; they want to believe in their work. They want work they can feel good about when they get up in the morning, that they look forward to and that they think is worthwhile" (Collins & Porras, 1993, p. 83). An organization's vision or direction ought to be a reflection of the needs, values, and motivations of organizational members; it must be a personal commitment; and it must be communicated and reinforced. Implementing a coherent strategy and effective tactical decisions requires a clear overarching goal which all organizational members can keep in sight.

Engaging in dialogue requires more than clearly phrased directives, open discussions, or polite greetings. It requires a different kind of attention to and awareness of others. James Autry (1991), a CEO and poet, talks about how his organization lives within the paradoxes of profit and caring. In his poem, "Threads," Autry wrote about leadership in turbulent times:

> Listen.
>
> In every office
>
> you hear the threads
>
> of love and joy and fear and guilt,
>
> the cries of celebration and reassurance,
>
> and somehow you know that connecting those threads
>
> is what you are supposed to do
>
> and business takes care of itself. (p. 26)

Although most leaders want reform, they are not certain how to go about making it. How best can a leader who speaks from a position of power significantly affect the power distribution in the organization? The literature offers several proposals. One such proposal is organizational stewardship. "Stewardship, the exercise of accountability as an act of service, requires a balance of power to be credible" (Block, 1993, p. 28). Stewardship questions our assumptions that accountability and control are synonymous. Although managers step back, they continue to struggle with the managerial control they and others expect them to wield. Caught within webs of power, organizations free themselves by first changing the thinking of those in power. "What is unique about this revolution—and gives us hope—is that it is being initiated by the ruling class, the managerial class. Stewardship is a revolution initiated and designed by those in power" (p. 45).

A managerial revolution reveals the paradoxical tension between wanting partnership, yet needing those currently in power to change. Block (1993) wrote his book for organizational executives, yet his advice runs counter to conventional managerial wisdom. For Block, organizations are not made up of parents and children, but rather "adults making decisions together with full responsibility and accountability, but without systems of control and compliance" (Deetz, 1995, p. 169). Echoing Eisler, the stewardship relationship moves leaders from a parental role to that of a partner. This change characterizes the dialogic approach and distinguishes it most clearly from the monologic and the transactional. In dialogue, everyone has an equal right to voice their experience. Similarly:

> Partnership means each of us at every level is responsible for defining vision and values. Purpose gets defined through dialogue. Let people at every level communicate about what they want to create, with each person having to make a declaration. *Let the dialogue be the outcome.* (Block 1993, p. 29; emphasis added)

Experiencing work as community reflects a particular view of communication and change, one that takes a long-term perspective and struggles to make some kind of democratic governance work. Such organizations are challenged to develop structures of democratic learning that check the "tendency of any human organization to develop factions which hoard power" (Bellah et al., 1992, p. 100). In this kind of work community, we may in fact see more socially grounded people in a more democratic economy. "Community, in its basic form, involves a group of people who have committed themselves to a process of ever-deepening levels of communication" (Gozdz, 1993, p. 111). This committed group communicates in uncharacteristically respectful and risky ways. In the process of building community, people learn to take greater responsibility for their own behavior.

However, a lasting organizational community requires more than commitment and communication. It requires discipline and mastery. This mastery is achieved as each person makes his or her contributions and assumes responsibility for them. Instead of a solitary leader responsible for performance, each member becomes the leader depending on the skills, knowledge, and experience needed in each situation. "Leadership in community is more a context than a person" (Gozdz, 1993, p. 113). Because each member makes his or her own contribution, the experience of work in community becomes a creative and enriching part of life.

How does a dialogic perspective on communication and change differ from the monologic and transactional perspectives? Taking a monologic approach, the manager or leader is responsible for creating a vision and then clearly interpreting it for the organization. "The leader's goal is not mere explanation or clarification but the creation of meaning" (Bennis, 1993, p. 78). In other words, the vision and its interpretation are constructed by the leader. Although the transformational leader does encourage the two-way flow of communication, he or she is still the instigator and power behind change efforts. He or she has the first, final, and most powerful voice. In contrast, dialogue shifts control from any one person to the community. For organizations to move from dominance to partnership and from dependency to empowerment, managers must give up control and recognize order in its many present forms. A dialogic relationship requires give and take; as a result, it can inspire creativity. Conversely, monologue minimizes risk and surprise, and hence stifles creativity.

Complex decision making requires employee participation in generating ideas, suggestions, and innovative thinking. This kind of participation encourages better social choices, builds better citizens, and provides important economic benefits. Yet we need to be suspicious of programmatic solutions to reach these democratic goals. Simply implementing new management programs won't work because these programs are managerially imposed. Words like empowerment, participation, and quality become mere slogans (Deetz, 1995), and they increase the effectiveness of bureaucracy, rather than change the system. Empowerment and participatory management programs have been tainted with elements of consent or concertive control. Paradoxically, employees want to make decisions about their workplace, yet they must conform to managerial programs that reward the current faddish behavior or work processes. The greatest threat to genuine participation comes in subtle control or consent, rather than in lack of opportunity for involvement which would most likely be resisted. To counteract the forces of consent, organizations must be open to a discourse of resistance:

> The existence of consent in pluralistic society calls for different kinds of activities, the force of more participatory discourse and the studies that aid it can no longer be a discourse of affirmation and conviction. It must be a discourse of resistance on the way to co-determination. This would be a micro-practice of resistance to consent and opposition to discussion closure. (Deetz, 1995, p. 171)

In other words, organization members at every level must speak up and ask questions to create a new kind of discourse which seeks to question rather than to convince.

Despite our obvious appreciation for the dialogic approach, we are nonetheless left with some questions. Most important, under what circumstances is dialogue most effective? When is it more trouble than it's worth? What place do skill and expertise play in a dialogic organization? Are all voices equally skilled in speaking (clearly not), and what difference does this make in the outcome? What about those who are not comfortable talking? Do all voices carry the same authority and weight? Are we attempting to substitute community at work for community at home or in our neighborhood? What about those who prefer silence?

Conclusion

This chapter began with the idea that in approaching organizational change, it is stability that most needs explanation. Furthermore, in describing reasons for resistance to change and the persistence of current patterns, we observed that our present day is unique in its openness to revision of canon-ical stories both in and outside of work. The path this revision ought to take is toward holistic, second-order change.

We continued by maintaining that the problem of organizational change management resides within a larger context of control traceable to the heart of Western culture. By entertaining alternatives to taking control of the change process—such as identifying sources of order that are already there and capitalizing on them—we may not only change the field of organiza-tional behavior but the larger domain of social life.

The final section of the chapter sought to contrast three models of orga-nizational change based on differing models of communication: monologic, transactional, and dialogic. Each of these models is progressively less direc-tive in its approach to control and change management, so much so that in dialogue, change emerges through the joint collaboration of empowered managers and employees talking and acting together. Although all three models are in place today, we wish to argue for the special relevance of the dialogic approach in the development of environmentally adaptive, holisti-cally oriented, high-involvement work communities.

References

Autry, J. A. (1991). *Love and profit: The art of caring leadership*. New York: William Morrow.

Avolio, B. J., & Bass, B. M. (1988). Transformational leadership, charisma, and beyond. In J. G. Hunt, B. R. Baliga, H. P. Dachter, & C. A. Schreisheim (Eds.), *Emerging leadership vistas* (pp. 29–49). Boston: Lexington.

Avolio, B. J., Waldman, D. A., & Einstein, W. O. (1988). Transformational leader-ship in a management game simulation. *Group and Organizational Studies, 13*, 59–80.

Barnet, R., & Cavanaugh, J. (1993). *Global dreams*. New York: Simon & Schuster.

Bartunek, J. M., & Louis, M. R. (1988). The interplay of organizational development and organizational transformation. In W. A. Pasmore & R. W. Woodman (Eds.), *Research in organizational change and development: Vol. 2* (pp. 97–134). Greenwich, CT: JAI Press.

Bass, B. M. (1981). *Stogdill's handbook of leadership: A survey of theory and research*. New York: The Free Press.

Bass, B. M., Waldman, S. A., Avolio, B. J., & Bebb, M. (1987). Transformational leadership and the falling dominoes effect. *Group and Organizational Studies, 12*, 73–87.

Beer, M., Eisenstat, R. A., & Spector, B. (1990). *The critical path to corporate renewal*. Cambridge, MA: Harvard Business School Press.

Bellah, R. N., Madsen, R., Sullivan, W. M., Swidler, A., & Tipton, S. M. (1992). *The good society*. New York: Vintage.

Bennis, W. G. (1984). Transformative power and leadership. In T. J. Sergiovanni & J. E. Corbally (Eds.), *Leadership and organizational culture* (pp. 64–71). Chicago: University of Illinois Press.

Bennis, W. G. (1993). Learning some basic truisms about leadership. In M. Ray & A. Rinzler (Eds.), *The new paradigm in business: Emerging strategies for leadership and organizational change* (pp. 72–80). New York: Putnam.

Bennis, W. G., & Nanus, B. (1985). *Leaders: Strategies for taking charge*. New York: Harper & Row.

Block, P. (1993). *Stewardship: Choosing service over self-interest*. San Francisco: Berrett-Koehler.

Bohm, D. (1980). *Wholeness and the implicate order*. London: Ark Paperbacks.

Bohm, D., & Edwards, M. (1991). *Changing consciousness: Exploring the hidden source of the social, political, and environmental crises facing our world*. San Francisco: HarperSan Francisco.

Burns, J. M. (1978). *Leadership*. New York: Harper & Row.

Cheney, G., & Tompkins, P. K. (1988). On the facts of the text as the basis of human communication research. In J. A. Anderson (Ed.), *Communication yearbook 11* (pp. 455–481). Newbury Park, CA: Sage.

Chilton, K., & Weidenbaum, M. (1994). *A new social contract for the American workplace: From paternalism to partnering* (Center for the Study of American Business, Policy Study 123). St. Louis: Washington University.

Collins, J. C., & Porras, J. I. (1993). Purpose, mission, and vision. In M. Ray & A. Rinzler (Eds.), *The new paradigm in business: Emerging strategies for leadership and organizational change* (pp. 82–89). New York: Putnam.

Conger, J. A., & Kanungo, R. N. (Eds.). (1987). *Charismatic leadership: The elusive factor in organizational effectiveness*. San Francisco: Jossey-Bass.

Covey, S. R. (1989). *The 7 habits of highly effective people: Restoring the character ethic*. New York: Simon & Schuster.

Daft, R. L., Bettenhausen, K. R., & Tyler, B. R. (1993). Implications of top managers' communication choices for strategic change. In G. P. Huber & W. H. Glick (Eds.), *Organizational change and redesign: Ideas and insights for improving performance* (pp. 112–146). New York: Oxford University Press.

Deetz, S. A. (1995). *Transforming communication, transforming business: Building responsive and responsible workplaces*. Cresskill, NJ: Hampton Press.

Deluga, R. J. (1988). Relationship of transformational and transactional leadership with employee influencing strategies. *Group and Organization Studies, 13,* 456–467.

Eisenberg, E. M., & Goodall, H. L. (1997). *Organizational communication: Balancing creativity and constraint* (2nd ed.). New York: St. Martin's Press.

Eisler, R. (1987). *The chalice and the blade*. San Francisco: Harper.

Goodall, H. L., Jr., & Eisenberg, E. M. (1997). The dispossessed. In B. Sypher (Ed.), *More case studies in organizational communication*. New York: Guilford.

Gozdz, K. (1993). Building community as a leadership discipline. In M. Ray & A. Rinzler (Eds.), *The new paradigm in business: Emerging strategies for leadership and organizational change* (pp. 107–119). New York: Putnam.

Hammer, M., & Champy, J. (1993). *Reengineering the corporation.* New York: HarperCollins.

Handy, C. (1994). *The age of paradox.* Boston: Harvard Business School Press.

Hater, J. J., & Bass, B. M. (1988). Superiors' evaluations and subordinates' perceptions of transformational and transactional leadership. *Journal of Applied Psychology, 73,* 695–702.

Henderson, H. (1993). Age of light. In M. Ray & A. Rinzler (Eds.), *The new paradigm in business: Emerging strategies for leadership and organizational change* (pp. 267–275). New York: Putnam.

House, R. J. (1977). A 1976 theory of charismatic leadership. In J. G. Hunt & L. L. Larson (Eds.), *Leadership: The cutting edge* (pp. 189–207). Carbondale: Southern Illinois University Press.

Isaacs, W. N. (1993a). Dialogue: The power of collective thinking. *The Systems Thinker, 4,* 3.

Isaacs, W. N. (1993b). Taking flight: Dialogue, collective thinking, and organizational learning. *Organizational Dynamics, 22*(2), 24–39.

Kanter, R. M. (1983). *The change masters: Innovation and entrepreneurship in the American corporation.* New York: Simon & Schuster.

Kanter, R. M., Stein, B. A., & Jick, T. D. (1992). *The challenge of organizational change: How companies experience and leaders guide it.* New York: The Free Press.

Kouzes, J. M., & Posner, B. Z. (1987). *The leadership challenge: How to get extraordinary things done in organizations.* San Francisco, CA: Jossey-Bass.

Kuhnert, K. W., & Lewis, P. (1987). Transactional and transformational leadership: A constructive/developmental analysis. *Academy of Management Review, 12,* 648–657.

Land, G., & Jarman, B. (1993). Moving beyond breakpoint. In M. Ray & A. Rinzler (Eds.), *The new paradigm in business: Emerging strategies for leadership and organizational change* (pp. 250–266). New York: Putnam.

Landers, L. (1978). *Defective medicine.* New York: Farrar, Straus & Giroux.

Lyotard, J. F. (1984). *The postmodern condition: A report on knowledge* (G. Bennington & B. Massumi, Trans.). Minneapolis: University of Minnesota Press.

Mandel, T. (1993). Giving values a voice: Marketing in the new paradigm. In M. Ray & A. Rinzler (Eds.), *The new paradigm in business: Emerging strategies for leadership and organizational change* (pp. 164–177). New York: Putnam.

Osterburg, R. V. (1993). A new kind of company with a new kind of thinking. *The new paradigm in business: Emerging strategies for leadership and organizational change* (pp. 67–71). New York: Putnam.

Peck, M. S. (1993). *A world waiting to be born: Civility restored.* New York: Bantam.

Quinn, D. (1992). *Ishmael.* New York: Bantam.

Quirke, B. (1995). *Communication change.* London: McGraw-Hill.

Rashford, N. S., & Coghlan, D. (1994). *The dynamics of organizational levels: A change framework for managers and consultants.* Reading, MA: Addison-Wesley.

Ray, M. R. (1993). What is the new paradigm in business? In M. Ray & A. Rinzler (Eds.), *The new paradigm in business: Emerging strategies for leadership and organizational change* (pp. 1–10). New York: Putnam.

Seltzer, J., & Bass, B. M. (1990). Transformational leadership: Beyond initiation and consideration. *Journal of Management, 16,* 693–703.

Stata, R. (1988). The role of the chief executive in articulating the vision. *Interfaces, 18*(3), 3–9.

Tichy, N. M., & Devanna, M. A. (1986). *The transformational leader.* New York: Wiley.

Tichy, N. M., & Ulrich, D. O. (1984). SMR Forum: The leadership challenge—A call for the transformational leader. *Sloan Management Review, 26,* 59–68.

Watts, A. (1967). *The book: On the taboo against knowing who you really are.* New York: Vintage.

Weick, K. E. (1979). *The social psychology of organizing* (2nd ed.). Reading, MA: Addison-Wesley.

Wheatley, M. J. (1992). *Leadership and the new science: Learning about organization from an orderly universe.* San Francisco: Berrett-Koehler.

White, O. F., & McSwain, C. J. (1983). Transformational theory and organizational analysis. In G. Morgan (Ed.), *Beyond method: Strategies for social research* (pp. 292–305). Beverly Hills, CA: Sage.

Yammarino, F. J., & Bass, B. M. (1990). Transformational leadership and multiple levels of analysis. *Human Relations, 43,* 975–995.

Zaleznik, A. (1977). Managers and leaders: Are they different? *Harvard Business Review, 55*(5), 67–80.

Zaleznik, A. (1990). The leadership gap. *Academy of Management Executive, 4*(1), 7–22.

12

Flirting With Meaning

This invited essay considered communication more broadly (not only in organizations) and was a frank critique of any theory that presumes the possibility of "fixing" meaning. I argued instead for a view of language and meaning that both privileges and celebrates ambiguity and contingency and that, in so doing, views individuals as having a flirtatious relationship with any particular interpretation or identity.

This paper began as a panel discussion held at the National Communication Association that featured current work on language in communication. My co-panelists likely expected a very different paper, one focused specifically on the language of work. But when I agreed to write, I was beginning to articulate what seemed like some important observations about language and the development of identity. The papers were later published in a special issue of the Journal of Language and Social Psychology; *this essay is easily identifiable as the one "least like the others" in that issue of the journal.*

SOURCE: Eisenberg, E. M. (1998). Flirting with meaning. *Journal of Language and Social Psychology, 17,* 97–108. Copyright © 1998, Sage Publications, Inc.

Only in the realm of fiction do we find the plurality of lives we need.

—Sigmund Freud

C onsiderations of equivocality and ambiguity inevitably begin with speculation about how one might use these attributes of language to do things to others. Whether one's motives are nefarious (as in certain well-known instances of plausible deniability) or pure (as in some religious and spiritual discourse), the attitude is the same—that ambiguity is a property of language that individuals may exploit to accomplish their communicative goals (Eisenberg, 1984).

Although there is nothing wrong with this strategic perspective, there is an alternate view of ambiguous communication that attends to the lived consequences of various ways of speaking—and in particular, of equivocal ways of speaking—for one's sense of identity. This approach makes a connection between the epistemic and the ontological and, in so doing, draws together the problems of linguistic and existential meaning. Put another way, this angle on communication highlights the close relationship between the possibility of being clear about what we mean, and the associated likelihood of knowing who we are.

Writers focusing on the ontological significance of linguistic ambiguity hail from diverse disciplines and are largely unaware of each other's work. This essay seeks to present the key features of such a perspective on communication, to highlight how the approach differs from others, and to describe three concrete programs of research in which the approach has been usefully applied to social situations.

Departures: Ambiguity, Identity, and the Postmodern

As sociologist Donald Levine (1976) observed, Western civilization is marked by a "flight from ambiguity" associated with the rationalization of the world. Whereas in traditional cultures, magic, ritual, and faith played a central role in sense making, in modern Western society, these activities are for the most part seen as inferior to the scientific method as routes to reliable knowledge. Central to the modernist project is the elevation of two related notions: truth and identity. The modern world consists of distinct, unified subjects perceiving a knowable, objective reality (Spretnak, 1997). In service of this worldview, the express purpose of communication is to discover what is true about the world and to transmit this valuable information to others. When knowledge is defined this way, communication necessarily appears as discrete messages traveling an inert conduit between self and other.

In recent years, the modernist project has come under considerable attack. Criticisms have been far-reaching, focusing on the existence of a multiplicity of truths and identities that are themselves unstable and ever changing. The implications of this postmodern perspective for communication are dramatic. Lacking a coherent and fixed notion of self, is communication possible? And if there are no foundational truths apart from human culture, language, and sense making, what is communication for? And perhaps most important, if we exist as individuals communicating only in language, could alternate ways of speaking suggest other viable options for being alive?

The search for literal, fixed, and representational meaning in language is most likely futile, inasmuch as there is "no natural end, either in the form of literal meanings of expressions or ultimate knowledge of the world, to the explication of linguistically mediated meaning" (Rommetveit, 1974, p. 125). The postmodern critique of fixed meaning offers some clear lessons for zealots of certainty, wherever they reside. Battles over who has access to the "truth" are bloody markers in the history of the world—each holocaust finds its reasons in certainty and in separation. All efforts to fix meaning— to establish certainty in some area of knowledge—are also acts of power and control (Foucault, 1988). In this way, a certain rigid attitude toward communication is always implicated in our capacity to hate and to kill.

I do not, however, mean to suggest that human beings can somehow opt out of the struggle for reliable knowledge. On the contrary, the structure of human consciousness makes the pursuit of certainty inevitable and the development of a separate identity equally predictable. But, acknowledging this tendency reveals only part of the story. Just as people say that "plans don't work, but planning does," we all pursue truth but find mostly contradiction; we struggle for authenticity and a coherent self but find life fraught with surprises (Phillips, 1994).

This said, the *particular attitude toward truth and certainty* that is encouraged by a society or community matters greatly. This is because a community's view of language and communication reveals a great deal about the kinds of human beings who can grow and develop there. For example, a view of communication that idealizes clarity and unisignative meaning tends to construct people who define themselves in narrow ways. The modernist worldview urges us to tell a unified story of who we are (e.g., doctor, lawyer, secretary, Democrat, student) and insists that internal contradictions are problematic and in need of fixing. Alternatively, a more constitutive, contingent, provisional view of communication would lead us to identify not with our present story but with the storyteller; not with one's current identity but with the generative process of sense making from which numerous possible life stories might arise. Such a perspective once again shifts the purpose of communication, this time from a process dedicated to describing the past to one designed to entertain future possibilities.

Communication, Identity, and Interpersonal Relationships

A contingent approach to communication and identity has significant implications for close relationships. According to Adam Phillips (1994), "It is through desire, in language . . . that the potential for connection between people is stored and kept safe" (p. 81). Similarly, reflecting on the work of Kenneth Burke (1984), Payne (1995) maintains that "the 'substance' and meaning of our language is the set of relationships we carry on with each other and the world. . . . We desperately need to devise provisional and poetic language that renders and evokes understanding of these relationships" (p. 337).

Full appreciation of this perspective demands a view of communication that goes well beyond the symbolic transmission of information and is both dialogic and ontological in nature (cf. Hyde, 1995). Put this way, the most critical function of communication is transformation, or the capacity to suggest new possibilities for individuals to be together. Following Rommetveit (1974),

> Once the other person accepts the invitation to engage in that dialogue, his [sic] life situation is temporarily transformed. What is meant and understood is from that moment on determined by a joint commitment to a temporarily shared social reality, established and continually modified by acts of communication. (p. 79)

Seeing communication ontologically—in terms of its impact on alternate ways of being in the world—foregrounds the possibilities inherent in *all* interaction. This view is more forward looking and less concerned than most with either intentionality or representation, both of which reference the past. In essence, ontological distinctions are acts of hope, clearings for new ways of thinking and being that "expand the possibility of the world's meaning" (Hyde, 1995, p. 11). The ultimate goal of ontological communication is the "freedom to be" (Hyde, 1995, p. 2).

Everyday communication, from this perspective, is more music than mathematics, more plural than singular (Goodall, 1991). One cannot establish with finality the meaning of any utterance (or of any relationship or identity), because "no language act is perfectly able to constitute or legislate the conditions of being and doing" (Payne, 1995, p. 338). Consequently,

> Students of human communication who abandon monistic assumptions will accordingly have to redefine their trade in some important respects: To explicate the ambiguities of life will not only be considered a legitimate, but possibly even the most important part of their task. (Rommetveit, 1980, p. 146)

From Ambiguity to Action: The Importance of Commitment

Yet, despite this inherent ambiguity of communication, our faith in the possibility of clarity and the existence of shared meaning permits us to carry on. Put differently, "whether or not all meaning can be made explicit or not is perhaps less critical than the belief that it can" (Olsen, 1977, p. 275). One might say that the true genius of humanity is the capacity to *act as if* meaning and identity were fixed or fixable, as if communication were possible. We persist in this belief, fully aware that our business with meaning is never finished, that every communicative act has a fundamentally emergent and unpredictable quality, and that we must always await "the next turn in the dialogue, the next moment in the dialectic" (Payne, 1995, p. 338).

Nevertheless, our commitment to live as if communication were possible—and to the ideology of "shared meaning"—is essential to understanding our relationship with language and with each other. I am not suggesting the acceptance of an ambivalent, wholly relativist view of meaning and identity that leaves us unable to choose among alternative constructions of reality. Quite the contrary, living well requires the ability both to envision new ways of being and to commit to a chosen course of action for a period of time. It is to regard one's self—and one's life choices—with a certain degree of lightness, detachment, and humor—while continuing to play the game.

Ontological Approaches to Communication and Identity

If our faith in the possibility of communication is a singular strength, perhaps our greatest weakness is the tendency to take constructions of self, other, and the world too seriously and allow our attachment to a chosen worldview irreparably to divide us from diverse others. One could argue that the central crisis of our species is fragmentation and division, or the inability to see the forest for the trees (Senge, 1990). In Western society, this tendency is fueled by centuries of unchecked nationalism and a philosophy of individualism (Bellah, Madsen, Sullivan, Swidler, & Tipton, 1985). Public life as most Westerners have come to know it—in which individuals and families seek to maximize their personal gain and well-being—has, for many, led to a profound sense of meaninglessness and of fear.

The consequences of maintaining an isolated view of the self—emphasizing both difference and separation—are disastrous for individuals and for society. Psychologically and emotionally, such fragmentation is unhealthy for body and soul. Socially and ecologically, it is precisely our ability to imagine humanity as somehow separate—in, rather than of, the world—that allows us to commit acts of terrifying violence on others and on nature (Watts, 1972).

So why does the quest for clarity and a consistent self continue with such enthusiasm? What does talking about certainty help us to avoid talking about? When people struggle to hold onto the possibility of certainty, when they identify with the current story they are telling and not with the storyteller, it is a way of not thinking about what might happen to their sense of self were it truly open to co-construction through communication with others. Whereas a worldview characterized by certainty and stability appears relatively resistant to change, one that is open to multiple meanings risks profound personal and societal transformation. Simply put, authentic dialogue is always chancy, because identity, not just meaning, is always at stake.

Although a detailed history of the philosophical underpinnings of this view of communication is well beyond the scope of this article, some very brief references will help to contextualize my argument. In the 20th century, the role of language in philosophy has grown in prominence, as writers of various backgrounds have struggled to draw connections between the symbolic and existential realms. Notable in this regard are Ludwig Wittgenstein's (1972) "language games," Martin Heidegger's (1994) view of language as the "house of Being," and Suzanne Langer's (1951) "philosophy in a new key." Among contemporary philosophers, John Searle's (1992) theory of speech acts and Richard Rorty's (1979) epistemological pragmatism come closest to the view of communication that I have been advancing here. Although there are many important differences among these authors, they share a view of language that goes beyond the representational and focuses on the ways in which communication constructs, transforms, and allows people to cope with an emerging reality. In the field of communication, John Stewart (1996), Don Ellis (1986), and Bruce Hyde (1995) have been struggling with many of the same issues.

Central to this work is the assumption that the relationship between communication and identity is a recursive one. Changes in our experience of the world, which many today characterize as "moving in multiple directions all at once," require a new language of coping that is largely equivocal. At the same time, changes in the mode of communication—from less to more equivocal forms—can open up space for new ways of being in the world. Put differently, this approach requires

> approaching texts and human events as moments of emergence, contingency, and purposive creativity, moments that have already come and gone, and whose "meaning" can only be found by tracing their influence upon the next moment of transformational action. (Payne, 1995, p. 338)

Three Examples

Some concrete examples may be helpful. A number of projects are under way that invoke communication, not for its ability to fix meaning or promote understanding but rather for its capacity to problematize accepted meanings as a means of creating new kinds of people capable of an expanded range of actions. The projects I discuss below have two commonalities. First, each starts with the assumption that it is natural for humans to get stuck in interpretive ruts, to reproduce shopworn plots, occasionally with dire consequences. Second, each offers specific methods for creating space between people and their worldviews through special forms of communication. The three projects I will discuss are Friedman's (1993) new language of change, Peter Senge's (1990) theory of organizational dialogue, and Phillips's (1994) contingent view of the self.

Friedman's New Language of Change

It is by now commonplace to claim that the self is socially constructed (Berger & Luckmann, 1967). But, what does this really mean? In a superficial sense, we use the ideas and words of others to describe our own experiences and, over time, may come to adopt these descriptions as our own. In a deeper sense, however, language itself constructs the idea of being, of existing as beings, of the very possibility of individual selves. In this sense, following Heidegger (1994) and Gadamer (1994), it may be said that our language "speaks us."

The relevance of this deeper view of language lies in the felt discontinuity between what we know about ourselves and our lived experience. Life is a more or less conscious exploration of this discontinuity. From this perspective, our identities can be seen as social constructions, typifications we have appropriated and found useful but that never quite fit. Slippages around the edges of who we think we are alert us to the existence of borders that separate us from what else we might someday become. Although we grasp the steering wheel of our carefully constructed lives, our real passion is for the road ahead. This is what Joseph Campbell (Campbell & Moyers, 1988) meant when he said that what people want most is not to know the meaning of life but to have an experience of life that resonates with their total being.

Although we may catch glimpses of an alternative reality, it takes considerable courage to abandon an established worldview. The difficulty of breaking free from negative patterns of self-definition is the impetus for Friedman's (1993) approach. In this book, he describes a class of therapies designed to help people "re-story their lives" by bringing forth new possibilities through communication. These therapeutic approaches take an expressly ambivalent attitude toward history and the client's self-description of problems. Instead, when the client raises negative examples (e.g., "My mother never paid attention to me"), the therapist asks for exceptions (e.g., "Tell me about a time when you felt comfortable around your mother."). By searching for exceptions to problems, the practitioner strives to reframe the therapeutic conversation from one saturated with problems to one full of possibility (Friedman & Fanger, 1991).

In addition to identifying exceptions, this "therapy of possibility" further accentuates the positive by asking the client to construct an ideal image of the future. This is accomplished through the "miracle question": "If a miracle happened tonight while you were sleeping, and tomorrow you awoke to a perfect world, what would this world be like? What would people be thinking, doing, or saying?" Consistent with the optimism of this approach, these therapists see their clients as *experts* capable of change.

In an essay titled "Escape from the Furies," Friedman's (1993) summary of his therapeutic approach is well worth quoting at length.

> I think of myself as a "possibility therapist" [who] . . . views language as the key to therapeutic change. Therapy is a conversation in which dialogue between therapist and client leads to the generation of new meanings, understandings, and options for action. The goal is to engage in conversations with the client in which alternative views of the "self-in-context" become possible and even inevitable. . . . Since meanings in language are inherently unstable (i.e., negotiable), opportunities exist for co-creating ideas that support client competence and allow for the construction of new more empowering stories. As Parry (1991) puts it so well, "A narrative therapist seeks to raise into the foreground of the person's attention, alternative stories . . . in order to challenge the received text or life-story in its constraining role" (p. 52). (pp. 272–273)

Finally, in their analysis of an adolescent girl attempting suicide, Hoffman-Hennessy and Davis (1993) stress the importance of "holding a position of ambiguity" in the service of change. Their clinical work leads them to conclude that not only epistemology but also psychology are flawed models from which to change human behavior:

> For us, most of the beliefs that surround the concept of psychology deserve to be challenged. . . . In fact, it might not be such a bad idea to decide that psychology is a flawed field and replace it with a new emphasis on human communication. (p. 362)

Senge's Organizational Dialogue

For Senge (1990) and his colleagues, fragmentation of perception and unchallenged "mental models" are at the root of many social and organizational problems. Inspired by visionary physicist David Bohm (1983), Senge describes our current predicament as one in which the vast majority of people are incapable of seeing the systems in which they are a participant, and consequently overidentify with their worldview, which is by definition partisan and partial (Eisenberg & Goodall, 1997). From this starting point, Senge calls the typical communicative exchange among organizational members "discussion," during which people share ideas in oppositional ways, seeking to dominate, failing to listen, unwilling to compromise, and ultimately being blind to opportunities for learning from one another.

An alternative to the discussion model of organizational communication is "dialogue" (Bakhtin, 1981; Bohm, 1983; Buber, 1970; Eisenberg & Goodall, 1997; Senge, 1990). Dialogue begins with participants agreeing to suspend their certainties and to disconnect their egos from their ideas. In so doing, mutual exploration of creative solutions becomes possible. Common ground can be found because identifying points of agreement is no longer seen as a sign of weakness. Dialogue constitutes a kind of learning by expanding, through which multiple perspectives are not offered as competing but rather combine for a richer understanding of the situation.

Senge's (1990) view of organizational communication is especially timely given the blinding speed at which organizations and their environments are changing. Experts on business strategy, for example, have all but given up on competitor analysis as a means for defining the direction of a business (Hamel, 1997). The problem with focusing on competitors is that it limits one's thinking to the ideas and assumptions that already exist somewhere. Success in business today requires people to think outside of the frame, to challenge industry orthodoxies, and in so doing to reinvent one's company.

Imagination is the scarce resource. Consequently, the ability to engage in creative dialogue—and through communication, to systematically question and abandon prior actions, practices, and mental models—is *the* critical leadership competency. Attachment to accepted historical principles and personal investments in the long-standing story of the firm will more often than not prove one's undoing. Essential is the ability to engage in the organized abandonment of accepted practices (Drucker, 1997), to self-consciously and systematically replace the old theory of the business with a new one.

Phillips's Contingent View of the Self

For Phillips (1994), the good life appears as a never-ending flirtation with various modes of being. In this light, the struggle to establish a single, coherent self is beside the point—living well means mastering movement in multiple, often conflicting directions. Nonetheless, most people do not share this point of view; fantasies of coherence, clarity, and single meaning are "hypnotic like the horizon" (p. 44). Phillips is highly critical of the monolithic view and its psychological consequences. Alternatively, he sides with his colleague, Ferenczi, who maintains that "a patient is not cured by free association, he is cured when he *can* free-associate" (as cited in Phillips, 1994, p. 67). What Phillips takes this comment to mean is that the goal of recovery is not understanding but possibility, freeing the potentially endless process of reinvention, and indulging in the significant pleasures of misunderstanding. By gaining a freedom of perspective, the primary "instinct to elaborate oneself" is advanced (Bollas, as cited in Phillips, 1994, p. 158).

Despite centuries of scientific, philosophical, and political efforts to purify language and "save" human beings from ambiguity, we have found the world profoundly resistant to any such final solution. Following Weedon (1987),

> We are neither the authors of the ways in which we understand our lives, nor are we unified rational beings. . . . It is language in the form of conflicting discourses which constitutes us as conscious thinking subjects and enables us to give meaning to the world. (p. 32)

Furthermore, these divergent discourses need not and cannot be fully integrated or resolved. What one can do is complicate one's own sense-making capabilities as a means of opening oneself to a broader range of stories (Weick, 1979). For Phillips (1994), the ability to carry on a flirtation with one's place in the world, while at the same time committing to a selected course of action, is the essence of mental health.

Implications: Playing Ball on Running Water

Rigid attachment to one's worldview on one hand and openness to reinvention on the other are ends of a continuum along which people of various cultures, personalities, and perspectives can be placed. Just as certain
authors could be characterized as relatively more sympathetic to a representational view of communication, people in various professions (e.g.,
lawyers, writers, politicians) are keenly aware of how meaning is constantly
negotiated. What is more, attitudes toward communication may be self-perpetuating; throughout the life span, the general tendency is for dogmatic
individuals to become even more set in their ways, whereas those open to
renewal reap the rewards of this stance and seek ever widening possibilities
later on. Or, in the words of my protean colleague, Linda Andrews (personal communication, October 31, 1997), "I never ask what I should be
doing, only what's next."

By now, I have hopefully made the point that in all realms of life, it is
essential to recognize when a particular story line (paradigm, worldview,
philosophy, theory of the business) has run its course and needs to be
replaced. The problem with doing so is that it can leave people feeling
groundless. What can substitute for a familiar story? And, the problem may
be deeper still: For example, Phillips (1996) claims that our taboos about
marital infidelity are less about a mate who strays than they are about our
"fidelity to fidelity," to the idea of a center that holds. Without such a reliable center, life is like playing ball on running water (Reynolds, 1984), in
which we must continually find ways to keep the game going despite an
ever-changing context.

The view of communication described in this essay, then, requires a
different source of emotional stability, one found not in clarity or coherent
identity but in a reliable mode of being. After all, what remains constant in
a world of ever-changing jobs, careers, technologies, residences, and relationships? It is the storyteller, the core of being that never changes. Essential
to the survival of the storyteller is what Bennis (1997) calls "hardiness," the
ability to cultivate a continued sense of perspective that is solid and liquid,
stable and flexible. This sense of stability requires a commitment to living
both within and beyond the current frame, to both make clear choices and
to maintain a healthy detachment from each of them.

Implications for pedagogy are clear. An appreciation of diversity in all of
its forms requires that individuals understand the difference between how
things are now and how they might be tomorrow, and a further appreciation
for the power of transformation and openness to alternative constructions of
reality in today's turbulent social environment. Successful living in the world

today requires an adaptive, contingent, dialogic approach to identity and communication. In the end, it can hardly be any other way. Were we to try to end our provisional relationship with language and communication, there is every indication that meaning would continue its flirtation with us.

AUTHOR'S NOTE: An earlier version of this article was presented at the annual meeting of the Speech Communication Association, San Antonio, Texas, November 1995. Many thanks to Lisa Tillmann-Healy, David Payne, Paul Mineo, Bruce Hyde, and Mark Hamilton for their insight and inspiration.

References

Bakhtin, M. (1981). *The dialogic imagination.* Austin: University of Texas Press.

Bellah, R., Madsen, R., Sullivan, W., Swidler, A., & Tipton, S. (1985). *Habits of the heart.* Berkeley: University of California Press.

Bennis, W. (1997, October). *The essence of leadership.* Paper presented at the Global Institute for Leadership Development conference, San Diego, CA.

Berger, P., & Luckmann, T. (1967). *The social construction of reality.* New York: Anchor.

Bohm, D. (1983). *Wholeness and the implicate order.* New York: Ark Paperbacks.

Buber, M. (1970). *I and thou.* New York: Scribner's.

Burke, K. (1984). *Permanence and change.* Berkeley: University of California Press.

Campbell, J., & Moyers, B. (1988). *The power of myth.* Garden City, NY: Doubleday.

Drucker, P. (1997, October). *Leadership past and present.* Paper presented at the Global Institute for Leadership Development, San Diego, CA.

Eisenberg, E. (1984). Ambiguity as strategy in organizational communication. *Communication Monographs, 51,* 227–242.

Eisenberg, E., & Goodall, H. L., Jr. (1997). *Organizational communication: Balancing creativity and constraint,* 2nd edition. New York: St. Martin's.

Ellis, D. (1986). *Contemporary issues in language and discourse processes.* Hillsdale, NJ: Lawrence Erlbaum.

Foucault, M. (1988). Strategies of power. In L. Kritzman (Ed.), *Michel Foucault: Politics, philosophy, culture.* New York: Routledge.

Friedman, S. (1993). *The new language of change.* New York: Guilford.

Friedman, S., & Fanger, M. (1991). *Expanding therapeutic possibilities: Getting results in brief psychotherapy.* New York: Lexington.

Gadamer, H. (1994). *Ruth and method* (2nd rev. ed.). New York: Continuum.

Goodall, H. L. (1991). *Living in the rock n' roll mystery.* Carbondale: Southern Illinois University Press.

Hamel, G. (1997, October). *The search for strategy.* Paper presented at the Global Institute for Leadership Development, San Diego, CA.

Heidegger, M. (1994). *Basic questions of philosophy.* Bloomington: Indiana University Press.

Hoffman-Hennessy, L., & Davis, J. (1993). Tekka with feathers: Talking about talking (about suicide). In S. Friedman (Ed.), *The new language of change* (pp. 345–373). New York: Guilford.

Hyde, B. (1995, February). *An ontological approach to education.* Paper presented to the annual meeting of the Western Speech Communication Association, Portland, OR.

Langer, S. (1951). *Philosophy in a new key.* New York: New American Library.

Levine, D. (1976). *The flight from ambiguity.* Chicago: University of Chicago Press.

Olsen, D. (1977). From utterance to text: The bias of language in speech and writing. *Harvard Educational Review, 47,* 257–281.

Payne, D. (1995). Kenneth Burke and contemporary criticism. *Text and Performance Quarterly, 15,* 333–341.

Phillips, A. (1994). *On flirtation.* Cambridge, MA: Harvard University Press.

Phillips, A. (1996). *Monogamy.* New York: Pantheon.

Reynolds, D. (1984). *Playing ball on running water.* New York: Quill.

Rommetveit, R. (1974). *On message structure, a framework for the study of language and communication.* London: Wiley.

Rommetveit, R. (1980). On "meanings" of acts and what is meant and made known by what is said in a pluralistic social world. In M. Brenner (Ed.), *The structure of action* (pp. 108–149). New York: St. Martin's.

Rorty, R. (1979). *Philosophy and the mirror of nature.* Princeton, NJ: Princeton University Press.

Searle, J. (1992). *The rediscovery of the mind.* Cambridge, MA: MIT Press.

Senge, P. (1990). *The fifth discipline.* New York: Doubleday Currency.

Spretnak, C. (1997). *The resurgence of the real.* Reading, MA: Addison-Wesley.

Stewart, J. (1996). *Beyond the symbol model.* Albany, NY: State University of New York Press.

Watts, A. (1972). *The book: On the taboo against knowing who you really are.* New York: Vintage.

Weedon, C. (1987). *Feminist practice and poststructuralist theory.* London: Basil Blackwell.

Weick, K. (1979). *The social psychology of organizing.* Reading, MA: Addison-Wesley.

Wittgenstein, L. (1972). *On certainty.* New York: Harper.

PART III

A New Communication Aesthetic

I n this final part of the book, I take the contingent model of communication and seek out useful practical applications. In so doing, I move beyond an exclusively organizational focus to look more generally at the relationship between views of meaning and perspectives on human identity and relationships. Specifically, I emphasize the value of examining how we are attached to various interpretations of our lives and how the strength of these attachments affects our attitudes and behavior. I conclude with a prescription for a new aesthetics of contingency, the pursuit of which has the potential to promote a more peaceful coexistence among diverse individuals.

13

The Kindness of Strangers

Hospitality in Organizational Communication Scholarship

This invited essay sought to apply the aesthetics of ambiguity and contingency to my own subdiscipline, organizational communication. The hospitality metaphor illustrated the overriding importance of coordinated action—of kindness to one's colleagues, regardless of scholarly perspective—as a positive alternative to focusing on intellectual coherence and the elusive shared meaning.

The goal of the volume in which this paper appeared (Foundations of Organizational Communication: Finding Common Ground) *was to call a much-needed truce between various factions within organizational communication. The editors had the ingenious idea of asking various scholars "representing" different perspectives to write about how their interests connect to those who take an alternate view. Once the major perspectives were discussed, a number of people (myself included) were asked to comment on the exchange, and this essay is what emerged. I thought it would be interesting to apply the organizing theme of the book to our field in particular. In so doing, I sought another opportunity to both explain and argue for a view of organizing that privileges coordinated action over mutual disclosure.*

SOURCE: Eisenberg, E. M. (2000). The kindness of strangers: Hospitality in organizational communication scholarship. In S. Corman & M. S. Poole (Eds.), *Foundations of organizational communication: Finding common ground* (pp. 113–119). New York: Guilford. Copyright © 2000, The Guilford Press. Reprinted with permission.

Our common future depends upon our capacity to welcome the
stranger, that is, our capacity for hospitality.

—Darrell Fasching (1996)

Perspective

In times past, religions, cultures, and individuals lived in relative isolation—
there were many traditions but no single world tradition. Today, with the
help of revolutionary communication technology, we are in the process
of creating a global civilization. As such, we are challenged to design new
ways of relating to one another that eschew simple agreement in favor of
"unified diversity" (Eisenberg, 1984). Religious studies scholar Darrell
Fasching (1996) characterizes these contemporary approaches as requiring a
renewed hospitality toward strangers, one that includes an active willingness
to temporarily "pass over" into another's world and see things through their
eyes. When we do this, according to Fasching, we return to our own tradition enriched with new insight.

The primary authors of this collection are committed to some version of
this ideal, the details of which are likely to be familiar to students of communication. In essence, Miller, Cheney, and Mumby each propose some sort
of dialogue among perspectives, one that makes possible respectful communication among widely varying points of view (Arnett, 1986; Buber, 1965a,
1965b; cf. Eisenberg, Andrews, Laine-Timmerman, & Murphy, 1999). In this
way, they call us to traverse the narrow ridge between self and other, simultaneously recognizing our own subjectivity and making room for people who
are most unlike us. Dialogue holds promise not only for individual relationships but for the total research enterprise. Rather than regarding our scholarly perspectives as opposed, we can treat them as different but additive, each
contributing a new way of seeing organizational communication. Cheney's
metaphor is apt—in a dark cave, each new flashlight promises to illuminate
a detail or passageway that was heretofore invisible.

It is no accident that our colleagues in the field of organizational behavioral
are engaged in a similar conversation concerning multiparadigm relations.
Central to this exchange is the notion of *incommensurability*: the idea that different perspectives employ different languages, and hence are beyond reconciliation. Recently, however, there have been some positive signs. Responding
to a journal forum on organizational theory, Karl Weick (1999) remarked that
"reflexive conversation about organizational theory is possible" (p. 804), and
recommended that, like smart firefighters, scholars "drop their heavy tools
of paradigms and monologues" to communicate more effectively. In support

of this idea, he offers the following quote from Czarniawska's (1998) essay, "Who Is Afraid of Incommensurability?":

> There are much more serious dangers in life than dissonance in organization theory. Crossing the street every day is one such instance. We may as well abandon this self-centered rhetoric [about incommensurability] and concentrate on a more practical issue: it seems that we would like to be able to talk to one another, and from time to time have an illusion of understanding what the other is saying. (p. 274)

Put differently, if there is anything like "common ground" to be explored here, it can only be found in dialogue (Anderson, Cissna, & Arnett, 1994; Eisenberg & Goodall, 1997; Senge, 1990). The focus of this dialogue, at least initially, should be an organizational practice, the micropolitics of everyday communication. No matter what our perspective, we share a desire to link our viewpoint to meaningful action. From personal narratives to performance management, the proof of any perspective's power is in the practice's pudding.

Comments on the Chapters

In her chapter, Kathy Miller argues persuasively that the interpretive turn in organizational communication created a caricature of positivism, one that no longer describes the vast majority of social scientific practitioners. Furthermore, she suggests that while communication researchers for the most part recognize the impossibility of value-free inquiry, this is not sufficient reason to abandon objectivity as a goal. She calls for an end to the "vilification" of an outmoded positivism that no longer exists. This seems most sensible, and I look forward to conversing with those colleagues in search of important overlap in our work. At the same time, at least to me, there were some revealing slips in Miller's otherwise exemplary performance. For example, I had some anxious moments when she casually referenced "progress" as a goal of modified objectivists (one could ask, "Progress toward what?" "By what criteria?" "In whose interest?"), as well as when she tried to pry apart individuals' "lenses" from the "real world out there." With regard to this latter distinction, she quotes Phillips (1990), who in discussing Freudian concepts asserts that "believing in these things [like ego and id] does not make them real" (p. 43). I would beg to differ: it is precisely beliefs of this kind that are *most* real in their consequences, both for their adherents and for others (Jackson, 1989).

George Cheney is equally inspiring in his reflexive look at the many meanings of interpretation. While rejecting relativism, he argues convincingly for a multiparadigm approach to revealing the many different sides of any story, and for placing these versions in conversation with one another. For me, the best thing about his chapter was its light touch, which somehow manages to engage significant questions about communication while modeling the very openness he is advocating. Also helpful is Cheney's admonition that interpretive scholars must "come to terms with the material world," as well as his passing suggestion to look more closely at distributed cognition, which promises to provide a more useful operationalization of intersubjectivity than we have yet seen.

Finally, Dennis Mumby is on target in his interrogation of the binary oppositions that have perpetuated the functionalist-interpretivist debate for nearly two decades. Using a variety of examples, he affirms what for communication scholars is by now commonplace: that individual identity and social structure arise together through everyday communicative praxis. The push and pull inherent in this structurational process *is* power in action, neither purely objective nor purely subjective, neither fully cognitive nor behavioral. He further suggests that the proper object of communicative study is the communicative act, which in every case is a complex nexus of creativity and constraint (Eisenberg & Goodall, 1997; Martin, 1992). Finally, his four candidate "problematics"—voice, rationality, organization, and the organization-society relationship—seem to me fruitful avenues for future research with relevance across a range of disparate perspectives.

Along the way, Mumby references Habermas's (1984) description of three "quasi-transcendental" human interests: technical (toward prediction and control), practical (toward understanding and community), and emancipatory (toward autonomy and empowerment). These three capture nicely the various urges to study organizational communication, and one would be hard-pressed to find anyone in organizational studies who would challenge their importance. Moreover, these terms reflect the politics of epistemology that underlies the deployment of such terms as "functional," "interpretive," and "critical" to describe research programs. That we endorse these goals as a collectivity does not, of course, mean that *each* of us foregrounds *each* one in his or her work! Instead, the *set* of interests is maintained through a kind of division of labor, through which individual members and groups carry certain commitments on behalf of the field. I wish to discuss this process next.

Projective Identification in Organizational Communication

Those familiar with family systems theory will recognize the notion that while in theory each person has the capacity to display the total spectrum of possible behaviors, in practice important characteristics are distributed throughout the system, such that individual members "carry" certain key attributes for the whole. For example, while everyone needs privacy, nurturing, and the ability to express anger, these behaviors may be "assigned" or "taken on" by different family members, such that only dad can get angry, only mom can withdraw, and only big sister gets nurtured (Hoffman, 1982).

Members take on roles. At first, this distribution of qualities may serve a useful organizing function both for the individual and for the group. Over time, however, such divisions become caricatures as people can get stuck in a one-dimensional existence. Moreover, because the system needs the whole set of qualities, it resists change on the part of any one member—the quiet child is chastised for speaking up, the wild one for withdrawing, the smart one for taking time out to rest or to play. While the preservation of the *set* of capacities may sometimes be functional for the family, the method by which they are distributed takes its toll on individuals and relationships.

The communicative process by which this uneven distribution of qualities occurs has been called "projective identification" (Scarf, 1987). By enacting a limited side of ourselves, we suppress qualities with which we are uncomfortable, what Jung called the "shadow" self. Hence the "macho" male disdains any signs of personal sensitivity, the "organized" woman all evidence of weakness or chaos. Over time, we become lopsided in our orientation and behavior.

What is more, we are both ambivalent and unconscious about our shadow selves; we both consciously disdain that which we have abandoned, and unconsciously seek it so that we may recover balance. This is why we tend to associate with others who are one-sided in ways that *complement* our own tendencies, often without knowing why we do it. We project onto the other person those qualities we have repressed in ourselves, and if we have chosen "well" they are all too happy to oblige. The nurturer pairs with someone in need of nurturing; the raging boss finds subordinates who are willing to be yelled at. In time, we revive our lifelong project of repressing our shadow side, only now with a more tangible target: the other person (or group). It is far easier to blame someone else (for being lazy, unmotivated, immoral, too sensitive, out of control) than it is to confront our internal conflicts over being unbalanced. War is declared, and given the right conditions everyone faults everyone else for expressing qualities they have repressed in themselves. Taken to an (il)logical extreme, the system disintegrates, and each individual is free to start again with a new cast of characters, chosen again for their willingness to embody the shadow side. Learning and personal growth are impossible. *It is only when people become conscious of their tendency to attack in others what they most fear in themselves that this cycle may be interrupted.*

Arguments over research perspectives in organizational communication show many of the features of projective identification. By this I mean that researchers associated with various "camps" often display strong emotions and attachments to their perspectives, accompanied by an unwillingness to listen to other perspectives with anything remotely resembling an open mind. It is as if they are afraid that allowing a multiplicity of approaches would somehow contaminate or pollute the field as a whole, and reflect badly on all of us. This is an especially ironic stance for a communication scholar to take, given our presumed understanding of the value and importance of dialogue across difference.

From this viewpoint, it is easy to see that while certain groups and individuals have chosen to emphasize one or another of Habermas's interests, taken together we have managed to retain them all. Along these lines, and with an appreciative and generous spirit, Miller, Cheney, and Mumby have made a breakthrough in thinking about our community of scholars. They have reconsidered our field as embodied by all three interests, then worked to show how different scholars have chosen to foreground different themes.

For example, the neo-positivists Miller describes help us to remember that, taken to unreasonable extremes, social constructionism becomes a naive sort of hubris, inasmuch as one rarely gets the reality one seeks to create (Ortner, 1984). Cheney's meditation on the multiplicity of meanings of interpretation recalls the many ways personal agency matters, and how patterns of interpretation have serious consequences. Finally, Mumby's recapitulation of the critical agenda provides a valuable reminder of how meaning and interpretation, knowledge and communication never exist apart from hierarchy, and that hierarchy always translates into an unequal distribution of power. Taken together, we could hardly ask for more; our collective memory is strengthened by the way each scholar has framed their contribution not as oppositional, but as additive. But many readers will have a different response, which I address next.

Scholarship as Attachment

Some of you appreciate the idea of projective identification in principle, but are unwilling to see it working in this instance; instead, you insist on the incommensurability of perspectives and find distasteful the mixing of goals, metaphors, and epistemological and ontological assumptions. But where does this desire for perspectival purity come from? It is one thing to argue *from* a perspective, quite another to insist that one's view is superior to all others.

Indeed, the sort of loyalty to a perspective that requires the denial or denigration of alternative perspectives is all too familiar in human relationships, visible in discussions of religion, ethnicity, and national origin. But why with regard to scholarship?

For most of us, our professional perspectives serve as important resources for our identities. As a result, the usual risks associated with ego development apply: we tend to take ourselves too seriously, to confuse our reality with "the" reality, and to become overly attached to our perspective or worldview. I have stated elsewhere that the history of this way of thinking about the world is deeply troubling, in that "every holocaust finds its reasons in certainty and in separation" (Eisenberg, 1998). Our quest for purity is as a rule motivated by fear of the "other," and by what openness to difference might do to our sense of self, and to the integrity of our institutional "homes" (Calás & Smircich, 1999b). The worst-case scenario: Insecure in our own position, unconsciously recognizing our repressed tendencies in others, we caricature (and may seek to silence) opposing perspectives, in the hope of remaking the world in familiar imagery. When we succeed even partially (and, thankfully, we are rarely successful in silencing the other), the result is anticlimactic. Inasmuch as we rely on the "deviant" to prove our normalcy, once the other is gone we have nowhere to turn but inward, and what we find there is not comforting. New scapegoats must be found, and the cycle begins again.

But there is another way. To me, a respectful dialogue among differences in perspective is the best choice we have for perpetuating individuality and community, difference and cohesion. Philosopher Alan Watts (1972) described this process as playing "the game of black and white": We each form attachments and make distinctions only to return at some point to their source, to recognize the unity of all opposites and the fundamentally relational quality of human experience (Bateson, 1972). To wit: good is meaningless without bad; a table is only hard because flesh is soft; there are no mountains without valleys. Seen like this, attachment and loyalty to egos, relationships, and schools of research is to be expected, even encouraged. Where we must improve, however, is in our tendency to hold on too tightly to what we believe. We should examine how an excess of certainty impacts negatively on our attitudes and behaviors toward others with differing worldviews. To regard one's own attachments as superior to others is more fetish than identity, and closes off the possibility of communication. But there is another way, where the strength of our commitments is rivaled only by the strength of our compassion, resulting in a more complete understanding of important organizational issues.

Conclusion: Hospitality Redux

In sum, the arguments I have presented here reflect my own peculiar aesthetic, through which I have always privileged beauty over truth, fragrance over formula, community over calculation. As I have become more confident as a scholar, I have become acutely aware of two paths through the academic forest, one narrow and steep, and the other broad and level. While I have known many solo climbers, I have always sought the romance of the clearing, of handshakes and hugs and stories to tell and listen to. Perhaps this is also why I have a great affection for hotels, and for the very idea of hospitality, that we might extend kindness to persons whom we know nothing about, and whose personal commitments are irrelevant to our welcoming attitude. Others of you will see things differently, but I remain hopeful that at least some of the spirit of hospitality can take hold in the academic world. The answer may not be common ground, but rather a common orientation toward each other as fellow travelers in the world. If we are willing to risk it, the benefits will far outweigh whatever it is that we are afraid of losing.

References

Anderson, R., Cissna, K., & Arnett, R. (1994). *The reach of dialogue: Confirmation, voice, and community.* Cresskill, NJ: Hampton Press.

Arnett, R. (1986). *Communication and community.* Carbondale, IL: Southern Illinois University Press.

Bateson, G. (1972). *Steps to an ecology of mind.* New York: Ballantine Books.

Buber, M. (1965a). *Between man and man.* New York: Macmillan.

Buber, M. (1965b). *The knowledge of man: A philosophy of the interhuman.* M. Friedman (Ed.). New York: Harper & Row.

Calás, M., & Smircich, L. (1999b). Past postmodernism? Reflections and tentative directions. *Academy of Management Review, 24,* 649–671.

Czarniawska, B. (1998). Who's afraid of incommensurability? *Organization, 5,* 273–275.

Eisenberg, E. (1984). Ambiguity as strategy in organizational communication. *Communication Monographs, 51,* 227–242.

Eisenberg, E. (1998). Flirting with meaning. *Journal of Language and Social Psychology, 17,* 97–108.

Eisenberg, E., Andrews, L., Laine-Timmerman, L., & Murphy, A. (1999). Transforming organizations through communication. In P. Salem (Ed.), *Organizational communication and change* (pp. 125–147). Cresskill, NJ: Hampton Press.

Eisenberg, E., & Goodall, H. L. (1997). *Organizational communication: Balancing creativity and constraint,* 2nd edition. New York: St. Martin's Press.

Fasching, D. (1996). *The coming of the millennium: Good news for the whole human race.* Valley Forge, PA: Trinity Press International.

Habermas, J. (1984). *The theory of communicative action, Volume I.* (T. McCarthy, Trans.). Boston: Beacon Press.

Hoffman, L. (1982). *Foundations of family systems theory.* New York: Basic Books.

Jackson, M. (1989). *Paths toward a clearing.* Bloomington: Indiana University Press.

Martin, J. (1992). *Cultures in organizations: Three perspectives.* New York: Oxford University Press.

Ortner, S. (1984). Theory in anthropology since the sixties. *Comparative Studies in Society and History, 26,* 126–167.

Scarf, M. (1987). *Intimate partners.* New York: Random House.

Senge, P. (1990). *The fifth discipline.* New York: Doubleday.

Watts, A. (1972). *The book.* New York: Vintage.

Weick, K. (1999). Theory construction as disciplined reflexivity: Tradeoffs in the 90s. *Academy of Management Review, 24,* 797–807.

14

Building a Mystery

Communication and the Development of Identity

This essay provided further exploration of the relationships among aesthetics, contingency, and identity. In it, I brought together three disparate but compatible literatures encompassing life history, dialogue, and the biochemical bases of mood. A comparative reading of these literatures revealed a common mechanism at work in each: attachment. I used this notion to advance a new theory of communication and identity that valorizes contingency and eschews fundamentalism and fixed meaning.

Of everything I have written, this piece receives the most fan mail, and often from unexpected places. This is partly because of its placement; the Journal of Communication *has a large and diverse readership, one that I do not often reach. I suspect that people like the piece because it brings together themes that are prominent in the contemporary zeitgeist, marshalling them in service of a vision of planetary peace. I will build on the ideas in the paper for the remainder of my career.*

SOURCE: Eisenberg, E. M. (2001). Building a mystery: Communication and the development of identity. *Journal of Communication, 51,* 534–552. Copyright © 2001, Oxford University Press.

When the fit is too tight, there may be only one mutual position that is compatible with the binding of the two molecules; the probability for binding is low and, hence, the information required for finding that position is high. On the other hand, when the fit is too loose, we again get a low probability for binding. Somewhere in between lies the optimal, sloppy fit where the binding probability is highest and the information required, lowest.

—Werner Loewenstein (1999)

Certainty is fatal.

—Harry Beckwith (2000)

The Challenge of Identity

A primary challenge of human being is living in the present with the awareness of an uncertain future. Perhaps the most extreme form of this dilemma is knowledge of our own mortality (Becker, 1997), but life is full of occasions where we must make important decisions with limited information. The fundamental indeterminacy of the future is an essential quality of human experience. We can never know precisely what is in store for us, yet we nonetheless try to live a good and meaningful life.

How we respond to the fundamental uncertainty of life shapes everything we do and is driven in part by how we think about our place in the world, our sense of identity. Some people think of identity as a kind of answer, an ideal or end-state, achieved progressively through an ongoing examination of one's character and qualities. Others see identity as a question, an open-ended journey that is always shifting and changing. For this latter group, the development of self requires a kind of "enlightened indeterminacy"—a willingness to embrace ambiguity and uncertainty as an integral part of everyday life (Babrow, Kasch, & Ford, 1998; Varela, Thompson, & Rosch, 1991). For all kinds of people, however, identity is a significant accomplishment. Coping with the uncertainties of one's positionality in the world is key to ontological security, which is another name for emotional or mental health. Bolstering this claim is the argument that human emotions are largely determined by our beliefs about the future, by our degree of confidence that things will turn out well for us (Barbalet, 1999).

Contrasting Approaches to Identity Across Cultures

Broadly speaking, notions of identity in the West have been largely individualistic; people are taught to feel that they are born *into* the world, and that they must establish and maintain boundaries between themselves and others. Seeing the self in this way creates predictable opportunities and challenges and has led on the one hand to stunning developments in economics and industry, but on the other to significant levels of alienation, anxiety, and social division.

Alternatively (and again broadly speaking because much of this is shifting today), Eastern cultures teach their members that the collective is paramount, and that the individual is important only to the extent that they are part of a web of socially meaningful relationships. Some cultures even lack the vocabulary to speak of individual intentions (Duranti, 1984). In such cultures, people are more apt to feel that they come *out* of the world and are part of a broader web of life (Capra, 1997; Watts, 1989). This worldview also has predictable effects; families are strong (but traditional) and crime rates are low, but there is little tolerance for individual creativity, difference, or dissent.

Taking an historical perspective, the contrasts are even more dramatic. In her landmark work on ecofeminism, Eisler (1988) characterized all contemporary societies as variations on the "dominator" model, in which hierarchy is the prevailing metaphor and women, nature, and animals (other than human beings) are subjugated. It has not always been so; she contrasts this model with a "partnership way" of organizing that is nearly lost from memory but existed in a number of ancient, matriarchal cultures. Eisler's ecofeminism model—and the possibility of radical alternatives to hierarchy as an organizing model for society—has significant appeal and has impacted many contemporary writers (e.g., Quinn, 1992; Spretnak, 1997; Starhawk, 1993).

The Role of Spirituality and Religion

Returning to the present day, the worldviews described above are associated with differences in spiritual and religious orientation between the East and the West. Spiritual systems usually seek to address two questions: (a) What is the human being's place in the world? and (b) How does one live a good and meaningful life? Moreover, spiritual traditions share a similar response to these queries, as suggested by the translation of the word *religion* (from Latin) as "to bind into one." At their core, spirituality and religion serve as reminders to human beings of the interconnectedness of all life, whether we call this pattern of connection "nature," "energy," or "God."

Despite the fact that this is the intent of most spiritualities—to promote unity consciousness in humans, which in turn may shape their decisions and actions—our actual behavior as a species suggests that the message is a hard one to follow. In most civilizations (including our own), the spiritual urge has proven too weak to discourage the perennial quest for a single, literal, fundamental truth, whether it be found in nationalism, capitalism, or religious fundamentalism. I have written elsewhere that "every holocaust finds its reasons in certainty and in separation" (Eisenberg, 1998), and this remains true today, when no fewer than 50 wars are being fought on Earth, all of them over truth claims of one kind or another. Despite unprecedented advances in science and culture, brutal dictatorships, medieval forms of torture, and genocide persist. Although the notion of a transcendent love of all creatures is appealing in the abstract, there is no denying that humans are quick to move from an inclusive "story" of tolerance and meeting to a series of more practical, exclusive, and potentially pernicious "lists"—of memberships, boundaries, and rules (Browning, 1992; Buber, 1965).

Why is this so? I think Watts (1989) was correct in his assessment that most people have a faulty notion of who they are, identifying with an isolated ego inside a bag of skin, rather than seeing themselves as a living expression of an interconnected universe. Watts sees this dramatic failure of imagination—at least in the West—as emanating from a widespread cultural taboo against more expansive and interdependent constructions of identity. Once bounded, what follows is a nearly irresistible tendency toward self-grasping, toward a strong attachment to the idea of an independent, fixed, unitary self. Moreover, this belief works in concert with prevailing economic models of human behavior. From this perspective,

> the self is seen as a territory with boundaries. The goal of the self is to bring inside the boundaries all of the good things while paying out as few goods as possible and conversely to remove to the outside of the boundaries all of the bad things while letting in as little bad as possible. Since goods are scarce, each autonomous self is in competition with other selves to get them. (Varela et al., 1991, p. 246)

This mode of being in the world is unsatisfactory for a number of reasons. First, grasping after an independent self produces anxiety and frustration because such separation is impossible to find in experience. Secondly, this worldview effectively pits us against one another and blocks the "embodiment of concern" that is necessary for preservation of our species and the planet (Varela et al., 1991, p. 247).

If the main challenge of living is sense making—developing a workable narrative about the self and the world for dealing with existential/ontological uncertainty—it is crucial to ask where people find both their motivations and the resources to construct such a narrative. The purpose of this essay is to examine more closely this process and to identify the ways in which people draw upon biological, interpersonal, organizational, societal, and cultural resources in the development of identity. In this way, I hope to show both how certain patterns of thought, talk, and action reinforce the prevailing view of the self as a separate entity, as well as those points of leverage that might be identified as useful for "undoing" or modifying this pattern (Krippendorff, 1995). This in turn may open up possibilities for real dialogue and planetary thinking.

Emerging Perspectives on Identity

At least in theory, there is ample readiness for an alternative view of identity that eschews a fixed sense of self with rigid boundaries and more closely aligns with the shifting and fragmented quality of lived experience. This new notion of self has alternatively been called "protean" (Lifton, 1999), "saturated" (Gergen, 2000), "flirtatious" (Phillips, 1994), "improvisational" (Barrett, 1998; Eisenberg, 1990; Hatch, 1999) and even "groundless" (Varela et al., 1991). Although there are significant differences among these formulations, they each begin by rejecting the notion of an individual as an isolated physical entity with a singular, core identity. Each approach in one way or another celebrates the "multiplicity of selves" that each one of us may perform at any given moment. Raul Espejo and Keith Pheby (2000) link this multiplicity to a feeling of openness to others and, by implication, to possibility itself:

> The human subject should be construed as a multiplicity rather than a discrete identity. "It" is always open to "otherness" in its constitution. This proximal encounter with alterity takes place in a domain of pure potentiality . . . human selves are provisional blocks of becoming. (p. 2)

Moreover, there is ample evidence to suggest a kind of primordial, biological element of subjectivity that is the result of having corporeal presence in the world, that is, having a body (Merleau-Ponty, 1962). It is "at the level of one's bodyhood that the habitual intentionality of the world is given" (Espejo & Pheby, 2000, p. 2).

Varela and his colleagues (1991) have provided perhaps the most detailed consideration of the role of the body in the construction of identity. They offer "cognition as embodied action" as an alternative to foundational, representational views of human behavior. Central to their argument is the controversial idea that whenever people "look inside themselves" for a fixed, unitary self, no such animal can be found. Instead, we find that who we are is completely bound up with and relative to our environment. The inability to catch one's self without a perception, to separate the self from the world, can lead to anxiety, restlessness, and self-grasping. Yet there is no hard wood without soft skin, no brilliant colors without fine-tuned ocular receptors. Our lay epistemologies are, for the most part, ill equipped to cope with such a groundless, relational existence. Our theories are not much more helpful:

> Science has shown us that a fixed self is not necessary for mind but has not provided any way of dealing with the basic fact that this no-longer needed self is precisely the ego-self that everyone clings to and holds most dear. (Varela et al., 1991, p. 80)

Taking the long view, it would appear that we are just learning how to be human beings, to live in an interdependent world with reflexive consciousness.

Shifting Portrayals of Identity in the Popular Media

These changes in how people think about identity are not solely theoretical, but are reflected in the popular media. Three recent examples are instructive. First, compare the police officers of the television series *NYPD Blue* with those from *Hill Street Blues,* an earlier series by creator Steven Bochco. On *Hill Street,* the captain regularly exercised moral and legitimate authority against a turbulent and unpredictable outside world. Officers struggled to pass their sergeants' exams and move up the precinct hierarchy, and people who refused to play by the rules (like Officer Buntz) were demonized and expelled from the system. Years later, the world of *NYPD Blue* could hardly be more different. All talk of rules and hierarchy has disappeared, the precinct leader stays in the background, and officers are challenged to survive each day through improvisation, relying mainly on their relationships with trusted coworkers. In this world, Buntz becomes Sipowicz (even played by the same actor), and his creative police work, however marginally legal or moral, is routinely celebrated.

A second example can be seen in the critically acclaimed, Academy Award–winning western, *Unforgiven.* In this film, actor/director Clint Eastwood deconstructs the traditional western genre to reveal the inner contradictions of his character, which in the past would have been cast one-dimensionally as a romantic outlaw in search of justice in an unjust world. The traditional outlaw, like the men and women of *Hill Street,* sought to return integrity to a world gone mad. In contrast, Eastwood's protagonist is full of uncertainty and self-doubt. Eastwood's character finds that the old stories no longer work for him, but at the same time it is exceedingly hard to imagine who he is without them.

A final dramatic example of the changing nature of identity in the media is found in the enormously successful organized crime series, *The Sopranos*. In striking contrast to every other crime series ever made, the writers have crafted a mob boss whose identity is constantly in question. Moreover, Tony Soprano's challenges go far beyond the usual "enemies" to include his mother, his family, and his mental health. Tony survives by improvising, by making use of cultural resources and scripts that fall well outside those traditionally available to this character (e.g., psychotherapy, Prozac). In this way, each protagonist struggles with his or her frustration over old scripts that no longer fit and the need to continually create and re-create themselves in a dynamic and uncertain world.

Perhaps we can better understand the pragmatics of identity development through a renewed emphasis on language and social interaction. Some writers—notably Martin Buber, Adam Phillips, and Kenneth Gergen—make radical proposals that challenge many of our received notions about the functions of communication. For example, Phillips (1998) celebrates the "virtues of inarticulateness" that accompany infancy, and bemoans what is lost in possibility when a child learns to speak. Gergen (1985) offers a critique of individualism and sees knowledge not as something people "have," but rather as something they do together. In this paper, I seek to bring together what I see as an emerging aesthetic of identity and to articulate the implications of this new formulation for communication. This is a very large undertaking, and this paper should be read as a detailed outline for a forthcoming book on the subject (Eisenberg, 2001).

Communication and the Development of Identity

Most theories that seek to link communication to identity do so with an overly simplistic view of the communication process. Specifically, these theories have insisted that the main—if not the sole—function of human communication is uncertainty reduction, accomplished through the maximization of clarity, openness, and understanding. This decidedly partial view characterizes ambiguity and concealment as to be avoided at all costs, and has been described in broad terms as a cultural "flight from ambiguity" (Levine, 1985). This perspective is closely aligned with the notion of communication as information transfer, or what one observer has called the "conduit" metaphor (Axley, 1980).

Put differently, the definitions of communication that have dominated both academic and public discourse since WWII have emphasized instrumentality, intentionality and the autonomous self, fitting well with the challenges of the 20th century but not so well with those of the 21st. From now on, social life will be characterized by a much broader view of information exchange (including intercellular, interspecies, and between animals and machines), less concerned with persuasion than connection, less focused on self than system, and less preoccupied with maintaining a fixed identity (of persons, organizations, nation-states) than with developing a robust but dynamic conception of identity that continually adapts to a turbulent environment.

In many ways, the foundations of such an approach have been a long time in coming. A closer study of the pragmatics of human communication worldwide over the past two decades reveals a broadening of perspective. Studies of communicative competence outside of Europe and the U.S. (e.g., Asia, Scandinavia) show that many of the world's peoples do not share our ideological commitment to clarity, but instead evaluate communicative effectiveness by one's ability to maintain face needs or otherwise facilitate interpersonal relationships. Moreover, it now appears that multiple goals in interaction are the rule, not the exception—people do want to be understood, but this is not all they want, and not at any cost.

Part of the difficulty has been the inevitable gap between what we think we *should* do and what we actually do as communicators. In the interpersonal realm, Arthur Bochner (1984) was among the first to question whether our beliefs about effective communication reflected actual practice or felt ideology. Specifically, he argued that although people say close relationships should be open and highly disclosive, in reality the longer one is in a relationship the more one has to lose, which in turn can inhibit disclosure or make it less necessary. In organizational theory, Karl Weick (1979) championed the virtues of equivocality and randomness in decision making, showing how such practices both inspired creativity and confused the competition. In my own work, I have tried to expose the ideology of openness in discourse about organizational communication and, in so doing, demonstrate the potential benefits of ambiguity in certain situations (Eisenberg, 1984, 1990; Eisenberg & Witten, 1987). Although I rightly have been criticized for minimizing the uses of ambiguity in fostering domination of the powerless (e.g., Deetz, 1992), I continue to believe that there is much to be gained from redirecting our notions of competence to include the strategic uses of ambiguity.

Although I am gratified that most contemporary communication textbooks no longer promote an uncritical endorsement of clear and open communication, I nevertheless feel that the critique has not gone deeply enough into our understandings of the role of communication throughout the lifespan, exploring the relationship between how we communicate and our sense of our "self" in the world. The ideology of clarity continues to assert undue influence on our ideas about human development and specifically on the development of identity. The notions of "one true meaning" and "one true self" are closely related, with belief in the possibility of the former providing crucial groundwork for the acceptance of the latter. Put another way, to "fix" identity, one must first believe it possible to "fix" meaning (Ellis, 1995). The possibility of a singular, literal interpretation is a fitting handmaiden to the notion of a core self—both are a kind of wishful fundamentalism. Both are unverifiable in practice (Varela et al., 1991), and the pursuit of each can lead well-meaning people into a life of anxiety and frustration associated with feelings of multiplicity often expressed as "not knowing who I really am." A view of identity as multiple and dynamic is more in line with the experience of living today. Put differently, it is always a mistake to treat identity as a noun; rather, "we live in the identity process" (Altheide, 2000, p. 4).

Reframing Uncertainty as Mystery

In no way do I wish to minimize the importance of "understanding" as an accomplishment between people. Rather, I see understanding as highly perishable, a receding roadside marker along the relational journey. Seen this way, understanding exists in a dialectical relationship with mystery, and a primary function of communication is to promote movement between the two (Goodall, 1991). An exclusive focus on understanding and uncertainty reduction tells only some of the story and often not the most interesting part. Reframing certainty as failed mystery casts uncertainty as a potentially positive state, as a source of possibility and potential action. We use communication to work our way back and forth along this dialectic, with the degree of uncertainty, or mystery, in relationships always in flux.

We run into trouble, both individually and collectively, when we seek clarity at all costs, or when we aspire to establish some transcendent truth "once and for all." Harboring such aspirations leads people to "lock in" to a particular way of thinking and being, that is, to a specific role, text, lifestyle, worldview, or identity. Having done this, what we may gain in certainty we lose in possibility, in equal and predictable amounts. Any attempt to fix meaning and identity for the long haul is an ontological circling of the wagons, a turning inward to defend a way of life. This strategy can work for a short period of time for isolated individuals in relatively closed systems, but this is not our present situation. Instead, most of us struggle to find meaning in interdependent, open systems in which we are challenged each day to know who we are and what we believe amidst an endless barrage of alternatives. For the zealot and the fundamentalist, these alternatives appear as threats and challenges, not opportunities. Over time, this limited approach to identity can lead people to engage in defensive behavior that becomes self-fulfilling, evoking similarly defensive and dogmatic responses in others.

In fact, defensiveness and attachment by anyone in an interdependent social system tends to lead others to respond in the very same way. More formally, the circulation of possibility in a system is impeded by the hardening of any individual's position. We see this clearly in the classroom, where defensiveness on the part of a teacher or an especially vocal student can negatively affect everyone else's experience. We also witness it in families where dogmatic members insist on their definition of reality to the exclusion of all others. One primary way the system becomes limited and dysfunctional is through "projective identification" (Scarf, 1996). As one person overly attaches to their worldview, they denigrate alternative perspectives and assign them to others in the system, who, depending upon power relations, often find themselves trapped in an unsatisfactory and diminished role. Frustration then prompts a search for possibility elsewhere, which all too often leads people to conflict, gangs, cults, depression, drug abuse, and even suicide.

Reasons for Defensiveness

Why does this happen? For sure, each of us has at one time or another grown weary and intolerant of others and looked to withdraw from the interpersonal world. Tolerance and forgiveness are by no means easy to achieve. Consider the recent implementation of zero-tolerance policies in schools, English-only policies in some communities, and the sentiment on the part of many citizens to punish rather than rehabilitate those sentenced to our correctional system. A recent study of the public mental health system in the U.S. reveals how stigma and beliefs about "normal" functioning keep people with various mental illnesses trapped in cruel labyrinths that never fully address their suffering. Drawing solid lines around what is "normal" or "acceptable" may at first seem like an effective defense, but it has costs—in limiting possibility, it also makes us a little less human. In effect, the other's unfolding is reframed as a problem, a violation, a foreign object, and, in this state, cannot make a difference in one's worldview. The prevailing cultural attitude is something like this: "When our way of life is threatened . . . if only we can succeed in classifying the other as irreparably deviant—as another species, really, not at all like ourselves—then we will be safe."

Naturally, every society requires that limits be set, and certain behaviors can never be tolerated. But there is a difference between discipline and demonization (in schools, organizations, between nations), and it is the latter that ends up destroying not just the other but the possibility of connection itself. In an interdependent world, some degree of interpersonal contact is always necessary. There is no private language, no human being who is not already in relationship. Moreover, in the memorable words of composer Frank Zappa, "we *are* the other people." What seems natural and taken for granted to us about our own behavior most assuredly will seem unnatural to someone else.

So, where does this leave us? Even in the most seemingly homogenous community, the cost of possibility in an interdependent world is vulnerability to others. It is fear of this vulnerability—which can be physical, emotional, economic, or psychological—that makes people want to lock in.

Toward a New Theory of Communication and Identity

Thus far in this paper, I have described how a pervasive alienation from and apprehension toward others can lead into a desire for certainty, rigid boundaries, and even physical separation. But what can be done to move things in a different direction, to support people in recognizing their potential, their interconnectedness, and to promote planetary thinking? The sense of separation and division that accompanies fundamentalist ways of thinking can only be bridged through new forms of communication. Throughout most of the 20th century, philosophers and communication theorists have struggled to articulate the nature of these forms, the best developed of these being dialogue (Buber, 1965). Stewart (2000) recently described the practice of dialogic communication as "the willingness to let others happen to you while holding your own ground." Dialogue acknowledges the human being's twofold nature, our persistent oscillation between individuation and communion.

Unfortunately, dialogue is exceedingly rare and unlikely to occur where it is most needed. Although dialogue is rooted in a definition of identity that values multiple perspectives and embraces possibility, few people are oriented in this way. Whereas the experience of dialogue inspires some to consider a different worldview, it is equally important to examine the factors that might predispose a person either for or against dialogic communication.

Specifically, I propose a theory of communication and identity that connects a person's communicative choices with their personal narratives, their personal narratives with their bodily experience of emotionality and mood, and each of the above with the environmental resources available for the creation and sustenance of particular identities. In so doing, I specify a cyclical relationship among these diverse elements (communication, personal narrative, and mood) such that they are mutually reinforcing in the service of identity building and uncertainty management. I then propose various points of leverage in the system where interventions have the potential to shift the overall pattern.

A graphic representation of my proposal is given in Figure 14.1. A few features are especially noteworthy. First, this conceptualization includes both thoughts and emotions in the construction of identity, highlighting the role of mood and the body. Second, I have dissolved the boundary between symbolic and biological information, maintaining that identity has significant biological underpinnings that are in one sense communicative, but are expressly non-linguistic. Taking this approach allows me to show how elements of our physical environment (e.g., what we eat, how we move) shape our identities, and lays important groundwork for adapting the theory to include interaction with other life-forms and machines. Third, I have added macroeconomic and institutional forces, inasmuch as they have been shown to exert a "surround of force" that is pervasive in shaping people's moods, life stories, and communication (Shorris, 1997). Taken together, these elements constitute a new aesthetic of communication and identity, one that reveals how more restricted patterns of thought and behavior are self- reinforcing and suggests ways that new patterns can be introduced into the system.

The Surround

At birth, each of us emerges from the womb into a social world already in motion, complete with preexisting languages, relationships, social networks, and culturally prescribed patterns of behavior. In this sense, the world is external to the individual, inasmuch as the traces of other people, both living and dead, exert an influence on each of our lives (Archer, 1995). Following Shorris (1997), I will refer to the sum total of environmental influences, as the "surround." Although there are many ways to characterize elements of the surround, a number are easily identifiable:

- Spiritual: cosmological concepts, values, and behaviors
- Economic: ideas and behaviors regarding exchange of material resources
- Cultural: assumptions, values, rituals characterizing social groupings
- Societal: acceptable rules, roles, and laws that pertain to membership in a society
- Interpersonal: rules, values, and patterns of behavior that define intimate relations
- Biological: electrochemical and genetic patterns that shape human development

Each of these dimensions has its own set of "lists" and "stories" (Browning, 1992); each is a collection of laws, rules, norms, and canonical narratives suggesting acceptable (or deviant) patterns of behaviors. People draw from the surround to make sense of their lives and, in so doing, construct their identities (Giddens, 1979). As is commonly argued in postmodern

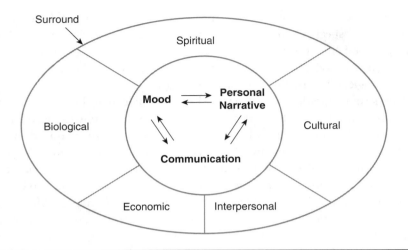

Figure 14.1

philosophy, what passes for a "person" today is a collection of stories, a pastiche of sensibilities drawn from disparate aspects of the surround (Gergen, 2000).

Yet another way to characterize the surround is as an information field that contains both symbolic and biological information. This means that some of its effects on the person will occur consciously, but many others occur at the cellular level and will never enter into discursive consciousness (Giddens, 1979; Loewenstein, 1999). Nevertheless, it is the interplay among all these sources of information that provides the raw material for the sense-making processes described next.

Sense-Making Processes

Within the surround, there are three closely related subprocesses that comprise the ongoing process of identity formation. The first, having to do with emotions, brain chemistry, and mood, is mainly biological. It can be expressed as a person's orientation toward time, whether they are hopeful or anxious, happy or depressed about their possible futures (Barbalet, 1998). By the future, I am referring to everything from the next moment to the rest of one's life. The second process is the ongoing authorship (and editing) of one's personal narrative or life story, which tells a great deal about our attachments, interpretations, and view of our own possibilities. Personal narratives vary in many ways, not the least of which in how open they are to change. The third process is one's approach to communicating with others, which I characterized above as varying in degree of defensiveness and openness to others' worldviews.

Each element of the process is shaped by (and also shapes) elements in the surround. For example, people who are raised in poverty or victims of domestic abuse as a rule experience a surround of force (Shorris, 1997) that colors every aspect of their lives. Alternatively, people of privilege may experience a pervasive surround of opportunity. Considered this way, identity is a complex process of drawing lists and stories from the surround that complement or otherwise inform one's mood, personal narrative, and communicative style.

As I stated earlier, these processes are mutually reinforcing, and repeated patterns tend to get locked in, with varying consequences. When change is desirable, it is possible to disrupt the system from almost any angle, so long as one understands the subprocesses and their interrelated, self-reinforcing character. Failure to attend to these interrelationships limits the possibility of lasting change. Interventions designed to change communication behavior have no lasting effect when they fail to become integrated into a person's life story. Similarly, directly changing moods through specialized drugs can be hard to sustain when no new communication skills are learned. Positive change is most likely to occur when each subprocess is taken into account. Similar to what occurs at the societal level, policy changes have little or no impact on social life until the average person experiences a shift in consciousness concerning their positionality in the world (Havel, 1951).

In the next section, I offer a more detailed description of each of the three subprocesses, emphasizing their interrelatedness. I then go on to summarize the implications of this model for thinking about uncertainty in human relationships, drawing out questions and lessons for communication theory and practice.

Identity Process One: Mood

Recently, there has been a resurgence of interest in the ways in which biological factors may affect communication (cf. Condit, 2000; McCroskey & Beatty, 2000). Whereas for many years any discussion of biology was considered suggestive of racism or sexism, today a more complex picture is emerging, one that acknowledges that genetics play a key role in personality development and in determining a person's overall mood. Both research and clinical practice report significant successes in the chemical manipulation of serotonin levels in the brain as a means of treating anxiety and depression. People who had struggled for years to think and act differently (but with little success) were shocked by the biochemical fix. Many reported "feeling like themselves" for the first time in their lives (e.g., Kramer, 1997). Moreover, many of these same people also said that their newfound emotional stability at long last permitted them to modify their communicative behaviors (e.g., to become less irritable, self-conscious, or defensive), which in turn allowed them to author a new life story (Kramer, 1997).

The willingness to see changes in brain chemistry as a legitimate determinant of mood and, in turn, of behavior suggests many other possibilities for the biological underpinnings of communication. For example, McKenna (1993) describes how our development as a species is closely tied to the plants we have chosen to consume. Certain psychoactive plants, such as cannabis and psilocybin mushrooms, deflate the ego and promote playful, holistic thinking. These plants are illegal in most cultures. Other plants, like tobacco and coffee, reinforce ego boundaries and are compatible with hard work. McKenna's point is that we have developed a cultural aversion to any plant that might be "mind expanding" and has the potential to distract us from our roles as efficient producers and consumers of goods and services. In this way, his argument resembles those of scholars in cultural studies who see a primary role of the media as reinforcing people's view of themselves as consumers (e.g., Grossberg, Wartella, & Whitney, 1998). No fan of opiates, McKenna draws a neat parallel between the effects of heroin and television. There are numerous cultural mechanisms that encourage the development of a well-bounded self, so long as that self most wants to go shopping.

Certain mood states encourage particular interpretations of the events in one's life, and a set of life stories and communicative choices. A person who is anxious about his or her future is less likely to perceive multiple narrative possibilities and will likely communicate in ways that are self-defeating. Alternatively, someone who is feeling good about life is more likely to tell a positive story, which in turn leads to less defensive, more open communication. Our patterns of thought flow from our bodily experiences, and this relationship is reflected in our language and metaphors (Lakoff & Johnson, 1999). Recent scientific research further confirms the role of biology in shaping behavior and the distributed nature of intelligence. In actual brains,

> there seem to be no rules, no central logical processor, nor does information appear to be stored at precise addresses. Rather, brains can be seen to operate on the basis of massive interconnections in a distributed form, so that the actual connections among ensembles of neurons change as a result of experience. (Varela et al., 1991, p. 85)

This "experience" is that of the body in the world, in continuous contact with a dynamic environment that includes other people.

Identity Process Two: Personal Narrative

Studies of social life reveal that people live according to stories, and that we are guided more by narrative rationality than by formal logic (Fisher, 1984; Parry & Doan, 1994). Personal narrative is the primary tool people use in sense making, and our autobiographies are highly resistant to change. Moreover, even when people claim to behave in accord with objective rationality, this is itself a construction that is made to look otherwise— objectivity is just another kind of story, complete with its own set of emotions (Barbalet, 1999).

A new branch of psychotherapy has developed that has as its goal to help people "re-story" their lives (Friedman, 1993; Parry & Doan, 1994). Its theory states that once the story changes, behavior will follow, and that attachment to a dysfunctional story—that is, one in which one consistently plays the victim—is a significant obstacle to positive change. Life stories, however, can have great inertia. Narrative therapists try to help replace "problem-saturated" life stories with ones that are more "possibility focused" to varying results (Friedman, 1993).

The notion of narrative possibility is central to my argument. People vary in the felt quality of their interior life, and this perception of quality is a function of their perceived personal power and feelings of possibility about the future. Some of these feelings come mainly from biology; even moderate levels of anxiety and depression can greatly diminish one's sense of personal power and effectiveness. When constantly confronted with a surround of force, the poor often feel especially limited in power and possibility. It makes sense that a person would have to feel some basic level of personal power and possibility in order to take the next step, which is responsibility—literally the "ability to respond" to others. A decreased sense of personal power and the feeling of being trapped lead to rigid, defensive, fearful communication. This behavior in turn elicits fear and defensiveness from others, which over time reinforces negative self-regard.

In making this argument, I distinguish between two types of power, each associated with a different approach to life. Those who prefer certainty, rationality, and sharp boundaries are most concerned with the power they do or do not have over other people and things (and what others have over them). By contrast, those who are inclined to value interrelatedness define power as "the ability to define a situation for self and others," emphasizing the importance of mutual influence and communication (Altheide, 2000, p. 5). Whereas "power over" is bounded, instrumental, and attached, "power of" is limitless, inclusive, nonstrategic, and open. This distinction is also a cornerstone of feminist thinking, which seeks to sponsor voice and participation as alternatives to hierarchy.

Therapeutic approaches to rewriting personal narratives succeed when they are supported by aspects of the surround and the other subprocesses. New life stories are meaningful for people because they lead to new patterns of relationships and enhanced moods. Moreover, enacting a more functional plot injects new elements into the surround—such as new spiritual beliefs or new rules about close relationships—that are available to be drawn upon in the future.

More than simply being about exchanging one story for another, attention to one's personal narrative can lead to an entirely new orientation toward one's autobiography. Consider the difference between being the protagonist in a particular story, on the one hand, and the storyteller, on the other. When we inhabit a particular story as a protagonist, we feel the ontological security of knowing where and who we are. If it is a good story, one in which we feel we belong, in which we have satisfying relationships with others along with some sense of our own heroism, we may even become smug and passive. We may come to feel that our story *is* the world, forgetting what may be happening to people not included in our narrative. This could apply equally well to the stock market, a local neighborhood, a school, a family, or a gang. Even if it is not a good story for us, we may still feel trapped by it, doomed to live out our impoverished and unhappy part, or perhaps taking dramatic action as a means of escaping the role. The protagonist lives mainly in the past.

In contrast, the enlightened storyteller always keeps one metatruth in mind: *I am not the story.* The good storyteller inhabits each story for a time, enough to feel the emotional connection, to experience the heroics and the relationships, but the storyteller always reserves the right to tell a different story. In this sense, whereas the protagonist's resources always are limited by the context, the storyteller's resources are limited only by his or her imagination. The storyteller believes above all in possibility and the future. When things become intolerable, one always can tell a different story.

An analogy to a solar eclipse is helpful in understanding this shift in perspective. Objectively, one can determine that the sun is many times bigger than the moon. Seen from a particular perspective, however, the smaller moon can completely eclipse the sun, despite its relatively small size. So it is with those stories to which we are most attached. Although the world may be huge with possibility, our adopted story blots out everything that is not in the present story. Fortunately, even a small shift in perspective can reveal what was previously hidden. Unfortunately, such a shift can be profoundly difficult to achieve, as is evident in the challenges of many of the mentally ill to gain insight into the realities of their own conditions, or in the struggle to get abused spouses to leave home.

Yet the possibility of a broader perspective on our lives—of "floodlight consciousness" (Watts, 1989)—remains. We catch a glimpse of it now and again, and this may be sufficient to sustain a conversation about the benefits of uncertainty and mystery. This mode of consciousness is a birthright of human beings, but the surround as a rule encourages us to trade possibility for certainty, the floodlight for ego's narrow spotlight. This limitation is in a sense a public health problem, not qualitatively different from mothers bathing children each day in a polluted river. As people develop, we expose them to patterns of thinking that are harmful. These thought patterns in turn manifest themselves as dysfunctional patterns of behavior.

Identity Process Three: Communication

Much has been written in the past decade about the need for new patterns of communication in society (cf. Isaacs, 1999; Tannen, 1998). Concentrated interest in the subject reflects a deep dissatisfaction with traditional ways of dealing with disagreement, from argument to debate to lawsuits to violence. There is growing consensus that there must be a better way, and furthermore that the better way has a lot to do with learning new communication skills such as mediation and facilitation. The idea is not to eliminate vigorous dissent but to make it possible, by replacing violence and avoidance with robust relationships that can tolerate productive disagreement.

A typical contrast is between discussion and dialogue (Bohm, 1996). In discussion (coming from the same roots as "concussion"), people square off in defense of their positions, which leads to a "hardening" of attachments that limits the flow of possibility. Alternatively, in dialogue, each party shares a commitment to both voice their experience and be open to others. When successful, dialogue reinforces both the competency of the individuals and the power of the relationship or group.

As one can imagine, there are numerous complexities associated with the pragmatics of dialogue, including who gets to participate and what effect existing power and status relations have on the resulting communicative encounters. Whenever people communicate with one another, there is much at stake. The main point I wish to make here, however, is that changing communication is rarely enough to change social systems of relationship, unless these changes can also be tied to altered moods, narratives, and elements of the surround.

Another take on alternatives to a defensive communicative style can be found in the interplay among jazz musicians. Recently, a number of researchers have shown how principles of jazz improvisation can provide promising models for relationships outside the music world. While remaining attentive to and respectful of some basic rules of music, jazz players constantly challenge themselves to be innovative without alienating the others. Well-worn riffs are called "comps," which is short for "competency traps," and a player who chooses them is seen as weak (Barrett, 1998; Hatch, 1999). Unlike the usual pattern in relationships, jazz musicians "fail" when they steer clear of uncertainty and fall back on what they know best.

Putting It All Together: Communication and the Development of Identity

Is it possible to imagine a race of humans for whom nothing on Earth is "other," for whom the whole web of life feels like home? We must abandon our reckless fundamentalism if we hope to accomplish anything of the kind. Cultivating a planetary identity, of course, contains a paradox. Philosopher Karl Popper (1966) once said that we must reserve the right not to tolerate the intolerant. Similarly, planetary consciousness requires that we be certain about our commitment to uncertainty, about maintaining a questioning attitude and a beginner's mind in our dealings with all creatures (and, soon enough, with machines). If we have learned anything from the 20th century, it is that technology alone is not the solution. Even dramatic increases in interconnectivity can be destructive if accompanied by a defensive and limited worldview.

Moreover, interconnectivity is not simply a matter of drawing lines between dots; it is about changing the nature of the dots altogether. Merleau-Ponty (1962) fashioned a lovely expression of the notion of identity as distributed possibility when he said that in the future, identity will be found:

> not in self-identity but in autodispersion; it is being beyond oneself, outside oneself, ecstatically; it is existing in multiple location; it is existing not as a point-occupancy in space and time, but as a radiation, a dimension, as a world-ray; it is not to be in-itself, but always further on.

Easier said than done. Fear and anxiety draw us away from planetary thinking by impacting our sense of power and possibility, raising our need to be right, which in turn leads to attachment, dysfunctional communication, and destructive conflict. For our future, we require a global declaration of interdependence, a central tenet of which must be the release of grasping after self and tribal identity, "grasping for a ground as the territory that separates one group of people from another" (Varela et al., 1991, p. 254).

Of course, our usual solution to feelings of fragmentation is to seek a new grounding. This endless attraction to absolutism and its seeming opposite, nihilism, is in fact fueled by the same fire—objectivism. Once we give up the idea of a fixed truth, one that is separate from our making—and of a fixed self, separate from the world—we can begin the process of world building from a new and unprecedented perspective. Varela and his colleagues call this new way "laying down a path in walking," and it begins with the presumption that all things, including people, lack an intrinsic nature. Instead, it is *relationships* that matter most, because the history of joint action of organisms and environments over time is what creates the world (Bateson, 2000; Varela et al., 1991). This does not mean that life is meaningless or unbounded, only that these boundaries are not reified. Put another way: "We are always constrained by the path we have laid down, but there is no ultimate ground to prescribe the steps that we take" (Varela et al., 1991, p. 214).

Writers across diverse disciplines struggle today to name and describe those qualities of being that can give our lives stability without invoking certainty. Discussions of ethics, values, and morals and of hardiness and emotional intelligence are all examples of "playing ball on running water" (Reynolds, 1984), of crafting a livable life in a dynamic, groundless world. The challenge with each of these is our tendency to convert them gradually from purposefully ambiguous signifiers into dogma.

That brings us full circle to the value of uncertainty. In this essay, I have described both the reasons why people are drawn to certainty as a solution to life's problems and the specific ways this solution has been applied to the development of the self. Mood, personal narrative, and typical patterns of communication all tend to reinforce this prevailing view. Recently, however, a new aesthetic of identity is emerging. Close examination of the desire for separation and for certainty reveals it to be fruitless because meaning cannot be fixed and there is no experience of self that is completely separate from the world. The challenge is to develop new ways of living in a world without foundations. In such a world, it is the structural relations between people that matter most, and for all of our sakes, these relationships ought to be entered into with a compassionate spirit: "Planetary building requires the embodiment of concern for the other with whom we enact a world" (Varela et al., 1991, p. 247). Communication is the heart of this effort.

When transience is not merely an occasion for mourning, we will
have inherited the Earth.

—Adam Phillips (2000)

Out beyond fields of wrongdoing and rightdoing, there is a field.
I will meet you there.

—Jelaluddin Rumi (1997)

AUTHOR'S NOTE: The author thanks Lori A. Roscoe for advice on this paper and
Sarah McLachlan for suggesting the title.

References

Altheide, D. (2000). Identity and the definition of the situation in a mass-mediated
context. *Symbolic Interaction, 23,* 1–28.

Archer, M. (1995). *Realist social theory: The morphogenetic approach.* Cambridge,
UK: Cambridge University Press.

Axley, S. (1980). Managerial and organizational communication in terms of the conduit metaphor. *Academy of Management Review, 9,* 428–437.

Babrow, A. S., Kasch, C. R., & Ford, L. A. (1998). The many meanings of "uncertainty" in illness: Toward a systematic accounting. *Health Communication, 10,*
1–24.

Barbalet, J. (1998). *Emotion, social theory, and social structure.* Cambridge, UK:
Cambridge University Press.

Barrett, F. (1998). Creativity and improvisation in jazz and organizations:
Implications for organizational learning. *Organization Science, 9,* 605–622.

Bateson, G. (2000). *Steps to an ecology of mind.* Chicago: University of Chicago Press.

Becker, E. (1997). *The denial of death.* New York: Free Press

Beckwith, H. (2000). *The invisible touch.* New York: Warner Books.

Bochner, A. (1984). The functions of human communication in interpersonal bonding. In C. Arnold & J. Bowers (Eds.), *Handbook of rhetoric and communication
theory* (pp. 544–621). Newton, MA: Allyn & Bacon.

Bohm, D. (1996). *On dialogue.* New York: Routledge.

Browning, L. (1992). Lists and stories as organizational communication. *Communication Theory, 2,* 281–302.

Buber, M. (1965). *Between man and man.* New York: Collier Books.

Capra, F. (1997). *The web of life.* New York: Doubleday.

Condit, C. (2000). Culture and biology in human communication: Toward a multi-
causal model. *Communication Education, 49,* 7–24.

Deetz, S. (1992). *Democracy in an age of corporate colonization.* Albany: State
University of New York Press.

Duranti, A. (1984). Intentions, self, and local theories of meaning: Words and actions in a Samoan context. *Center for Human Information Processing, 122,* 1–20.

Eisenberg, E. (1984). Ambiguity as strategy in organizational communication. *Communication Monographs, 51,* 227–242.

Eisenberg, E. (1990). Jamming: Transcendence through organizing. *Communication Research, 17,* 139–164.

Eisenberg, E. (1998). Flirting with meaning. *Journal of Language and Social Psychology, 17,* 97–108.

Eisenberg, E. (2001). *Building a mystery.* Unpublished book manuscript.

Eisenberg, E., & Witten, M. (1987). Reconsidering openness in organizational communication. *Academy of Management Review, 12,* 418–426.

Eisler, R. (1988). *The chalice and the blade.* San Francisco: HarperSan Francisco.

Ellis, D. (1995). Fixing communicative meaning. *Communication Research, 22,* 515–544.

Espejo, R., & Pheby, K. (2000). Transduction, recursive logic, and identities of the self, [Online], 1–10. Available: www.syncho.com/papers/transduction.htm.

Fisher, W. (1984). Narration as a human communication paradigm: The case of public moral argument. *Communication Monographs, 51,* 1–22.

Friedman, S. (1993). *The new language of change.* New York: Guilford Press.

Gergen, K. (1985). The social constructionist movement in modern psychology. *American Psychologist, 40,* 266–275.

Gergen, K. (2000). *The saturated self.* New York: Basic Books.

Giddens, A. (1979). *Central problems in social theory.* Berkeley: University of California Press.

Goodall, H. L., Jr. (1991). *Living in the rock n' roll mystery.* Carbondale: Southern Illinois University Press.

Grossberg, L., Wartella, E., & Whitney, D. (1998). *Media-making: Mass media in a popular culture.* Thousand Oaks, CA: Sage.

Hatch, M. (1999). Exploring the empty spaces of organizing: How improvisational jazz helps redescribe organizational structure. *Organization Studies, 20,* 75–100.

Havel, V. (1991). *Disturbing the peace.* New York: Vintage Books.

Kramer, P. (1997). *Listening to Prozac.* New York: Penguin.

Krippendorff, K. (1995). Undoing power. *Critical Studies in Mass Communication, 12,* 101–132.

Isaacs, W. (1999). *Dialogue.* New York: Currency Doubleday.

Lakoff, G., & Johnson, M. (1999). *Philosophy in the flesh.* New York: Basic Books.

Lennie, I. (1999). *Beyond management.* London: Sage.

Levine, D. (1985). *The flight from ambiguity.* Chicago: University of Chicago Press.

Lifton, R. J. (1999). *The protean self.* Chicago: University of Chicago Press.

Loewenstein, W. (1999). *The touchstone of life.* New York: Oxford University Press.

McCroskey, J. C., & Beatty, M. J. (2000). The communibiological perspective: Implications for communication in instruction. *Communication Education, 49,* 1–6.

McKenna, T. (1993). *Food of the gods.* New York: Bantam Books.

Merleau-Ponty, M. (1962). *Phenomenology of perception.* Colin Smith, Trans. London: Routledge & Kegan Paul.

Parry, A., & Doan, R. (1994). *Story re-visions: Narrative therapy in the post-modern world.* New York: Guilford Press.

Phillips, A. (1994). *On flirtation.* Cambridge, MA: Harvard University Press.

Phillips, A. (1998). *The beast in the nursery.* Cambridge, MA: Harvard University Press.

Phillips, A. (2000). *Darwin's worms.* New York: Basic Books.

Popper, K. (1966). *The open society and its enemies.* Princeton, NJ: Princeton University Press.

Quinn, D. (1992). *Ishmael.* New York: Bantam.

Reynolds, D. (1984). *Playing ball on running water.* New York: Quill.

Rumi, J. (1997). *The essential Rumi.* San Francisco: HarperSanFrancisco.

Scarf, M. (1996). *Intimate partners.* New York: Ballantine Books.

Shorris, E. (1997). *New American blues.* New York: Norton.

Spretnak, C. (1997). *The resurgence of the real.* Reading, MA: Addison-Wesley.

Starhawk. (1993). *The fifth sacred thing.* New York: Bantam.

Stewart, J. (2000, April). *The pragmatics of dialogue.* Annual Grazier Lecture, Department of Communication, University of South Florida.

Tannen, D. (1998). *The argument culture.* New York: Random House.

Varela, F., Thompson, E., & Rosch, E. (1991). *The embodied mind.* Cambridge, MA: MIT Press.

Watts, A. (1989). *The book.* New York: Vintage.

Weick, K. (1979). *The social psychology of organizing* (2nd ed.). Reading, MA: Addison-Wesley.

15

Creating Clearings for Communication

This essay was first presented at the Aspen Conference on Organizational Communication, a gathering of scholars and practitioners dedicated to translating communication research into action. Like my earlier paper dealing with planned change (Chapter 11, "Transforming Organizations Through Communication"), this piece addressed the goals and methods associated with effective communication training. Consistent with my core argument, I maintained that effective communication training is less about learning new skills and more about reflecting on persistent patterns of existing behavior, with the goal of "unfreezing" old patterns and making room for new ones.

The Aspen conference marked an important step in the development of the organizational communication discipline. The overarching purpose of this annual meeting is to tighten the connection between theory and practice and to demonstrate how work done in communication can have real value for communication practitioners. This essay reflects the influence of my thinking about identity on the very tangible challenge of employee training and development. Real behavioral change always begins with honest self-reflection.

SOURCE: Eisenberg, E. (2005). Creating clearings for communication. In Simpson, J. L., & Shockley-Zalabak, P. (Eds.), *Engaging communication, transforming organizations: Scholarship of engagement in action* (pp. 113–125). Cresskill, NJ: Hampton Press. Copyright © 2005, Hampton Press.

Introduction: Something Worth Learning

When critics assert that communication faculty should do a better job of contributing to communicative practice, they usually have in mind some set of concepts or principles that have been supported by research and may be of use to practitioners. Implicit in this view is the assumption that practitioners both desire and would benefit from learning more about communication, and that a more engaged professoriate would be better positioned to provide this knowledge.

While this conclusion seems logical and appealing, it rests on two related assumptions, namely that communication (a) is a learned skill, and (b) is something worth learning. Unfortunately, not all practitioners share these assumptions. Many engineers, bank managers, doctors, lawyers, and other working professionals think of a person's communication as largely driven by his or her personality and not easily influenced by formal education and training. This belief is attributable in part to the general absence of communication education in schools, and in part to the vast number of communication training programs that have failed to create lasting behavioral change.

But this does not mean that the importance of communication is unrecognized by practitioners, only that communication skill is seen as either innate or as developing experientially, and not through formal education. It is important to consider the possibility that it is not communication itself but the way we have chosen to engage with practitioners about communication that is problematic. Specifically, most communication education is additive in nature; it focuses on providing individuals with a defined set of concepts and skills to apply in their daily life. Framed this way, we may also be implying that communication skill is something that working professionals are lacking that we might provide. By contrast, if we begin by acknowledging that successful practitioners have always found ways to communicate that work for them, a different (and potentially more successful) approach to engagement may emerge.

But what would this approach be like? How do you educate people about something when they are suspicious about the legitimacy or teachability of the subject matter? Most if not all of us would agree that to succeed, a teacher must meet the students "where they are" both emotionally and intellectually. Not only have few working professionals received formal training in communication, consider the current business environment. Intense pressures to save time, cut costs, and increase productivity often push communication education to the back burner. One typical comment that I have heard from executives is: "I already know how to communicate, so I can't get much out of additional education. And even if I believed this was incredibly valuable, I can't take this time away from my [real] work to focus on this right now."

An additional example will clinch the point. Some years ago, I was facilitating a workshop on organizational dialogue and decision making for staff members who had been appointed to cross-functional teams at my university. Not 10 minutes into the first session, a participant who worked in financial affairs asked whether the communication workshop was really necessary, stating that she had an enormous amount of important work on her desk and would prefer to address communication issues as they arose in her daily work. Her question troubled me, and I quickly figured out why. Having recently become scuba certified, I responded with a question of my own: "Would you ask a scuba instructor to skip the up-front instruction and wait to address problems as they occurred 100 feet underwater?" The answer was obvious to everyone in the room, including the questioner. We all can see that waiting to learn about diving would be a bad idea because we understand that scuba diving is a learned skill. The same awareness doesn't always exist when it comes to communication.

Given this background, the purpose of this chapter is to explore an alternative way of engaging with practitioners about communication that may not elicit the same kind of response. My specific objectives are twofold: (a) to propose a coherent alternative to the additive, acquisitive model of communication training and development, one that emphasizes reflexivity with regard to one's current patterns over the learning of new skills; and (b) to suggest how this newfound reflexivity creates possibilities for a different way of living and working that both encourages and affirms a life of contingency and uncertainty that resists all foundationalism, courts otherness, and views progress as "laying down a path in walking" (Varela, Thompson, & Rosch, 1997).

Emptying the Cup: An Alternative Approach to Communication Education

How do most communication researchers approach their engagement with practitioners? As stated earlier, communication training and development often has an acquisitive quality, focusing mainly on the active addition of new concepts, principles, and techniques as the main route to enhanced effectiveness. But what if "learning new things" is precisely the wrong place to begin? In my experience, the most important "thing" practitioners can gain from communication education is not a new technique for communication, but a deeper understanding of and appreciation for how they are *already* communicating. This broadened understanding can in turn create clearings for more intelligent and sensitive communicative choices. Without this kind of insight, the likelihood of real behavioral change is minimal.

Recent research examines why people do or don't change their behaviors, describing the unconscious, competing commitments that undermine people's best efforts to change (see Kegan & Lahey, 2002). What emerges from this work is the realization that positive change happens only when a number of related conditions are met. A lack of alignment among organizational systems is deadly to any change effort; communication educators often have the experience of promoting ideas and concepts that are not reinforced or are even contradicted by other systems within the organization (e.g., a week-long training in team dynamics immediately followed by the introduction of an individually focused compensation plan). What you or I might call "good" communication is not a winning strategy in many organizations. And if forced to choose between the two, lessons learned through communication education are no match for organizational norms that support a different set of behaviors.

When approaching a group with the aim of communication development, I am reminded of Salvador Dali's well-known painting *Persistence of Memory*. The canvas is littered with melted clocks, remnants of the past that remain part of the present landscape. In much the same way, people approach communication education with established habits of communicating that they are (understandably) reluctant to abandon. These persistent patterns are not of themselves an obstacle to learning new communication skills. But they do become problematic when left unacknowledged (i.e., if the individual thinks of his or her behavior as right, normal, and appropriate, and *not* as embodying a series of personal choices). We all reside in worlds that are largely socially constructed, and what varies the most is our degree of *awareness* of the fact that we are living but one of an infinite number of possible stories.

Put another way, the main work of communication education is to help individuals become aware of their habitual patterns of interaction, to make persistent patterns both visible and discussable by moving communication from practical (tacit) to discursive consciousness (Giddens, 1986). This is not really a new idea. Think of the famous Zen story in which the teacher pours tea into an already full cup, causing it to overflow. The point of the story is that to make room for new lessons, one must first empty one's cup.

The challenge to communication education that derives from a lack of awareness of habits, then, is not *resistance* to change but rather a kind of *inertia* (Bean & Eisenberg, 2002). People are unconsciously attached to ways of being in the world that are for the most part taken for granted.

In the absence of reflexivity (and meaningful feedback from others), the best predictor of how someone will communicate tomorrow is their communication today. In this conservative context, new information about how to communicate has little chance of making a real impact.

Improving as a communicator may have more to do with extinguishing old patterns than with the acquisition of new ones. A famous American composer was interviewed on the occasion of his 105th birthday. When asked for the "secret" of his long life, he responded, "I have a poor memory." Anthropologist and noted systems thinker Gregory Bateson frequently held up a blackboard eraser during his talks, commenting that "you can't live without this."

"Laying Down a Path in Walking": Seeking a New Ontology of Communication

Making current communication patterns visible through enhanced reflexivity, however, is only the first part of the story. Once a person has gained some rudimentary insight into their own style and behavior (no small achievement!) and communication choices become more conscious and less taken-for-granted, there remains a need for guidance regarding how to live with these new choices. Increased reflexivity undermines simple reliance on taken for granted rules and recipes; it is no longer possible to hide behind statements like "that's just how I am" or "this is the right thing to do." Life as a conscious, reflexive communicator holds a greater potential for openness to both different people and behaviors, but with this openness comes increased anxiety, uncertainty, and confusion. How can one learn to live this way?

Put another way, conscious communication often prompts an identity crisis. Moreover, this crisis often goes well beyond the need to change one's overt communication behavior. In an earlier paper on this subject, I argued that behavioral change is unlikely to result from an isolated focus on dialogic communication style and techniques (Eisenberg, 2001). There is no reason to expect that people will change their style of communicating when a myriad of other factors—personality, experience, and material working conditions, for example—reinforce the status quo. A better approach would take into account a number of other factors that shape individual behavior, including personality, life history, and socioeconomic background.

In this earlier paper, I advanced the idea that there are three mutually reinforcing subprocesses that comprise the process of identity formation. They are as follows:

Soma: Emotions, brain chemistry, and other biological processes combine to result in a general emotional orientation toward the world, hopeful or anxious, happy, or depressed.

Story: The way we choose to narrate our life story tells a great deal about our attachments, interpretations, and view of our own potential and possibilities.

Style: Style refers to one's approach to communication encounters, with emphasis on how one experiences, thinks about, and relates to others.

All three of these identity sub-processes exists in the context of a fourth "s," what Shorris (1997) called the "surround." The surround is the sum total of biological, economic, interpersonal, cultural, and spiritual factors that influence a person's perceived sense of self. The complete model appears in Chapter 14 (Figure 14.1).

Only when all of these overlapping systems are considered can we hope to impact actual communication behaviors. What is most interesting about this model is that there is a common tension throughout each of the sub-processes, a dialectic of vulnerability and defensiveness. In each case, anxiety about communication leads to a contraction and a kind of protectiveness, whether that anxiety is driven by biology, impoverished life narrative, communication apprehension, or a disadvantaged surround. Moreover, these processes are mutually reinforcing, and repeated patterns tend to get locked in. Changes in any part of the process will likely be met with inertia from other sub-processes. This is why any number of narrowly conceived interventions—moving to a new area, going on a new drug, or learning to use a new communicative tool—are likely to fail unless they are supported by changes in other parts of the model. For example, teaching people about the elements of effective communication without also providing a supportive climate for communication is like trying to grow plants without soil—the new practices have nowhere to take root.

Techniques for Increased Reflexivity

If you accept the idea that becoming aware of one's present way of communicating is a necessary condition for further communication education, it seems reasonable to ask how a more reflexive awareness might be cultivated. I have had experience with a number of different kinds of techniques, from the subtle to the highly confrontational. I describe some of these next.

Surface Styles

Of all the techniques I discuss here, this one is most widespread in both communication education and training programs. Surfacing styles means making peoples' explicit tendencies visible both to themselves and to those around them. Typically, an instrument such as DISC (Voges & Braund, 1995) or the Myers-Briggs Type Indicator (Keirsey, 1998) is used, and online temperament sorters are now available and somewhat improved over their predecessors. Through the use of these tools, individuals learn whether they are an extrovert or an introvert, along with the conditions within which they are most likely to thrive.

Surfacing styles does more than simply provide vocabulary for people to describe their tendencies, but also reveals the many differences that exist between people with regard to social interaction. Recognizing this difference is the first step toward any kind of change; by examining your persistent habits, you free yourself to set off in new directions.

A cautionary note is in order. Classifications of this sort can be easily misused, both by the individual subject and the powers that be. The distinctions made by these tests themselves reflect an implicit system of values, and individuals may use their "style" or "type" as something to hide behind and to avoid deeper analysis (Holmer Nadesan, 1997). Nonetheless, they can also be a crucial first step in a person's journey toward greater self-awareness with regard to their communication.

Strange Questioning

A staple of the human potential movement (associated with the 1960s counterculture and surviving today under new labels) is the query that is unanswerable from one's taken for granted worldview. For example, I often ask people to describe how they are "already always listening" to others. Inevitably, they resist the suggestion that they have a common orientation to listening that cuts across all aspects of their lives; they are determined to convince me that how they listen "depends on the situation." Once I give them some examples, however, they warm to the possibility of a more general pattern. I tell them that like most teachers, I tend to listen "how can I help you" in most every interaction. Others listen like "how is this person out to get me" and still others "I know this already."

Once participants are willing to consider the possibility that they have a generic approach to listening, they have also begun to see more clearly the alternatives that could exist to the way they do things. Through strange questioning, a small crack can be created between taken-for granted patterns (in this case, of listening) and a range of alternative communicative styles and practices. In systems language, what this technique does is allow the participants to move beyond first-order to second-order change, and in so doing consider the effectiveness of their generic approach to communication.

Take a Hike

The setting in which communication education takes place can make a difference in the degree to which participants will be willing to be reflexive. At a superficial level, effective communication is easy to intellectualize (and also to fake!). It is much different to understand how to communicate than it is to consistently do it; the most common criticism of managerial communications is an inability to "walk the talk."

When it comes to communication, many people talk a good game, and this same deception can continue in training seminars that lack a behavioral dimension. In my work, I involve participants in a range of activities (indoors and out) that activate multiple learning styles and require the performance of new communication behaviors. The benefit of such an expanded approach is that over time, participants can usually identify disconnects between their espoused theory of communication (what they think they do) and their theory in use (what they actually do when faced with a challenge) (e.g., Argyris, 1993).

A final advantage of communication education in a nontraditional setting is that any distance from the workplace helps to loosen role expectations and give participants permission to get to know one another as people. Encouraged to rely less heavily on role relationships as a guide for their communicative choices, participants may also experiment with alternative ways of relating to co-workers that can set a positive precedent once everyone returns to the office.

Accentuate the Positive

One of the most common patterns of organizational communication emphasizes breakdowns and disconnects, leading to frustration and a sense of discouragement. While honest perception of communication challenges is essential, they may be framed in a way that both acknowledges the problems and evokes the many possible ways out.

Narrative possibility therapy (Friedman, 1991) was developed to combat the "problem-centered narratives" that populate most people's accounts of their life and work. Similar to strange questioning, this approach gently challenges participant's taken-for-granted view of their present situation, in so doing inviting them to consider alternatives. One example is the use of the "miracle question," which asks people to describe a world without problems. Another is called "exception-seeking"—when the person complains about a boss's communication style, the facilitator pushes the individual to identify a time when the person had a positive experience with the boss, and to build from there. The idea is that framing challenging situations as "problems" acts as a kind of self-fulfilling prophecy, which may be counteracted by inviting individuals to consider alternative possibilities.

Resist the Rescue

As teachers or consultants, many of the people reading this book already tend to listen "how can I help you?" and are very likely to intervene in a training group when things appear to be going sour. An inherent part of good communication education is that difficult issues do come up and must be handled somehow by the facilitator and/or the group. Most thorny of all is the poor communicator who is constantly derailing the group and has little to no insight into their own behavior.

There is a huge temptation, in dealing with participants of this kind, to intervene, to do damage control and set ground rules for the future. But there is a significant problem in doing so. Inasmuch as the facilitator/trainer is always in some sense part of the system, stopping an offending participant constitutes a kind of rescue. In one sense, the facilitator is rescuing the other group members from having to put up with the offending one; in another, they are rescuing the offender from sustained repercussions from the group. It is this latter sense of rescue that is potentially most problematic. If greater reflexivity is the goal, does it really make sense to protect participants from direct feedback? Practitioners of group therapy are clear on the recommended protocol here; they suggest that people not only be permitted to continue their offending behaviors, but that they be encouraged to repeat them. They may be called on the carpet by the others in the group, but over time they are more likely to see what it is in their behavior that is inspiring anger in others. Rescuing someone from this feedback hampers, and does not help the cause of encouraging greater reflexivity (e.g., Ormont, 1991).

Consult the Body

It takes a great deal of work to sustain a strong attachment to a worldview or set of practices, and a large percentage of this weight is carried by the body. One successful route to behavior change is biofeedback (e.g., Murphy, 1993). Biofeedback works by providing either audible (beep) or visible (flash) signals whose intensity varies with the level of tension in your body. For example, one common form of biofeedback attaches electrodes to a person's neck and jaws, measuring degree of muscle tension and beeping (or flashing) at a pace to match the level of tension. A typical first reaction to this treatment is that participants are surprised to learn that they were in fact tense when they felt relaxed. This is due to the fact that when faced with a moderate baseline level of stress, the body accommodates and comes to feel like it is normal.

But this sense of what is normal can also be changed. People undergoing biofeedback are next taught progressive relaxation techniques to release muscle tension (which in turn slows the beeps or the flashes until they finally stop). Moreover, it is unlikely that the same insight (and change) could have been accomplished through counseling or any other kind of talk therapy. Using other parts of the body—other learning modalities—creates a unique opportunity for reflecting on what one believes to be normal.

Make Peace With Uncertainty

This has become a truism of organizational theory, as writers for decades have encouraged practitioners to "ride whitewater" and "thrive on chaos." At the same time, a large part of what is frustrating about teaching communication to practitioners is the desire for simple recipes and easy answers. One well-known training company obliged by printing its "key principles" for effective communication on the side of a coffee mug.

But the pursuit of solid certainty when it comes to organizational behavior is both a mirage and a trap (Lennie, 1999). Decisions about how to interact vary widely by audience and by situation. Life and work are both fundamentally unmanageable. Communication education is defeated when participants insist on simple prescriptions or rules of thumb. When and if we succumb to this temptation, it is these very prescriptions that further deflate our reputation among savvy and experienced practitioners.

In challenging taken-for-granted habits of communication, it is critically important to resist replacing them with new foundations. Our usual antidote to anxiety is to seek out certainty wherever we can find it, to establish a new grounding. But this may not be a winning strategy in today's world. An alternative might look like this:

> Once we give up the idea of a fixed truth, one that is separate from our making—and of a fixed self, separate from the world—we can begin the

process of world building from a new and unprecedented perspective. Varela and his colleagues call this new way "laying down a path in walking," and it begins with the presumption that all things, including people, lack an intrinsic nature. Instead, it is relationships that matter most, because the history of joint action of organisms and environments over time is what creates the world (Bateson, 2000; Varela et al., 1991). This does not mean that life is meaningless or unbounded, only that these boundaries are not reified. Put another way: "We are always constrained by the path we have laid down, but there is no ultimate ground to prescribe the steps that we take" (Varela et al., 1991, p. 214; Eisenberg, 2001).

The present challenge is to develop ways of living in the world without fixed truths or foundations. Effective communication requires a high level of sensitivity to the emerging social context, which leads in turn to the ability to choose consciously among optional responses. If attachment to practices that are no longer effective is the problem, learning to live with multiplicity and ambiguity may well be part of the solution. This kind of openness to others is invariably rewarded and even celebrated. When it comes to human relations, a measured vulnerability turns out to be the best means of control. It would be a positive step toward a more peaceful society if our attempts at communication education reflected this worldview.

Summary

Literally millions of pages have been dedicated to the subject of organizational development and training, with a smaller but still significant subset focusing specifically on communication. Much of what is reported in these pages is ingenious, and new ideas and activities are being developed all the time. But despite this embarrassment of riches, what has been the experience of academics and others attempting to teach about these ideas? With few exceptions, the reach of these programs far exceeds their grasp. New concepts and skills are imparted only to be forgotten immediately by participants. Sponsoring executives release participants for the classes, but do little else to follow up or to reinforce valuable lessons learned.

For these and other reasons, I have chosen to develop and implement a form of communication education that has little to do with these formal programs. My approach does not entail bringing new knowledge about communication or anything else. Instead I see my role as holding up a mirror to their taken for granted interactions and using their observations to expand their communicative repertoire.

I recognize that calling for this kind of self-reflection can be stressful and highly threatening to individuals who are strongly attached to a version of themselves. Consequently, I design activities that make use of multiple learning styles and modalities to try to get past the anxiety and defensiveness to a place where the participant understands the nature and source of their own communicative style, and subsequently can make use of this understanding to make different choices.

Change does not have to be negative to be frightening; development of any kind can prompt anxiety by potentially threatening taken-for-granted practices and beliefs. Nevertheless, for many people it is precisely this anxiety and defensiveness that stands in the way of personal growth. And what keeps the whole process at a standstill is the undiscussability of what is happening.

Once current patterns of communication become both visible and discussable, then it is possible to introduce a range of communication principles and techniques. Once groups acquire the capacity for reflexivity and self-organization—to live consciously with conscious communication—they become smarter and more resilient. Throughout their life, the average person grows increasingly inflexible, attached, and closed as a misguided defense against change. A better strategy would be to cultivate a flexible, playful, open stance that better maps onto our dynamic environment.

References

Argyris, C. (1993). *Knowledge in action*. San Francisco, CA: Jossey-Bass.

Bean, C. J., & Eisenberg, E. (2002). *Employee sensemaking in the transition to nomadic work*. Paper presented at the annual meeting of the National Communication Association, New Orleans, LA.

Eisenberg, E. (1991). Tuesday for Bruce. In S. Banks & A. Banks (Eds.), *Fire and ice* (pp. 195–202). San Francisco: Alta Mira Press.

Eisenberg, E. (2001). Building a mystery: Toward a theory of communication and identity. *Journal of Communication, 51*(3), 534–552.

Friedman, S. (1991). *The new language of change*. New York: Guilford.

Giddens, A. (1986). *The constitution of society: Outline of the theory of structuration*. Berkeley: University of California Press.

Holmer Nadesan, M. (1997). Constructing paper dolls: The discourse of personality testing in organizational practices. *Communication Theory, 7*(3) 189–218.

Kegan, R., & Lahey, L. (2002). *How the way we talk can change the way we work*. San Francisco, CA: Jossey-Bass.

Keirsey, D. (1988). *Please understand me II: Temperament, character, intelligence*. New York: Prometheus Nemesis Books.

Lennie, I. (1999). *Beyond management.* London: Sage.

Murphy, M. (1993). *The future of the body: Exploration into the further evolution of human nature.* New York: J. P. Tarcher

Ormont, L. (1991). *The group therapy experience.* New York: St. Martin's.

Shorris, E. (1997). *New American blues.* New York: Norton.

Varela, F., Thompson, E., & Rosch, E. (997). *The embodied mind.* Cambridge, MA: MIT Press.

Voges, K., & Braund, R. (1995). *Understanding how others misunderstand you.* New York: Moody.

16

Karl Weick and the
Aesthetics of Contingency

This essay was commissioned as part of a special issue of the journal Organization Studies, *in honor of the work of management scholar Karl Weick. Ever since I first read him in the 1970s, Weick has had enormous influence on both my work and my worldview. Weick sang the praises of equivocality long before it was acceptable to do so, and this paper both celebrates his unique vision and conducts a thorough assessment of the ways in which contingency is an exemplary framework for certain kinds of organizational communication.*

This paper contains my latest thinking about the relationship between organizational communication and sensemaking. Although I take Weick to task some for his unwillingness to take on issues of power and politics, the broader message lies in his implicit theory of identity. Specifically, I wish to extend Weick's work to develop a more robust aesthetics of contingency with the potential to improve human relations across a broad range of institutions. As Weick is a central figure in organizational studies, this essay has the potential to impact a large group of scholars and their conceptions of communication.

SOURCE: Eisenberg, E. (2006). Karl Weick and the aesthetics of contingency. *Organization Studies, 27*(11), 1–15. Reprinted by permission, Sage Publications, Ltd.

The emergence of Western culture has been characterized as a "flight from ambiguity" (Levine, 1985). Expansion of global capitalism is fueled by a reliance on technology and a belief in the possibility of unfettered progress. Taylorism is but one example of Newton's "single vision"—we moderns need little encouragement to dream of discovering the "one best way" to work, love, and live. A massive self-help industry from Dr. Ruth to Dr. Phil offers candidate solutions to life's most vexing problems. Mega-churches dot the American landscape preaching an increasingly fundamentalist message. Many Westerners long for a simpler time where life-paths were clear. What we experience instead is a world of contradiction and confusion, wherein rampant subjectivity and diversity make plural that which was once self-evident and certain, leaving us with a multiplicity of truths, reasons, and realities. Each of the paradigms central to Western civilization is undergoing major transformations today, at the start of the 21st century (Ventura, 1993).

It is against this dynamic backdrop that I take stock of the scholarly contributions of a leading American intellectual, Professor Karl E. Weick. When Weick began writing in the 1960s, most organizational observers were confused and disoriented by the radical changes described above and for the most part persisted with traditional models and concepts. Others acknowledged the new reality of unrelenting change, but did little more than comment upon it. Weick's body of work is unique in that he both identified the fragmented, turbulent, at times counter-rational quality of organizational life and struggled to make sense of it. His legacy is a rich set of concepts and tools for appreciating the turbulent quality of contemporary organizing.

More specifically, I reflect on Weick's work with the aim of illuminating his impact on my chosen sub-field of *Organizational Communication*. Far from being a parochial decision, however, I will show that the sensibility that captured the imagination of the Communication discipline impacted the whole of Organizational Studies. The wide reach of his scholarship is largely the result of his approach to organizations being less a technique than a new way of thinking about communicating and organizing.

This essay is motivated by the following question: In accepting Weick's invitation to think his way, to what exactly have we agreed? In the next section, I describe the historical and intellectual context within which Weick's ideas first emerged, chronicling his attempts to evoke a new kind of order in the wake of the collapse of a facile modernism. Against this historical backdrop, I undertake a closer analysis of Weick's scholarly contributions, focusing specifically on his enduring effect on the field of Organizational Communication.

Organizing After Modernism: A Certain Equivocality

Scholarly reactions to this erosion of certainty in contemporary life have been mixed. The first, more pessimistic view pronounces the death of grand narratives, of God, meaning, authorship and the autonomous self, putting in its place "situation ethics" and deconstruction without end. The second, more optimistic perspective sees the proliferation of meanings as an opportunity for world-building. This latter project has been dubbed the "re-enchantment" of the world (Berman, 1981), and it is also Weick's project, as he aims to celebrate equivocality and a plurality of perspectives while at the same time avoiding moral or intellectual relativism.

A *seeming* contradiction characterizes Weick's work. While his writings are chocked full of potentially destabilizing concepts such as randomness and equivocality, they are presented in the service of elaborated sense-making, increased understanding, or as precursors to improving practices of organizing. Sporting an anarchist's vocabulary, he deploys it both constructively and appreciatively, shedding more light than heat. And as much as Weick's ideas are challenging to the status quo, he remains a card-carrying organizational scientist in pursuit of ever more compelling and reliable explanations.

Much of Weick's appeal is traceable to his keen ability to speculate about the future. He reveals in his work the "charm of the scout," a moniker once applied to Gregory Bateson for his unique ability to challenge the status quo with ideas that were decades ahead of their time (Toulmin, 1983). He appears comfortable in the role of a guide and his talent is in the wandering. His body of work represents a long intellectual bridge between a linear, hierarchical, and avowedly rational world to one that is circular, participative, and unabashedly improvisational.

All told, Karl Weick has made great strides in the struggle to re-enchant the world of organizations, returning to them the mystery that resides at their core (Goodall, 1991). He has done so without ever falling prey to easy answers or fundamentalisms. Rather than seeking to purify human action through the development of a more perfect belief system (cf. Burke, 1969), Weick rejoices in the choppy humanness of action, and in the ways in which belief and action are consistently out of alignment (e.g., when a fire-fighter struggles to choose between dropping his tools and ignoring the advice of his squad leader). In this way, his thinking foreshadows Giddens's (1986) preoccupation with unintended consequences and the limits of practical consciousness; i.e., in practice, we do so many things that we don't fully understand, at least when we are doing them.

For Weick, organizing is improvisation without end, set in a world where our actions have serious consequences but lack solid foundations.

Whether consumed with hospital handoffs, secondary education, or air traffic control, Weick sustains his focus on belief-in-action and on the ongoing interplay between thought and behavior. In this sense, he responds to the hopelessness that can accompany paradigms lost by redoubling his faith in human ingenuity and the endless possibilities of human organizing.

Put another way, Weick's work reveals a wellspring that exists just beyond the concepts at hand, a worldview that transcends human organizing and reflects a strong view of the human spirit. In addition to the many intellectual contributions Weick has made in his career, his legacy will include the advancement of a particular aesthetic, one that construes the world as contingent and multifaceted and conceives of effective communication as heedful interrelating across a diversity of perspectives.

Communicating and Organizing: Tracing Weick's Influence

I begin with an obligatory caveat: Since an exhaustive view of Weick's writing is beyond the scope of this essay, my more modest aim is to identify three historical moments in Weick's work, each characterized by a particularly influential set of ideas. For ease of discussion, these three moments can be associated with his three most popular books, *The Social Psychology of Organizing* (1969/1979), *Sensemaking in Organizations* (1995), and *Managing the Unexpected* (2001, with K. Sutcliffe). Weick's influence on organizational communication centers on sensemaking, the process by which people enact equivocal environments and interact in ways that seek to reduce that equivocality. His first book (1969/1979) lays the groundwork for a theory of sensemaking by introducing the notion of equivocality and affirming the importance of collective action. His second book (1995) presents the theory itself and adds more detail to sensemaking properties and the cognitive processes they reflect. Finally, his most recent volume (2001) applies the sensemaking vocabulary to a specific genre of organizing, and in so doing valorizes the importance of "heedful interrelating" as a model of effective organizational communication.

Equivocality and Interaction

The first edition of *The Social Psychology of Organizing* (1969) was a short book whose influence grew exponentially over time. I was first introduced to it while in graduate school in the 1970s, when a member of my doctoral committee (Vince Farace) declared it to have "more good ideas per page than anything he had ever read." The impact of this book stems from presenting equivocality reduction as a driving force in social life, identifying social interaction as the substance of organizing, and linking systems thinking to meaning-based models of organizing. Each of these elements is described below.

Prior to Weick, organizational analysts regarded equivocality as inherently problematic and to be either ignored or expunged from organizational life. Weick turned this idea on its head, arguing instead that equivocality is *the* engine that motivates people to organize. In Weick's model, individuals enact environments that vary in their degree of equivocality, which in turn leads everything that "happens" in and around organizations to be subject to multiple (and often competing) interpretations. People communicate in an effort to reduce the number of possible interpretations, and in so doing make coordinated action possible. Notably, these insights pre-date Goffman's (1974) work on the "framing" of social situations. Some representative quotes from the first edition (Weick, 1969):

> [Actors] create and constitute the environment to which they react; the environment is put there by the actors within the organization and by no one else. (p. 28)

> Organizing is concerned with removing equivocality from information and structuring processes so that this removal is possible. (p. 29)

An important consequence of this argument was the centering of communication in the processes of organizing. Weick's work showed communication practitioners a genuine alternative to the transmissional model of human interaction (cf. Putnam, 1983). But however conceptually appealing, it was hard to imagine how to study a phenomenon that was at once shapeless and fleeting. Where was one to look for the "double-interacts" that were purported to characterize organizational communication? Surely not in the research literature at that time. In the 1960s, organizational communication research was dominated by paper and pencil studies of manager and employee attitudes regarding communication. No one looked directly at social interactions.

In the field of communication, the first empirical test of Weick's approach came in the late 1970s (Bantz & Smith, 1977). Bantz and Smith conducted a laboratory experiment to assess the relationship between equivocality and cycles of communication. Non-significant findings caused the researchers to reflect critically on Weick's initial conceptualization. In particular, they noted a conflict between two very different definitions of process (linear and non-linear) evident in Weick's theory. Bantz and Smith rejected the linear version of equivocality reduction represented in Weick's specified model and argued instead for a gestalt explanation for the way organizing resembles sociocultural evolution.

A few years later, Kreps (1980) studied the relationship between the equivocality of motions made in a university Faculty Senate and the cycles of interaction that ensued, and concluded that more equivocal messages *did* in fact lead to greater numbers of cycles. Adding support to this conclusion was an experimental study conducted by Putnam and Sorenson (1982). Using students as subjects, they created zero-history simulated organizations and exposed them to messages that varied in ambiguity. Participants used more assembly rules and involved more people in processing ambiguous messages than they did with those that were relatively clear. A unique finding of this study was that how participants responded to ambiguity varied by their job level in the simulated organization. Lower level "employees" responded to ambiguity by generating multiple interpretations, while "managers" moved more directly to action as means of reducing equivocality. The authors observe that conflict may ensue in organizations when different employee groups use differing strategies for sensemaking.

All three of these studies demonstrated the considerable challenges associated with operationalizing Weick's model. Despite some positive empirical results, Bantz and Smith's first insight seems on the right track. Weick's formulation works best as a theory of dynamic systems, one that is difficult to test through simplified linear representations or the relatively primitive methodological approaches popular at the time (i.e., cross-sectional data collection, general linear model of analysis).

Recently, organizational communication scholars have picked up Weick's model yet again, this time with the aim of modifying it to reflect changes both in academic sensibilities and contemporary organizations. Weick's initial formulation was developed in the 1960s to describe organizations and environments, both of which were stable in ways that now seem quaint (for example, airline corporations and the banking industry were examples of stable industries that occupied placid environments at that time). Seen in this light, the notion of requisite variety seems chimerical—how can organizations today develop internal processes that match the complexity of external forces? Taylor and Van Every (1999) conclude that there is a profound ambiguity that characterizes Weick's early thinking, traceable to his work at the intersection of two very different vocabularies and sensibilities: systems and cultures.

And there is the rub. In combining the two great tropes of the 20th century—system and culture—Weick entertains strange bedfellows.

Whereas systems thinking holds out hope for the precise mapping and managing of complexity, cultural approaches are less focused on outcomes and more on understanding and appreciating the meanings people ascribe to collective behavior, and how these meanings help constitute communities and societies. Some clear overlaps exist, namely, contemporary cultural and systems approaches to organizational communication share an interest in developing holistic understandings of the dynamics of organizing. However, important differences distinguish the two arenas, both in the aims of people doing this work and the aesthetics that underlie it. Weick incorporates elements of both vocabularies, but remains unreconciled to either. This duality is visible in contrasting the 1969 definition of organizing with his 1979 definition in the 2nd edition:

> Organizing consists of the resolving of equivocality in an enacted environment by means of interlocked behaviors embedded in conditionally related processes. (Weick, 1969, p. 91)

> Organizations keep people busy, occasionally entertain them, give them a variety of experiences, keep them off the streets, provide pre-texts for story telling, and allow socializing. They haven't anything else to give. (Weick, 1979, p. 264)

In this latter quote—which concludes the 2nd edition of *The Social Psychology of Organizing*—Weick foreshadows the next turn in his career, one that would focus much less on the structure of interaction and more on the sense people make of these exchanges.

Fueling the "Interpretive Turn"

In Weick's universe, enactment is the starting point for organizing. Drawing on research that documents the selectivity of human perception, Weick makes an unconscious human activity both conscious and discussable. He insists that the first step in understanding how social reality is constructed and reproduced is grasping the nature of *attention*, of identifying which elements in one's surroundings are most worthy of focus.

Weick's discussion of enactment in his first book was eventually developed into a comprehensive theory of sensemaking (Weick, 1995; Weick, Sutcliffe & Obstfeld, 2005). The roots of this thinking can be traced to Wittgenstein (1972), Heidegger (1962), and Langer (1968), each of whom underscore the centrality of language in human existence. Decades later,

Gergen (1985) famously summarized the constitutive view of communication with the statement "knowledge is something we do together." Weick's theory of sensemaking is in many ways a logical extension of this worldview. It stems from his treatment of language less as a tool for sharing information and more as a resource for creating reality.

The first half of *Sensemaking in Organizations* (1995) preserves Weick's earlier emphasis on cycles of interaction aimed at reducing equivocality. Furthermore, he insists that the reader acknowledge that sensemaking is mainly about *enactment*:

> Sensemaking is about authoring as well as interpretation, creation as well as discovery. (p. 8)

> Problems do not present themselves to the practitioners as givens. They must be constructed from the material of problematic situations which are puzzling, troubling, and uncertain. (p. 9)

> Sensemaking is about the ways people generate what they interpret. (p. 13)

The interpretive turn in the social sciences (Rabinow & Sullivan, 1979) surfaced in organizational communication in the early 1980s, first appearing in a series of conference papers presented in Alta, Utah that were eventually published as a book (Putnam & Pacanowsky, 1983). Weick was aware of these conversations, knew about the growing interest within organizational communication, and even attended some of these meetings (cf. Weick, 1983). Consequently, research on sensemaking in organizations both proceeds and follows the publication of his 1995 book, which was a summation of Weick's research program at the time. Weick's theories and concepts have been applied to a wide range of organizational phenomena (e.g., negotiation, public relations) with the intent of revealing how communication is constitutive of organizational culture. A special issue of *Communication Studies* that appeared around this time (1989) provides a number of examples of this trend. Weick's theory and concepts permeated much of the published writing in organizational communication in the 80s and 90s.

More recent communication research that uses Weick's theory of sensemaking includes studies of university search processes (Eisenberg, Murphy, & Andrews, 1998); nomadic work (Bean & Eisenberg, 2006); sexual harassment (Dougherty & Smythe, 2004); and environmental destruction from flooding (Sellnow, Seeger, & Ulmer, 2002). Within organizational studies, promising applications of sensemaking appear in studies on institutionalization

(Lounsbury & Glynn, 2001), organizational change (Mills, 2003) and emotion at work (Magala, 1997). In each case, researchers select key concepts from the sensemaking model and use them to generate new insights about how organizations enact problematic situations and how communication addresses them.

More recently, Weick and his colleagues (Weick, Sutcliffe, & Obstfeld, 2005) highlight the implications of the sensemaking concept for organizational communication. Relying heavily on the Taylor and Van Every (1999) book, Weick maintains that communication is central to sensemaking, and supports this claim with a quote from their text:

> We see communication as an ongoing process of making sense of the circumstances in which people collectively find themselves and of the events that affect them. The sensemaking, to the extent that it involves communication, takes place in interactive talk and draws on the resources of language. . . . As this occurs, a situation is talked into existence and the basis is laid for action to deal with it. (Taylor & Van Every, 2000, p. 58)

Even though the core notions in the theory of sensemaking fit with Weick's earlier model of equivocality (now called the "enactment model"), Weick provides some important updates. In the 1995 volume, Weick sharpens the distinction between decision making and sensemaking by revealing that the former prompts us to blame bad actors who make bad choices while the latter focuses instead on good people struggling to make sense of a complex situation. This systemic sensibility with regard to error and accountability foreshadows his later work on high reliability organizations. In addition, he places more emphasis on the pivotal role of plausibility over accuracy by highlighting the improvisational quality of organizational behavior.

A second area of emphasis that emerges in the theory of sensemaking is the connection between sensemaking and individual/organizational identity. Struggles over meaning invariably have implications for identity, that is, particular explanations and courses of action evoke certain images of the organization while eroding others. It is no accident that Weick lists *identity* as the first property of sensemaking. He references Dutton and Dukerich's (1991) study of the New York Port Authority as an example of how positive and negative perceptions of organizational identity affect members' interpretations of "who they were, what they felt, what they faced, and what they were doing" (Weick, 1995, p. 21). Furthermore, he contends that sensemaking is "triggered by a failure to confirm one's self" and that "people learn about their identities by projecting them into an environment and observing the consequences" (p. 23). In this way, the development of identity and its link to communication surface in one's attachment to explanatory narratives of self in organizing (Eisenberg, 2001).

True to his politically neutral stance, Weick has written copiously on the subject of enactment but makes scant reference to questions of hegemony or agenda control (Gramsci & Buttgieg, 1991). One notable exception is his discussion of premise controls (Perrow, 1986), which he characterizes as vocabularies of organizing that may constrain thought and action. The enactment idea, however, provides explanatory power for understanding the motivations behind human behavior, and it can account for why certain voices are or are not heard within and outside the organization (see Weick, Sutcliffe, & Obstfeld, 2005, for an update). The demise of Enron, for example, could be traced to one CEO's ability to enact a world within which illegal and unethical practices "made sense," and where alternate definitions of reality were at best not tolerated and at worst actively punished.

Other historical echoes reverberate but never quite penetrate Weick's conceptual universe. For example, parallels exist between Weick's work and the Soviet school of literary criticism and philosophy, as represented by Vygotksy (1980) and Bakhtin (1983). One senses Vygotsky's "social theory of mind" and his contention that meaning is "always rented, never owned" in Weick's discussion of retrospective sensemaking. Weick's favorite description of how cognition works in practice is the recipe "How can I know what I think until I see what I say?" But Bakhtin might have asked: "Does this question go far enough?" Inasmuch as what we say makes sense only *in relationship to others* (there is, after all, no private language [Wittgenstein, 1972] or monologic imagination), the saying, seeing, and thinking in this sentence are *already social* and, to use Bakhtin's term, fundamentally and forever dialogic. The last section of this essay shows how this dialogic sensibility is now appearing in Weick's recent work on high reliability organizations.

Finally, one potentially fruitful line of argument that first appears in the sensemaking book casts interruptions as emotional triggers for sensemaking. Weick, Sutcliffe, and Obstfeld (2005) concur with Magala (2003) that research to date only scratches the surface of what might become a full-blown theory of organizational *sentiments* in sensemaking. The contention that disruptions to expectations or routines could trigger strong emotions and the need for sensemaking is both compelling and provocative.

In their study of sexual harassment in an academic setting, Dougherty and Smythe (2004) describe the offending incident as unexpected and emotionally jarring, serving as a trigger for retrospective sensemaking. They use Weick's seven properties of sensemaking to explain the harassment incident and its aftermath. In a related vein, Sellnow, Seeger, and Ulmer (2002) build upon

Weick's characterization of the Mann Gulch fire as a nomic rupture, a collapse of sensemaking "when people suddenly and deeply feel that the universe was no longer a rational, orderly system" (Weick, 1993, p. 634). They use this example to illuminate the sensemaking that followed the 1997 Red River Valley floods in Manitoba, Canada, thus, linking this ineffective institutional response to an emotional bias for seeing novel and threatening occurrences in a routine way. They conclude by advocating that organizational actors recognize these challenging emotions and embrace equivocality as both more ethical and more effective than a false certainty (Sellnow, Seeger, & Ulmer, 2002).

But even this treatment of emotion is still somewhat mentalistic and bloodless. It misses a complete consideration of emotions from the neck down, one that incorporates the whole body and in particular the senses other than the thinking. Scholars could argue, for example, that the theory of sensemaking fits with the work on organizing as joint performances (e.g., Murphy, 1998). Specifically, it is exciting to imagine the hybrid understandings that might occur from the marriage of Weick's ideas and the performance ethnography of Conquergood (1991) or the autoethnography of Goodall (1989), both of whom have taken great pains to document the sounds, touch, smells and feel of organizational life.

Dialogue and Heedful Interrelating

In effect, Weick's three most influential books serve less as separate scores and more as movements within a larger symphony. While written for a practically-minded audience of intellectually curious executives, *Managing the Unexpected* continues with many of the major motifs that appeared in Weick's earlier work. In describing how high reliability organizations (such as nuclear power plants and hospital emergency departments) work, Weick and Sutcliffe (2001) feature the concept of mindfulness, defined as

> the combination of ongoing scrutiny of existing expectations, continuous refinement and differentiation of expectations based on newer experiences, willingness and capability to invent new expectations that make sense of unprecedented events, a more nuanced appreciation of context and ways to deal with it, and identification of new dimensions of context that improve foresight and current functioning. . . . Mindfulness exploits the fact that two key points of leverage in managing the unexpected are expectations and categories. People who persistently rework their categories and refine them, differentiate them, update them, and replace them notice more and catch unexpected events earlier in their development. That is the essence of mindfulness. (p. 42, p. 46)

This concept is in essence a new way of talking about enactment. What carries through from Weick's earlier work is the idea that communication creates social reality through the "reworking of categories." For the organizational communication researcher, there is much at stake in persuading practitioners to appreciate this premise. If on the one hand language and communication are simply tools for sharing information, organizational communication offers little more than the development of effective communication skills. On the other, if language and communication function as the ways in which people call reality into being through their choice of categories, then organizational communication has great significance for work on organizational strategy, alignment, and change.

A second theme present in the 1969 book that has gained currency in 2001 is the need to acknowledge and learn to cope with complexity. Describing how to do this is the central contribution of *Managing the Unexpected*. Three ideas with direct implications for communication receive close attention in this book: (1) a preoccupation with failure; (2) loosening of hierarchical control; and (3) encouraging heedful interrelating. I discuss each in turn.

In arguing for the value of a preoccupation with failure, Weick and Sutcliffe (2001) underscore the dramatic difference between high reliability organizations and their less risky counterparts. In most organizations, success breeds routine, which leads to confidence and complacency. It takes great effort to challenge the human tendency to seek out confirming information and ignore failures. In practice, it requires a radical change in what typically passes for organizational communication, even among leaders. Sustained conversations about failure are difficult because they are mined with threats to identity. In Western cultures at least, talk of systems failures is still closely shadowed by hushed talk of incompetence and blame.

But Weick and Sutcliffe (2001) maintain that high reliability organizations do not conceive of failure in terms of blame. They recognize the tendency to scapegoat and suggest how institutions can make it normative to speak openly about failures and near misses as a way of developing a deeper understanding of and coping with complexity. One obvious example of this idea is medical error, in which open communication about missteps is essential to avoid them in the future (Eisenberg et al., 2005; Leape, 2004). But by far the most comprehensive example of the challenges associated with remaining vigilant to potential failures is Tompkins's (2005) career-long study of NASA's space shuttle program, in which he suggests that the loss of a culture of open communication (and the mechanisms to support it) was a significant contributor to multiple disasters and the steady decline of the space program.

A second theme of this book is the need for loosening hierarchical control. Even though this sensibility appears in Weick's earlier work, it is not clearly articulated. To cope with complexity, an organization must be mindful; that is, all its members must take responsibility for both remaining vigilant and doing something when they sense a deviation from expectations (Tompkins [2005] refers to this idea as "automatic responsibility" in the old NASA culture). This desirable cultural characteristic is also described as "coordinate leadership" (Westrum, 1997) in which the leadership role shifts "to the person who currently has the answer to the problem at hand" (Weick & Sutcliffe, 2001, p. 75). Executives in high reliability firms seek to develop a climate in which expertise is respected and communication is encouraged, irrespective of a member's status. Drawing from generations of research on empowerment, effective organizational communication, and high-involvement organizations, Weick and Sutcliffe (2001) encourage executives to "Work to create a climate where people feel safe to question assumptions and to report problems or failures candidly" (p. 66).

In a recent paper, Browning and Boudes (2005) compare Weick's approach with Snowden's (2000) work at the Cynefin Centre for Organizational Complexity. An important common characteristic of both approaches is an emphasis on self-organization, that is, on creating systems of control that are loose enough to permit significant involvement and improvisation by all employees. They conclude that both Snowden and Weick's models:

> direct us toward developing enough trust that we can empower people to participate in local complex conditions, including the right to respond instantly. If complex change can begin with small, local forces, then having the ears and eyes of observers acting on these forces follows as a strategy. (Browning & Bourdes, 2005, p. 38)

Loosened hierarchical control makes more room for employee improvisation. Notions of improvisation run throughout Weick's (Weick, Gilfillan, & Keith, 1973) work on jazz orchestras, in which he provides a subtle and detailed account of the interplay between structure and improvisation in musical performances. This work has influenced a number of communication scholars to look further at how a musical performance can serve as a metaphor for organizing (e.g., Barrett, 1998; Bastien & Hostager, 1992; Hatch, 1999). My essay on jamming (see Chapter 5, this volume) follows in these footsteps in adopting this metaphor to explain coordinated action (Eisenberg, 1990). This work promises to provide alternative vocabularies for conceiving of new organizing structures, processes and forms.

Finally, *Managing the Unexpected* introduces "heedful interrelating" as a goal for effective communication in complex environments. Weick and

Sutcliffe (2001) wade carefully into these waters, seeming to acknowledge how challenging this mode of interaction can be. They urge practitioners to become mindful of negative information in their environments and to carry the whole of their knowledge and experiences lightly, remaining open to surprise. Reprising one of his earliest insights, Weick concludes by reminding the reader that "ambivalence builds resilience" (Weick & Sutcliffe, 2001, p. 167).

Stated even more positively, Weick maintains that the key to successful organizing—particularly in high reliability organizations—is to create a culture of *resilience*. Such a culture is one in which the boundaries between functions and levels are permeable; where employees are unafraid to speak up, even when they are less than certain; and where members develop the systemic awareness that promotes heedful interrelating and catches the precursors of adverse events before they cascade out of control. To succeed in this task, individuals must hold on loosely to their beliefs and remain open to hearing disparate perspectives from others. In this kind of world, people must not only be less certain, but also less certain about the value of certainty (Phillips, 1994).

Weick and Sutcliffe (2001) make a few suggestions concerning the importance of "skill in interpersonal relations" (p. 163), but in this realm, they seem out of their element. Luckily, organizational communication scholars have conducted considerable work on the pragmatics of organizational dialogue, which is a close cousin to the sort of open communication that Weick links to mindfulness and heedful interrelating (cf. Eisenberg & Goodall, 2005). At the close of Weick and Sutcliffe's book (2001), the reader experiences a clear tension between two powerful movements, one focusing on cognition and the other on practice. Weick and Sutcliffe invoke notions of organizational culture to bridge this gap, and while they are successful in part, I would prefer a more dramatic embracing of distributed cognition in action. Needless to say, organizational scholars should examine the pragmatics of heedful interrelating closely, especially for what mindfulness or resilience looks like in practice.

Conclusion

Throughout his career, Weick has been a proponent of appreciative inquiry. His critical take on overly rationalized, prospective thinking is softened by his passionate commitment to cultivating flexibility, openness, and a diversity of thought. Weick embodies the spirit of dialogue, in that he holds out hope for the in-between and for the possibilities that can emerge against a backdrop of certain equivocality. He further recognizes, as does noted child psychologist Adam Phillips, that there "is no cure for multiple plots" (Phillips, 1994, p. 75), nor should there be.

This essay makes connections between the major works of Karl Weick and our unique historical moment. I began by suggesting that Weick's original juxtaposition of system and culture was an apt tonic for post-modern society, inasmuch as it was both framed as scientific but at the same time offered new possibilities for the re-enchantment of the world. In Weick, readers found a contrary voice willing to question some of the more deeply held assumptions about social life.

While Weick's work is radical in an intellectual sense, he has not participated in the groundswell of critical scholarship in organizational studies and has managed to stay resolutely apolitical in his research and writings. Weick might see this stance as a kind of politics, not focused on models of economic power but deeply critical of accepted models of rationality and decision-making. This stance has worked for him as he has made a comfortable home for himself on the inner border of the margins of organizational science.

In this essay, I have reviewed Weick's three most influential books with a goal of identifying how they have influenced my sub-field of organizational communication. What I find is that the core ideas have not changed much over three decades, but have built upon each other. The enactment model that is introduced in his first book re-appears in the second, this time with greater emphasis on the plausibility of explanations and the impact of particular sensemaking outcomes on individual and organizational identities. The third book recasts the enactment and sensemaking models in term of mindfulness and heedful interrelating, with an explicit effort to produce actionable guidelines for interested practitioners.

From the standpoint of organizational communication, Weick's most valuable contributions have been his insistence on the centrality of language and communication in the construction of organizational reality, and his sustained focus on communicative practice as a site for improving our understanding of cognition, culture, and social interaction. In the 1960s, the field of communication was mired in psychological views of interaction, and Weick's approach pointed the way to a different path.

A further Weickian contribution to organizational communication study comes less from his models and more from his metaphors, which consistently evoke an aesthetic of contingency. Like Lifton's idea of the "protean self" (1993), Weick's notions of equivocality and contingency in social life shine a beacon of real hope for humanity at a time when greater numbers of people seek to allay their fears of uncertainty through the pursuit of various fundamentalisms.

My extreme gratitude for Weick's unique perspective, however, does not stop me from wishing that he would go even further. I encourage Weick and those who make use of his work to take the next steps and consider the possibility of enacting a world without grounding, one lacking in foundations altogether (Eisenberg, 2001). Such a world requires heedful interrelating, to be sure, and compassion toward one's own and others' futile attempts to grasp for new absolutes. In their masterful essay that links Buddhism to cognitive science, Varela et al. (1997) state this case most elegantly:

> our historical situation requires not only that we give up philosophical foundationalism but that we learn to live in a world without foundations . . . to lay down a path of thinking and practice that gives up foundations without transforming them into a search for new foundations. . . . the solution for the sense of nihilistic alienation in our culture is not to try to find a new ground; it is to find a disciplined and genuine means to pursue groundlessness. (p. 252)

I find in the work of Karl Weick the building blocks for the pursuit of groundlessness, for understanding human organizing as "laying down a path in walking" (Varela et al., 1997, p. 237). To the extent that this worldview takes hold, Professor Weick may turn out to be the most radical scholar of them all.

References

Bakhtin, M. (1983). *The dialogic imagination*. Austin: University of Texas Press.

Bantz, C., & Smith, D. (1977). A critique and experimental test of Weick's model of organizing. *Communication Monographs, 44*(3), 171–184.

Barrett, F. J. (1998). Creativity and improvisation in jazz and organizations: Implications for organizational learning. *Organization Science, 9*(5), 605–622.

Bastien, D., & Hostager, T. (1992). Cooperation as communicative accomplishment: A symbolic interaction analysis of an improvised jazz concert. *Communication Studies, 43*, 92–104.

Bean, C. J., & Eisenberg, E. (2006). Employee sensemaking in the transition to nomadic work. *Journal of Organizational Change Management, 19*(2), 210–222.

Berman, M. (1981). *The reenchantment of the world*. Ithaca, NY: Cornell University Press.

Bochner, A. (1994). Perspectives on Inquiry II: Theories and stories. In M. Knapp and G. R. Miller (Eds.), *Handbook of interpersonal communication*, 2nd ed. (pp. 21–41). Thousand Oaks, CA: Sage.

Browning, L., & Boudes, T. (2005). The use of narrative to understand and respond to complexity: A comparative analysis of the Cynefin and Weickian models. *E:CO, 7*, 32–39.

Burke, K. (1969). *A grammar of motives*. Berkeley: University of California Press.

Campbell, D. (1997). From evolutionary epistemology via selection theory to a sociology of scientific validity. *Evolution Cognition, 3*(1), 5–38.

Communication Studies (1989). Special issue applying the work of Karl Weick. 40(4).

Conquergood, D. (1991). Rethinking ethnography: Towards a critical cultural politics. *Communication Monographs, 58*, 179–194.

Deetz, S. (1992). *Democracy in an age of corporate colonization*. Albany, NY: SUNY Press.

Dougherty, D., & Smythe, M. J. (2004). Sensemaking, organizational culture, and sexual harassment. *Journal of Applied Communication Research, 32*(4), 293–317.

Dutton, J., & Dukerich, J. (1991). Keeping an eye on the mirror: Image and identity in organizational adaptation. *Academy of Management Journal, 34*(3), 517–554.

Eisenberg, E. (1990). Jamming: Transcendence through organizing. *Communication Research, 17*, 139–164.

Eisenberg, E. M. (2001). Building a mystery: Communication and the development of identity. *Journal of Communication, 51*(3), 534–552.

Eisenberg, E., & Goodall, H. L., Jr. (2005). *Organizational communication: Balancing creativity and constraint*, 4th edition. New York: St. Martin's Press.

Eisenberg, E. M., Murphy, A., & Andrews, L. (1998). Openness and decision-making in the search for a university provost. *Communication Monographs, 65*, 1–23.

Eisenberg, E., Murphy, A., Sutcliffe, K., Wears, R., Schenkel, S., Perry, S., & Vanderhoef, M. (2005). Communication in emergency medicine: Implications for patient safety. *Communication Monographs, 72*(4), 390–413.

Fairhurst, G., & Sarr, R. (1991). *The art of framing*. San Francisco: Jossey-Bass.

Farace, R. V., Monge, P., & Russell, H. (1977). *Communicating and organizing*. Reading, MA: Addison-Wesley.

Gane, N. (2005). *Max Weber and postmodern theory: Rationalization versus re-enchantment*. New York: Palgrave MacMillan.

Gergen, K. (1985) The social constructionist movement in modern psychology. *American Psychologist, 40*, 266–275.

Giddens, A. (1986). *The constitution of society: Outline of a theory of structuration*. Berkeley: University of California Press.

Goffman, E. (1974). *Frame analysis*. Boston, MA: Northeastern University Press.

Goodall, H. L., Jr. (1989). *Casing a promised land*. Carbondale: Southern Illinois University Press.

Goodall, H. L., Jr. (1991). *Living in the rock 'n' roll mystery*. Carbondale: Southern Illinois University Press.

Gramsci, A., & Buttgieg, J. (1991). *Prison notebooks, Vol I*. New York: Columbia University Press.

Hatch, M. J. (1999). *The jazz metaphor for organizing: Historical and performative aspects*. Paper presented at the Critical Management Studies Conference, Manchester, July 1999.

Heidegger, M. (1962). *Being and time*. San Francisco: HarperSan Francisco.

Koestler, A. (1983). *Janus: A summing up*. New York: Pan Macmillan.

Kreps, G. L. (1980). A field experimental test and revaluation of Weick's model of organizing. In D. Nimmo (Ed.), *Communication yearbook 4* (pp. 384–398). New Brunswick, NJ: Transaction Press.

Langer, S. (1968). *Philosophy in a new key*. New York: Signet.

Lanzmann, C. (1985). *Shoah*. New Yorker Films Video.

Leape, L. (2004). *To do no harm*. San Francisco: Jossey-Bass.

Lennie, I. (1999). *Beyond management*. London: Sage.

Levine, D. (1985). *The flight from ambiguity*. Chicago: University of Chicago Press.

Lifton, R. (1993). *The protean self*. Chicago: University of Chicago Press.

Lounsbury, M., & Glynn, M. (2001). Cultural entrepreneurship: Stories, legitimacy, and the acquisition of resources. *Strategic Management Journal, 22*(6), 545–564.

Magala, S. (1997). The making and unmaking of sense. *Organizational Studies, 18*(2), 317–338.

Mills, J. (2003). *Making sense of organizational change*. London: Routledge.

Murphy, A. (1998). Hidden transcripts of flight attendant resistance. *Management Communication Quarterly, 11*, 499–535.

Perrow, C. (1986). *Complex organizations* (3rd ed.). New York: Random House.

Phillips, A. (1994). *On flirtation*. Cambridge, MA: Harvard University Press.

Putnam, L. (1983). The interpretive perspective: An alternative to functionalism. In L. L. Putnam & M. E. Pacanowsky (Eds.), *Communication and organization: An interpretive approach* (pp. 31–54). Beverly Hills, CA: Sage.

Putnam, L. & Pacanowsky, M. (1983). *Communication and organization: An interpretive approach*. Beverly Hills, CA: Sage.

Putnam, L., & Sorenson, R. (1982). Equivocal messages in organizations. *Human Communication Research, 8*(2), 114–132.

Rabinow, P., & Sullivan, W. M. (1979). The interpretive turn: Emergence of an approach. In P. Rabinow & W. M. Sullivan (Eds.), *Interpretive social science: A leader* (pp. 1–21). Berkeley: University of California Press.

Sellnow, T., Seeger, M., & Ulmer, R. (2002). Chaos theory, informational needs and natural disasters. *Journal of Applied Communication Research, 30*(4), 269–292.

Taylor, B. (1990). Reminiscences of Los Alamos: Narrative, critical theory, and the organizational subject. *Western Journal of Speech Communication, 54*(3), 395–419.

Taylor, J., & Van Every, E. (1999). *The emergent organization: Communication as its site and surface*. New York: Lawrence Erlbaum.

Tompkins, P. (2005). Apollo, Challenger, Columbia: *The decline of the space program*. Los Angeles: Roxbury.

Toulmin, S. (1983). The charm of the scout. In C. Wilder (Ed.), *Rigor and imagination*. New York: Praeger.

Varela, F., Thompson, E., & Rosch, E. (1997). *The embodied mind*. Cambridge: MIT Press.

Ventura, M. (1993). *Letters at 3 AM: Reports on endarkenment*. New York: Spring Publications.

Vykgotsky, L. (1980). *Mind in society: The development of higher psychological processes*. Cambridge, MA: Harvard University Press.

Weick, K. (1969/1979). *The social psychology of organizing*. Reading, MA: Addison-Wesley.

Weick, K. (1976). Educational organizations as loosely coupled systems. *Administrative Science Quarterly, 21*, 1–19.

Weick, K. (1983). Organizational communication: A research agenda. In L. Putnam & M. Pacanowsky (Eds.), *Communication and organization: An interpretive approach* (pp. 13–29). Beverly Hills, CA: Sage.

Weick, K. (1995). *Sensemaking in organizations*. Thousand Oaks, CA: Sage.

Weick, K. (1998). Improvisation as a mindset for organizational analysis. *Organization Science 9*(5).

Weick, K. (2001). Leadership as the legitimation of doubt. In W. Bennis, G. Spreitzer, & T. Cummings (Eds.), *The future of leadership* (pp. 91–102). San Francisco: Jossey-Bass.

Weick, K., Gilfillan, D., & Keith, T. (1973). The effect of composer credibility on orchestra performance. *Sociometry, 36*, 435–462.

Weick, K., & Sutcliffe, K. (2001). *Managing the unexpected*. San Francisco: Jossey-Bass.

Weick, K., Sutcliffe, K., & Obstfeld, D. (2005). Organizing and the process of sense-making. *Organization Science, 16*(4), 409–421.

Westrum, R. (1997). Social factors in safety-critical systems. In R. Redmill & J. Rajan (Eds.), *Human factors in safety critical systems* (pp. 233–256). London: Butterworth-Heinemann.

Wittgenstein, L. (1972). *On certainty*. New York: Perennial.

Conclusion

Beyond Fundamentalism

We are born of the world as flesh, straining for
connection. Language appears
to wrest us from this world, to construct humans-as-beings.
We are called to name, to approach being through naming.
We also seek the spaces around the names, an experience
of life that is meaningless but resonant.

Wherever we turn as human beings, language has gotten there first.
Language seeks to define us through two kinds of names:
subject/object and past/present/future.
Subject/object constructs "self" and "other" and the possibility of theories
about "other people and things." Past/present/future
constructs history and the future. Theory and history are
constructed through communication.

Communication, theory, and history are efforts to develop a deeper
understanding of our positionality in the world, the very positionality made
both possible and problematic by communication. Theory and history are
attempts through communication to heal the wounds of
separation torn open by communication.

Communication is both sentence and salvation. The material manifestation of
reflexive consciousness, communication both creates the possibility of theory
and history and harbors the seeds of something beyond them.

Although we have created these ideas to access "there and then," theory
and history are conversations that we have right here, right
now. Theory is a conversation about how things work here and there,
but it always happens here. History is a conversation about how
things worked before, but it always happens now. Talking about
theory and history as if they were actually "there and then" wrongly
reinforces the power and univocality of these categories.

The houses we construct with theory and history
(our theories and histories) may be
well-furnished, but they are lonely and windowless.
They are fine for the occasional visit but not as permanent residences.

Sometimes we try to escape theory and history through communication.
We aim toward the experience of larger being, of
transcending our paltry stories and identities and
feeling at one with the Earth. In these moments, we readily
offer our theories, histories, and identities in
exchange for a world that needs none of these things.

When we are lucky, we find such a world in music.
We find it in love.
We find it in nature.
We find it in God.
We find it whenever we finally stop looking.

A common failing of books such as this one is that, while they provide a thorough critique of all that is wrong with the current state of affairs, they are less useful in helping to imagine what to do next. In this concluding chapter, I pick up on clues and suggestions from throughout these readings that seek to evoke a new and different way of seeing and being in the world. My goal is to provide as explicit a description as possible of the kind of world I envision and the forms of communication, organization, and identity that would make up such a a world.

The essays in Part I of this volume make a strong argument for the organizing value of strategic ambiguity. In their zeal to create "optimal" interpersonal relationships, fundamentalists and progressives alike have embraced a radically ideological view of the "authentic" self that has some conceptual appeal but negative practical consequences for real people and real communication (Bochner, 1982; Taylor, 2005). If nothing else, experience teaches us that the twin goals of total clarity and complete openness are both chimerical and naïve. Both are impossible to achieve, impossible to measure if they have been achieved, and often not even desirable. So let us call off the search, halt the "flight from ambiguity" (Levine, 1988), and recognize once and for all that uncertainty has "the advantage of keeping the imagination open and thereby protecting one from emotions that are monolithic, suffocating, [and] inauthentic" (Lifton, 1993, p. 102). Instead, we should take Burke's (1962) sage advice that appears at the front of this book, and seek to "clarify the resources of ambiguity" (p. xxi) available to support both individual and social transformation.

Written with this in mind, Part II of this collection includes essays that examine the practical implications of embracing ambiguity. Through a diverse set of examples, multiple interpretations of reality are shown to be productive for organizing, providing a broader universe of perceptions upon which to draw. At the most extreme, one of these essays ("Jamming") explores the possibility of self-transcendence through noninterpersonal means, via loosely coordinated activities in the absence of shared meaning. Insistence on shared meaning as a standard for effective communication works against our ability to collaborate across significant differences. Our future depends to a large degree on our capacity to navigate precisely those relationships in which shared meaning is least likely to be realized.

Of course, not all perceptions have equal standing. Although there will always be narrative asymmetries in social systems, lessening our reliance on shared meaning as a goal makes a big difference in how we approach these relationships. The importance of shared meaning has been overstated in communication studies, and these essays help shift the emphasis toward effectively coordinated action among individuals who hold widely varying attitudes and interpretations. Strategic ambiguity is useful in promoting these relationships.

Finally, Part III of this volume argues that, taken together, these ideas constitute a new "aesthetics of contingency" for communication. In pursuing such a conclusion, I find myself in good company; writers from various fields are calling for new ways to gauge the success of human relationships and the integrity of human identities (e.g., Appiah, 2005; Pearce, 1989). Rather than treat ambiguity and shifting meanings as signs of failure, as a group these authors suggest instead that they may be the cornerstones of a new definition of human being, one better suited to the demands of a globalizing yet persistently diverse and fragmented world.

The Problem: Narrative Attachment and Projective Identification

Being just contaminates the void. (Hitchcock, 1999)

In the next few pages, I summarize a modest proposal for a new version of human identity, one with a unique relationship to language and communication. In the most definitive statement to date on the subject, Lifton (1993) made a persuasive case for refiguring the self as "protean," thereby reframing its persistent changeability as a desirable feature rather than a flaw. As each of us is driven to differentiate as a recognizable being, we can do so only in relationship to particular institutions, belief systems, and existing social narratives (Taylor, 1991). These narratives are versions of reality (Ochs & Capp, 1996) that are born from and give meaning to experience.

The reason why these various contexts and the stories they inspire are important can be found in our species' lifelong hunger for meaning, a seemingly unavoidable adjunct to reflexive consciousness. The human animal has been characterized as social and symbolizing; our lack of strong instincts requires us to enact meaningful worlds to inhabit. Whereas other animals rely more on unambiguous signs, language leads us to construct a symbolic universe of ideas, stories, and plots, all of which we use as resources for composing our lives.

From the moment of birth, we are engaged in an autopoetic process of self-development against a shifting background. The only way we can know who we are is by orienting ourselves to one or more of the various social systems in which we are participants—our relationships, families, organizations, societies. Philosopher Charles Taylor (2005) calls these orientation points "horizons of significance." But *none* of these identifications is stable or uncontested. Instead, with identification comes expectations of how our lives can be lived, and with expectations come attachments to how we—and others—*should* live. We see this every day as people struggle to position themselves successfully in marriages, jobs, and communities. But the sense that is made each moment is also always in the process of coming apart.

Although identification with such narratives is essential to personal development, no single story can encompass the entirety of one's life experience. The stories we tell about what we value in relationships, institutions, and society overlap and often conflict. Consequently, we are challenged to somehow make sense of those situations in which our ready explanations conflict or fall short, and in which the application of our avowed beliefs presents problems or inconsistencies. This dilemma tends to produce two types of outcomes:

> Faced with such a challenge, narrators alternate between two fundamental tendencies—either to cultivate a dialogue between diverse understandings or to lay down one coherent, correct solution to the problem. The first tendency is associated with relativistic and the second with fundamentalistic perspectives. (Ochs & Capp, 1996, p. 29)

Although it is inevitable that individual identity develops through apprehension of and identification with select social narratives, the stance one takes in the identification process is highly variable. The challenge, then, is not interpretation as much as interpretation of our interpretations, the beliefs we have about the relative standing of our beliefs in the life of the world. To the extent that one engages a fundamentalist style of thinking, one becomes deeply attached to a single narrative as the sole, unassailable truth. Summarizing Sigmund Freud's view of this tendency, Edmundson (2006) says, "We want a strong man with a simple doctrine that accounts for our sufferings, identifies our enemies, focuses our energies and gives us, more enduringly than wine or even love, a sense of being whole" (p. 18). This recalls the dark side of Buber's (1971) "I-it" relationship, wherein we see ourselves as enlightened subjects and regard those who do not share our worldview as misguided, disposable objects. Humans are spiritual beings capable of great love, of cultivating the sacred connections that unite us all despite our apparent differences. But it is also true that, when poked with a sharp stick, we poke back, and then set out for a bigger stick, and when assaulted, we invariably become defensive.

This defensiveness leads us to the further objectification of others as disposable, inferior, and deserving to die. Black, white, gay, straight, Christian, Jew, Hutu, Tutsi, German, Israeli, Iraqi, Serb—these are all arbitrary categories created by humans to shore up identity and distinguish ourselves from others. But these increasingly inaccurate and imprecise linguistic characterizations are too often brandished along with real blades that tear through the human family and leave deep scars. Moreover, we cannot keep thinking and acting this same way and expect to see different results. The hope of establishing a complex peace rooted in unified diversity (Eisenberg, 1984) is barely visible from where we sit today, at the bottom of a deep, dark, and bloody well. Wrapped in our present darkness, we are dimly aware of the light above, reminding us of the possibility of a single human family and the call of species, if not planetary, identity. Moving in this direction is incredibly hard; despite breathtaking advances in technology, we remain beginners at human relationships.

Hate is a relationship. Adopting a relational worldview leads us to recognize that no identity ever develops in a vacuum. Attaining a particular position in a system or culture simultaneously requires constructing the "other" who is outside of the identified group. This has much to do with the polarizing power of language (e.g., to be normal, I must create deviance; to become holy, I must invent the infidel). I alluded to this process in Chapter 8 in my discussion of projective identification, an unconscious process by which we identify disliked aspects of ourselves, break them off, and locate them in an "other" who can then carry these negative qualities for us and serve as an object of our hatred and disgust (there are similarities here to Burke's notions of scapegoating and purification, which he also links to the hierarchical nature of language). Put another way, projective identification turns a vital internal struggle into a false external one between individuals and groups whose knowledge of each others' characters, cultures, and motivations is minimal.

To be even more direct, I connect our species' latest flirtation with world war and annihilation squarely to our conception of human identity and the impact of this conception on human relationships. Drawn as we are by language to see ourselves as isolated egos perched nervously inside bags of skin (Watts, 1989), there is a sad sense of inevitability to our situation. Our efforts at self-definition and self-protection only serve to increase our anxiety and vulnerability. The more rigidly I identify with the concepts I choose to describe myself and my life—e.g., male, American, Democrat, Jew—the more vulnerable I become to feelings of fear, anger, and alienation from society as a whole. By contrast, the more open I am in conceiving of my self and my life, the more resilient I can be, the more readily I can adapt to new people and new situations. Fixity of belief impedes the health of the human organism just as surely as blocked arteries stop the flow of blood.

Conceiving of ourselves as isolated individuals (or groups of individuals) in a hostile world, our situation is far worse than having taken a wrong turn onto the wrong road. A more apt metaphor adds the fact that we are in the wrong car with the wrong map. Philosopher Hannah Arendt (1994) famously described the banality of evil; along the same lines, fundamentalism is perhaps best seen as a failure of imagination, a desperate retreat to unworkable historical scripts that no longer function in a globalizing world. The invention of new scripts and notions of individual and cultural identity are key to the development of healthy, sustainable relationships and societies.

A New Vision: Laying Down a Path in Walking

Just because a thing can never be finished doesn't mean it can't be done. (Young, 2002)

So we at last come to the hardest question, one that became urgent for Americans after 9/11: How can we remain open to the world, to embrace others who hold different worldviews, while at the same time standing firm in our values and beliefs? How can we respond to a violent fundamentalism without becoming violent fundamentalists ourselves?

The usual response to adversity of this kind is to seek a deeper or stronger level of grounding or foundation. The problem is that there isn't any, and to the extent that we act as if there were, we deepen our sense of alienation and the divisions among us. But let me be clear about what I am saying about the value of faith, spirituality, or religion. I see all of these as historically valuable and personally powerful modes of experience, facilitating as they do the transcendence of self and material reality. The difference is that I see these as modes of experience, not knowledge. The moment we seek to bring this experience into the world of language, to translate the truth of our experience into the "Truth" about the world, we turn religion on its head. Whereas the etymology of the word *religion* reflects the act of "binding into one," extending the religious experience into the realm of literal meaning leads ironically only to division.

An interesting example of how one might live with a multiplicity of possible truths can be found in different perspectives toward hurricane preparedness. Like much else in life, the path of a hurricane is ultimately unpredictable—the best we can do is to identify a "cone" that encompasses a range of possible paths and assigns probabilities to different paths within the range. In choosing how to describe their predictions in forecasts, meteorologists favor reports that show only the cone of probabilities, arguing that this does the best job of reflecting the actual level of uncertainty and does not encourage a false sense of either urgency or complacency. The general population, of course, seems desperate for forecasters to identify a likely path. But even though the identification of a single path can reduce anxiety for some in the short term ("At least we know whether to evacuate or not," etc.) it can be disastrous in the long term (as was the case when a storm whose path ran due north made a sudden turn to the east, devastating a largely unprepared community). Reliable ambiguities are, in the long run, preferable to false certainties; in the world of human relations, there is much to be said for cultivating ambivalence and doubt (Weick, 1979, 1995). They are the cornerstones, for example, in creating a culture of safety in high-reliability organizations (cf. Tompkins, 2006; Weick & Sutcliffe, 2001).

Fortunately, there is some precedent for thinking this way in American culture, although one would hardly know it from today's headlines and political debates. We continue to live in the long shadows of Watergate and Vietnam and in the backlash toward liberalism that seeks to cast all attempts at authentic dialogue as invitations to moral relativism. When Ronald Reagan first became president, he famously announced, "The era of self-doubt is over." Although at the time this seemed to many like America finding its way again, the consequences of this kind of thinking have now come home to roost.

The alternative to this misguided sense of certainty was articulated in the 1940s and 1950s by such intellectuals as Reinhold Niebuhr, cofounder of Americans for Democratic Action. "Americans," Niebuhr argued, "should not emulate the absolute self-confidence of their enemies. They should not pretend that a country that countenanced McCarthyism and segregation was morally pure. Rather, they should cultivate enough self-doubt to ensure that, unlike the Communists', their idealism never degenerated into fanaticism" (Beinhart, 2006, p. 42). Open-mindedness, Niebuhr maintained, is not "a virtue of people who don't believe anything. It is a virtue of people who know . . . that their beliefs are not absolutely true." Our ability to bring freedom and democracy to the world is inseparable from our commitment to encourage these same ideals closer to home. Contrary to fundamentalist thinking, the moral high ground rests on a foundation of ambiguity and humility.

We must reject the objectivism that underlies both nihilism and fundamentalism, and learn to accept that (1) there is no single Truth, and (2) all things and all people lack an intrinsic nature (Varela, Thompson, & Rosch, 1991). Meaning exists only in relationship; the only reason my keyboard feels hard is that the skin on my fingers is relatively soft. Beautiful sunsets rely on species capable of certain kinds of vision. There is no meaning beyond meaning; the human experience occurs on the narrow ridge between self and other, in the navigation of the in-between (Arnett, 1986).

Astute readers will see a clear connection between the approach to life I favor and what has been described as a cosmopolitan form of communication (Pearce, 1989). Pearce identified four forms of communication, each of which acts to bring into being a particular kind of social world. The four forms are monocultural, ethnocentric, modernistic, and cosmopolitan, and Pearce argues that "[t]he primary differences among them are whether they are prepared to put their resources (stories that make the world coherent) at risk in any new encounter and whether they treat others as natives (that is, hold them accountable to the same interpretive and evaluative criteria that they would apply to their own behavior)" (Pearce, 2005, p. 13). Cosmopolitan communicators view difference in perspective as an opportunity to learn and expand one's practical repertoire for living in the world, and not as an occasion to either synthesize or choose between differing worldviews (Brown, 2005).

Along these same lines, Appiah (2005) argues for a new form of "rooted cosmopolitanism" that both values interaction across world views and recognizes that sometimes it is "the differences we bring to the table that make it rewarding to interact at all" (p. 271). In globalization, he sees the positive side of what others call cultural contamination, and resonates with Salman Rushdie's celebration of hybridity, impurity, and intermingling as the main way that newness enters the world. If the golden rule of cosmopolitanism is that "I am human: nothing human is alien to me" (Appiah, 2006, p. 37), the practical implications of this revelation are both mundane and profound. Appiah urges us to learn about people in other places, to seek understanding and get used to one another, without expecting to agree. "Understanding one another may be hard; it can certainly be interesting. But it doesn't require that we come to agreement" (Appiah, 2006, p. 37).

But if not agreement, then what? I believe that we should conceive of life as "laying down a path in walking" (Varela et al., 1991), which is not a life without narratives or boundaries but one in which these provisional truths are not reified as transcendent or supernatural. David Reynolds, a brief therapist in the Japanese tradition, calls this style of being "playing ball on running water," the ability to engage in the world and at the same time see it as transient and void of ultimate truth. Such a life is passionate but not polarized, engaged but not fanatical, committed but capable of holding space for differences. By doing so, we are well on our way toward inventing new ways to live in a diverse, and increasingly interdependent world.

References

Appiah, K. A. (2005). *The ethics of identity.* Princeton, NJ: Princeton University Press.

Appiah, K. A. (2006, January 1). The case for contamination. *New York Times Magazine,* pp. 30–37, 52.

Arendt, H. (1994). *Eichmann in Jerusalem: A report on the banality of evil.* New York: Penguin Classics.

Arnett, R. (1986). *Communication and community.* Carbondale: Southern Illinois University Press.

Beinhart, P. (2006, April 30). The rehabilitation of the cold-war liberal. *New York Times Magazine,* pp. 41–45.

Bochner, A. P. (1982). On the efficacy of openness in close relationships. In M. Burgoon (Ed.), *Communication Yearbook 5.* New Brunswick, NJ: Transaction Books.

Brown, M. T. (2005). *Corporate integrity: Rethinking organizational ethics and leadership.* Cambridge, MA: Cambridge University Press.

Buber, M. (1971). *I and thou.* New York: Free Press.

Burke, K. B. (1962). *A grammar of motives.* Berkeley: University of California Press.

Campbell, J., & Moyers, B. (1991). *The power of myth.* New York: Anchor.

Edmundson, M. (2006, April 30). Freud and the fundamentalist urge. *New York Times Magazine,* pp. 15–18.

Eisenberg, E. (1984). Ambiguity as strategy in organizational communication. *Communication Monographs, 51,* 227–242.

Hitchcock, R. (1999). Antwoman. *Jewels for Sofia* (Track 8). Los Angeles: Warner Brothers.

Levine, D. (1988). *The flight from ambiguity.* Chicago: University of Chicago Press.

Lifton, R. (1993). *The protean self.* Chicago: University of Chicago Press.

Ochs, E., & Capp, L. (1996). Narrating the self. *Annual Review of Anthropology, 25,* 19–43.

Pearce, W. B. (1989). *Communication and the human condition.* Carbondale: Southern Illinois University Press.

Pearce, W. B. (2005, April). Toward communicative virtuosity. Paper presented at "Modernity as a Communication Process (Is Modernity 'On Time'?)" seminar sponsored by the Department of Communications and Social and Political Theories, Russian State University for Humanities, Moscow.

Phillips, A. (1997). *On flirtation.* Cambridge, MA: Oxford University Press.

Phillips, A. (1998). *The beast in the nursery.* New York: Pantheon.

Taylor, C. (2005). *The ethics of authenticity* (Rev. ed.). Cambridge, MA: Harvard University Press.

Varela, F., Thompson, E., & Rosch, E. (1991). *The embodied mind.* Cambridge: MIT Press.

Watts, A. (1989). *The book: On the taboo against knowing who you really are.* New York: Vintage.

Young, D. (2002). *Skid.* Pittsburgh, PA: University of Pittsburgh Press.

Index

About the Author

Eric M. Eisenberg is Professor of Communication at the University of South Florida. Dr. Eisenberg received his doctorate in Organizational Communication from Michigan State University in 1982. After leaving MSU, he directed the Master's program in Applied Communication at Temple University before moving to the University of Southern California. Over a ten-year period at USC, Dr. Eisenberg twice received the National Communication Association award for the outstanding research publication in organizational communication, as well as the Burlington Foundation award for excellence in teaching. In 1994, Eisenberg joined the faculty of the University of South Florida, honoring a lifelong pledge always to live within driving distance of a Disney park. He is recipient of the 2000 Ohio University Elizabeth Andersch Award for lifetime contributions to the field of Communication.

Eisenberg is the author of more than 60 articles, chapters, and books on the subjects of organizational communication, health communication, and communication theory. His most recent work focuses on handoffs in health care and how improved communication can reduce the likelihood of medical error. Dr. Eisenberg is an internationally recognized researcher, teacher, facilitator, and consultant specializing in the strategic use of communication to promote positive organizational change.